Learning and Teaching

Learning and Teaching

A Constructivist Approach

Noushad Husain

SHIPRA

(First Published in India 2016)

Rs. 1500; US$ 60

ISBN: 978-81-7541-857-8

2022 Impression

Learning and Teaching: A Constructivist Approach

Published by:
SHIPRA PUBLICATIONS
LG 18-19, Pankaj Central Market
I.P. Ext., Patparganj, Delhi 110092, India
+91 11 2223 5152/6152; 96500 28065
info@shiprapublication.com
www.shiprapublication.com

The Author Gratefully Acknowledges His
Indebtedness to
God
For His Mercy

Dedicated to
My Wife Razda Khan and
Son Arsh Husain

Learning is more than absorbing facts, it is acquiring understanding.
Teaching is more than imparting knowledge, it is inspiring change.

Preface

The progress and development of any society or nation is largely depends on the development and well being of its young generation. Education is a powerful means and method of bringing required development and introducing desired modification in the behavior of the children for preparing them an effective and productive member of the society. For this purpose, we need to organize the teaching-learning process of our schools in a properly coordinated way resulting into desirable educational outcomes. Learning outcomes are central to the teaching and learning process. All the teaching efforts and endeavour of the teachers should concentrate over arranging the most suitable learning experiences for the learners in most appropriate way.

The contemporary view of learning is defined as knowledge construction. Psychological research shows that the most effective learning occurs when students build their own associations between new information and their previous knowledge-base, not when they memorize how others have framed it. Teachers need to be acquainted with the very concept and nature of the learning, factors affecting the learning and styles of learning suitable to very nature and capabilities of their students.

The teachers should understand how learning occurs, how learners construct knowledge, acquire skill and develop disciplined thinking processes and know how to use instructional strategies that promote student learning. Teachers should also understand that each learner's cognitive, linguistic, social, emotional and physical development influences learning and know how to make instructional decisions that build on learners' strengths and needs.

Teachers should understand that all teaching is directed at learning and the learner is at the heart of teaching. They should critically question the widespread belief that teaching is telling (informing/demonstrating) and understand culturally responsive teaching approaches that support learning. They should explore the activity of teaching in a formal setting and appreciate it as a contextually located, highly complex enterprise that cannot be reduced to techniques.

Learning encompasses many dimensions: knowledge, skills, values, beliefs, attitudes and habits. Student-teachers will understand theories of learning as conceptualized currently within psychology and cognitive science. They should engage critically with theories that reduce learning to behaviorural and testable components, which have been influential in education, but which narrowly limit the perspective on education. The centrality of curiosity, interest, active engagement and inquiry in learning at all levels should be emphasized. Teachers should engage theoretically and through observation with the notion of learning as construction of knowledge. They should also investigate the differences and connections between learning in school and learning outside school

Values, personal relationships between teacher and learners, relationships among the learners themselves, autonomy, self-esteem and freedom experienced by learners, all shape and are shaped by the work of teaching. Student-teachers will analyze teaching as a profession; reflect on their beliefs and practices, multiple responsibilities located in an institutionalized setting, and the need and opportunities for professional growth.

The present book entitled as "Learning and Teaching" is based on the new syllabus of two yearly B. Ed. Programme (Semester 2, Course 3) directed by NCTE and applied by the various Universities of India. This book provides a comprehensive understanding about the different concepts related to learning and teaching. The subject matter of the book deals with the complete concepts of learning and teaching. This is a core course that brings together perspectives from many other courses and draws upon theoretical frames from psychology, philosophy, sociology and language learning. It offers a site for prospective teachers to reflect on and critique notions of learning and teaching that they have formed from their own experience and to move beyond them.

This book is based on latest Curriculum Framework-2014 developed by NCTE and has 33 important chapters namely – understanding learning, behaviourist approach to learning, cognitivist approach to learning, constructivist approach to learning, child growth and development, individual differences, transfer of learning, development of adolescent, constructivist learning, introduction to reflection, learning in and out of school in diverse environments, understanding teaching, variables of teaching, phases of teaching, levels of teaching, models of teaching, teaching skills, micro-teaching, practicing teaching skills through micro-teaching, traditional and constructivist lesson planning, identification and formulation of teaching or instructional objectives, modification of teacher behavior and analysis of classroom interaction, team teaching, classroom communication, measurement and evaluation in education, pedagogy and pedagogical analysis, teacher's diary, constructivist teaching, multicultural education, teaching as a profession and mission, learning style vs. teaching style, ICT, and e-learning and m-learning.

This book is prepared to serve the educational purposes of students, teachers, teacher-educators, student-teachers, parents etc. for developing a better understanding about the learning and teaching. I hope that after reading the present book, the readers will be able to better understand the different concepts related to learning and teaching. The teachers will make the teaching-learning process interesting and goal oriented.

First of all, I thank a lot of my indebtedness to 'God for His Mercy', because without the mercy of God, the present book could not be completed. God gave me a direction, knowledge, support and patience to write this book.

I would like to take this opportunity to thanks my father Mr. Zakir Husain and Mother Mrs. Aiysha Begum, who are always a source of inspiration for my academic work. I would also like to thanks my wife Razda Khan and my beloved son Arsh Husain because without the help and support of my family members this would not have been possible.

The author is grateful to the various authors, writers and editors of the books and journals or any other type of published work for preparing the manuscript of this book. I would like to show my gratitude towards all those authors and publishers, whose works have been consulted, quoted and abstracted to make, the book up-to-date and useful.

With great pleasure, I want to express my grateful appreciation to my wife Razda Khan beloved son Arsh Husain for inspiring me to write this wonderful book.

In the end, I am thankful to Mr. D. Kumar, Shipra Publications for the meticulous processing of the manuscript and give the book a nice look.

Dr. Noushad Husain

Contents

1
Understanding Learning

All complex behaviours are learned. Learning is a theoretical concept. Hence, it is not directly observable. We can infer that learning has taken place if an individual behaves, reacts as a result of experience in a manner different from the way formally behaved.

Learning has no universally agreed definition. The way one defines it emanates from, as well as influences, the way one theorizes learning. Thus, there are as many definitions as there are theories of learning. For instance, cognitive theories of learning, which emphasize the thought process and the role of the mind in learning, view it as the mind's ability to acquire, process, and retain new knowledge and information. Thus cognitive psychologists studying learning are interested in unobservable mental activities such as thinking, remembering, creating, and solving problems. On the other hand, behavioural psychologists view that the outcome of learning is change in behaviour and emphasizes the effects of external events on the individual. But experiential theories, which emphasize the role of action and experience in learning, conceptualize it in terms of competencies generated among learners.

MEANING OF LEARNING

Learning is the primary reason for the existence of schools and a means by which socialization is affected. It is difficult to imagine how human beings can be separated from learning, for the two are not separated. Think for a moment a state that human being would be in if there was no learning or he/she did not have capacity to learn. Without learning people would not know their names; their parents and children would not even know where they came from. In this chapter we are going to discuss in detail about learning.

By definition *learning* involves a change of behaviour as a result of what one has experienced, and this may be shown in the way a person thinks, acts and feels (Hilgard and Bewer, 1975). This definition claims that there are certain behaviours that may not be the result of learning but an outcome normal biological development just like walking and seeing.

Learning is a continuous process lasting from the moment a person is born to the end of his/her life on the surface of the earth (Mwamwenda, 1996). Learning may also be defined as relatively permanent change in behaviour following practice or experience. Many of us think of learning as the process of only acquiring facts and that it is only taking place in schools. But, there are many kinds of learning taking place at all times, although our discussion is basically on school learning.

DEFINITIONS OF LEARNING

The important definitions of learning are as follows:

1. *Gates and Others* (1946) — "Learning is the modification in behaviour to meet environmental requirements."

2. *F.S. Freeman* (1958) —"Learning is the process of developing the ability to respond adequately to a situation which may or may not have been properly encountered."

3. *H. Faigan* (1958) —"Learning is a sequence of mental events or conditions leading to changes in the learner. As a sequence of events, the learning process is as follows: (1) The individual has needs and is therefore in a state of readiness to respond. There are antecedent conditions within the learner. (2) He meets a learning situation or problem. A new interpretation is required because previously learned responses are not adequate for reaching the goal and satisfying his need. He encounters something new or unexpected and must search for a different response. (3) He interprets the situation with reference to his goals and tries a response or responses which seem to satisfy his need. The way he perceives the situation and the response he makes depends both on his 'readiness' and on external conditions of the situation. (4) If his response leads to devised goals or satisfaction, he will tend to interpret and respond to similar future situations in the same way. If not, he keeps on trying and reinterpreting until consequences are attained. The learning process is this whole sequence.

4. *H.J. Klausmeir* (1961) —"Learning is a process whereby a change in behaviour results from some form of experience, activity, training, observation and the like."

5. *E.A. Peel* (1962) —"Learning is a change in the individual following upon changes in the environment."

6. *Blair, Jones and Simpson* (1964) —"Any change of behaviour which is a result of experience and which causes people to face later situations differently may be called learning."

7. *W.C. Morse and G.M. Wingo* (1967) —"Learning can be defined as changing one's potential for seeing, feeling and doing through experiences, partly perceptual, partly intellectual, partly emotional and partly motor.

8. *J.F. Travers* (1972) —"Learning is a process that results in the modification of behaviour."

9. *Dictionary of Education by C.V. Good* (1973) — The term 'learning' has been interpreted to mean: "Change in response or behaviour (such as innovation, elimination or modification of responses, involving some degree of performance) caused partly or wholly by experience, such experience being in the main conscious, but sometimes including significant unconscious components, as is common in motor learning or in reaction to unrecognized or subliminal stimuli; includes behaviour changes in the emotional sphere, but more commonly refers to the acquisition of symbolic knowledge or motor skills, does not include psychological changes, such as fatigue or temporary sensory resistance or non-functioning after continued stimulations."

10. *M.L. Bigge* (1976) — "Learning may be considered as a change in insights, behaviour, perception, motivation or a combination of these."

11. *Bernhardt* —"Learning is more or less permanent modification of an individual activity in a given situation, due to the practice in attempts to achieve some goal or solve some problem."

12. *Colvin* —"Learning is the modification of the reactions of an organism through experience."

13. *Cronbach* —"Learning is shown by a change in behaviour as a result of experience."

14. *Eason* —"Learning includes changes in behaviour that are determined primarily by the individual's interaction with his environment."

15. *Gooch* —"Learning as we measure it is a change in performance which occurs under the condition of practice."

16. *Harrimn* —"Learning is the improvement in efficiency of adjustment as a result of practice, insight, observation, imitation and conditioning."

17. *Heidgerken* —"Learning is not an addition of new experience per se, nor is it old experience summed up, rather it is the synthesis of old and the new experiences which result in completely new organisation or pattern of experience."

18. *M.H. Marx* —"Learning is a relatively enduring change in behaviour which is a function of prior behaviour (usually called practice).

19. *Gardner Murphy* (1968) —"The term learning covers every modification in behaviour to meet environmental requirements."

20. *Henry P. Smith* (1962)—"Learning is the acquisition of new behaviour or the strengthening or weakening of old behaviour as the result of experience."

21. *Woodworth* (1945) —"Any activity can be called learning so far as it develops the individual (in any respect, good or bad) and makes him alter behaviour and experiences different from what they would otherwise have been."

22. *Kingsley and R. Garry* (1957) —"Learning is the process by which behaviour (in the broader sense) is originated or changes through practice or training."

23. *Pressey, Robinson and Horrocks* (1967) —"Learning is an episode in which a motivated individual attempts to adapt his behaviour so as to succeed in a situation which he perceives as requiring action to attain a goal."

24. *Crow and Crow* (1973) —"Learning is the acquisition of habits, knowledge and attitudes. It involves new ways of doing things, and it operates in an individual's attempts to overcome obstacles or to adjust to new situations. It represents progressive changes in behaviour...... it enables him to satisfy interests to attain goals."

25. *Hilgard* (1958) —"Learning is the process by which an activity originates or is changed through reaching to an encountered situation, provided that the characteristics of the changes in activity cannot be explained on the basis of native response, tendencies, maturation, or temporary states of the organism (e.g. fatigue or drugs, etc.)."

26. *Kimble* (1961) —"Learning is a relatively permanent change in behavioural potentiality that occurs as a result of reinforced practice."

27. *Skinner* (1960) —"Learning is a process of progressive behaviour adaptation."

28. *Leagans* (1961) —"Learning is a process by which a person becomes changed in his behaviour through self-activity."

29. *Kolb* (1984) —"Learning is the process whereby knowledge is created through the transformation of experience."

30. *Van den Ban & Hawkins* (1988) defined learning as —"the acquiring or improving the ability to perform a behavioural pattern through experience and practice."

31. *Weiss* (1990) —"Learning is any relatively permanent change in behaviour that occurs as a result of experience or practice."

32. *Atkinson et al.* (1993) —"Learning is a relatively permanent change in behaviour that results from practice."

33. According to *Woolfolk* (1995), "learning occurs when experience causes a relatively permanent change in an individual's knowledge or behaviour."

That above definitions reveals the following facts about learning:

- Learning is a process and a product (outcome).
- It involves all those experiences and training of an individual (right from birth) which help him to produce changes in his behaviour.
- Learning leads to changes in behaviour but this does not necessarily mean that these changes always bring about improvement or positive development. One has an equal chance to drift to the negative side of human personality.
- Instead of change in existing behaviour or acquisition of new behaviour, learning may also result in discontinuance or abandonment of existing behaviour. Though it is referred to as unlearning, actually unlearning is also a learning process.
- Learning prepares an individual for any adjustment and adaptation that may be necessary.
- Learning is purposeful and goal-oriented. In case there is no purpose, there would hardly be any learning.
- The scope of learning is too wide to be explained in words. It is a very comprehensive process which covers nearly all fields—conative, cognitive and affective - of human behaviour.
- Learning is universal and continuous. Every creature that lives learns. In human beings, it is not restricted to any particular age, sex, race or culture. It is a continuous, never-ending process that extends from the womb to the tomb.
- As maintained by Crow and Crow, learning involves new ways of doing things but there is no limit to adopting these ways and means. All learning does not take place in the same manner. Therefore, learning as a process is of different types and involves different methods.
- As mentioned by Hilgard, the concept of learning excludes changes in behaviour on the basis of native response tendencies like instincts and reflexes, etc. Instinctive or species specific programmes cannot be termed as learned behaviour. Similarly, reflexes, the innate involuntary responses

to stimulation, e.g. blinking at bright lights and the infant's sucking behaviour, cannot be attributed to learning.

- Learning does not include changes in behaviour on account of maturation, fatigue, illness or drugs etc.

NATURE OF LEARNING

The nature of learning is as follows:

Learning is universal: Every creature that lives learns. Man learns most. The human nervous system is very complex, so are human reactions and human acquisitions. Positive learnings is vital for children's growth and development.

Learning is through experience: Learning always involves some kind of experience, direct or indirect (vicarious).

Learning is from all sides: Today learning is from all sides. Children learn from parents, teachers, environment, nature, media etc.

Learning is continuous: It denotes the lifelong nature of learning. Every day new situations arise and the individual has to bring essential changes in his style of behaviour to tackle them. Learning is from birth to death.

It results in change in behaviour: It is a change of behaviour influenced by previous behaviour. It is any activity that leaves a more or less permanent effect on later activity.

Learning is an adjustment: Learning helps the individual to adjust himself adequately to the new situations. Most learning in children involves modification, adaptation, and development of their original nature. In later life the individuals acquire new forms of behaviour.

It comes about as a result of practice: It is the basis of drill and practice. It has been proven that students learn best and retain information longer when they do meaningful practice followed with repetition. Every time practice occurs, learning continues.

Learning is a relatively permanent change: Even after a rat wakes up from sleep, he remembers the way to reach to his food. Similarly, a human being can become proficient in cycling after little practice, even though he had left it for years.

Learning as growth and development: It is a never ending growth and development. At each stage the learner acquires new vision for his future growth and new ideals for achievement of his goal. According to Woodworth, "All activity can be called learning so far as it develops the individual."

Learning is not directly observable: The only way to study learning is through some observable behaviour. Actually, we cannot observe learning; we see only what precedes performance, the performance itself and the consequences of performance.

PRINCIPLES OF LEARNING

There are some principles of learning, which are very much applicable in extension. These principles are generalized guidelines, which form the basis for taking action. Following are some of the principles of learning along with their implications for teaching:

1. Principle of Association: Learning is growth-like and continuous. The kind of learning that takes place is the result of the kind of experience, we have. Previous learning always sets the stage for subsequent learning. New learning may be associated with previous successful and satisfying responses. For example, if the farmers have obtained profitable return by the application of nitrogenous fertilizer, they may be motivated to use balanced fertilizers containing phosphate and potash, for still higher return.

Implications for Teaching: Implications of this principle are:

- Begin at the level of the learner.
- New must be related to the old.
- Adjust the pace to the learner's capacity—one idea at a time.
- Bring the idea to the attention of the learner repeatedly (in a variety of ways) and over a period of time.

2. Principle of clarity of Objectives: Learning is more effective, when it is purposeful. It has to be useful to the learners. Objectives must be clear and meaningful to the learners. What is to be learnt must be important to a relatively large number of participants in the group and must be attainable.

Implications for Teaching

- Learning must make sense to the learner.
- Progress must be constantly appraised and redirected.
- Purpose must be kept in sharp focus (objectives must be clear to the learner and teacher).

3. Principle of Self Activity: Learning is an active process on the part of the learners. The instructor can create a situation and stimulate a person to learn. The door to learning is "locked from inside" and unless the learner opens the door herself/himself, learning cannot take place. Activities appropriate to the specific learning must be used. For example, conducting demonstration by the farmers in their own fields provides opportunity for self-activity, that is, *learning by doing*. This makes learning effective and permanent.

Implications for Teaching

- Activities appropriate to specific learning situation must be used.
- Learning activities should engage a maximum number of senses.

4. Principle of Motivation: To learn, people need to feel the need for learning. When this desire exists, the learner will exert a high level of effort. The learning experience, therefore, should be so designed that learners can see how it will help them achieve the goals they have set for themselves.

Implications for Teaching

- Teacher motivation of the student is essential in making learning more challenging.
- Standards demanded of the learner should be suitable to their ability or capacity.
- Appropriate and timely recognition should be given to student achievement.

5. Principle of Practice: When learners actually practice what they have read, heard, or seen, they gain confidence and are less likely to make errors or to forget what they have learned. Active involvement through practice, therefore, should be made part of the learning process.

Implications for Teaching

- Course content should be organized into meaningful units.
- Theory should be related to practice.
- Emphasis on provide activities that stimulate actual use situation.

6. Principle of Disassociation: Learning is affected by emotions. The most effective way of eliminating an undesirable response is to set up a desirable substitute that must be more satisfying than the original reaction.

Implications for Teaching

- Strive to increase pleasant emotions and decrease unpleasant emotions of students in connection with the learning process.
- Train the expression of emotions in the right direction.

7. Principle of Readiness: Learning takes place more effectively when one is ready to learn.

8. Principle of Set or Attitude: An unfavourable attitude or set retards learning and a favourable attitude accelerates it.

9. Principle of Reinforcement: Behaviours that are positively reinforced (rewarded) are encouraged and sustained. When the behaviour is punished, it is temporarily suppressed but is unlikely to be extinguished.

10. Principle of Transfer of Learning: It does not make much sense in perfecting a particular skill in the classroom that cannot be successfully transferred later to a related job. Therefore, learning should be designed to foster transferability.

11. Principle of Feedback: Learning is facilitated when the learners are provided with knowledge of progress of learning.

12. Principle of Abilities: Learning abilities varies widely among individuals. The level of communication and the level of understandability of the subject matter taught must be in line with the learner's ability.

CHARACTERISTICS OF LEARNING

The main characteristics of learning are discussed below:

Learning is Growth: The word 'growth' is generally associated with the body which is growing, but through the mental growth of the learner. Although it is latent, yet we can perceive its growth. Through his daily activities the child grows both mentally and physically. Therefore, we say that learning is growth through experience.

Learning is Experience: The individual lea ns through experiences. Human life is full of experiences. All these experiences provide new knowledge, understanding, skills and attitudes. Learning is not mere acquisition of the knowledge, skills and attitudes. It is also the reorganization of experiences or the synthesis of the old experiences with the new.

Motivation is a Key Component in Learning: Motivation does not merely help learning. It is essential for learning. Motivation, as described here, is broadly conceived to include an understanding of ways in which the knowledge can be used. Unless we know "the reasons–why", we may not be very involved in using the knowledge that may be instilled in us, even by the most serious and direct teaching.

Learning is Adjustment: Learning helps the individual to adjust himself adequately to new situations. Children meet with new situations which demand solution. Repeated efforts are required to react to them effectively. Life is full of experiences and each experience leaves behind some effects in the mental structure. These effects modify our behaviour.

Learning is Organizing Experience: Learning is not mere addition to knowledge. It is not mere acquisition of facts and skills through drill and repetition. It is the reorganization of experience.

Learning is Purposeful: All true learning is based on purpose. Purpose plays a big role in learning. According to Ryburn, "This purpose is always connected with the use of some instinctive power, with the use of the energy with which we are endowed with birth". We do not learn anything and everything that comes in our way, in a haphazard manner. All school activities should be purposeful so that the child can feel the real urge for learning.

Learning Involves Language: The language we use influences learning. On the empirical level, researchers have noted that people talk to themselves as they learn. On a more general level, there is a collection of arguments, presented most forcefully by Vigotsky that language and learning are inextricably intertwined.

Learning is Intelligent: Meaningless efforts do not produce permanent result. Any work done mechanically is without any soul. When a child learns something unintelligently, he is likely to forget it very soon. He does not assimilate through late learning. Only efforts made intelligently have lasting effects.

Learning is an Active Process: Learning is an active process in which the learner uses sensory input and constructs meaning out of it. The more traditional formulation of this idea involves the terminology of the active learner (Dewey's term) stressing that the learner needs to do something; that learning is not the passive acceptance of knowledge which exists "out there". It also engages the learner with the world.

Learning does not take place without a purpose and self-activity. In the teaching-learning process, the activity of the learner counts more than the activity of the teacher. The principle of learning by doing is the main principle and it has been recommended by all modern educationists. It is the basis of all progressive methods of education such as the Dalton, the Project, the Montessori and the Basic.

Learning is Both Individual and Social: Learning is more than an individual activity. It is also a social activity. Individual mind is affected by the group mind consciously as well as unconsciously as individual is influenced by his friends, teachers, peers relatives, classmates, parents, etc. and learns their ideas, feelings and notions. Social agencies like the family, church, film etc.

have a tremendous influence on the child and are always moulding and re-moulding him.

Much of traditional education, as Dewey pointed out, is directed towards isolating the learner from all social interactions, and towards seeing education as a one-on-one relationship between the learner and the objective material to be learned. In contrast, progressive education (to continue to use Dewey's formulation) recognizes the social aspect of learning and uses conversation, interaction with others, and the application of knowledge as an integral aspect of learning.

Learning is the Product of the Environment: Environment plays an important role in the growth and development of the individual. Therefore, the Environment should be healthy and rich in educative possibilities. The individual interact with people in the society. Particularly, environment plays an important part in the growth and development of the individual. The physical, social, intellectual and emotional development of the child is moulded and remoulded by the objects and individuals in his environment. Therefore, the child should be kept away from unhealthy environment which could otherwise be detrimental to his learning.

People Learn to Learn as they Learn: Learning consists both of constructing meaning and constructing systems of meaning. For example, if we learn the chronology of dates of a series of historical events, we are simultaneously learning the meaning of a chronology. Each meaning we construct enables us to give meaning to other sensations which can fit a similar pattern.

The crucial action of constructing meaning is Mental: It happens in the mind. Physical actions, hands-on experience may be necessary for learning, especially for children, but it is not sufficient; we need to provide activities which engage the mind as well as the hands.

True learning affects the conduct of the Learner: There is a change in the mental structure of the learner after every experience. Learning is called the modification of behaviour. It affects the learner's behaviour and conduct. Therefore attempts are made to provide such learning experiences which can mould the desired conduct and habits in the learners.

Learning is Contextual: We do not learn isolated facts and theories in some abstract ethereal land of the mind, separate from the rest of our lives: we learn in relationship to what else we know, what we believe, our prejudices and our fears. On reflection, it becomes clear that this point is actually a corollary of the idea that learning is active and social. We cannot divorce our learning from our lives.

One needs knowledge to Learn: It is not possible to assimilate new knowledge without having some structure developed from previous knowledge to build on. The more we know, the more we can learn. Therefore any effort to teach must be connected to the state of the learner. Teaching must provide a path into the subject based on the previous knowledge of the learner.

It Takes Time to Learn: Learning is not instantaneous. For significant learning we need to revisit ideas before applying them. This cannot happen in the 5-10 minutes usually spent in a gallery (and certainly not in the few seconds usually spent contemplating a single museum object.) If you reflect on anything you have learned, you soon realize that it is the product of repeated exposure and thought. Even, or especially, moments of profound insight, can be traced back to longer periods of preparation.

LAWS OF LEARNING

On the basis of research findings, Thorndike (1932) formulated three Laws that govern learning:

The Law of Effect: This law states that a satisfying state of affairs leads to repetition of a given behaviour, whereas an annoying state of weakness delays a response. If raising a hand by student attracts the teacher's attention and recognition, his behaviour has resulted in a satisfying state of affairs and this is likely to repeat. On the other hand, if a pupil raises hand to attract teacher's attention and the teacher does not recognize it, the pupil is less likely to repeat such behaviour. This, too, shows how learning occurs.

The Law of Readiness: Given a situation where a person is ready or prepared to engage in certain behaviour and is provided with an opportunity, the whole experience will be a pleasing or satisfying one. Therefore it is important to note that learner's readiness is important in learning. Secondly, if a person is denied the chance to engage in behaviour for which he/she is prepared, this will result in frustration and annoyance. Third, if a person is forced to engage in certain behaviour for which he is not ready, the end result will be annoying.

The Law of Exercise: A strong connection or bond is established between a stimulus and a response as a result of practice. Indeed, as it is often said, "*practice makes perfect*". The more the skill or body of information is practiced the more it will be mastered, applied and retained in memory. In Tanzanian primary schools for example, it is a common practice for pupils to memorise multiplication tables. This practice applies the law of exercise.

LEARNING CURVE

A learning curve is a graphic representation, which is drawn to represent the progress of learning of an individual or a group in a given period. Usually the abscissa (x-axis) of a learning curve is described in terms of number of trails or some measure of time. The ordinate (y-axis) is usually represented by scores (latency, frequency, etc). The slope of the curve indicates the rate of progress (increase or decrease).

Two telegraphists, namely Bryan and Harter were the originators of a learning curve. While transmitting telegrams, they came across this phenomenon.

If we take trails on X-axis and progress on Y-axis and join the points, we have with us a learning curve (Figure 1.1).

The learning curves connected with child learning are almost confined entirely to the sensory-motor types of learning. They represent acquisition of skills such as telegraphy, typewriting, learning (memorization) and retention or forgetting of practice material like nonsense syllables. Since such material is divisible into units and is capable of quantitative expression, the drawing of learning curves representing these skills is possible.

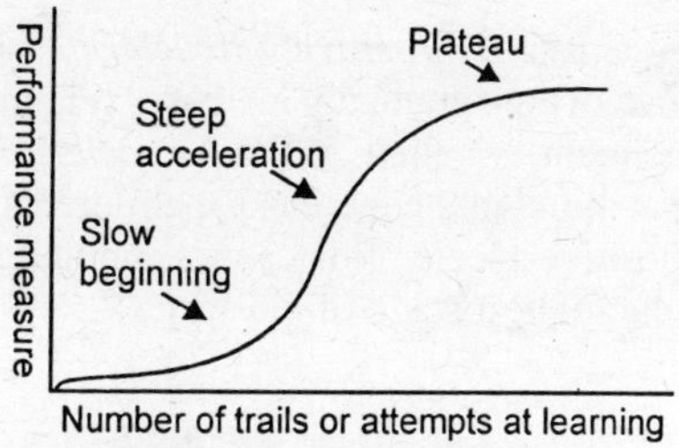

Figure 1.1: Learning Curve

Types of Learning Curves

The progress made in the acquisition of skills when graphically plotted takes the form of several types of curves. The different types of learning curves are as follows:

Straight Line Curve: Such a curve shows a constant or uniform rate of progress (Figure-1.2). This type of curve is seldom found. Here the increment of gain is the same for each successive trail.

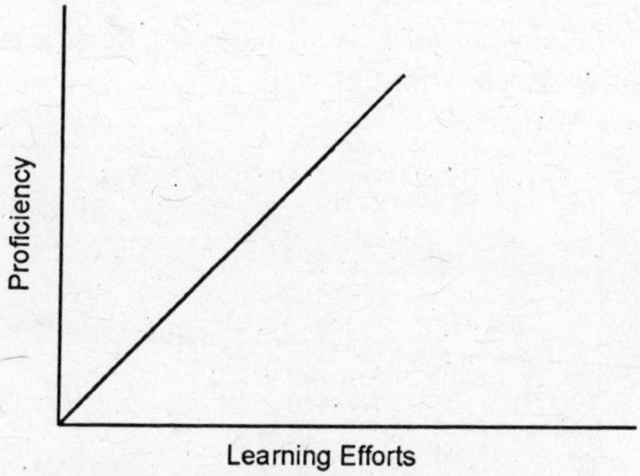

Figure 1.2: Straight Line Learning Curve

Convex Learning Curve or Negatively Accelerated Learning Curve: In convex curve, there is the fastest rate of gain in the beginning but decreases as practice continues. Such a rate is called *negative acceleration.* Improvement is still being made but the increment of gain decreases in successive trails. (Figure-1.3). Such learning curve is frequently found.

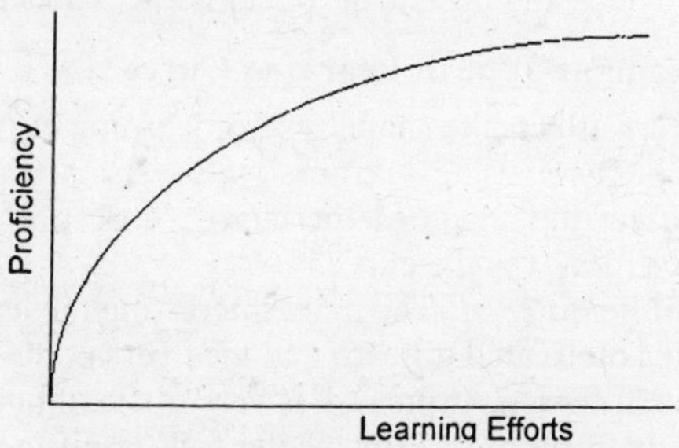

Figure 1.3: Convex Learning Curve

Concave Learning Curve or Positively Accelerated Curve: This curve shows that the initial rate of gain gradually increases (Figure-1.4). This increase in the rate of improvement is called *positive acceleration*. An example of positive acceleration is found in the increase of children's vocabulary. It must be remembered that positive acceleration cannot continue indefinitely. Sooner or later one reaches the highest stage of mastery.

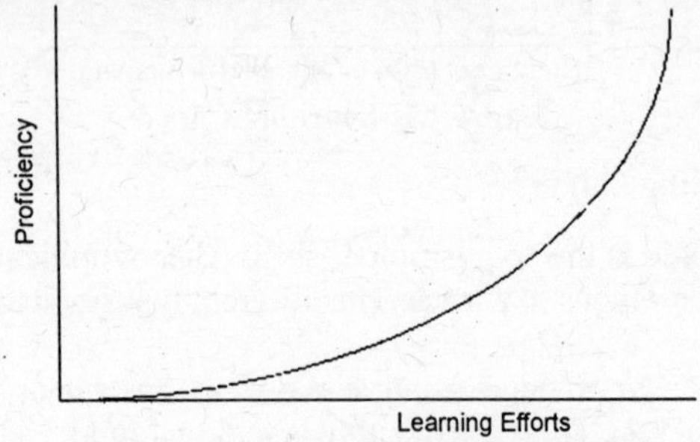

Figure 1.4: Concave Learning Curve

Combination of Convex and Concave Curve: Such a curve represents negative and positive accelerations as well.

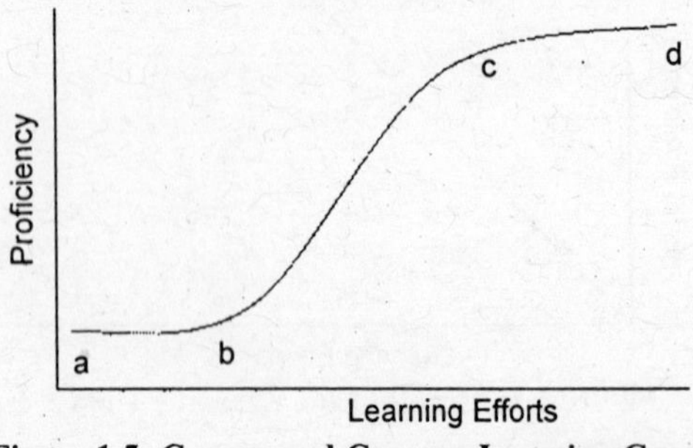

Figure 1.5: Convex and Concave Learning Curve

On account of individual differences, these curves vary from person to person and from subject to subject. The form of the curve depends partly on the nature of the work and partly on the learner's ability to perform a task, his method of work, previous training and the circumstances under which he works.

Factors Affecting Shape/Type of Learning Curve

The following factors affects the shape/type of learning curve:

Nature of the Learner: The learners' interests, attitudes, potentials capabilities etc. affect the shape of the curve., e.g- more interests, more learning, more upward moves the curve.

Nature of Learning Material: The more interesting the learning materials, the more the child is motivated to learn and vice versa.

Length of Practice Period: If the task is very difficult but is also given lot of time then it leads to progress. But, if the task is difficult and not given enough time than the progress is affected; it may lead to less or even no learning.

Previous Learning: It adopts the principle of moving from the Known to Unknown. This leads to progress in learning.

Environmental Factors: Factors like proper ventilation, lighting, seating arrangements etc. lead to better learning as they help a child to pay more attention. It leads to progress in learning. On the other hand, poor environmental condition affects learning and leads to downward moving curve.

To Know the Extent to Which Objectives have been Achieved: Objectives achieved lead to progress—curve moves upward. Objectives not achieved—lead to no or less learning, decline in the progress.

Drawbacks/limitation of Learning Curve

The main drawbacks of learning curve are as follows:

- The data for learning curve is very limited, e.g. acquisition of skills, memory, forgetting (how much one forgets, after each interval)
- Disregard to individual learning in its environment, i.e. it ignores the learning environment.
- It does not show progress in terms of learning that has taken place as per unit time, i.e. how much learning has taken place in each interval.
- Learning curve does not show latent learning, i.e. hidden learning. For example, a small child learning to speak in the initial phases of life. The learning of language cannot be measured.

Phases of Typical Learning Curve

The phases of a typical learning curve are:

A Period of Slow Progress: Here, since the learning material is new or because the child has just started learning, the rate of progress in this initial stage is very slow. e.g. child learning types of noun for the first time—slow learning.

A Period of Rapid Progress: Now slowly-slowly the child gets involved into the process of learning. In case of new material with more practice the child gains mastery over it, showing a rapid progress in learning, thereby accelerating the curve upward.

Period of No Progress: Now, since the child has gained mastery over the learning material, he may revise some of the material or may take some rest because of which no new learning takes place and therefore the curve stays stable.

Period of Sudden Rise: Now, again the child takes up something new and learns because of which learning has taken place which leads to rise in learning curve.

Leveling Off: The phase of leveling off is reached when the physiological limits are reached, when the brain are saturated and one is not physically and mentally ready to do any more learning. At such time one needs to take a break from learning.

FACTORS THAT MAY AFFECT THE LEARNING PROCESS

Some of the important factors which may affect the learning process are as follows:

Intellectual Factor

The term refers to the 'individual' mental level. Success in school is generally closely related to the level of the intellect. Pupils with low intelligence often encounter serious difficulty in mastering schoolwork. Sometimes pupils do not learn because of special intellectual disabilities. A low score in one subject and better scores in other subjects indicate the possible presence of a special deficiency. Psychology reveals that an individual possesses different kinds intelligence. Knowledge of the nature of the pupil's intellect is of considerable value in the guidance and the diagnosis of disability. The native capacity of the individual is of prime importance in determining the effectiveness of the learning process.

Learning Factors

Factors owing to lack of mastery of what has been taught, faulty methods of work or study, and narrowness of experimental background may affect the learning process of any pupil. If the school proceeds too rapidly and does not constantly check up the extent to which the pupil is mastering what is being taught, the pupil accumulates a number of deficiencies that interfere with successful progress.

In arithmetic, for instance, knowledge of basic addition is essential to successful work in multiplication. Weakness in addition will contribute directly to the deficiency in multiplication. Likewise, failure in history may be due to low reading ability or weakness in English. Similarly, because of faulty instruction, the pupil may have learned inefficient methods of study. Many other kinds of difficulty which are directly related to learning factors may interfere with progress.

Physical Factors

Under this group are included such factors as health, physical development, nutrition, visual and physical defects, and glandular abnormality. It is generally recognized that ill health retards physical and motor development, and malnutrition interferes with learning and physical growth.

Children suffering from visual, auditory, and other physical defects are seriously handicapped in developing skills such as reading and spelling. It has been demonstrated that various glands of internal secretion, such as the thyroid and pituitary glands, affect behaviour. The health of the learner will likely affect his ability to learn and his power to concentrate.

Mental Factors

Attitude falls under mental factors. Attitudes are made up of organic and kinesthetic elements. They are not to be confused with emotions that are characterized by internal visceral disturbances. Attitudes are more or less of definite sort. They play a large part in the mental organization and general behaviour of the individual.

Attitudes are also important in the development of personality. Among these attitudes are interest, cheerfulness, affection, prejudice, open mindedness and loyalty. Attitudes exercise a stimulating effect upon the rate of learning and teaching and upon the progress in school. The efficiency of the work from day to day and the rapidity with which it is achieved are influenced by the attitude of the learner. A favourable mental attitude facilitates learning. The factor of interest is very closely related in nature to that of symbolic drive and reward.

Emotional and Social Factors

Personal factors, such as instincts and emotions; social factors such as cooperation and rivalry are directly related to a complex psychology of motivation. It is a recognized fact that the various responses of the individual to various kinds of stimuli are determined by a wide variety of tendencies.

Some of these innate tendencies are constructive and others are harmful. For some reason a pupil may have developed a dislike for some subject because he may fail to see its value, or may lack foundation. This dislike results in a bad emotional state. Some pupils are in a continuing state of unhappiness because of their fear of being victims of the disapproval of their teachers and classmates. This is an unwholesome attitude and affects the learning process to a considerable degree. Often, this is the result of bad training.

Environmental Factor

Physical conditions needed for learning comes under environmental factor. One of the factors that affect the efficiency of learning is the condition in which learning takes place. This includes the classrooms, textbooks, equipment, school supplies, and other instructional materials.

In the school and at the home, the conditions for learning must be favourable and adequate if teaching is to produce the desired results. It cannot be denied that the type and quality of instructional materials and equipment play an important part in the instructional efficiency of the school.

It is difficult to do a good teaching in a poor type of building and without adequate equipment and instructional materials. A school building or a classroom has no merit when built without due regard to its educational objectives and functions.

Teacher's Personality

The teacher as an individual whose personality is an important element in the learning environment or in the failures and success of the learner. The way in which his personality interacts with the personalities of the pupils being taught helps to determine the kind of behaviour which emerges from the learning situation.

The supreme value of a teacher is not in the regular performance of routine duties, but in his power to lead and to inspire his pupils through the influence of his moral personality and example. Strictly speaking, personality is made up of all the factors that make the individual what he is, the complex pattern of characteristics that distinguishes him from the others of his kind. Personality is the product of many integrating forces.

In other words, an individual's personality is a composite of his physical appearance, his mental capacity, his emotional behaviour, and his attitude towards others. Effective teaching and learning are the results of an integrated personality of the teacher.

Generally speaking, pupils do not like a grouchy teacher who cannot control his temper before the class. It is impossible for a teacher with a temper to create enthusiasm and radiate light and sunshine to those around him.

Pupils love a happy, sympathetic, enthusiastic and cheerful teacher. Effective teaching and learning are the results of love for the pupils, sympathy for their interests, tolerance, and a definite capacity for understanding.

The teacher must therefore recognize that in all his activities in the classroom he is directly affecting the behaviour of the growing and learning students.

FACTORS ASSOCIATED WITH LEARNER THAT AFFECTS LEARNING

Learner is the key figure in any learning task. He has to learn to bring desired modification in his behaviour. How he will learn or what he will achieve, through a particular learning act, depends heavily upon his own characteristics and ways or learning. Such things or factors associated with this can be described as follows:

Learner's Physical and Mental Health

Learning is greatly affected by the learner's physical and mental health maintained by him, particularly at the time of learning. A simple headache or a stomach pain can play havoc with the process and products of learning. A child who does not maintain satisfactory physical health, has to suffer adversely in term of learning. Similarly, the mental state and the health of a learner at the time of learning become potent factors in deciding the outcome of his learning. A tense, emotionally and mentally disturbed learner cannot show satisfactory results in learning.

Basic Potential of the Learner

The results achieved by the learner through a process of learning depend heavily upon his basic potential to undergo such learning. Such potential may consist of the following:

- Learner's innate abilities and capacities for learning.
- Learner's basic potential in terms of general intelligence and specific knowledge, understanding and skills related to a particular learning area.
- Learner's basic interests, aptitudes and attitudes related to the learning of a particular thing or area.

Level of Aspiration and Achievement Motivation

Learning is greatly influenced by the level of aspiration and nature of achievement, motivation possessed by a learner. How can we expect a learner to achieve something for which he has no aspiration? Also, too much aspiration makes it impossible for an individual to achieve. A person has to maintain the level of his aspiration and achievement motivation at a reasonable level. His aspirations should be neither too high which could result in non-achievement of his goals, nor too low that could dissuade him from achieving what he can.

Goals of Life

The philosophy of immediate as well as ultimate goals of one's life affects the process and product of learning. His mode and ways of looking towards things, his inclination towards learning a particular subject and patience and persistence in pursuing his learning despite the heavy odds—all depend upon his goals and philosophy of life.

Readiness and Will Power

A learner's readiness and power to learn is a great deciding factor of his results in learning. No power on earth can help a learner if he is not ready to learn. If he has a will to learn anything, he will himself find ways for effective learning.

FACTORS ASSOCIATED WITH THE TYPES OF LEARNING EXPERIENCES THAT AFFECT LEARNING

The type of changes or modifications found in learner's behaviour depends much on the type of learning experience and training received by him for this purpose. This task involves a variety of factors given below.

Nature of Learning Experience

Learning is influenced by the nature of the subject matter and the learning experiences presented to a learner such as the following:

- Whether the nature of learning experience is formal or informal, incidental or well-planned, direct or indirect.
- Whether learning experiences are suitably selected on the basis of the principle of child-centeredness, principle of activity, criterion of activity, age, grade and experiences of a learner.
- Whether learning experiences are suitably organised for the attainment of desired educational objectives or not.

Methodology of Learning

Learning depends upon the methods, techniques and approaches employed for the teaching and learning of the selected contents. Let us think about the truth of this statement from various angles:

Linking the Recent Learning with those of the Past: The quality of result in learning depends much on the abilities of a teacher and a learner to link the present new learning with the past experiences of the learner. Past experiences help the learner to assimilate and understand the new learning.

Correlating Learning in one Area with that of Another: Correlation facilitates the task of learning as it allows maximum transfer of training or learning from one area to another. Accordingly, one can expect good results in learning, if learning experiences are given in view of seeking correlation (a) among the different subjects on areas, (b) within the branches or experiences of the same area and (c) with real life happenings and situations.

Utilization of Maximum Number of Senses: Senses are said to be the gateway of knowledge and consequently the results in learning are very much influenced by the nature and type of utilization of one's senses in the acquisition of learning experiences. A learner who learns through utilization of his maximum senses like sense of sight, hearing, touch, smell, taste and also tries to learn by doing things for himself, always has an advantageous edge over others.

Revision and Practice: Review and practice always brings good results in the achievements of learning. A learner who makes use of sufficient drill work, practice work, revision and review of his learning can be expected to harvest a good yield in terms of his good retention, reproduction and utilization at the proper time.

Provision of Proper Feedback and Reinforcement: Learning yields are dependent upon the nature and quality of the reinforcement provided to the learner in his learning task. One must be acquainted with the progress of his learning in term of his strength and weakness and remedial action if needed may be taken at the proper time. Knowledge of the results and the progress may work for providing immediate reinforcement to the learner. In addition to it, learning process can be suitably designed if we take due care to make planning of proper reinforcement schedules.

The Selection of the Suitable Learning Methods of Techniques: There are sufficient methods and a number of good techniques available for the teaching and learning of different subjects and areas of experiences. The results of learning are always influenced by the nature and quality of the methods and techniques employed for the teaching and learning of a particular content, subject matter or learning experiences.

FACTORS ASSOCIATED WITH THE MEN AND MATERIAL RESOURCES THAT AFFECT LEARNING

A learner is helped by the available resources (men and material) for bringing desirable changes in his behaviour. How effectively such changes will take place in his behaviour depends much on the quality and management of these resources. Certain factors which affect learning may be listed in the following manner:

- Quality of teacher in term of his mastery over the subject matter, teaching skills, rich experiences, teacher qualities and behaviour.
- Socio-emotional climate available in the institution in the form of teacher-pupil relationships, pupil-pupil relationships and school-staff relationships and the like.
- Availability of appropriate learning material and facilities like teaching-learning aids, text books, library and laboratory facilities, project works etc.
- Availability of proper conducive environment and learning situations like:
  - Proper seating arrangement
  - Calm and peaceful environment
  - Management and control of the factors leading to distraction
  - Cooperative and competitive group situations
  - Congenial learning environment at home
  - Provision of proper change, rest and recreation
  - Provision of opportunity for creativity and self expression

Classroom Implications of Learning

Classroom implications of learning may be summarized as under:

Who is to Learn?: The child is to learn and therefore, his age, abilities, aptitudes and interests may be taken note of by all those who are responsible for the learning of the child.

From Whom to Learn?: Learning is from the teacher. Therefore, a teacher must present a good model of teaching-learning.

Why to Learn?: Learning is not merely in terms of the traditional 3 R's, i.e. reading, writing and arithmetic but in terms of 7R's, i.e. reading, writing, arithmetic, rights, responsibilities and their relationships and recreation. Learning is for individual good as well as for the good of the society.

How to Learn?: It involves various methods of learning, for instance learning through rote memory, learning through imitation, learning through insight etc.

When to Learn: This is concerned with motivational situations for the learner.

Where to Learn?: Learning takes place in the classroom, on the playfield, in the workshop, in the neighbourhood, etc. School is not the only place of learning.

2
Behaviourist Approach to Learning

According to behaviourism, learning is a mechanical process of associating the stimulus with response, which produces a new behaviour. Such behaviour is strengthened by the reinforcement. Behaviourists view the learner as a passive person, who responds to the stimuli. According to them, the learner starts as '*tabula rasa*' (which means clean slate) and the behaviour is shaped by reinforcement. Positive as well as negative reinforcement increase the probability of the repetition of behaviour. However, the punishment decreases the chance of repetition of the behaviour. Learning is therefore defined as a change in the behaviour of the learner.

The behaviourist school sees the mind as a "black box," in the sense that a response to a stimulus can be observed quantitatively, totally ignoring the effect of thought processes occurring in the mind. The school, therefore, looks at overt behaviours that can be observed and measured as indicators of learning.

KEY IDEAS OF BEHAVIOURISM

The key ideas of behaviourism are as follows:

- Behaviourism focuses on observable learning events as demonstrated by stimulus and response relationships.
- Learning always involves a change in behaviour.
- Mental processes should be excluded from the scientific study of learning.
- The laws governing learning apply equally to all organisms, including human organisms.
- Organisms begin life as blank slates: there are no innate laws of behaviour.
- Learning results from external events in the environment.
- Behaviourism is a deterministic theory: the subject has no choice but to respond to appropriate stimuli.

BEHAVIOURIST ASSUMPTIONS ABOUT LEARNING

The main assumptions of behaviourist learning are as follows:

- Observable behaviour is more important than understanding internal activities;
- Behaviour should be focused on simple elements: specific stimuli and responses;
- Learning is about behaviour change.

KEY PRINCIPLES OF BEHAVIOURISM

The key principles of behaviourism are as follows:

Reinforcement: Positive or negative feedback which will lead the learner to form a strong association between the stimulus and the desired behaviour.

Contiguity: The more immediate the feedback, the stronger the association.

Repetition: The more frequent the stimulus-response the more likely is the desired outcome.

Variation: Varying the pattern of the stimulus generalizes the response.

Intermittent Reinforcement: Not rewarding the response every time is found to be more effective than constant reward; it helps keep the learner guessing.

Extinction: If the stimulus-response bond is not reinforced the association will die.

BEHAVIOURAL APPROACHES TO LEARNING

Common behavioural approaches to learning are as follows:

- The learner takes on a predominantly passive and reactive role.
- Instruction is structured and systematic.
- Concrete and defined instructional goals, objectives and strategies aimed at learners in general and not on the individual learner.
- Learning can be measured.
- It assumes that a well-planned instructional intervention can result in a desired learning outcome.
- Focus on simplification (start with easy and progress to more difficult) and repetition (rote learning/drill and practice).
- Instruction is instructor-controlled.

STRENGTHS OF BEHAVIOURISM

The main strengths of Behaviourism are as follows:

- It can be used to formulate behavioural contracts in the school as well as at home.
- It is helpful in bringing about behaviour modification (desired outcome) with the help of reinforcement, punishment and extinction.
- Cueing responses to behaviour allow the learner to react in a predictable way under certain conditions.
- Success of outcomes is easily measurable.
- Guarantees specific learning.
- Ease of application.

WEAKNESSES OF BEHAVIOURISM

The main weaknesses of Behaviourism are as follows:

- It is an extrapolation of animal behaviour to humans.
- Behaviourism fails to explain the development of human languages.
- Effect of environment in shaping the behaviour of a human, is not taken into account by the behaviourists.

IMPLICATIONS OF BEHAVIOURISM

- Learners should be told the explicit outcomes of the learning, so that they can set expectations and can judge for themselves, whether or not they have achieved the outcome of the day's lesson.
- Learners must be tested to determine whether or not they have achieved

the learning outcome. Testing and assessment should be integrated into the learning sequence to check the learner's achievement level and to provide appropriate feedback.

- Learning materials must be sequenced appropriately to promote learning. The sequencing could take the form of simple to complex, known to unknown, and knowledge to application.
- Learners must be provided with feedback so that they can monitor how they are doing and take corrective action if required.
- The techniques of reinforcement and punishment have been employed by the teachers in the classrooms to promote desirable behaviour and discourage unwanted behaviour of the learners.

PRACTICAL IMPLICATIONS OF BEHAVIOURISM

Current educational practice is influenced by behaviourist features like:

Curriculum Planning

The following list outlines curriculum-planning steps commonly undertaken by teachers at different educational levels:

- identify the need for the programme;
- determine the aims and instructional objectives of the programme;
- define the characteristics of the target group;
- list the precise learning outcomes;
- categorize learning outcomes according to Bloom's taxonomies;
- break the material down into small units;
- carefully sequence these units;
- provide frequent practice to strengthen the stimulus–response bond;
- ensure that the learner responds (does things);
- observe and assess any behavioural changes;
- provide opportunities for frequent learner feedback;
- reinforce 'correct' behaviour with immediate rewards;
- evaluate the effectiveness of the programme;
- modify and improve the programme.

Learning Outcomes

Learning outcomes, which have developed from the behavioural educational objectives described above, are increasingly used at all levels of education, although their application is more straightforward when the behaviours are easily observed. Their use is more difficult when applied to complex and internal thought processes. A learning outcome is an explicit statement of what a learner will be able to do as a result of completing a course of study. A learning outcome statement includes:

- action, expressed using precise behavioural verbs;
- context, which requires reference to the conditions of performance;
- threshold, which is an indication of acceptable performance—that is, a statement about the performance threshold required.

Learning outcomes help learners at all levels to understand exactly what is expected of them and to tailor their learning activities accordingly. One of the major contributions of behaviourism to contemporary educational practice has been to remove the mystique and vagueness that has frequently characterized the discourse of educational aims and objectives.

Assessment

It is commonly held that effective assessment tasks should test the performance of behaviours stated in learning outcomes under the same conditions as those under which they were learnt. For example, if the learning outcome states that apprentice carpenters will be able to hang a door, the assessment should require them to hang a door rather than describe the technique in a written examination, which is what often happens.

Behaviourist principles are useful as part of formative assessment, which is a kind of assessment designed to provide feedback for the learner and teacher, rather than to record or certify achievement. Formative assessment may be seen as a form of reinforcement, designed to motivate and encourage learners. To be effective, the reinforcement of desired behaviour must be provided consistently and in a timely manner so that the correct response is reinforced. When it comes to assessment, therefore, learners should receive feedback as quickly as possible after the assessment task.

Behaviour Management

Changing or strengthening learners' behaviours is the aim of most elementary learning programmes. The strengthening of specific behaviours act as a precursor to the development of cognitive skills. As part of the process of behaviour management, teachers can use operant conditioning techniques, which Skinner claims work best in providing motivation for learning. Indeed, positive reinforcement or the use of praise as a motivator lies behind practices that seek to reward learners when they demonstrate the behaviour the teacher has set out to inculcate. Reinforcers may be:

- material, such as prizes and awards;
- social, such as teacher attention, approval or praise;
- activity-related, such as an opportunity to engage in a favourite activity;
- intrinsic, such as feelings of self-actualization or pride.

MAJOR LEARNING THEORIES RELATED TO BEHAVIOURISM

I.P. Pavlov's Classical Conditioning or Conditioning Response Learning Theory

Behaviourism had its origins in the last years of the nineteenth century, when physiologists such as Ivan Pavlov investigated animals' automatic and involuntary responses to stimuli. Classical behaviourists believe that all learning conforms to observable scientific laws governing behavioural associations and patterns; the learner simply responds to external stimuli in a deterministic manner.

What is Classical Conditioning?

Classical conditioning proposes that we learn through association. This was first discovered by Pavlov in his experiments with dogs. Pavlov first established that meat caused dogs to salivate, but a neutral stimulus such as the tone of a bell did not cause the dog to salivate. However, when Pavlov presented several pairings of the tone and food, the dog began to salivate to the tone when it was presented alone. The dogs learnt to associate the tone with food, and responded accordingly. Within classical conditioning there are certain stimuli and responses which make up the results seen in Pavlov's dog. These are: unconditioned stimulus, conditioned stimulus, unconditioned response and conditioned response.

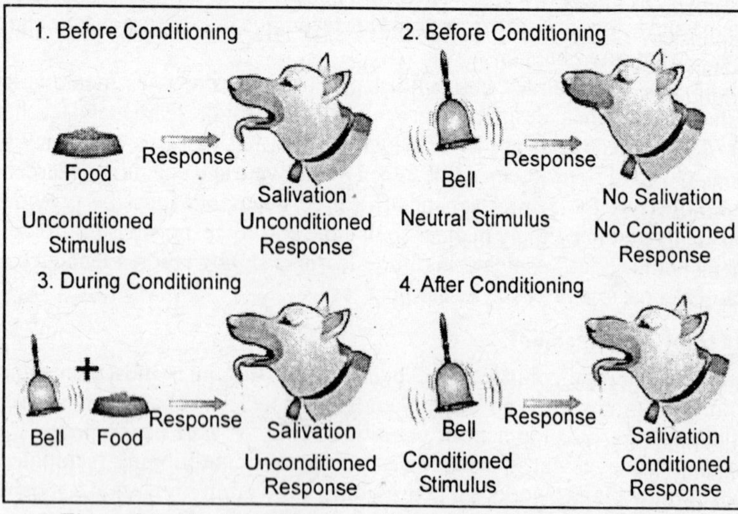

Figure 2.1: Illustrates Pavlov's Classic Experiments with Dogs

Pavlov noted that the smell of food caused dogs to salivate. This is an 'unconditional response' because the dogs reacted naturally to the food (the 'unconditional stimulus'). Pavlov began ringing a bell (a 'conditional stimulus') immediately prior to providing the food, and discovered that after a certain number of repetitions, the bell alone was sufficient to cause salivation. This is a 'conditional' or trained response and needs to occur contiguously, or close in time, to the unconditional.

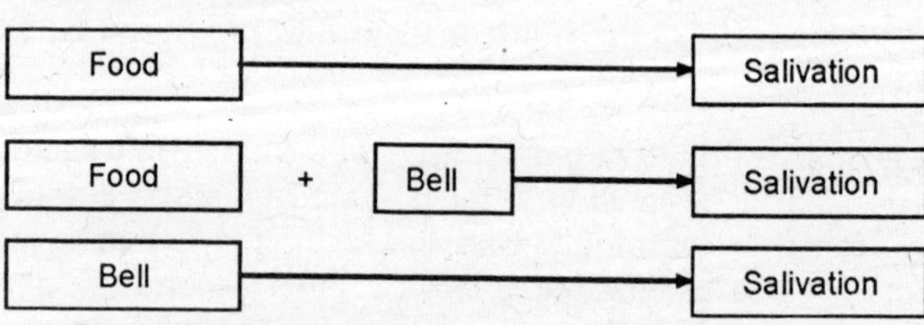

Figure 2.2: Unconditional and conditional responses

When the conditional stimulus (the bell) is repeatedly presented without the associated unconditional stimulus (the food), the conditional response (salivation) declines until it is non-existent. This is called 'extinction'. The principle of conditional response underpins the behaviour modification called 'classical conditioning', which is at the heart of behaviourism. Behaviourists tend to use the term 'conditioning' instead of 'learning' to indicate that the subject is changed by external rather than cognitive events.

The theory of classical conditioning can be used to explain how people learn a variety of involuntary responses, especially those associated with physiological functioning or the emotions. For example, most people experience darkness as an unconditional stimulus for going to sleep; therefore, in particular environmental settings, darkness may elicit a 'go-to-sleep' response. Classical conditioning is also useful for explaining the development of fears and phobias. For example, a person who is bitten by a dog may become afraid of that breed of dog, or even of all dogs.

Characteristics of Classical Conditioning

Some important characteristics of classical conditioning are as follows:

Intensity: There is positive relationship between intensity of the stimulus and magnitude of the response but there is negative correlation between intensity of the stimulus and latency of the response. It has also been reported that if the CS is too weak there may be no conditioning.

Temporal Relationship between CS and UCS: Classical conditioning experiments have been conducted in control conditions in psychological laboratory. Psychologists have manipulated systematically the time interval between the CS and UCS that produces the greatest amount of conditioning. If the time interval is shorter than half a second and particularly if the interval is negative so that the Cs follows UCS, a dramatic failure of conditioning is typically found. Studies suggest that there may be very different optimum interval for different responses. The following types of temporal relationships have been studied:

Simultaneous Conditioning: When CS and UCS occur either at the same time or just after the onset of the conditioned stimulus, the conditioning is more effective.

Delayed Conditioning: In this procedure the onset of UCS is delayed, following the onset of the CS. It is less effective than simultaneous conditioning. The delayed conditioning procedure becomes more difficult when the interval between UCS and CS increases.

Trace Conditioning: In this procedure, the CS termination precedes UCS. Essential feature is that both should not overlap. It is not effective and is difficult to achieve.

Backward Conditioning: In this procedure, UCS precedes CS. It is also not a success for conditioning.

Stimulus Generalization: In this sense, the person does not only give response to the same stimulus but to the similar or identical stimulus also. For example, if a child is afraid of white rabbit, he may also get afraid of the spinned cotton.

Extinction: If CS (sound of the bell) is not followed by UCS (food), it means there is no reinforcement. A stage comes when the dog stops to secrete saliva. This process is known as extinction. Pavlov reported in his experiments that when the spacing to test trails was increased, the response extinguished rapidly.

Spontaneous Recovery: It has been experimented that when the dog is withdrawn out of the experimental set-up and again put in the set-up after a lapse of time, the dog responds to conditioned stimulus (CS) by gastric secretion. This process is called spontaneous recovery. The phenomenon of spontaneous recovery explains that there is no complete extinction due to time interval but there is inhibition of CR. It can, thus, he said that reconditioning following extinction occurred more rapidly than first conditioning.

Differentiation: As the child grows up, he starts discriminating the differences between different types of stimulus. Pavlov also experiments that the saliva comes in the mouth of the dog with the ringing of the specific bell only. It did not do so when some other bell was rung. That is why the child discriminates the noise of the foot of the mother and changes his behaviour accordingly.

Inhibition: Inhibition may be defined as a process in which a stimulus inhibits a response that would otherwise occur. Pavlov described two types of inhibitions as given below:

1. External Inhibition: It is a process of inhibiting CR by external factors in the environment as noise or any other distraction which may draw the attention of the dog. It has been further reported that if the novel stimulus is presented on series of experimental trails, the CR will return to its full strength.

2. Internal Inhibition: It was observed by Pavlov that if complete extinction of CR is obtained by not providing food to the dog and it is then given a period of 24 hours rest, CR will show spontaneous recovery when the dog is tested again. The extinction does not permanently weaken the CR. Pavlov argued that spontaneous recovery proves that CR in extinction does not represent dying of the reflex or any real weakening of the learned S-R connections. It is blocked by some internal inhibitory processes.

Motivational Factors: Pavlov found that the strength to ease with which the conditioning is done also depended upon motivational factors like hunger, sec etc. In case the response of animal is related with some organic needs, conditioning will be better.

Educational Implications of Classical Conditioning Learning Theory

The educational implications of Classical Conditioning Learning Theory are as under:

- The formulation of positive attitudes, fears, love, prejudices or hatred towards an object, phenomenon or event can be developed through conditioning. Thus, classical conditioning can be used to develop favourable or unfavourable attitude towards learning, teacher and the school.
- We should associates faults with punishment so that whenever a child feels like committing faults, he/she anticipates the punishments. Thus, reward and punishment may be given right at the time of the act and not to be delayed.

- Repetition and habit formation is to be strengthed in the process of learning.
- Most of our learning is associated with the process of conditioning from the beginning. Thus, the teacher is to develop good reading habits through conditioning.
- This learning theory is helpful for developing good habits such as cleanliness, respect for elders, honesty, punctuality etc. in the learners.
- It can be used to eliminate bad habits and conditioned fear from the behaviour of the students.
- The principle of classical conditioning can be used in removing complexes from the minds of abnormal children.
- The principle of Stimulus Generalization and Differentiation is used to select the subjects of study in schools.
- The use of conditioning can be used to do away with old bad habits and to create new good habits.

Watson Theory of Learning or Theory without Reinforcement

The way Pavlov conducted his experiment on his dog, Watson did the same experimentation with his child of nine months, who was not afraid of white rats. When the child was crawling towards the rat, Watson made a loud voice with the dropping of a hammer. As a result of it the child was afraid. This was done a number of times. In this way a connection was made between the loud voice and the rat. As a result of this, the child started feeling afraid of the sight of the white rat, even when the loud noise was not raised by the dropping of the hammer. In this way the artificial stimulus (white rat) took the place of ordinary response (loud voice).

Watson developed a simple theory of learning. He proposed that when a stimulus and response occur at the same time, learning is strengthened. The strength of connection between stimulus-response (S-R) depends upon the frequency of S-R repetitions.

Watson's theory of learning was primarily a protest against Thorndike's theory of learning. He said that Thorndike's Law of Effect was mentalistic in nature; it was nothing but an update version of the old hedonistic principle of behaviour.

His second contribution is the *Law of Recency*. This most recent response is strengthened more by its frequent occurrence than is an earlier response. He made conditioning the basis for learning.

Thorndike's Trial-and-Error Learning Theory

The experimental study of animal learning by E.L. Thorndike (1874-1949) in the United States and his theory on trial-and-error learning provided the impetus for Skinner's experiments on instrumental or operant conditioning. Thorndike's doctoral research on *'Animal Intelligence'* in 1898 provided the psychological world the first miniature system of learning known as trial-and-error learning.

Trial & Error is based on random activities to reach the goal. Thorndike's research on animals showed that learning is a matter of connecting responses to stimuli in a very mechanical way. There is no involvement of consciousness, thinking, reasoning or understanding. The animal performs responses mechanically. The responses that bring reward are learned; the responses that do not bring reward are not learned. The animal does not show ability to understand, think and reason. The animal learns mechanically through trial-and-error.

Indeed many forms of human learning, particularly the learning of sensory-motor skills, are achieved through trial-and-error. Learning to walk, to swim, or to ride a bicycle is based on trial-and-error. At the beginning, we make wrong movements and commit errors. As we go through a series of practice trials, errors are reduced and responses are mastered. The gradual reduction of errors over trials gives the term, 'trial-and-error' form of learning.

Features of Trial and Error Learning

- Learning by trial and error is gradual process.
- For learning to occur, the learner must be definitely motivated.
- The learner makes random and variable response.
- Some responses do lead to the goal (annoying response)
- Some responses lead to the goal (satisfying responses)
- With the increase in number of trials, the annoying responses will tend to be eliminated and the satisfying responses will be strengthened and repeated.
- The time taken to perform the task (to repeat the satisfying response) decreases with successive trials.

Thorndike's Laws of Learning

On the basis of his experimentation with different animals, Thorndike coined his laws of learning, which have been divided into two parts:

(A) Primary Laws of Learning

These are five as listed below. At first only three laws listed at serial no. 1, 2 and 3 were worked out. Later on, the next i.e. 4 and 4 were added in 1935.

1. Law of Readiness
2. Law of Exercise
3. Law of Effect
4. Law of Belongingness
5. Law of Spread of Effect

(B) Secondary Laws of Learning

These are also five in number as listed below:

1. Law of Multiple Response
2. Law of Set or Attitude
3. Law of Partial Activity or Pre- potency of Elements
4. Law of Response by Analogy
5. Law of Associative Shifting

Primary Laws

(i) Law of Readiness: First primary law of learning, according to him, is the *'Law of Readiness'* or the *'Law of Action Tendency'*, which means that learning takes place when an action tendency is aroused through preparatory adjustment, set or attitude. Readiness means a preparation for action. If one is

not prepared to learn, learning cannot be automatically instilled in him. For example, unless the typist, in order to learn typing prepares himself to start, he would not make much progress if he is lethargic or unprepared.

(ii) Law of Exercise: The second law of learning is the *'Law of Exercise'*, which means that drill or practice helps in increasing efficiency and durability of learning. According to Thorndike's S-R Bond Theory, the connections are strengthened with trail or practice and the connections are weakened when trial or practice is discontinued. The 'law of exercise', therefore, is also understood as the 'law of use and disuse' in which case connections or bonds made in the brain cortex are weakened or loosened. Many examples of this case are found in the case of human learning. Learning to drive a motor-car, typewriting, singing or memorizing a poem or a mathematical table, and music etc. need exercise and repetition of various movements and actions many times.

(iii) Law of Effect: The third law is the *'Law of Effect'*, according to which the trial or steps leading to satisfaction stamps in the bond or connection. Satisfying states lead to consolidation and strengthening of the connection, whereas dissatisfaction, annoyance or pain leads to the weakening or stamping out of the connection. In fact, the 'law of effect' signifies that if the response satisfies the subject, they are learnt and selected, while those which are not satisfying are eliminated. Teaching, therefore, must be pleasing. The educator must obey the tastes and interests of his pupils. In other words, greater the satisfaction, stronger will be the motive to learn. Thus, intensity is an important condition of 'law of effect'.

(iv) Law of Belongingness: This principle was added by Thorndike later in 1935. It stated that learning is basically concerned with two things. One is the concern with the situation and the other is with the later result of that. In case both these things are clear then learning takes place in a better way. In accordance with this principle only those rewards and punishments carry positive or negative which give a sense of belongingness with the situation so created at the time of getting response.

(v) Law of Spread of Effect: This principle was also added by Thorndike to his principles in 1935. The reward does not confirm the relationship of the situation of belongingness only, but also upon the priority and later situations. If the reward is given at the time of the result, it not only strengthens the present situation of S-R but also the situation created prior to that and also after that situation. This principle strengthens the ideology of Thorndike that the results of rewards are more of mechanical type than mental process.

Secondary Laws

Besides these three basic laws, Thorndike also refers to five subordinate laws which further help to explain the learning process. These are:

(i) Law of Multiple Response: According to it, the organism varies or changes its response till an appropriate behaviour is hit upon. Without varying the responses, the correspondence for the solution might never be elicited. If the individual wants to solve a puzzle, he has to try in different ways rather than mechanically persisting in the same way. Thorndike's cat in the puzzle

box moved about and tried many ways to come out till finally it hit the latch with her paw which opened the door and it jumped out.

(ii) Law of Set or Attitude: Learning is guided by a total set or attitude of the organism, which determines not only what the person will do but what will satisfy or annoy him. For instance, unless the cricketer sets himself to make a century, he will not be able to score more runs. A student, similarly, unless he sets to get first position and has the attitude of being at the top, would while away the time and not learn much. Hence, learning is affected more in the individual if he is set to learn more or to excel.

(iii) Law of Partial Activity or Pre-potency of Elements: According to this law, the learner reacts selectively to the important or essential in the situation and neglects the other features or elements which may be irrelevant or non-essential. The ability to deal with the essential or the relevant part of the situation makes analytical and insightful learning possible. In this law of pre-potency of elements, Thorndike is really anticipating insight in learning which was more emphasized by the Gestaltions.

(iv) Law of Response by Analogy: According to this law, the individual makes use of old experiences or acquisitions while learning a new situation. There is a tendency to utilize common elements in the new situation as existed in a similar past situation. The learning of driving a car, for instance, is facilitated by the earlier acquired skill of driving a motor cycle or even riding a bicycle because the perspective or maintaining a balance and controlling the handle helps in stearing the car.

(v) Law of Associative Shifting: According to this law we may get a response of which a learner is capable, associated with any other situation to which he is sensitive. Thorndike illustrated this by the act of teaching a cat to stand up at a command. A fish was dangled before the cat while he said 'stand up'. After a number of trails by presenting the fish after uttering the command 'stand up', he later ousted the fish and the overall command of 'stand up' was found sufficient to evoke the response in the cat who standing up on her hind legs.

Educational Implications of Thorndike's Laws of Learning

In brief, the educational implications of the Thorndike's Theory are:

- The task can be started from the easier aspect towards its difficult side. This approach will benefit the weaker and backward children.
- A small child learns some skills through trial and error method only, such as sitting, standing, walking, running etc. In teaching also, the child rectifies the writing after committing mistakes.
- More emphasis has been laid on motivation. Thus, before starting teaching in the classroom the students should be properly motivated.
- Practice leads a man towards maturity. Practice is the main feature of trial and error method. Practice helps in reducing the errors committed by the child in learning any concept.
- Habits are formed as a result of repetition. With the help of this theory the wrong habits of the children can be modified and the good habits strengthened.

- The effects of reward and punishment also affect the learning of the child. Thus, the theory lays emphasis on the use of reward and punishment in the class by the teacher.
- This theory may be found quite helpful in changing the behaviour of the delinquent children. The teacher should cure such children making use of this theory.
- With the help of this theory the teacher can control the negative emotions of the children such as anger, jealousy etc.
- The teacher can improve his teaching methods making use of this theory. He must observe the effects of his teaching methods on the students and should not hesitate to make necessary changes in them, if required.
- It pays more emphasis on oral drill work. Thus, a teacher should conduct oral drill of the taught contents. This helps in strengthening the learning more.

Skinner's Operant Conditioning Learning Theory

Burhaus Frederic Skinner (1938) is the best-known psychologist in the US behaviourist tradition. In the 1930s, he adopted a carefully structured approach called *'operant conditioning'* in which the behaviour of the subject determines the response to the subject's own actions.

What is Operant Conditioning?

B.F. Skinner (1938) coined the term operant conditioning; which means roughly changing of behaviour by the use of reinforcement given after the desired response. Skinner identified three types of responses or operant that can follow behaviour:

- *Neutral Operants:* Responses from the environment that neither increase nor decrease the probability of a behaviour being repeated.
- *Reinforcers:* Responses from the environment that increase the probability of a behaviour being repeated. Reinforcers can be either positive or negative.
- *Punishers:* Responses from the environment that decrease the likelihood of a behaviour being repeated. Punishment weakens behaviour.

Operant conditioning proposes that we learn through consequence. It works on the assumption of learning through reward and punishment. Behaviour which is positively reinforced tends to be repeated, whereas behaviour which is negatively reinforced tends to be avoided. This learning theory was first investigated by Skinner, who developed the "Skinner box" in which rats were placed in a box and required to press a lever for food to be dispensed (the reward). The consequence of receiving food if they pressed the lever caused the rats to repeat this behaviour again and again.

Skinner (1948) studied operant conditioning by conducting experiments using animals which he placed in a '*Skinner Box*' which was similar to Thorndike's puzzle box.

In his *Skinner Box*, Skinner used positive reinforcement to train rats to press a lever to obtain food pellets. The positive reinforcement provided by

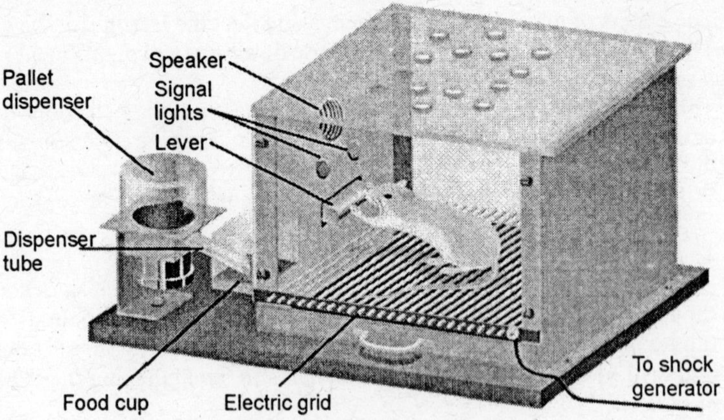

Figure 2.3: Skinner Box

the food increases the probability that the rats will press the lever again. Negative reinforcement removes an aversive stimulus after the correct response—for example, rats press a lever to remove an electric shock. The relief from painful experience also increases the probability that the lever will be pressed again. Skinner uses the term 'reinforcer' rather than 'reward' because 'reinforcer' has an association with behaviour whereas 'reward' does not. A response followed by a reinforcing stimulus is strengthened and is therefore more likely to occur again. The larger and more appealing the reinforcer, the faster a response will be learned. A response that is not followed by a reinforcing stimulus is weakened, and is therefore less likely to occur again. The link between stimulus and response gradually becomes weaker and subsequently dies. For example, rats repeatedly pressing a lever without receiving food pellets will eventually abandon that behaviour. This results in extinction. Therefore:

- desired behaviours are rewarded causing their frequency to increase;
- undesired behaviours are punished causing their frequency to decrease.

Although Skinner did not consider punishment as effective as reinforcement in modifying behaviour it is still commonly used as a deterrent. Types of reward and punishment are shown in Figure 2.4.

Skinner experimented with what he called continuous and variable reinforcement schedules. In continuous reinforcement, every correct response is reinforced; in variable reinforcement, only some are. Skinner found that variable reinforcement schedules lead to steadier response rates because of the possibility that the next response will pay off.

In other experiments, Skinner (1958a) trained pigeons to play a type of table tennis by a process called 'shaping'. At first pigeons were rewarded when they performed an action that vaguely approximated to the target behaviour. Then the reward was restricted to actions that more closely matched the target behaviour. Gradually their behaviour was 'shaped' until it was satisfactory. A summary of the key terms used in operant coniditong is given in Table 2.1.

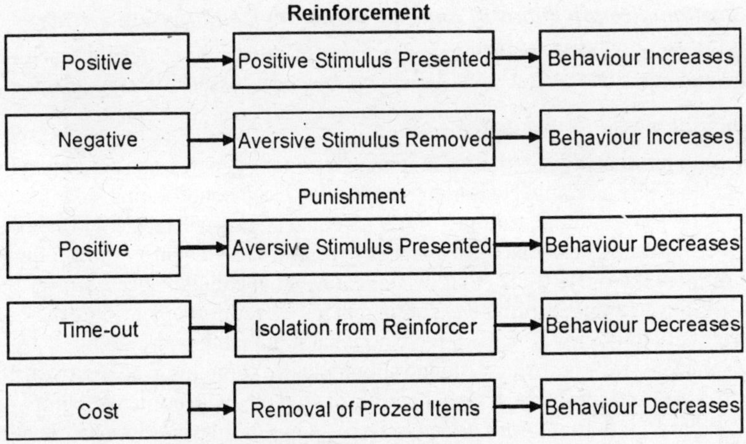

Source: *based on Oates* et al. *(2005: 55).*

Figure 2.4: Reinforcement and punishment

Table 2.1: Key Terms in Operant Conditioning

Operant Conditioning	The process of shaping behaviour by following it with reinforcement that increases in frequency
Reinforcement	An event that increases the probability that the event preceding it will be repeated
Continuous Reinforcement	A pattern in which every desirable response is followed by reinforcement
Variable Reinforcement	A pattern in which only some desirable responses are followed by reinforcement
Magnitude	A term that describes the scale of a large and appealing reinforce that is likely to produce faster learning of responses
Repetition	The frequency of reinforced operant behaviour that strengthens association between stimulus and response
Extinction	The elimination of behaviour by removing reinforcement
Shaping	The process of reinforcing behaviour as it becomes more like the target behavior

Operant Conditioning in the Classroom

Behaviour modification therapy is much used in clinical and educational psychology, particularly with people with learning difficulties. In the conventional learning situation, it applies largely to issues of class, and student management, rather than to learning content. It is very relevant to shaping skill performance.

A simple way of giving positive reinforcement in behaviour modification is in providing compliments, approval, encouragement, and affirmation. A ratio of five compliments for every one criticism is generally seen as being the most effective in altering behaviour in a desired manner.

One familiar method of ensuring classroom control (particularly in Primary schools and with very disruptive children) is the use of sticker charts - an application known formally as a Token Economy.

Educational Implications of Skinner's Operant Conditioning Theory

Skinner's operant conditioning theory is of great importance in teaching-learning situations. A few situations have been discussed in detail as under:

Conditioning Study Behaviour

For Skinner, teaching is the arrangement of contingencies of reinforcement, which expedite learning. He is convinced that operant conditioning, so effectual when applied to animal, training promises equal success when used in schools. Furthermore, he thinks that the most effective control of human learning requires instru-mental aid. He thinks that, when teachers have taught successfully, they always have arranged effective contingencies of reinforcement, but they are more likely to do this if they understand what it is that they are doing.

Hence, if we want that student should learn something at his own, the teachers should reinforce such behaviour of students who come well prepared in the class, sit in the library and acts actively in school programmers through a variety of incentives such as prize, medal, praise, smile, affectionate patting on the back or even by giving higher marks in the examination.

Conditioning and Class-room Behaviour

In order to change the behaviour of the pupils in the class room and to bring desired change in their behaviours, conditioning is of immense importance. If a child's experiences in a certain classroom, while studying a certain subject with a particular teacher are predominantly unpleasant the unpleasantness becomes conditioned to the teacher, the subject and the classroom. If this is repeated, the child will develop a dislike for the subject as well as for the teacher. Hence, to check all these, suitable behavioural contingencies may be used and atmosphere of recognition, acceptance, affection and esteem may help the child in approaching the teacher and the subject with good will.

For instance, if a student is not serious in his studies, the teacher can control his behaviour by using negative reinforce-ment such as showing his negligence for the student by criticizing him in front of the whole class. On the other hand, a student who is serious in his studies should be provided positive incentives such as prize, medal, praise, smile etc. An interesting example is quoted here.

A student was having a mobile in classroom. The teacher neglected him totally and he was indulged in talking with other good students for a long time. The teacher even did not look once to the naughty boy. After a long time the naughty boy asked in the middle of conversation, Sir, till now you are receiving assignments, I will also submit you. Thus, the important behaviours are conditioned.

Managing Problem Behaviours

Generally, students perform a variety of behaviours that seems undesired and problematic form social conduct point of view. Hence, to utter them a great success may be achieved through the process of operant conditioning. Operant conditioning has established as an important behaviour therapy technique in the recent years. It use in schools in shaping student's behaviour is going on increasing day by day. In this regard Albert Bandura's views are of great significance.

But, one has to admit here that instead of making use of negative contingencies, such as punishment a teacher must make use of positive contingencies such as praise, appropriate encouragement for better learning prospects. Behaviour of the students is generally dominated by aversion (escape) stimulation. And, hence, they somehow want to run away from the dull and dreary classes.

Dealing with Anxieties through Conditioning

Students develop many fears, anxieties, prejudices, attitudes as well as perceptual meanings through conditioning. When we see that a train or a car stops whenever there is red light, we interpret the red light as a sign to stop. In war-time, when a siren is blown in a particular way, we interpret is as a signal for air raid. A child, who has received a painful injection from a doctor, may develop an aversion to or fear of any doctor. Such example causes anxiety in the human being.

To break such habits or fears, conditioning may be helpful. For this, the subject should be kept repeatedly in the situation that causes fear in him and he may be treated by controlling fear producing response. The technique is known as de-sensitization. In this technique firstly, we provide a very weak form of conditioned stimulus then gradually the strength of stimulus is increased.

Conditioning Group Behaviour

Conditioning is not useful only to make an individual learn something but it is equally important to make the entire group learn something and also in breaking out their undesired and unsocial behaviours. Generally, the complete behaviour of the entire group is changed on the basis of those reinforcements which form the basis of common expectations of students with their teachers.

For instance, if most of the students feel that putting questions to their teachers or telling a lie with them will make their teachers annoyed, then in such circumstances they learn to keep mum in the class and become conditioned by the teacher's authority. On the other hand, if their common expectation rests in the view that by asking questions to their teachers or taking active participation in class discussions will make the teacher feel happy, then in such conditions pupil-teacher interaction will increase remarkably and will help in making teaching-learning process more effective.

Conditioning and Cognitive Processes

Feed back or knowledge of progress is another form of reinforcement. The concept may be utilized in controlling the cognitive behaviours of the students. The concept demands such favourable conditions to be created for the students so that he may respond correctly and actively. Also, he must be kept well informed regarding his progress, as it will act as a source of motivation for him to reach his goal. Programmed Instruction and Teaching Machines are based on the same principle.

As regard knowledge of progress is concerned, we feel that too great a lapse of time exists between behaviour and its reinforcement. A boy who stands first in the class in the month of March or emerges as the all- around best Athlete even earlier in the month of January is rewarded in the month of December in the ceremonial annual prize distribution of the school.

Hence, in order to make effective use of operant conditioning principle the technique of programmed instruction is best suited. Programmed instruction is a system of teaching and learning within which pre-established subject matter is broken down into small, discrete steps and carefully organized into logical sequence in which it can be learned readily by the students. Each step builds deliberately upon the preceding one.

The learner can progress through the sequence of steps at his own rate and he is reinforced immediately after each step. Reinforcement (positive) comes when the response is correct. The pupil does not go ahead if his response is not correct. The technique is of great significance in the teaching of arithmetic, spelling, science etc. Hence, the need of a 'teaching-machine', which is the main instrument in carrying on programmed instruction, is must.

Shaping Complex Behaviour

To control such complex behavior, which exists in the form of a chain of small behaviour, the extended form of conditioning, known as shaping technique, is employed. In this technique, the smallest behaviour of an individual at the very initial stage is controlled. Then, gradually the next order of chain of behaviour is controlled or conditioned on behalf of different contingencies. In schools, the technique is widely accepted for its use to control students' behaviour.

Skinner recognizes the first 'task of teachers to shape proper response, to get children to pronounce and write responses properly. But, he sees their principal task as bringing proper behaviour under many sorts of stimulus control. According to Skinner- *"Teaching spelling is mainly a process of shaping complex form of behaviour. In other subjects, for example, arithmetic, response must be brought under the control of appropriate stimuli."* To achieve this task, Skinner recommends the use of programmed learning.

Comparison between Classical Conditioning and Operant Conditioning

The comparison between Classical Conditioning and Operant Conditioning is given in Table 2.2

Table 2.2: Comparison between Classical Conditioning and Operant Conditioning

Classical Conditioning	*Operant Conditioning*
It was developed by Russian Physiologist Ivan P. Pavlov.	It was developed by B.F. Skinner.
It is called Pavlovian or Type-1 learning (respondent).	It is called Skinnerian or type-2 learning (operant).
It is signal conditioning.	It is instrumental conditioning.
The occurrence of conditioned response (CR) is relaxively forced by unconditioned stimulus (UCS).	The response is more voluntary and spontaneous.
The unconditioned stimulus (UCS) occurs without regard to the subject's behavior.	The reward is contingent upon the occurrence of response.
It is described as preparatory or anticipatory response and is also called signal learning.	It serves primarily to emphasize or guide an organism which already has certain responses available in its repertoire.

Contd.

Classical Conditioning	*Operant Conditioning*
The association between stimulus and response (S-R) is on the basis of Law of Contiguity.	The association between stimulus and response (S-R) is on the basis of Law of Effect.
It is controlled by autonomic nervous system in the organism.	It is controlled by central nervous system in the organism.
Bondage between specific unconditioned stimulus (UCS)/conditioned stimulus (CS) is established	Tendency to respond in a specific manner is developed.
Reinforcement comes first as in Pavlov's experiment. Food is presented first to elicit the response.	Reinforcement is provided after the response is made by the organism.
Conditioned stimulus (CS) and unconditioned stimulus (UCS) can be placed in different temporal sequences, close contiguity is followed.	Close contiguity is followed and R-S chain is formed.
It focuses on the single (S-R) stimulus-response bondage.	It is concerned with sequences of response. A chain of responses is formed which leads to the desired goal.
We present the unconditioned response (UCS) irrespective of the behavior.	We present the stimulus only if the organism makes the desired response.
It presents different pictures of behavior and learning in which an arbitrary stimulus is associated with a high specific, elicitable response.	The situation describes the differentiation and discrimination of a response out of a mass behavior emitted in response to complex stimulus field.
The essence of learning is stimulus substitution.	The essence of learning is response modification.
The classical conditioned reflexes may have zero strength initially.	The operant cannot have zero strength because it has to occur at least once before it can be reinforced.
The classical conditioned response is correlated with and controlled by an antecedent event, an eliciting stimulus which is initially the UCS and subsequently the CS.	In operant conditioning, there is no antecedent and the behavior is controlled by its consequences.
Respondent behavior is internal.	Operant is external behavior.

3
Cognitivist Approach to Learning

How is it that, if someone speaks your name, you immediately hear it even though you are not consciously attending to it? Certain automatic brain processes have taken place for this to occur, and these processes are studied by cognitive psychologists.

Cognitivism involves the study of mental processes such as sensation, perception, attention, encoding and memory that behaviourists were reluctant to study, because cognition occurs inside the 'black box' of the brain. Cognitivists believe that learning results from organizing and processing information effectively. If educators understand how learners process information, they can design learning experiences that optimize this activity. For example, an awareness of how learners transfer short-term memories into meaningful knowledge is likely to be useful in the classroom.

Cognitivism refers to the study of the mind and how it obtains, processes and stores information. This theory was a response to behaviourism. It was argued that not all learning occurs through shaping and changing of behaviours. In this theory, learners are active participants in their learning and the mind functions like a computer processor. Information comes in as input, the mind processes the information for the time being and the information is stored away to be retrieved later. Learning is shaped by acquired learning strategies and prior knowledge and attitudes, called schemas. The cognitive view of learning is teacher-centered and information must be presented in an organized manner in order to achieve the most efficient learning.

KEY IDEAS OF COGNITIVISM

The key ideas of cognitivism are as follows:

- Learning does not always involve a change in behaviour.
- Cognitivism focuses on internal mental learning processes.
- The key metaphor in cognitivism is the computer model.
- This model assumes discrete stages through which information is processed.
- Learners actively process, store and retrieve information for use.
- Learners organize and interpret information to create knowledge.

KEY PRINCIPLES OF COGNITIVISM

According to Hartley (1998), the key principles of learning associated with cognitive psychology are:

- *Instruction should be well-organized:* Well-organized materials are easier to learn and to remember.
- *Instruction should be clearly structured*: Subject matters are said to have

inherent structures - logical relationships between key ideas and concepts, which link the parts together.

- *The perceptual features of the task are important:* Learners attend selectively to different aspects of the environment. Thus, the way a problem is displayed is important if learners are to comprehend it.
- *Prior knowledge is important*: Things must fit with what is already known if it is to be learnt.
- *Differences between individuals are important as they will affect learning:* Differences in 'cognitive style' or methods of approach influence learning.
- *Cognitive feedback gives information to learners about their success or failure concerning the task at hand:* Reinforcement can come through giving information -'knowledge of results' - rather than simply a reward.

STRENGTHS OF COGNITIVISM

The main strengths of cognitivism are as follows:

- Organized structure to learning: information comes in and is processed into short term memory before being stored away in long term memory.
- When problems are broken down into smaller parts, learners are not overwhelmed with incoming information and have time to process smaller bits.

WEAKNESSES OF COGNITIVISM

Because learning is very structured, it may become difficult to adapt to changes in what has already been processed and learned.

APPLICATION OF COGNITIVISM

Cognitivism is suited well for problem solving, where the concepts are complex and must be broken down into smaller parts. Ideas and concepts from these problems are linked to prior knowledge, which in turn helps the learner develop a stronger comprehension (Stavredes, 2011)

EDUCATIONAL IMPLICATIONS OF COGNITIVISM

- Learners should be told why they should take the lesson, so that they can attend to the information throughout the lesson.
- Information critical for learning should be highlighted to focus learners' attention.
- The difficulty level of the material must match the cognitive level of the learner, so that he/she can both attend to and relate to the material. Links to both simpler and more complicated materials can be used to accommodate learners at different knowledge levels.
- Strategies should be used to allow learners to retrieve existing information from long term memory to help make sense of the new information. Learners must construct a memory link between the new information and some related information already stored in long-term memory.
- Information should be chunked to prevent overload during processing in working memory (*Miller, 1956*). To facilitate deep processing, learners should be asked to generate the information maps during the learning process or as a summary activity after the lesson (*Bonk & Reynolds, 1997*).

- Other strategies that promote deep processing should be used to help transfer information for long-term storage. Strategies that require learners to apply, analyze, and evaluate promote higher-level learning, which makes the transfer to long-term memory more effective.
- Promote active listening;
- Don't overload short term memory by presenting too much material at once;
- Don't lecture for more than about twenty minutes without a break;
- Chunk material into groups or categories to facilitate retention;
- Make the structure and patterning of the material explicit for learners;
- Present material in more than one form to facilitate transfer to long term memory;
- Give learners the opportunity to revisit topics to strengthen retention;
- Use key words and terms as memory cues;
- Outline the metacognitive 27 strategies needed for a given subject.

MAJOR LEARNING THEORIES RELATED TO COGNITIVISM

Some important learning theories related to cognitivism are as under:

Robert Gagne's Theory of Learning

Robert Gagne (1916–2002) was an American educational psychologist who pioneered the science of instruction in the 1940s. His book *"The Conditions of Learning,"* first published in 1965, identified the mental conditions that are necessary for effective learning.

Gagné's Hierarchy or Conditions of Learning

Robert M. Gagné proposed a system of classifying different types of learning in terms of the degree of complexity of the mental processes involved. He identified eight basic types and arranged these in the hierarchy shown in Figure 3.1. According to Gagné, the higher orders of learning in this hierarchy build upon the lower levels, requiring progressively greater amounts of previous learning for their success. The lowest four orders tend to focus on the more behavioural aspects of learning, while the highest four focus on the more cognitive aspects.

The brief descriptions of Gagné's eight categories of learning are as under:

1. *Signal Learning:* This is the simplest form of learning and consists essentially of the classical conditioning first described by the behavioural psychologist Pavlov. In this, the subject is 'conditioned' to emit a desired response as a result of a stimulus that would not normally produce that response. This is done by first exposing the subject to the chosen stimulus (known as the conditioned stimulus) along with another stimulus (known as the unconditioned stimulus) which produces the desired response naturally. After a certain number of repetitions of the double stimulus, it is found that the subject emits the desired response when exposed to the conditioned stimulus on its own. The applications of classical conditioning in facilitating human learning are, however, very limited.

2. *Stimulus-Response Learning:* This somewhat more sophisticated form of learning, which is also known as operant conditioning, was originally

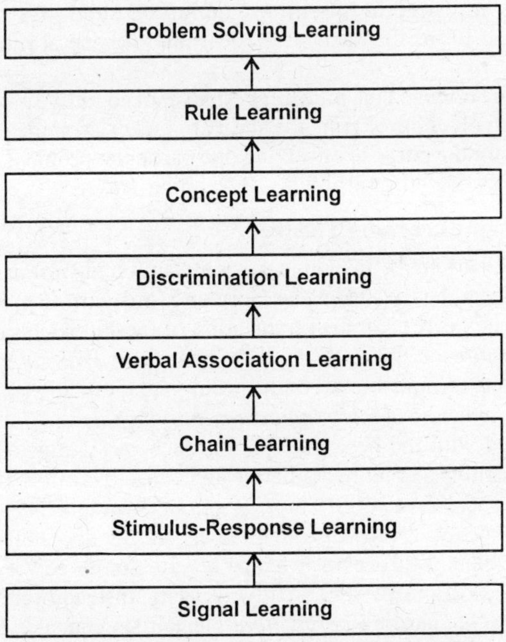

Figure 3.1: Gagné's Hierarchy of Learning

developed by Skinner. It involves developing desired stimulus-response bonds in the subject through a carefully-planned reinforcement schedule based on the use of 'rewards' and 'punishments'. Operant conditioning differs from classical conditioning in that the reinforcing agent (the 'reward' or 'punishment') is presented after the response. It is this type of conditioning that forms the basis of programmed learning in all its various manifestations.

3. Chaining: This is a more advanced form of learning in which the subject develops the ability to connect two or more previously-learned stimulus-response bonds into a linked sequence. It is the process whereby most complex psychomotor skills (eg riding a bicycle or playing the piano) are learned.

4. Verbal Association: This is a form of chaining in which the links between the items being connected are verbal in nature. Verbal association is one of the key processes in the development of language skills.

5. Discrimination Learning: This involves developing the ability to make appropriate (different) responses to a series of similar stimuli that differ in a systematic way. The process is made more complex (and hence more difficult) by the phenomenon of interference, whereby one piece of learning inhibits another. Interference is thought to be one of the main causes of forgetting.

6. Concept Learning: This involves developing the ability to make a consistent response to different stimuli that form a common class or category of some sort. It forms the basis of the ability to generalize, classify etc.

7. Rule Learning: This is a very-high-level cognitive process that involves being able to learn relationships between concepts and application of these relationships in different situations, including situations not previously encountered. It forms the basis of the learning of general rules, procedures, etc.

8. Problem Solving: This is the highest level of cognitive process according to Gagné. It involves developing the ability to invent a complex rule, algorithm or procedure for the purpose of solving one particular problem, and then using the method to solve other problems of a similar nature.

Kohler's Insight Learning Theory

The theory of learning by insight is the contribution of *Gestalt Psychologists*. Gestalt is a term derived from the German word *gestalten*, has no English equivalent. The nearest English translation of Gestalt is *configuration* or an *organized whole* or the *totality of a situation. Wolfgang Kohler, Max Wertheimer, Kurt Koffka* etc. were the prominent Gestalt Psychologists. They believe that *the whole is more important than its parts.*

Dissatisfied with the behaviourist approach of learning, the cognitivists tried to see learning as a more deliberate and conscious effort of the individual rather than a mere product of *habit formation* or a machine-like '*stimulus-response connection*'. According to them the learner does not merely respond to a stimulus, but also processes what he receives or perceives. Thus learning is a purposive, explorative and creative activity, instead of trial and error.

It is a theory regarding *perception.* Gestaltists consider learning as the development of insight, which is primarily concerned with the nature of perception. *Perception is a process by which an organism interprets and organizes sensation to produce a meaningful experience of the world.* It is the ultimate experience of the world and typically involves further processing of sensory input.

While learning, the learner always perceives the situation as a whole and after seeing and evaluating the different relationships takes the proper decision intelligently. Gestalt psychology used the term 'insight' to describe the perception of the whole situation by the learner and his intelligence in responding to the proper relationships. Insight refers the sudden flash in the mind about the solution of the problem.

Kohler conducted many experiments with his chimpanzee *Sulthan* to describe the term *insight.* Some of the Kohler's experiments for 'Learning by Insight' are:

1. In one experiment, Kohler put the chimpanzee Sulthan inside a cage and a banana was hung from the roof of a cage. A box was placed inside the cage. The chimpanzee tried to reach the banana by jumping but could not succeed. Suddenly he got an idea and used the box as a jumping platform by placing it just below the hanging banana.
2. In another experiment Kohler made this problem complicated that two or three boxes were required to reach the banana.
3. In a more complicated experiment, a banana was kept far outside the cage and two sticks, one larger than the other, were kept inside the box. When failed to reach the banana by one stick, with a sudden bright idea the chimpanzee tried to reach the banana by joining the two sticks.

These experiments demonstrated the role of intelligence and cognitive abilities in higher learning and problem solving situations.

Steps in the Insight Learning

Identifying the Problem: The learner recognizes the presence of intervening obstacles on his way to the goal.

Understanding the Problem: The learner observes the problematic situation, analyzes it and perceives the relation between the goal and the obstacles.

Incubation of Ideas: After analyzing the total situation he reaches conclusions by means of hesitation, pause, concentrated attention etc.

Trail of Mode of Response: The learner makes initial efforts in the form of a simple trial and error mechanism.

Sustained Attention: The learner maintains frequently recurrent attention to the goal and motivation.

Insight Development: In a certain moment there is a sudden perception of the relationship in the total situation and the organism directly performs the required acts.

Steady Repetition of Adaptive Behaviour: After getting an insightful solution, the individual tries to implement it in another situation.

Comprehension of Ability: The learner reaches the ability to understand the relevant parts of the situation, overlooking the irrelevant ones.

Educational Implications of Gestalt Learning Theory

Proceeding from Whole to Parts: The teacher should present the subject matter as a whole to facilitate insight learning. It means the teacher should teach the whole concept, i.e. begin from the globe and then come to country, state, district and block etc.

Integrated Approach: While planning curriculum, Gestalt principles should be given due consideration. A particular subject should not be treated as the mere collection of isolated facts. It should be closely integrated into a whole.

Importance of Motivation: The teacher should arouse the child's curiosity, interest and motivation. He should gain full attention of the whole class before teaching.

Emphasis on Understanding: It has made learning an intelligent task requiring mental abilities than a stimulus-response association. So the learner must be given opportunity for using his mental abilities.

Problem Solving Approach: This theory emphasises that as the learner is able to solve problems by his insight, meaningful learning, learning by understanding, reasoning, etc. must be encouraged in the school.

Checking of Previous Experiences: As insight depends upon the previous experiences of the learner. The teacher must check the previous experiences of the child and relate them with the new learning situation.

Goal Orientation: As learning is a purposeful and goal oriented task, the learner has to be well acquainted with these objectives. He should be fully familiar with the goals and purposes of every task.

Albert Bandura's Social Learning Theory or Observational Learning Theory or Learning by Imitation

Albert Bandura was born in Alberta, Canada in 1925. Bandura's early work in the 1960's represents one of the bridges from behaviourism to cognitive models for learning. He developed most of the principles of contemporary social learning theory/social-cognitive theory which is one of the more prominent and influential theories of development today.

Social learning theory argues that learning occurs within social situations and contexts. Social learning theory also considers how people learn from each other and includes related concepts such as observational learning, imitation and behavioural modeling.

In social learning, three variables of modeled behaviours, the person and the learning environment influence each other

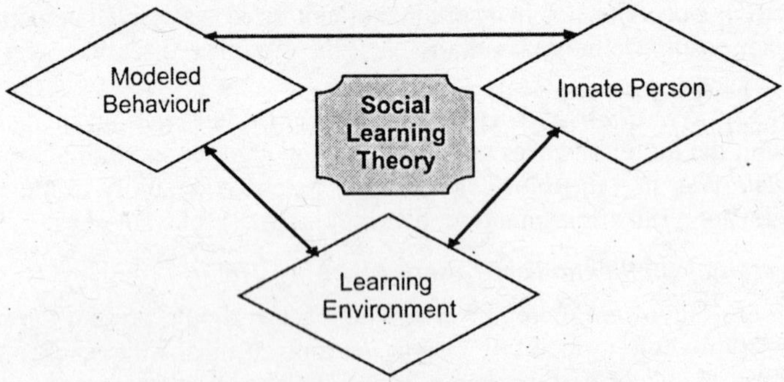

Figure 3.2: Variables of Social Learning Theory

Alfred Bandura's view of social learning emphasizes the value of observing and modeling behaviours, attitudes and emotional reactions of others. In 1977, he said that "...learning would be exceedingly laborious, not to mention hazardous, if [we] had to rely solely on the effects of [our] own actions to inform [our own understanding of something]... fortunately, most human behaviour is learned observationally through modeling: from observing others, one forms an idea of how new behaviours are performed, and on later occasions this coded information serves as a guide for action...". Bandura's work is related to the theories of Vygotsky and Lave which emphasize the central role of social learning in developing the intellectual and the social capacity of learners.

Principles of Observational or Social Learning Theory

There are several guiding principles behind observational learning or social learning theory:

- People learn by observing the behaviours of others and by observing the outcome of those behaviours
- According to social learning theorists, people are able to learn through observation.

- Cognition plays a certain role in learning. Awareness and expectations of future reinforcements or punishments have an impact on the behaviours people exhibit
- Social learning theory is a type of bridge or transition between behaviourist learning theories and cognitive theories
- The observer will imitate the model's behaviour, if the model possesses characteristics. It is attributes like talent, intelligence, power, good looks or popularity that the observer finds attractive or desirable.
- The observer will react to the way the model is treated and mimic the model's behaviour. When the model's behaviour is rewarded, the observer is more likely to reproduce the rewarded behaviour. When the model is punished (an example of vicarious punishment), the observer is less likely to reproduce the same behaviour.
- A distinction exists between an observer's "acquiring" a behaviour and "performing" a behaviour. Through observation, the observer can acquire the behaviour without performing it. The observer may then later, in situations where there is an incentive to do so, display the behaviour

Educational Implications of Social Learning Theory

Social learning theory has numerous implications for classrooms:

- Students learn a great deal simply by observing others
- Describing the consequences of behaviour increases appropriate behaviours, decreasing inappropriate ones. This includes discussing the rewards of various behaviours
- Modeling provides an alternative to teaching new behaviours. Instead of using shaping, an operant conditioning, modeling is a faster, more efficient means of teaching. To promote effective modeling, teachers must ensure the four essential conditions exist—attention, retention, motor reproduction and motivation
- Teachers must model appropriate behaviours and take care that they do not model inappropriate behaviours
- Teachers should expose students to a variety of models which is important to break down stereotypes
- Students must believe that they are capable of accomplishing a task; it is important to develop a sense of self-efficacy for students. Teachers can promote such self-efficacy by making students receive confidence-building messages, watch others being successful, and experience success on their own
- Teachers should help students set realistic expectations, ensuring that expectations are realistically challenging. Sometimes a task is beyond a student's ability
- Self-regulation techniques provide an effective method for improving student's behaviour.

4
Constructivist Approach to Learning

Some teachers take a great interest when their pupils offer an incorrect answer to a question. In such a situation, these teachers proceed by asking pupils to explain how they arrived at that answer. It is likely that these teachers are operating from a constructivist perspective, which sees learners as constructors of meaning. By investigating the origins of a wrong answer, the teacher can uncover the learner's thinking processes, subsequently challenging and refining faulty mental constructs.

It is difficult to draw a clear distinction between constructivism and cognitivism because constructivism is a natural progression from cognitivism and both are interested in cognitive processes. Whereas cognitivism focuses on how information is processed, constructivism focuses on what people do with information to develop knowledge. In particular, constructivism holds that people actively build knowledge and understanding by synthesizing the knowledge they already possess with new information. For constructivists, learning is an active process through which learners 'construct' new meaning.

Constructivism is the study of a learner's own construction of knowledge. This knowledge is constructed through one's own personal experiences and interactions with the outside world. The learner takes in new information and gives meaning to it, using his or her own prior attitudes, beliefs, and experiences as references. Learners are active participants in the construction of knowledge while the instructor serves as a facilitator.

Constructivists see learners as being active rather than passive. Knowledge is not received from the outside or from someone else; rather, it is the individual learner's interpretation and processing of what is received through the senses that creates knowledge. The learner is the center of the learning, with the instructor playing an advising and facilitating role. Learners should be allowed to construct knowledge rather than being given knowledge through instruction.

A major emphasis of constructivists is situated learning, which sees learning as contextual. Learning activities that allow learners to contextualize the information should be used in online instruction. If the information has to be applied in many contexts, then learning strategies that promote multi-contextual learning should be used to make sure that learners can indeed apply the information broadly. Learning is moving away from one-way instruction to construction and discovery of knowledge.

WHAT IS CONSTRUCTIVISM?

Constructivism is basically a theory, based on observation and scientific study about how people learn. It says that people construct their own understanding and knowledge of the world, through experiencing things and reflecting on those experiences. When we encounter something new, we have to reconcile it with our previous ideas and experience, maybe changing what we believe, or maybe discarding the new information as irrelevant. In any case, we are active creators of our own knowledge. To do this, we must ask questions, explore and assess what we know.

In the classroom, the constructivist view of learning can point towards a number of different teaching practices. In the most general sense, it usually means encouraging students to use active techniques (experiments, real-world problem solving) to create more knowledge and then to reflect on and talk about what they are doing and how their understanding is changing. The teacher makes sure that he understands the students' pre-existing conceptions, and guides the activity to address them and then build on them.

According to constructivism theory:

- learners construct knowledge (rather than acquiring it) individually through their interactions with the environment (including other learners) based on their current as well as prior knowledge, authentic experience, mental structures, and beliefs that are used to interpret objects and events in relation to the context and environment in which learning takes place.
- the learner is an active processor of information and creator of personal knowledge;
- instruction is a process of supporting than construction;
- knowledge is not purely objective; and
- the instructor's major role is that of a facilitator of learning.

DEFINING CONSTRUCTIVISM

Constructivism is *theory of learning* based on the idea that knowledge is constructed by the knower based on mental activity. Learners are considered to be active organisms, seeking meaning. Constructivism is founded on the premise that, by reflecting on our experiences, we construct our own understanding of the world consciously we live in. Each of us generates our own "rules" and "mental models," which we use to make sense of our experiences. Learning, therefore, is simply the process of adjusting our mental models to accommodate new experiences. Construction of meaning may initially bear little relationship to reality (as in the naive theories of children), but will become increasing more complex, differentiated and realistic as time goes on.

KEY IDEAS OF CONSTRUCTIVISM

The key ideas of constructivism are as follows:

- Knowledge is situated and constructed in social contexts.
- The learner is an active agent in the interpretation of the world.
- Constructivism focuses on meaning-making and the understanding of knowledge.
- Learning involves the interpretation of experience to construct meaning.
- Mental constructs may be modified as a result of confirmation or challenge.
- Other people are important in the formation and modification of mental constructs.

ASSUMPTIONS OF CONSTRUCTIVISM

According to Merrill's (1991), the assumptions of constructivism are:

- knowledge is constructed from experience;
- learning is a personal interpretation of the world;
- learning is an active process in which meaning is developed on the basis of experience;
- conceptual growth comes from the negotiation of meaning, the sharing of multiple perspectives and the changing of our internal representations through collaborative learning; and
- learning should be situated in realistic settings; testing should be integrated with the task and not a separate activity.

GUIDING PRINCIPLES OF CONSTRUCTIVISM

The guiding principles of constructivism are as follows:

- Knowledge is constructed, not transmitted.
- Prior knowledge impacts the learning process.
- Initial understanding is local, not global.
- Building useful knowledge structures requires effortful and purposeful activity.

HOW CONSTRUCTIVISM IMPACTS LEARNING

Constructivist learning theory does not necessarily imply that one must follow a "constructivist" pedagogical strategy. In other words, most researches firmly believe that knowledge is constructed, but some (e.g. mainstream instructional designers) do not adopt an instructional design that is labeled "constructivist".

Typically, a constructivist teaching strategy is based on the belief that students learn best when they gain knowledge through exploration and active learning. Hands-on materials are used instead of textbooks, and students are encouraged to think and explain their reasoning instead of memorizing and reciting facts. Education is centered on themes and concepts and the connections between them, rather than isolated information.

Instruction: Under the theory of constructivism, educators focus on making connections between facts and fostering new understanding in students. Instructors tailor their teaching strategies to student responses and encourage students to analyze, interpret and predict information. Teachers also rely heavily on open-ended questions and promote extensive dialogue among students.

Assessment: Constructivism calls for the elimination of grades and standardized testing. Instead, assessment becomes part of the learning process so that students play a larger role in judging their own progress.

COMPONENTS OF CONSTRUCTIVISM

The following components comprise the theoretical framework of Constructivism (Wilson, Teslow, and Osman-Jouchoux, 1995):

- mind is real: mental events are worthy of study;
- knowledge resides in the mind;

- knowledge is dynamic;
- meaning is constructed;
- reflection/abstraction is critical to becoming an expert;
- learning includes constructing representations;
- teaching is negotiating construction of meaning;
- thinking and perception are inseparable; and
- problem solving is central to cognition.

FACES OR SCHOOLS OF CONSTRUCTIVISM

The faces or schools of constructivism are given below:

Trivial (Cognitive) Constructivism

It is the concept that knowledge is actively constructed by the learner, not passively received by the environment. It is derived from the assimilation - accommodation and schema models of Piaget.

Von Glaserfeld's Radical Constructivism

Derived from Von Glaserfeld (1990). Von Glaserfeld put forth the notion that the learner's constructions do not necessarily reflect knowledge of a "real world." Coming to know is a process of dynamic adaptation toward viable interpretations of experiences. We have no way of knowing what "real" reality might be, since input is filtered. Previous constructs also influence our perceptions of current experience. We construct "viable" models of what reality is based on social and physical constraints.

Vygotsky's Social Constructivism or Socio-Constructivism

The social world of a learner includes the *people that directly affect that person, including teachers, friends, students, administrators and participants in all forms of activity*. This takes into account the *social nature of both the local processes in collaborative learning and in the discussion of wider social collaboration* in a given subject, such as science.

This was the theory of Vygotsky in the late 1970's. Vygotsky's point of view was that acquisition and participation were synergistic strategies in learning situations. Aspects of participation involved teaching in contexts that could be meaningful to students based on their personal and social history, negotiating class discussions, small group collaborative learning with projects and tasks, and valuing meaningful activity over correct answers. Social Constructivism emphasizes that learning takes place through interactions with other students, teachers, and the world-at-large.

Cultural Constructivism

Brings in a wider context to learning, including customs, religion, language, physiology, tools available (computers, books, etc.). Tools are used to redistribute the cognitive load between the learner and the tool, and can affect the mind beyond actual use by changing one's skills, perspectives, and responses.

Beyond the immediate social environment of a learning situation are the *wider context of cultural influences, including custom, religion, biology, tools and language*. For example, the format of books can affect learning, by promoting views about the organization, accessibility and status of the information they contain.

According to Vosniadou (1996) - *"[What we need] is a new conception of the mind, not as an individual information processor, but as a biological, developing system that exists equally well within an individual brain and in the tools, artefacts, and symbolic systems used to facilitate social and cultural interaction."*

Higher mental functions are, by definition, culturally mediated. They involve not a direct action on the world but an indirect one one that takes a bit of material matter used previously and incorporates it as an aspect of action. In-so-far as that matter itself has been shaped by prior human practice (eg it is an artefact), current action incorporates the mental work that produced the particular form of that matter.

Cobern (1993) writes of the world of subject matter and the internal mental world of the student as competing conceptual "ecologies", an image which invokes pictures of competing constructs, adaptation and survival-of-the-fittest. This is a somewhat more complex picture than radical constructivism. It highlights the need to consider both contexts fully, that of the student and the knowledge to be learned.

Critical Constructivism

Critical Constructivism adds a dimension of critical evaluation and cultural reform to the educational process. This approach incorporates the use of Communicative Ethics which defines the conditions for establishing dialogue, oriented toward mutual understanding among learners and teachers. Communicative Ethics promotes (1) primary concern for maintaining empathetic, caring and trusting relationships, (2) commitment to achieve reciprocal understanding of goals, interests and standards, and (3) concern for and critical awareness of the often-invisible rules of the classroom, including social and cultural myths.

Critical constructivism looks at constructivism within a social and cultural environment, but adds a critical dimension aimed at *reforming these environments in order to improve the success of constructivism applied as a referent*. Taylor (1996) describes critical constructivism as a social epistemology that addresses the socio-cultural context of knowledge construction and serves as a referent for cultural reform. It confirms the relativism of radical constructivism, and also identifies the learner as being suspended in semiotic systems similar to those earlier identified in social and cultural constructivism. To these, critical constructivism adds a greater emphasis on the actions for change of a learning teacher.

Cultural myths that are prevalent in today's education systems include (Taylor, 1996):

- The rationalist myth of cold reason - where knowledge is seen as discovery of an external truth. This can lead to the picture of the teacher in a central role as transmitter of objective truths to students. This philosophy does not promote clarifying relevance to the lives of students, but instead promotes a curriculum to be delivered.

- The myth of hard control - which renders the teacher's classroom role as controller, and "locks teachers and students into grossly asymmetrical power relationships designed to reproduce, rather than challenge the established culture".

Characteristics of Critical Constructivism

The main characteristics of critical constructivism are as under:

- Knowledge is socially constructed: world and information co-construct one another
- Consciousness is a social construction
- Political struggles: power plays an exaggerated role in the production of knowledge and consciousness
- The necessity of understanding consciousness—even though it does not lend itself to traditional reductionistic modes of measurability
- The importance of uniting logic and emotion in the process of knowledge and producing knowledge
- The inseparability of the knower and the known
- The centrality of the perspectives of oppressed peoples—the value of the insights of those who have suffered as the result of existing social arrangements
- The existence of multiple realities: making sense of a world far more complex that we originally imagined
- Becoming humble knowledge workers: understanding our location in the tangled web of reality
- Standpoint epistemology: locating ourselves in the web of reality, we are better equipped to produce our own knowledge
- Constructing practical knowledge for critical social action
- Complexity: overcoming reductionism
- Knowledge is always entrenched in a larger process
- The centrality of interpretation: critical hermeneutics
- The new frontier of classroom knowledge: personal experiences intersecting with pluriversal information
- Constructing new ways of being human: critical ontology

Trivial Constructivism

Knowledge is actively constructed by the learner, not passively received from the environment.

Constructionism

Constructionism is a constructivist learning theory and theory of instruction. It states that building knowledge occurs best through building things that are tangible and sharable. "Constructionism (in the context of learning) is the idea that people learn effectively through making things. Constructionism is connected with experiential learning and builds on some of the ideas of Jean Piaget." Constructionism asserts that constructivism occurs especially well when the learner is engaged in constructing something for others to see.

According to Papert (1990) - *"Constructionism shares constructivism's connotation of learning as `building knowledge structures' irrespective of the circumstances of the learning. It then adds that this happens especially felicitously in a context where the learner is consciously engaged in constructing a public entity, whether it's a sandcastle or a theory of the universe... If one eschews pipeline models of transmitting knowledge in talking among ourselves as well as in theorizing about classrooms, then one must expect that I will not be able to tell you about my idea of constructionism. Doing so is bound to trivialize it. Instead, I must confine myself to engage you in experiences (including verbal ones) liable to encourage your own personal construction of something in some sense like it. Only in this way will there be something rich enough in your mind to be worth talking about."*

Constructionism is not just learning-by-doing, but engaging reflexively and socially in the task. Both the creation process and the produced artifacts ought to be socially shared. Artifacts popular with constructionists include digital artifacts (e.g. things one can build with microworlds. "As adults, we all have time when we need to teach or explain something we know to someone else. To do this, we may have to hone up on the subject, talk with others, prepare notes and draw diagrams. In the process, we learn our subject well because we have to think hard about it and think of the best ways to convey it to others.

EDUCATIONAL IMPLICATIONS OF CONSTRUCTIVISM

Because constructivism is principally a theory about how people learn, we can draw many educational implications from the work of the key constructivist theorists, and those who have used constructivist principles. Some constructivist practices in education include:

- the diagnosis of learners' individual learning styles;
- the identification of learners' strengths or intelligences;
- curricular practices such as Individual Learning Plans (ILPs);
- attention to cultural inclusivity;
- innovative learning and teaching strategies such as problem-based learning;
- links between community-based learning and formal education;
- authentic assessment practices, which incorporate learners' views.

STRENGTHS OF CONSTRUCTIVISM

- Constructivist activities are generally relevant to the learner and real-world based.
- Learners construct knowledge and meaning as they can relate the information to their own experiences, beliefs, and attitudes.

WEAKNESSES OF CONSTRUCTIVISM

- Individual experiences and attitudes can vary.
- A specific, desired outcome may not always be achieved when different people approach the problem or task.

APPLICATION OF CONSTRUCTIVISM

Constructivism is best utilized when learners take control of the learning situation, such as in Problem-Based Learning. As learners engage themselves in an activity like this, they develop an understanding of the importance of the problem, comprehend the relevance of the topic, and construct knowledge through their experiences. It is more important to focus on the whole rather than the individual parts in constructivist learning. Constructivism is sometimes misconstrued as a theory that compels students to reinvent the wheel. Actually, it implores students to attempt to learn how it functions and apply it to real world learning.

IMPLICATIONS OF CONSTRUCTIVISM

- Learning should be an active process. Keeping learners active by doing meaningful activities results in high-level processing, which facilitates the creation of personalized meaning. Asking learners to apply the information in a practical situation is an active process, which also facilitates personal interpretation and relevance.
- Learners should construct their own knowledge rather than accepting that given by the instructor. Knowledge construction is facilitated by good interactive online instruction, since the students have to take the initiative to learn and to interact with other students and the instructor, and also because the learning agenda is controlled by the student.
- Collaborative learning should be encouraged to facilitate constructivist learning. Working with other learners gives real-life experience of working in a group, and allows them to use their metacognitive skills. Learners will also be able to use the strengths of other learners and to learn from others. When assigning learners for group work, membership should be based on the expertise level and learning style of individual group members, so that individual team members can benefit from one another's strengths.
- Learners should be given control of the learning process. There should be a form of guided discovery where learners are allowed to make decision on learning goals, but with some guidance from the instructor.
- Learning should be made meaningful for learners. The learning materials should include examples that relate to students, so that they can make sense of the information. Assignments and projects should allow learners to choose meaningful activities to help them apply and personalize the information.
- Learning should be interactive to promote higher-level learning and social presence, and to help develop personal meaning. Learning is the development of new knowledge, skills, and attitudes as the learner interacts with information and the environment.

MAJOR LEARNING THEORIES RELATED TO CONSTRUCTIVISM

Important constructivist learning theories are given below:

Situated Learning Theory

Situated learning theory is a theory developed by Jean Lave and Etienne Wenger and owes much to the work of John Dewey and Lev Vygotsky who believed students were more likely to learn by actively participating in their learning as opposed to listening to lecturers. Situated learning is a matter of creating meaning from the real activities of daily living where learning occurs in a pro-social but informal setting. This notion suggests that learning takes place through social relationships, within a cultural milieu, and by connecting prior knowledge to new contexts. Situated learning emphasizes the idea that what is learned is specific to the situation (context) in which it is learned. Wilson and Myers (2000) describe it as cognition that "emphasizes the web of social and activity systems within which authentic practice takes place."

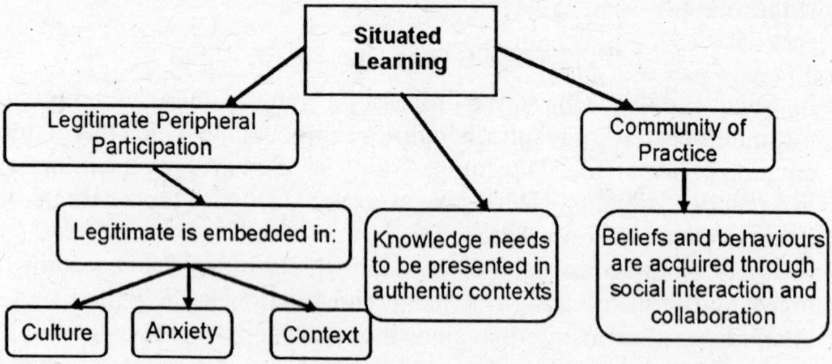

Figure 4.1: Schematic Diagram of Situated Learning

The situated model of learning is part of Lave and Wenger's theory of communities of practice which states that learning should not be viewed as mere transmission of knowledge but as a distinctly embedded and active process. They argue that this type of learning is stimulated by specific contexts (where learning is socially-situated) and within authentic social and physical environments.

Key Concepts of Situated Learning

The key concepts of Situated Learning are:

- Knowledge is not an object and memory is not a location; knowledge is socially-constructed
- Knowledge is thus located in the actions of people and groups of people; it evolves naturally as a result of individuals participating in and negotiating their way through new situations
- Knowing, learning and cognition are socially-constructed, expressed and reified in the actions of people and people interacting
- Construction of meaning is tied to specific contexts and purposes
- Mediation artifacts: cultural models are not held by individuals but live in the practices of a community and how people engage with each other, as well as any tools they use, and the specific cultural context
- As situations shape individual cognition, individual thinking and action shape the situation; the reciprocal influence constitutes an alternative conception of systemic causality to the more commonly assumed linear object causality (Wilson and Myers, 2000).

Lave's Situated Learning (1988)

Lave discusses the problem of *knowledge transfer* and argues that learning in natural settings occurs as a function of activities, context and culture in which it is situated. He examines cognition in everyday situations and provides descriptions for them:

- Cognition is socially defined, interpreted and supported
- Social contexts can both constrain and assist cognition: research should examine cognition to determine the generality of cognitive skills and articulate culture's role in developing skills
- People devise satisfactory opportunistic *in situ* solutions to problems; they don't employ formal approaches to problem-solving in everyday thinking
- Participation in interaction results in adaptive "survival" skills, as well as successful reasoning and learning

Brown, Collins and Duguid Situated Learning (1989)

According to Brown, Collins and Duguid (1989), different instructional goals such as *'knowing what'* and *'knowing how'* result in different practices in education. As a kind of decontextualized learning, it separates out the learning from the doing. They suggest that *"activity and situations are integral to cognition and learning"* and cognitive apprenticeship provides an *"authentic place to engage in activity and social interactions"*. He gives the importance of authenticity in situated learning. According to him:

- Knowledge, as a product of a meaning-making process, cannot be separated from its context
- Learning is a continuous, lifelong process from acting within (and reacting to) situations
- The tools of learning and their usage "reflect the particular accumulated insights of communities of practice"
- Learning is a process of acculturation: "...given the chance to observe and practice *in situ* the behaviours of members of a culture, people pick up relevant jargon, imitate behaviours"... and start to act in accordance with norms of that culture

Gibson's Affordance

Affordance is an ecological concept i.e., *how human beings perceive what something is or does within their environment*. The implications are that "affordance" is a term characterizing the impact of the environment on an organism's behaviour, and how it lives in its environment. Affordance emerges with the action of the organism, i.e. its direct perception of environmental affordances controls its behaviour. The idea of affordances suggests a reciprocal relationship between organism and environment. It is thus important to analyze behaviours in relation to environments. When affordances is considered by humans, our perception of affordance extends beyond the physical environment to conceptual states. Any theory of learning must therefore start with the cultural environment in which learners learn. If knowledge is co-produced within cultures, then the position of learners is a critical variable. Teachers need to respect knowledge communities and help learners to negotiate multiple worldviews.

Cognitive Apprenticeship

Cognitive apprenticeship is an important practical concept in *situated learning*. This type of learning apprenticeship engages learners to participate in communities of practice, and provides several advantages:

- The legitimacy of apprenticing and availability of community resources is important to learners
- Learners have strong goals and motivation in situated contexts
- Learners develop an understanding of the enterprise through an engagement in practice
- Communication among peers and near-peers also facilitates learning

Process of Cognitive Apprenticeship

The process of Cognitive Apprenticeship is given below:

- By beginning with a task embedded in a familiar activity, teachers show students the legitimacy of their implicit knowledge and its availability as scaffolding in unfamiliar tasks.
- By pointing to different decompositions, teachers stress heuristics are not absolute but assessed with respect to particular tasks; even algorithms can he assessed in this way
- By allowing students to generate their own solutions, teachers help them to be conscious creative members of the culture of problem-solving
- A cognitive apprenticeship helps students' acculturation acquiring culture's tools or a shared vocabulary and the means to discuss, reflect on, evaluate and validate community procedures is a collaborative process.

Legitimate Peripheral Participation

Legitimate peripheral participation (Lave, 1988, Lave & Wenger, 1991) refers to how learners engage in activities of socio-cultural practice and how they become increasingly competent in this practice. Participation provides students with ways to belong to a community of practice. Legitimate peripheral participation refers to the social organization of and control over resources. To get full access to resources takes time and experience. The word peripheral is used to *distinguish between new comers and old timers* (Driscoll, 2000) which *encompasses multiple, varied, more-or-less engaged and inclusive ways of being located in the fields of participation defined by a community*. Brown, Collins and Dugid (1989) support their propositions about situated learning and cognitive apprenticeship by addressing the following:

- There is a mismatch between the formal learning situations and real world situations
- There is a failure of knowledge to transfer
- Training by abstraction is of little use
- Learning is inherently a social phenomenon

5
Child Growth and Development

The aim of education is to bring about desired changes in the learner. Changes are taking place in an individual due to learning and also due to the natural growth and development. Development of proper attitudes, habits and patterns of behaviour formed during the early years determines to a great extent how successfully an individual adjusts himself as he grows older. Since the task of the teacher is to bring about desirable changes in the growing child, knowledge about growth and development is utmost important.

MEANING OF GROWTH AND DEVELOPMENT

The clear meaning of growth and development is as follows:

Meaning of Growth

The terms growth and development are often used interchangeably and regarded as synonymous. Growth is sheer increase in size, height, weight, power etc. It refers to the dimensional augmentation, cellular multiplication, or quantitative changes in size, weight and number. The process of gradual increase of an individual or animal or a seed, germ or root to its full size or maturity is called growth. According to Crow and Crow *growth refers to structural and physiological changes while development refers to growth as well as change in behaviour*.

Characteristics: The main characteristics of growth are given as follows:

- Growth is a complex process
- Growth follows a definite sequence or pattern
- Growth proceeds more rapidly in the early years of life
- Rate of growth is not uniform in different stages and parts
- Growth is not a continuous process. It stops with maturity
- Growth is cumulative in nature
- Growth is influenced by heredity and environment
- The tempo or speed of growth is not even
- There is marked individual difference in growth
- The rate and pattern of growth can be modified by conditions internal and external to the body

Meaning of Development

The term development refers to change in structure, form or shape and improvement in functioning. It does not consist merely of adding inches to one's height or improving one's ability but it is a complex process of integrating many structures and functions. In the words of Hurlock, the term *development means a progressive series of changes that occur in an orderly predictable pattern as a result of maturation and experience.*

Characteristics: The main characteristics of development are as follows:

- Development is the result of maturation and learning
- Development follows a definite and predictable pattern
- Each period of development involves certain hazards
- Certain characteristic traits are associated with each phase of development
- Development is not uniform in all individuals
- Development depends on both heredity and environment
- Development is gradual and it takes time

CORRELATION BETWEEN GROWTH AND DEVELOPMENT

Growth and development are correlated because both occur together. Growth takes place when a child grows taller; his bones, muscles and other parts of the body increase in size. As the child grows, his mind and body mature and he is able to function at a higher level. For example, as a child grows in age, the size of his fingers increases in length and in thickness. This is considered as growth. Along with this growth, the ability of the child to use his fingers with ease, speed and precision for various purposes also may increase. This change can be considered as development.

COMPARISON BETWEEN GROWTH AND DEVELOPMENT

The difference between growth and development can be seen with the help of the table-5.1 given below:

Table 5.1: Difference between Growth and Development

Growth	*Development*
Growth is quantitative	Development is qualitative
Growth is Structural	Development is functional
Growth is observable and measurable	Development is not observable and measurable
Growth is physical and external in nature	Development is internal and can be physical, social, emotional, moral, intellectual etc.
Growth is not a continuous process. It stops with the attainment of maturity	Development is a continuous process. It does not end with maturity
Growth may or may not bring development	Development is possible without growth
Growth refers to changes in the particular aspects of body	Development refers to over all changes resulting in improved functioning of the individual
growth does not depend upon maturation and learning	Development depends upon maturation and learning

PRINCIPLES OF GROWTH AND DEVELOPMENT

Following are the fundamental principles of growth and development:

Development Follows a Pattern or a Sequence

Development tends to proceed from the head downward. This is called the *'cephalocaudal principle'*. According to this principle, the child first gains control of the head, then the arms, and the legs. Infants gain control of head and face movements within the first two months after birth. In the next few months, they are able to lift themselves up using their arms. By 6 to 12 months of age, infants start to gain leg control and may be able to crawl, stand, or walk.

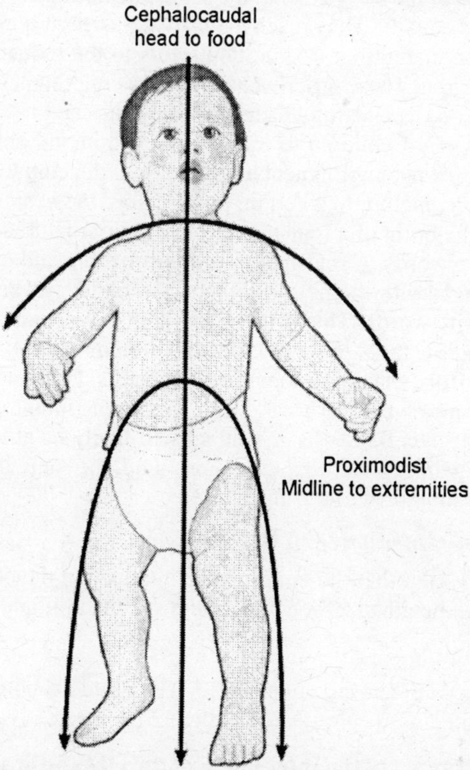

Figure-5.1: Pattern or Sequence of Development in Human

Development also proceeds from the centre of the body outward according to the *'proximodistal principle'*. Accordingly, the spinal cord develops before other parts of the body. The child's arm develops before the hands, and the hands and feet develop before the fingers and toes. Fingers and toes are the last to develop.

Development Proceeds from General to Specific Responses

It moves from a generalized to localized behaviour. The newborn infant moves its whole body at one time instead of moving only one part of it. It makes random kicking with its legs before it can coordinate the leg muscles well enough to crawl or walk.

Development is a Continuous Process

Development does not occur in spurts. Growth continues from the moments of conception until the individual reaches maturity. It takes place at slow regular pace rather than by 'leaps and bounds'. Although development is a continuous process, yet the tempo of growth is not even; during infancy and early years growth moves swiftly and later it slacken.

Different Aspects of Growth and Develop at Different Rates

Neither all parts of the body grow at the same rate nor do all aspects of mental growth proceed equally. They reach maturity at different times. Development also depends on maturation. Maturation refers to the sequence of biological changes in children. These orderly changes give children new abilities. Much of the maturation depends on changes in the brain and the nervous system. These changes assist children to improve their thinking abilities and motor skills. A rich learning environment helps children develop to their potential.

Children must mature to a certain point before they can gain some skills. For instance, the brain of a four-month-old has not matured enough to allow the child to use words. A four-month-old will babble and coo. However, by two years of age, with the help of others, the child will be able to say and understand many words. This is an example of how cognitive development occurs from simple tasks to more tasks that are complex. Likewise, physical skills develop from general to specific movements. For example, think about the way an infant waves its arms and legs. In a young infant, these movements are random. In several months, the infant will likely be able to grab a block with his or her whole hand. In a little more time, the same infant will grasp a block with the thumb and forefinger.

Most Traits are Correlated in Development

Generally, it is seen that the child whose intellectual development is above average is so in health size, sociability and special aptitudes.

Growth is Complex

All of its aspects are closely interrelated. The child's mental development is intimately related to his physical growth and its needs.

Growth is a Product of the Interaction of the Organism and Environment

Among the environmental factors, one can mention nutrition, climate, the conditions in the home, the type of social organization in which individual moves and lives.

There are Wide Individual Differences in Growth

Individual differences in growth are caused by differences in heredity and environment.

Growth is Both Quantitative and Qualitative

These two aspects are inseparable. The child not only grows in 'size'; he grows up or matures in structure and function too.

Development is Predictable

It is possible for us to predict at an early age the range within which the mature development of the child is likely to fall. However, mental development cannot be predicted with the same degree of accuracy.

MEANING OF CHILD GROWTH

Children are not just smaller versions of adults. They have very particular needs and capabilities. One of the major issues in children's education is lack of knowledge on the part of teachers about how children grow and develop. Good teachers know and understand the many changes that take place from child to adult and structure their learning experiences to best suit the needs of the children.

There are clear stages that children pass through from birth to adult. These stages are the same for boys and girls, but girls generally mature before boys. This is clearly shown in the Figure-5.2 given below:

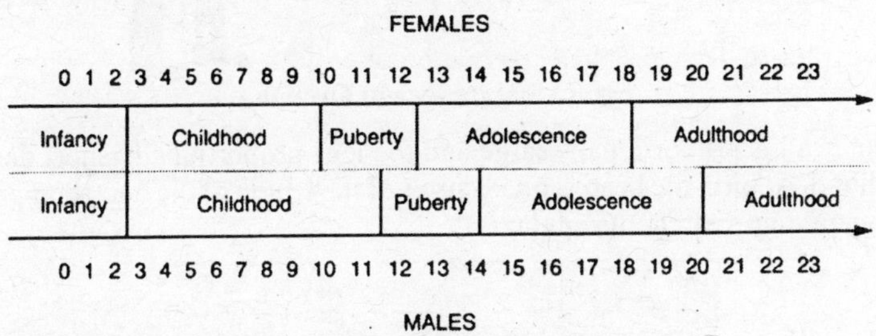

Figure 5.2: Child Growth Stages

Physical Growth

Physical growth is obviously important to performance. We will start by looking at how the body changes during development. There are important changes in body size and proportions. These changes affect the way children can perform different skills and activities.

Children grow in size at a very fast rate. At birth, infants are only about a quarter of their adult height. This final adult height is usually reached at about twenty years of age.

Characteristic Stages of Growth from Birth to Adult

There are four characteristic stages of growth from birth to adult:

1. Rapid growth in infancy and early childhood
2. Slow, steady growth in middle childhood
3. Rapid growth during puberty
4. Gradual slowing down of growth in adolescence until adult height is reached

Both sexes are of a comparable shape and size during infancy and childhood.

Patterns of Growth: Changes in Proportions

The physical proportions of the body at birth are very different from those of the adult. Some body parts grow more than others during development to reach the final adult proportions. The illustration shows the relative size of body parts at different ages.

Figure 5.3: Pattern of Growth

The head is proportionally large and the legs proportionally short during childhood. At birth the head is one quarter of the length of the body compared with about one sixth in the adult.

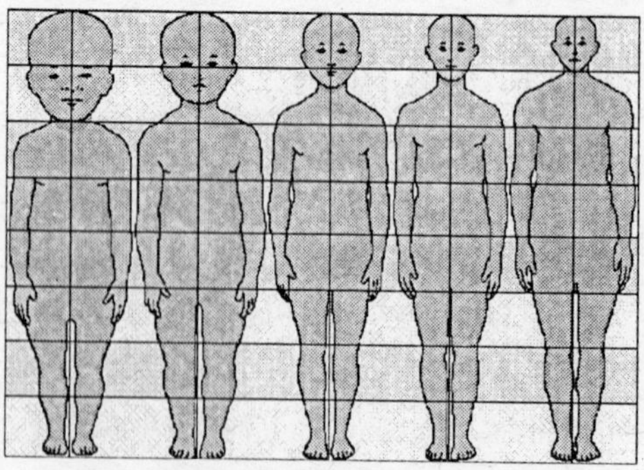

Figure 5.4: Changes in Proportions

The legs are about one third the length of the body at birth and one half in the adult. Because the body proportions change it means that not all the body segments grow at the same rate.

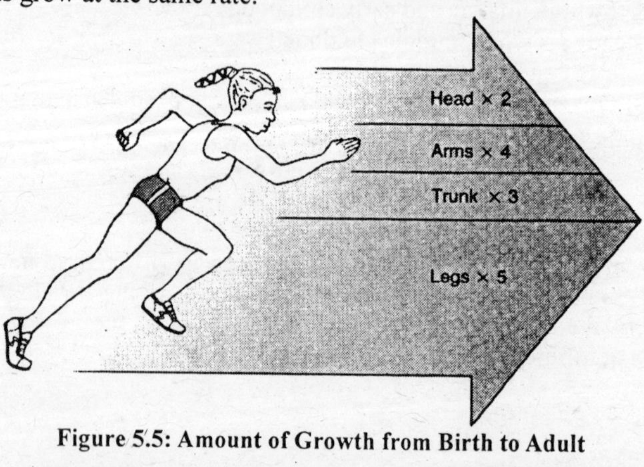

Figure 5.5: Amount of Growth from Birth to Adult

Changes in the size and shape of the body are caused by different segments growing at different times.

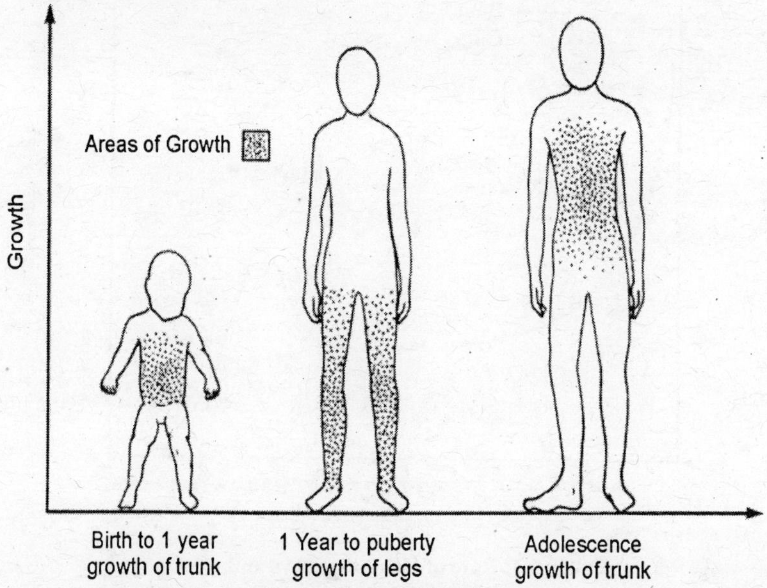

Figure 5.6: Areas of Growth

These changes in body proportions will have a great influence on how skills will be performed. For example, changes in the relative size of the head in childhood affects the balance of the body during movement and the relative shortness of the legs in the very young limits running ability. At the beginning of puberty, children have long arms and legs. They are better suited for running but the rapid growth may make them appear to be clumsy and to have difficulty in coordination.

Growth Spurts

When the rate of growth increases rapidly, it is called a growth spurt. The most important growth spurt is the one which occurs at puberty. This spurt produces a rapid increase in both weight and height.

The peak of this growth spurt occurs at about age 12 for girls and age 14 for boys. Before this growth spurt, there are no important differences between boys and girls in weight and height. During growth spurts, most of the child's energy is used for growing. Children will be easily tired and may not be able to keep up their usual volume or intensity of training. Light training will stimulate bodily growth if the child has enough energy.

Early and Late Developers

Each child develops at its own rate and some children develop earlier and some later than the average. For both boys and girls the age at the peak of the major growth spurt frequently occurs up to two years before or after the average age.

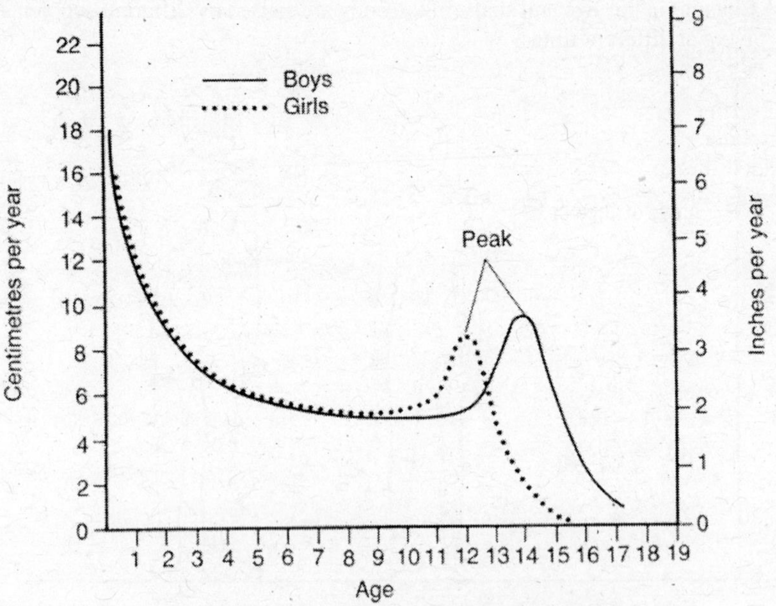

Figure 5.7: Rate of Height in Boys and Girls

Age for peak times for growth in height for boys and girls

	Peak growth		
	Early	*Average*	*Late*
Boys	12	14	16
Girls	10	12	14

Figure 5.8: Age for Peak Times for Growth in Height for Boys and Girls

There can easily be differences of four years in development between children of the same age. Thinking about growth stages and developmental age rather than age alone is perhaps one of the most important considerations when coaching young athletes. Early success may be due entirely to relative size and strength at the time. As other children catch up the early matures may be left behind. On the other hand, the late developers are frequently overlooked if they are judged only on their performances.

Structure of the Body

The changes in size and proportion are the easily observed signs of development. They are the result of changes in the skeleton inside the body. The skeleton of a child is mostly cartilage, which is softer than bone and can bend. The process by which cartilage becomes bone begins very early in life in special growth areas in the bones. These special growth areas are called growth plates.

These growth areas in the bone are the weakest part of the bone. They can be easily injured by a sudden force or a repeated force. Mild forces can stimulate bone growth, but excessive forces can cause damage and have serious long term effects.

Rebounding, repeated vigorous throwing and the use of weights should be avoided during periods of rapid growth. Once the body stops growing the growth regions become bone and are no longer weak areas.

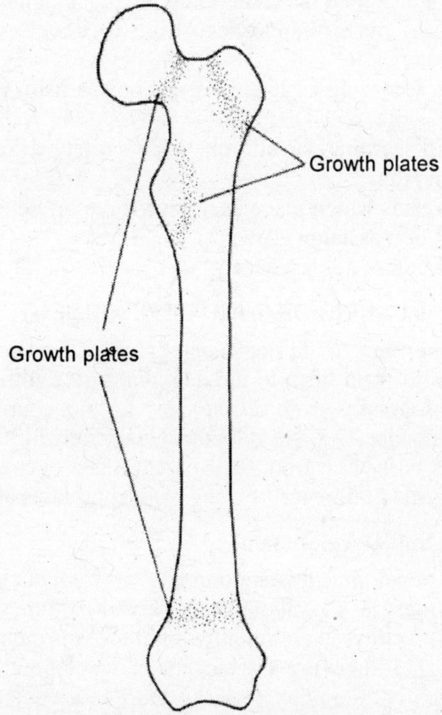

Figure 5.9: Growth Plates of the Thigh Bone— the Femur

Children and Exercise

Children do not tolerate exercise as well as adults. They are much less aware of their real limits. Children do not breathe as slowly or as deeply as adults. The average six year old child breathes in 38 litres of air to get one litre of oxygen. The average 18 year old needs only to breathe 28 litres of air to get one liter of oxygen. This means that the younger the athlete the harder their bodies must work to provide the oxygen their muscles need.

The body has three energy systems. Two of these are anaerobic, without oxygen, and the other is the aerobic system, using oxygen. Before adolescence children get a higher proportion of their energy from the aerobic system than adults do. In general, children are better at steady, extended exercises. Physical changes, during and after puberty will improve their anaerobic abilities. The amount of this improvement will help decide what event or distance is best for a young child.

Implications of Child Growth for the Teacher and Coach

The following implications will be useful for the teacher and coaches:

- Think about growth stages rather than ages
- Think how changes in physical proportions will affect performance
- Help children understand the changes taking place in their bodies
- Set standards of performance according to developmental age not chronological age
- Group children according to physical development, using height and weight as a guide
- Encourage skill learning for all your athletes, late developers could be very successful later
- Don't use exercises which place excessive force on bone growth regions during periods of maximum growth
- Avoid weights before adolescence

MEANING OF CHILD DEVELOPMENT

Child development refers to the sequence of physical and emotional changes that occur in a child from birth to the beginning of adulthood. During this process a child progresses from dependency on their parents/guardians to increasing independence. Child development is strongly influenced by genetic factors (the genes passed on from their parents) and events during prenatal life. However it is also influenced by environmental facts and learning.

Importance of Child Development

Monitoring child development is important to ensure that children meet their 'developmental milestones'. Although arbitrary time frames that are far from exact, checking that children are roughly 'on track' for their age is helpful in order to detect early if there are any hiccups in development. This is usually carried out through child/mother services and Paediatricians as infants and toddlers, and later through kindergartens and school term skills assessments.

The earliest possible detection (and treatment if appropriate) of developmental challenges is helpful as it can allow the early intervention to help minimize the impact these developmental hiccups can have on children's skill development and subsequently their confidence, or serve as an indicator of a possible diagnosis.

Developmental milestone checklist/charts are used as a guide as to what is normal for a particular age range and can be used to highlight any areas that a child may be delayed in. However, it is important to be aware that while child development has a predictable sequence, all children are unique in their development and the course in which each child follows to reach each milestone can vary.

Principles of the Development of Children

Human Development involves change. This change occurs at various stages of development and the development pattern at each stage has predictable characteristics. You might have observed that development is a product of maturity and learning. Maturity is more or less automatic, unfolding biological potential. It is an irreversible sequence and entails biological changes. Such changes are relatively independent of environmental factors as long as environmental factor remain normal.

Categories of Child Development

Categories of child development include:

- Cognitive Development (ability to learn and problem solve)
- Social development (interacting with others)
- Emotional development (Control over his emotions and self-control)
- Speech and Language development (understanding and using language, reading and communicating)
- Physical or Motor development (fine and gross motor skills)
- Spiritual Development (thinking about who we are and how we are in the world)
- Moral Development (development of proper attitudes and behaviours toward other people in society, based on social and cultural norms, rules and laws)
- Sensory Development (Maturing of the five familiar senses: hearing, smell, taste, touch, and vision)

Problems in Child Development

Problems in development can arise due to: genetics, prenatal circumstances, the presence of a specific diagnosis or medical factors, and/or lack of opportunity or exposure to helpful stimuli. Specific assessment by the best fit professional (which may initially be the GP or Paediatrician, and then Occupational Therapist, Speech Pathologist, Psychologist and/or Physiotherapist) can provide clarity about the issues and extent of concern and formulate a plan to overcome the challenge(s). In many cases, as the process of child development involves multiple skill areas developing at once, there may be benefit in consulting multiple professionals.

Overcoming the developmental challenges is crucial to maximizing the ease and speed of development, minimizing the gap that occur between a child's ability and those of their same ages peers, the confidence of the child as well as frustration that can be encountered by the child's parents and/or care-givers.

FACTORS INFLUENCING GROWTH AND DEVELOPMENT

Right from conception, the beginning of life in a mother's womb, the growth and development of human beings is influenced by a variety of factors categorized broadly as internal and external. They are (1) Internal Factors and (2) External Factors mentioned below:

Internal Factors

All those factors which lie within the individual are called internal factors. These include—

(1) Heredity, (2) Biological or constitutional,
(3) Intelligence, (4) Emotional and,
(5) Social factors.

1. Heredity Factors: Heredity is the process of transmitting biological traits from parent to offspring through genes, the basic units of heredity. Heredity also refers to the inherited characteristics of an individual, including traits such as height, eye colour and blood type.

Heredity factors play their part at the time of conception in the mother's womb. What is transferred to the offspring from its immediate parents in the form of genes and chromosomes at this time, constitute the hereditary contribution. This contribution is the real starting point and basis for all the growth and development that takes place later in the life of the child. The height, weight, colour of the eyes and skin, characteristics of the hair, are all decided by these hereditary influences.

The physical structure, nervous system and other things related to one's constitutional make-up, body chemistry and physical development are to a great extent decided by hereditary factors. If the hereditary contributions are satisfactory, then with minimum efforts, we get satisfactory results; otherwise we have to make tremendous efforts for achieving desired results or success in terms of child's satisfactory growth and development.

2. Biological and Constitutional Factors: A child's constitutional make-up, somatic or physical structure, body chemistry etc. influence his growth and development throughout his life.

- A child who is physically week or has internal deformities cannot achieve normal physical and mental growth and development.
- The nervous system which controls the body movement, affects the growth and development of a child in cognitive spheres.
- The endocrine or ductless glands or hormones have important role in growth and development. In case there is over activity (hyperactivity) or under activity (hypo activity) of these glands, it results in serious abnormality in growth and development.
- Defective constitutional make-up like ugly face, short stature and any other deformity of the body may give birth to feelings of inferiority and the person may face adjustment problems in the social environment.

3. Intelligence: Intelligence is considered as a major factor influencing development. Children of high intelligence develop in many aspects faster than that of low intelligence. Even the body movement and behaviour are regulated by his level of intelligence. It affects his social behaviour, moral adjustment and emotional growth. The physical, social, emotional, moral and language development of a child is greatly influenced and controlled by the level of his intelligence.

4. *Emotional Factors:* Emotional maturity and adjustability play a vital role in influencing a person's overall growth and development. A child who is found to be overwhelmed by negative emotions like fear, anger, jealousy, etc. is adversely affected in his physical, mental, social, moral and language development. If a person cannot exercise a reasonable control over his emotions, he has to suffer in terms of growth and development. He may find himself a failure in doing some serious mental activity.

5. ***Social Factors:*** A person's socialization helps him in achieving adjustment and advancement in other aspects of his growth and development. He may learn from his environment, by means of his social nature, which may prove to be a boon to him for his proper growth and development.

External Factors

The factors lying outside individual in his environment are collectively called the external factors influencing growth and development. These factors begin their role immediately after a baby is conceived. They are as follows:

Environment in the Womb of Mother

What is available to the child for his nourishment in its mother's womb from the time of conception till his birth is quite important from the angle of his growth and development. A few factors are cited below as examples:

- The physical and mental health of the mother during pregnancy
- Single child or multiple children getting nourished in the womb
- Quality and quantity of nutrition received by the embryo
- Normal and abnormal delivery
- Any damage or accident to the baby in the womb

Environment Available After Birth

What a child gets from different conditions and forces of his environment after his birth, influence his growth and development in many ways. These are described as follows:

(a) Accidents and Incidents of Life

The growth and development of an individual is greatly influenced by the good and bad incidents and accidents that occur in his life time. For example, if a child's nervous system is damaged in an accident, it will hamper his mental development and in turn it will affect his development in other spheres also.

(b) The Quality of Physical Environment, Medical Care and Nourishment

Child's growth and development is greatly influenced by the quality of physical environment and medical care and nourishment available to him for his living and working. These include open space, balanced diet, proper medical care etc.

(c) The Quality of the Facilities and Opportunities Provided by the Social and Cultural Forces

What a child gets from his social and cultural environment influences the entire course of his development. A few are mentioned below:

- Parental and family care received by a child
- Economic and social status of the parents and family
- The quality of schooling received by a child
- The quality of peer group relationships of the child
- The quality of neighbourhood and surrounding environment

THE DEVELOPMENTAL PROCESS

Change is the law of nature. Animate or inanimate objects are all subject to change. Seeds, after germinating in the soil grow as saplings, and then as specific plants and trees, which in turn flower and produce seeds or fruits for further germination. Similar is the case with birds, animals and human beings who can produce their own kind by the transmission of specific characteristics of the species through sexual union.

In all animals, including human beings, the pre-natal period resembles the time taken by a germinating seed to come out of the soil, which then grows and develops into a full-fledged plant or tree. *The process by which a germinating seed or conceived organism is turned into a mature plant or full-fledged being is collectively termed as growth and development.*

The process of growth and development are the medium and means for bringing about changes in the organism. In general, growth and development refers to the changes produced by the interaction produced by one's genetic and environmental factors as well as to the changes in the physical, mental, social, emotional and moral aspects involving one's individuality.

STAGES OF GROWTH AND DEVELOPMENT

Growth, development and behaviour of an individual have variations at different ages. Psychologists have divided the life span of an individual into different stages, each of which has certain common characteristics. Knowledge of various stages of development and its characteristics is essential for the teacher so as to make the teaching-learning process effective, appropriate, and meaningful.

Modern education is based on the psychology of the educand. The educand's psychology conforms to the stage of his development. By knowing the various stages of development through which an individual child is passing, the teacher can know his needs, interests and abilities and can plan his teaching strategy accordingly.

The different stages in the growth and development of an individual can be classified as follows:

Human Stage	Year
1. Pre-natal Stage	From conception to birth
2. Infancy	From birth to 3 years
3. Childhood	From 3 to 12 years (*in strict sense up to the onset of puberty)*
3.1. Early Childhood	3 to 6 years
3.2. Later Childhood	6 to 12 years
4. Adolescence	From 12 to 19 years (*from the onset of puberty to the age of maturity)*
5. Adulthood	From 20 to 60 years
6. Old Age	61 years and above

Although each stage is different from the other, we cannot draw a clear cut dividing line between different stages. Stage merges with the next and developmental process is a continuous one. A study of the pattern of growth and development exhibited by the individuals provides very useful data for parents and teachers to plan the development and education of the children.

Pre-natal Period

The pre-natal period extends from conception to birth, which is normally 280 days. The child's development within the womb is a very important phase of its entire development. During this period the developing organism is dependent upon the mother for the digestion of food, excretion of waste products, external respiration, body temperature etc. Factors like mother's health, food, emotional experiences and certain desires are some of the factors which influence the development during this period. Birth is merely an interruption of the normal development. This interruption is characterized by a change in the environment form that of the mother's womb to that of the world outside.

Infancy Period

The first 3 years of the life of a child is the period of infancy. The first two weeks is known as the period of *neonate* or the new-born. The period from the third week to the end of three years is known as *babyhood.* These 3 years of life are of tremendous importance in the progress of the individual. It is at this time that the infant adjusts to the totally new environment outside the mother's body and thus learns to be self-dependent.

Developmental Characteristics during Infancy Period

Physical and Motor Development: Rapid physical growth is marked in these years. Boys showed an increased rate in growth than the girls. The trunk grows faster than the head and the proportion between the two changes. The bodily functions tend to become stable and controlled.

Emotional Development: At birth, regarding the expression of emotions like pleasure and pain, the baby is able to cry only. Later he can express fear, anger, disgust, etc. The child feels pleasure in the company of his mother and distress in her separation.

Intellectual Development: There is rapid improvement in the structure and function of the sensory organs. Now the child is able to perform all functions of seeing, hearing, tasting, smelling, touching etc. almost as good as a mature individual.

Social and Moral Development: Mother is the first best friend who socializes with infant. Other family members are in the next in position. At the end of this period the child begins to establish contact with other infants.

Language Development: Language development of the infant begins from the birthcry. The 10 month old child is able to use one word. By the end of the first year he is able to use 3 or 4 words.

Early Childhood Stage (Pre-School Stage)

Early childhood that extends from 3-6 years, is labeled by the parents as the *problem age* or *toy age;* by the educators as the *pre-school age and by the psychologists as the pre-gang age.* During this stage children are obstinate, disobedient, negativistic and antagonistic. Hence most parents consider early childhood as a problem age. Educationally this is the most important and impressionable age. This stage plays a significant role in the development of character and personality. Exploratory age, questioning age, imitative age etc. are the other names of this period.

Developmental Characteristics of Early Childhood

Physical and Motor Development: Early childhood is a period of slow, steady and uniform physical growth. The average annual increase in height is three inches and in weight is three to five pounds. Eruption and replacement of teeth is a remarkable development in this period. Brain has developed 90 per cent of its adult weight. A variety of motor skills like crawling, walking, running, jumping, climbing etc. are also developed in this period.

Emotional Development: Emotions are especially intense during early childhood. The emotional behaviour of the child at this stage is further differentiated into shame, anxiety, envy, hope, disappointment and affection for parents and other members of the family. The most primitive sentiment is his love for his own self. Therefore this stage is called 'Narcissism', auto erotism or self-love. But soon the child extends his sentiments to his parents. According to Sigmund Freud, *Oedipus Complex* and *Electra Complex* are developed in this period. It is certain that, to a great extent, a boy has got great attachment to his mother and the girl to her father.

Intellectual Development: At this stage the child has got varied experiences connected with his immediate environment. He accumulates a heap of knowledge. He understands the basic functional relationship between things and events. He begins to form concepts of physical and social reality. *Ego-centrism* and fantasy are in a high degree at this stage. Gradual development in the perception of size, shape, colour, time; rapid increase in memory, thinking and reasoning, creativity and imagination etc. are also developed in this stage.

Language Development: During the first 8-10 months, the child's only mode of communication is babbling and cooing. The first words are uttered around child's first birth day. Then there is a rapid increase in vocabulary. Words are combined into phrases and sentences, and simple thoughts are communicated with ease.

Social Development

During early childhood the child acquires the preliminary training and experiences needed to become a member of a group in later childhood. During this stage, children become increasingly aware of their bodies and learn their sexual identities as male and female. This self awareness contributes to the development of their positive and negative self attitudes. During pre-school years children develop new inter-personal and appropriate relationship with others. They learn to share and compete with siblings and peers. The social qualities, such as co-operation, sympathy, social approval, teasing, quarrelling etc. are developed in this period. The important features of socializations during pre-school years are:

- Feelings of autonomy develops in children
- Social environment expands beyond home
- Child seeks social approval for his actions
- Children of both sexes play together without any discrimination

- They learn to co-operate with others and make friends on shared interests and similar personality traits

Later Childhood Stage (Primary School Stage)

Later, childhood extends from the age of six years to the time individual becomes sexually mature. It spreads from 6 to 12 years. Educationists call this age as *elementary-school age* and psychologists as *gang age* or *age of conformity.* The period is marked by rather slow and uniform growth. It is in this period, even the nicest child often begins to behave in the most awful way and hence requires proper guidance and counselling. At this stage several functional changes take place in the child. It gradually gains maturity in all physical and mental spheres. As regards sex, it remain dormant, but emerges with great force only at the end of this stage. It is why this stage is called *latency period.*

Developmental Characteristics of Later Childhood

Physical Development: Later childhood is a period of slow and relatively uniform growth until the changes of puberty begins. The growth is slowest for girls between nine and ten years, while boys grow slowest between ten and eleven years. The first teeth are replaced by permanent ones. Bones becomes harder and height and weight increase. Flattening of the forehead, sharpening of the nose and broadening of the chest are other notable changes. The most significant physical change occurring during this period is the lengthening of the limbs.

Motor Development: Motor abilities improve a great deal between sixth and twelfth year. Improving muscle co-ordination helps the child to acquire new skills and improve the already acquired ones. They have a reasonably good mastery over the basic motor skills of sitting, standing, walking and simple finger manipulation. By the age of twelve, muscle co-ordination is almost perfect.

Emotional Development: During this period the child learns to control emotional expression in social situations, especially the unpleasant ones and to use *emotional catharsis* to clear their pent-up emotions. Fear of many common things slowly disappears but fears caused by imaginary stimuli begin in this age. The child experiences more frustration and jealousy is intensified. Desire for acceptance as a member of the gang is developed and he likes to have company of his own sex. A catharsis is an emotional release. This emotional release is linked to a need to release unconscious conflicts. The individual may instead release these feelings in another way, such as through physical activity or another stress relieving activity

Intellectual Development: Primary school stage is the age of intellectual development. The child develops powers of observation, attention, reasoning and abstract thinking. They can focus on more than one aspect of a situation and can globally experience what happens around. His power of perception becomes keen and memory becomes keener. Here he learns the three R's—reading, writing and arithmetic. He is able to read books from which he gathers information and derives pleasure. Rote memory gives place to logical thinking. This is the period of physical and intellectual stability.

Social and Moral Development: This period is marked by greater degree of social awareness. He tires to loosen the control of the family and increasingly becomes more independent of his parents. He becomes an active member of a peer group. Peer group becomes an important agent of socialization during this period. He develops social qualities like co-operation, team spirit etc. to adjust with the social environment. He believes in group loyalty and tries to conform to the rules and values maintained by the group.

Speech and Language Development: During the later childhood, all areas of speech—*pronunciation, vocabulary, comprehension and sentence structure*—improve rapidly. By the age of 9–10, children develop an increasingly complex understanding of syntax. Grammatical errors are slowly eliminated and they talk fluently.

Adolescence Stage (Secondary or Higher Secondary School Stage)

Adolescence is that span of years wherein boys and girls move from childhood to adulthood mentally, emotionally, socially and physically. It is a period from the onset of puberty to the age of maturity. It is a period of rapid physical and biological changes which may lead to confusions, tensions, frustrations and feelings of insecurity. It is a period of transition when changes of attitude and behaviour are most rapid. Stanley Hall rightly calls it as the *period of stress and strain, storm and strife.* Holling Worth calls this the *period of temporary insanity.* It is because of the restlessness and disturbance due to the nature of development that takes place during this period.

Adolescence experiences create conflicts between the person and society. Change of role in society, shattered relations at home, failure to decide his status in social settings, difficulty in adjusting with the opposite sex, unnecessary restrictions on movement etc. give rise to tensions and worries. During this stage emotions fluctuate very frequently and quickly. The adolescent tries to oppose the views of parents and school authorities, but such efforts often fail.

The adolescent lives an intensely emotional life, in which the rhythm of positive and negative phases of behaviour gets lost. This results in constant alteration between intense excitement and deep depression. All these create a considerable degree of stress and strain in the adolescent.

Adolescence is also known as the *period of transition* because during this period an individual is neither a child nor an adult. During this period the individual's status is vague and there is confusion about the role he is expected to play. He is often looked upon in an ambiguous manner by the elders. Sometimes he is expected to behave as an adult and at other times he is treated as a child. This is the time when the individual is striving to wean himself away from the family in order to become a self-sufficient and autonomous person. Some may take drugs or get addicted to alcohol if their needs are thwarted or denied. Hence Holling Worth calls it a *period of temporary insanity.*

It is a very crucial period when the individual attains maturity physically, intellectually, emotionally, sexually and socially. The growth achieved, the experiences gained, the responsibilities felt and the relationships developed at this stage determine the complete future of the individual.

DEVELOPMENTAL TASKS FROM BIRTH TO OLD AGE

Havighurst (1953) prepared a developmental model in which he presented the list of developmental tasks from birth to old age. Every cultural group expects its members to master certain essential skills and acquire certain approved patterns of behaviour at various stages during the life span. Havighurst has labeled them developmental tasks.

According to him a developmental task is *a task which arises at or about a certain period in the life of the individual, successful achievement of which leads to happiness and to success with later tasks, while failure leads to unhappiness and difficulty with later tasks.*

Although most people would like to master these tasks at the appropriate time, some are unable to do so, while others are ahead of schedule. Though these tasks are applicable to American population, they are generally accepted to be applicable to all. They are as follows:

Developmental Tasks Related to Infancy

This stage covers approximately first two weeks of life. It is the shortest developmental period. It is a time for radical adjustment. The new born infant must make four major adjustments to post natal life viz.

- To temperature changes
- To sucking and swallowing
- To breathing
- To elimination.

Developmental Tasks Related to Babyhood and Early Childhood

The developmental tasks related to this stage are as under:

- Learning to take solid foods
- Learning to walk and talk
- Learning to control the elimination of body wastes
- Learning sex differences and sexual modesty
- Getting ready to read
- Learning to distinguish right and wrong and beginning to develop conscience.

Developmental Tasks Related to Late Childhood

The developmental tasks related to late childhood are as under:

- Learning physical skills necessary for ordinary games
- Building a wholesome attitude toward oneself as a growing organism
- Learning to get along with age-mates
- Beginning to develop appropriate masculine or feminine social roles.
- Developing fundamental skills in reading, writing and calculating.
- Developing concepts necessary for everyday living
- Developing a conscience, a sense of morality, and a scale of values
- Developing attitudes toward social groups and institutions.
- Achieving personal independence.

Developmental Tasks Related to Adolescence

The developmental tasks related to adolescence are as under:

- Achieving new and more mature relations with age-mates of both sexes
- Achieving a masculine or feminine social role
- Accepting one's physic and using the body effectively
- Desiring, accepting, and achieving socially responsible behaviour
- Achieving emotional independence from parents and other adults
- Preparing for an economic career
- Preparing for marriage and family life
- Acquiring a set of values and an ethical system as a guide to behaviour—developing an ideology.

Developmental Tasks Related to Early Adulthood

The developmental tasks related to early adulthood are as under:

- Getting started in an occupation
- Selecting a mate
- Learning to live with a marriage partner
- Starting a family
- Rearing children
- Managing a home
- Taking on civic responsibility
- Finding a congenial social group.

Developmental Tasks Related to Middle Age

The developmental tasks related to middle age are as under:

- Achieving adult civic and social responsibility
- Assisting teenage children to become responsible and happy adults
- Developing adult leisure-time activities
- Relating oneself to one's spouse as a person
- Accepting and adjusting to the physiological changes of middle age
- Reaching and maintaining satisfactory performance in one's occupational career
- Adjusting to aging parents.

Developmental Tasks Related to Old Age

The developmental tasks related to old age are as under:

- Adjusting to decreasing physical strength and health
- Adjusting to retirement and reduced income
- Adjusting to death of spouse
- Establishing an explicit affiliation with members of one's age group
- Establishing satisfactory physical living arrangements
- Adapting to social roles in a flexible way.

6
Individual Differences

In this world, all natural things—living or nonliving—are created in a unique way, as they have their unique features and characteristics, which differentiate them from one another. These differences and variations become more intense and remarkable as we draw our attention to human beings, who are one of the ultimate creations of the Almighty in the history of evolution. Human beings quite distinctly differ in size, shape, appearance, speed of reaction and innumerable other aspects of their personality makeup and behaviour. These differences in human beings are referred to as *individual differences*.

DEFINITION OF INDIVIDUAL DIFFERENCES

According to the Dictionary of Education, edited by Carter V. Good (1959), *"the term individual difference stands for the variations or deviations among individuals with regard to a single characteristic or a number of characteristics."*

Individual difference stands for those differences that in their totality distinguish one individual from another. Thus, the difference among individuals that distinguish or separate them from one another and make a person a unique individual may be termed *individual difference*.

According to the dictionary of education:

- Individual differences stand for the variation or deviations among individuals in regard to a single characteristic or number of characteristics.
- It stands for those differences which in their totality distinguish one individual from another. So, we can say that individual differences are the differences among humans that distinguish or separate them from one another and makes one as a single unique individual.

TYPES/AREAS OF INDIVIDUAL DIFFERENCES

Individuals have variety of differences. Some individual differences are natural to humans which cannot be controlled or changed, and some can be changed and controlled by human beings living in society. These are the differences which makes humans different in various fields of life. Psychology is academic discipline which studies these differences and prescribes the way of building effective personality of an individual.

Individual differences are observed among the human beings that may be grouped or classified into two broad categories, namely physical or physiological difference and psychological difference. Let us discuss the differences or variations among human beings in the following specific types of varieties:

Physical Differences: The observable differences that are majorly noted among people are the physical differences, such as height, weight, colour of skin, eyes and hair, size of hands and heads, arms, feet, mouth and nose, length of waistline, structure and functioning of internal organs, facial expression, mannerism of speech and walk, hair style and other physical characteristics.

Age Differences: This is visible difference. Age factor determines the characteristics of a person. Age five (5) students and age fifteen (15) students will have variety of differences in terms of height, strength, emotions and cognitive development.

Sex Differences: This is natural one. That is distinction between male and female individuals. This sex differences gives male and female their characteristics relating to body, psychology, mental abilities and cultural or social roles.

Intellectual and Mental Differences: People differ in their intellectual abilities and capabilities like reasoning and thinking, power of imagination, creative expression, concentration, etc. Generally, people are classified based on their intellectual difference as idiot, imbecile, moron, borderline, normal, bright, very superior and genius.

This is the vital areas as far as educational psychology is concerned. Because educational psychology mainly focusses on mental process and their manipulations in certain directions. Commonly, intellectual differences are checked by intelligence quotient (IQ) yard stick. This is clear difference that the IQ ability of one person (male or female) is different from another one. That's why psychologists have done IQ classification as given below:

Sl. No	*I.Q*	*Class*
1.	180/Above	Gifted Person
2.	140 to 170	Genius
3.	120 to 140	Very intelligent
4.	110 to 120	Intelligent
5.	90 to 110	Normal/Average
6.	80 to 90	Dull
7.	70 to 80	Borderline
8.	50 to 70	Feeble minded
9.	25 to 50	Imbecile
10.	0 to 25	Idiot

This information above helps a teacher to know his/her student's mental abilities.

Differences in Motor Ability: Wide differences are observed among people based on their motor abilities, such as reaction time, speed of action, hand steadiness, rate of muscular movement, manual dexterity and resistance to fatigue etc.

Emotional Differences: This is also a very important factor which gives a great distinguished status to a person against others. Those who have control over their emotional feelings, show better learning result as compared to those who are not a emotionally well balanced. This is one of the vital areas of individual differences where teacher and parents must work hard to produce and bring up sound personality in a student for social role.

It is observed that some people express more positive emotions, whereas some express negative emotions. Individuals also differ in the manner they express their emotions and manage their emotional behaviour. Some are emotionally stable in nature, while others are emotionally unstable and immature.

Different Aptitudes: Variation occurs among the individuals in relation to their specific aptitudes. For example, people are found to have different aptitudes; some are good in mechanical aptitude, while others have scholastic or verbal aptitude.

Different Interest: Variation occurs among the individuals in relation to their specific interest and aptitudes. For example, some people have more interest in social interaction and others are happy in solitude. Interest may be referred to as a motivating force that impels us to attend to a person, a thing or an activity. So, in educational field, differences in interest means that some are observed students like a particular subject, teacher, hobby or profession than other.

Difference in Attitude: Difference in attitude is psyche related to something. Few learners have positive attitude towards a specific topic, subject and profession than other. The role of education in society is to develop a positive attitude.

Difference in Values: Values are given importance by an individual. Some learners give value to materialist life style, others moral or religious life style etc. So, education must mould the mind of young generation to have a balanced value between materialism and spiritualism.

Study Habits: It is clearly observable that some students markedly differ from other students in study habits. Some students are studious and study all the subjects with interest but others are not. Some study in isolation and some in group.

Difference in Psychomotor Skills: Psychomotor skill is related to some skill acquisition. Some students differ in this area also. Some like football, others cricket etc. Some students easily learn operating a machine and some may not. A wise teacher should diagnose students' psychomotor skills abilities and encourage them in that direction.

Difference in Self Concept: Difference in self concept is the totality of attitudes, judgment and values of an individual relating to his behaviour, abilities and qualities. Thus, some students have positive self concept than boosts their confidence level and they perform better than those who have negative self image.

Learning Difference: Individual differences are also found in the field of learning. It is observed in a classroom that some students are very fast learners, some average and also slow learners. This difference is observed due to their individual difference in the pattern of studying or depends upon the individual nature of the learner.

Differences in Social and Moral Values: Individuals differ in respect of their social and moral development. Some are found to be more adjusted and have more interpersonal relationships, while others are not well adjusted socially and show more antisocial behaviour. This individual difference is due to their moral and social values.

This area of individual differences shows how an individual is able to adjust to the new changing environment. That adjustment degree varies from individual to individual. The role of environment or nurture is very vital. If, a child gets good environment in school and home, it will help a lot of students to have good adjustment. This social adjustment is a big indicator that makes the difference in individual to individual. The more you are socially adjusted to the role, the more you have balanced personality and social life.

Individual differences are natural, which make a person different from another. Now, it is the work of nature-education, training to maximize the good qualities of a student or person and minimize the bad ones in order to have good and peaceful social life for a person. The teacher's role in this regard is very vital.

Thus, all the above-discussed aspects distinguish an individual from others, as their personalities are unique. There are more dimensions to define the individual difference among the human beings.

ROLE OF HEREDITY IN GENERATING INDIVIDUAL DIFFERENCES

The role of Heredity in generating individual differences is as follows:

Heredity Determining the Sex of the Child: The autosomes (first 22 pair of Chromosomes) are responsible for deciding and determining the growth and development of most of the characteristics and structural composition of our body. Remaining one is the sex chromosome. That will be deciding the gender of the individual.

- There are two types of sex chromosomes, X and Y
- X + Y= Son, X + X = Daughter (X, Y-Male, X, X-female)
- Father is biologically more accountable for determination of the sex.

Heredity Contributes Significantly Towards Physical Constitution: Most of the attributes related to our body make-up, its constitution and functioning are well decided and guided by heredity.

- Ex: hair, facial look, blood type etc.
- Sometimes the role of heredity as determination of physical condition or body make up becomes questionable.

Contribution of Heredity towards the Birth of Twins and the Related Individual Differences: Sometimes two or more ova get fertilized resulting in the birth of two or more offspring's at a time. There are two distinctly different types of twins namely:

(i) ***Identical twins:*** Ova split in to two or more—each part develops in to complete individual. They carry exactly same genes.

(ii) ***Fraternal twins:*** Two or more ova may mature simultaneously and get fertilized simultaneously by two or more different sperms.

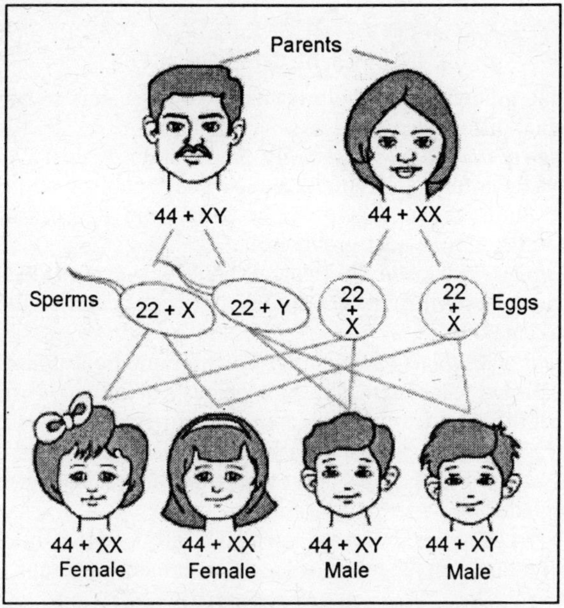

Figure 6.1: Sex Determination of the Child

ROLE OF ENVIRONMENT AS DETERMINANT OF INDIVIDUAL DIFFERENCES

The role of environment in individual differences is as under:

Internal Environment (inside the womb)

Whatever mother eats or drinks has an impact on the growth and development of the child. The quality of environment available during pregnancy is quite important for the baby. If the mother is tense, worried, anxious and emotionally upset, it may eventually have an adverse effect on the growth and development of the baby. Environment at the time of delivery will also affect the child (normal delivery or not? hygienic or not?)

External Environment (After Birth)

After birth, physical, sociological, cultural and psychological environment affects the growth and development of an individual.

RELATIVE IMPORTANCE OF HEREDITY AND ENVIRONMENT AS DETERMINES OF INDIVIDUAL DIFFERENCE

- Every phenomenon of life is the product of both. Each is as necessary to the result as the other. Neither can ever be eliminated or isolated.
- Nothing is more certain than that heredity and environment are co-acting influence and that both are essential.
- As a gift from heredity, we get our working capital but it is the environment which gives us the opportunity to invest it.

EFFECTIVE WAYS FOR TEACHERS/EDUCATORS DEALING WITH INDIVIDUAL DIFFERENCE

The following guidelines can help teachers and educators to cope and deal with individual differences:

Knowledge of Individual Personality: The first step to deal with individual differences is the information about an individual's choices, abilities, interest and attitudes. In this regard, help can be taken from various kinds of tests, personal records, family, peer group etc.

Adjustment in Curriculum: Curriculum should be rich in all kinds of subjects and co-curricular activities in order to take into consideration the individual interests and capabilities.

Adjustment of Methods of Teaching: Teachers and Educators are at liberty to adopt the proper teaching methods on the basis of individual differences in order to meet different learning styles of the learners.

Special Programmes or Individualized Instructions: School can arrange special classes for a specific group of learners or individualize coaching can also be adopted for a particular duration.

Grouping of Learners: Learners can also be grouped together on the basis of same individual differences in order to teach them in groups to save time and resources.

INDIVIDUAL DIFFERENCES AND EDUCATION

The teacher can make use of the knowledge of individual differences in education and teaching. The main features in this connection are the following:

Curriculum: In school, the curriculum should be modified to suit the needs of the dull children. Failure to achieve this adversely affects the development of this particular type of children

Limited Size of the Class: Keeping in mind the individual differences of the students, it is advisable that if they are to be taught properly, a class should not include more than 20 students. With 50 or more students, it is impossible to teach them, keeping in mind their specific requirements.

Method of Education: It is never advisable to use the same method of education in the case of all the children. It should be varied to suit and conform to their individual differences and mental requirements.

Educational Guidance: Knowing the personal differences between students, the teacher can render them signal service by guiding them in their educational career. It is the teacher who can tell them about the subjects, they should choose for their higher studies, if they are not injustice to their nature.

Vocational Guidance: Different professions require some specific physical, mental and personality traits of the individual. Hence, knowing their peculiar mental makeup and their tendencies, the teacher can guide the students regarding the vocation that they should adopt.

Contribution of School, Family and Community in Education: Knowledge of differences among children determines that education in school is not sufficient since many differences are due to the family and community. Hence, according to the modern educational psychologists, to attain the objective of all round development of individuals, prescribed by modern education, the co-operation of school, family, community and the religious institutions is sought.

Individual Training: Having knowledge of individual differences, now many methods of individual training have been devised. The Dalton plan, Project Method, Winnetka Method, Contract Plan and Activity Programme Methods have been devised for individual training. A brief resume of the various methods is given below:

Dalton Plan: In this method, children are not taught in class rooms. They are given subjects that suit their interests and they are given a project that covers a period of 15 days to a month. Such treatment leads to the development of neutrality, independence, co-operation and sociability etc.

Project Method: In this method, the children are required to do work in natural setting and in the process of this work, they are taught novel things.

Winnetka System: In this method, the student on his own tries to attain a certain definite objective and the teacher offers very little assistance. Later on, through some tests, the extent to which the student has attained his goal is discovered.

Contract Plan: In this method, similar to the Dalton Method, the subjects of study are determined and similar to the Winnetka method, the student's progress is measured through tests. In this manner, it is a synthesis of the Dalton and Winnetka method.

Activity Programme: In this method, keeping in mind the interests of the students, activities are prescribed in order to define the curriculum. These activities are based on democratic principles. This helps to develop democratic notion in the children.

7
Transfer of Learning

The ability of the individual to apply the previous experience to the new related experience is what we call transfer of learning. Unless students are able to transfer prior skills and knowledge to new ones, the continuity of learning will be difficult.

MEANING OF TRANSFER OF LEARNING

The essence of learning is that a previously learnt fact should be linked with a present experience. This is because human being must be dynamic and that the prior experience will help them to develop the new skills and knowledge. The influence that past experience has on the succeeding experience is called transfer of learning.

DEFINITIONS OF TRANSFER OF LEARNING

1. *M.J. Peterson* (1957), "Transfer is generalization, for it is the extension of idea to a new field."
2. *L.D. Crow and A.C. Crow* (1963), "The carry-over habits of thinking, feeling or working of knowledge or skills from one learning area to another usually is referred to as the transfer of training."
3. *B.L. Bigge* (1964), "Transfer of learning occurs when a person's learning in one situation influences his learning and performance in other situations."
4. *H.C. Ellis* (1965), "Transfer of learning means that experience or performance of one task influences performance on some subsequent task."
5. *K. Lovell* (1970), "Transfer of learning is the effect which some particular course of training has on learning or execution of a second performance. Such an effect may be helpful or it may hinder.
6. *Guthrie and Powers*, "Transfer may be defined as a process of extending and applying behaviour."
7. *Cormier and Hagman*, (1987) define transfer of learning as "the application of skills and knowledge learned in one context being applied in another context."
8. *Oladele* (1998) defines transfer of learning as the "effect of prior learning on the present."

Learning is meaningful when the past learning smoothens the progress of something else. For example, if a learnt experience refuses to aid the new learning, the goal of training has seized to be accomplished. In the school, the teacher teaches some subjects in order that the experience gained in those subjects could be transferred into another.

Charham (1987) affirms that human and animal learning is normally affected by the past experience, and that the various subjects are included in the school curriculum because of their utility and wide application to real life situations. For instance, the teacher who has taught his/her students some skills in Mathematics would believe that such skills be transferred to related subjects like Physics or Accounting. If the students fail to apply these skills in their subsequent learning, it means that the students have not been successful in transferring the learning.

TYPES OF TRANSFER OF LEARNING

The above example gives us clues into the different types of transfer of learning that we have. These are explained below:

Positive Transfer: When learning of one activity, it helps in the learning of another activity, it is called positive transfer e.g. Knowledge of typing is helpful to learn computer typing. This is a situation whereby a previously learnt fact or information aids in the understanding of a new task. Aside from aiding the learners in their subsequent learning, it also helps the learners to learn the new task effectively.

Negative Transfer: When previously learnt activity become obstacle in learning another activity, it is known as negative transfer. Pronunciation of mother tongue become obstacle while pronunciation of English language. This is a type of learning in which prior experience impacts negatively on the new one. In this case, the understanding of past skills inhibits the mastering of new ones. For example, if a student wrongly connects information, it can lead to negative transfer.

Zero Transfer: When learning of one activity neither facilitates nor interferes with the learning of a new work. It is said to be 'zero' transfer. There may be zero transfer in language and mathematics. This type of learning reveals no link between the previously learnt task and the recent one. The evidence of zero transfer is hardly seen, it reveals no clear positive or negative effect.

THEORIES OF TRANSFER OF LEARNING

The important theories of transfer of learning are as follows:

Theory of Mental Faculties or Formal Discipline Theory

This theory was propounded by the Greek Philosophers, notable among them was Aristotle. The basic tenet of the theory is that human mind is sub-divided into different powers of faculties like memory, judgment, reasoning or thinking. It is therefore believed that each of these faculties is reinforced and developed by continuous memorization of poetry/poem and similar works. This theory believes that exercises and regular practice will strengthen the mental faculties. It therefore dismisses the concept of transfer of learning. To it, a well trained and disciplined mind is the ingredient needed for understanding of new information.

Theory of Identical Elements

This theory was developed by Thorndike and Woodworth (American

Psychologists). It indicates that it is possible for an individual to transfer the prior skills and knowledge to recent ones because both experiences are identical (share things in common). This theory suggests that a successful or effective learning will happen if there are connections or interrelatedness between the old and the new experiences. For example, it is expected that a student who has learnt about anatomical parts of human being in a Biology lesson, should be able to do well when he/she is asked to name anatomical parts of a goat during Agriculture lesson.

Theory of Generalization

This theory was advocated by the Psychologist, Charles Judd. The assumption of the theory is that general principles aid transfer of learning better than segregated facts. This theory believes in Gestalt, an assertion which views learning from a whole or complete form rather than in isolated form. For example, the theory of generalization indicates that a learnt experience should be useful in other day-to -day related activities.

EDUCATIONAL IMPLICATIONS OF TRANSFER OF LEARNING

The knowledge and understanding of transfer of learning can be useful for the teachers for the following purpose:

- The teacher should know that transfer of learning will not take place when both the old and new are unrelated. Hence, the teacher should endeavour to teach his/her subject-matter in a more meaningful and detailed way rather than by rote.
- The teacher should provide the opportunity for his/her students to practice a subject-matter being discussed along with him/her. When the learners are allowed to take active part in teaching learning activities, they will be able to repeat the task at another time.
- For a transfer of learning to take place, the teacher should always emphasize the relationship that exists between one subject-matter and another.
- The teacher should endeavour to develop positive attitudes towards a learning task so that the students can be motivated to like the task rather avoiding it.
- It is believed that what students see, touch, feel or manipulate will be better remembered than the one they are not familiar with. Hence, for a meaningful transfer of learning to take place, the teacher should incorporate exercises that task the various senses of learners in the learning process.
- Transfer of learning takes place because of similarity of content and techniques and because of generalization hence teacher should show similarity in different content and teach how to use it.
- Teacher should provide varied experience to the student.
- Greater transfer from subject matter can be achieved by changing the methods of teaching. Teacher should use appropriate method as per demand of the subject matter.
- Emphasis be given on correlation is important. previous knowledge may be used in the new task.

- Coordination between theoretical knowledge and practical experience should be done in the classroom.
- The teacher should keep in mind that for maximum transfer, the generalization should be thoroughly mastered and completely understood.
- Teacher should make the use of law of association for providing different type of knowledge.
- Teacher should remember that transfer is not accomplished with equal facility or in equal amounts by all individuals. It depends upon one's ability to generalize his experience and the ability to perceive relationship between two situations.

8
Development of Adolescent

Adolescence is the period of developmental transition between childhood and adulthood, involving multiple physical, intellectual, personality and social developmental changes. The onset of puberty signals the beginning of adolescence. Puberty now occurs earlier, than it did in the past. The end of this developmental period is tied more to social and emotional factors and can be somewhat ambiguous.

IMPORTANCE OF ADOLESCENCE PERIOD

Adolescence period is very important because:

Adolescence is a Period of Transition or Role Confusion: Adolescence is known as the period of transition because during this period an individual is neither a child nor an adult. He has passed through childhood and yet is to become an adult. During this stage the status of the individual is vague and there is confusion about the roles which the individual is expected to play. Sometimes he is expected to behave as an adult and at other times as a child.

Adolescence is a Period of Stress and Strain: During adolescence the individual comes under social pressure and faces new conditions for which he had received little training during childhood. He experiences conflict between himself and with the society. Change of role in society, unfavourable relations at home, difficulty in adjusting with opposite sex, unnecessary restrictions on movements etc. give rise to tension and worries.

During this stage he tries to oppose the views of parents and school authorities. But he is not always successful and it makes him restless, moody and emotionally disturbed. As his emotions fluctuate very frequently, a considerable degree of stress and strain is created in the individual. That is why the adolescence is often viewed as a period of stress and strain or a period of storm and strife.

Peer Group influence during Adolescence: The most important social development during adolescence is the increased influence of peer group. The adolescent picks up the norms, habits and social qualities of his companion. His interests, attitudes and values are greatly influenced by his peers. Peer group is a very powerful instrument in moulding the social behaviour of the teenagers. As mentioned in an English proverb "*A cheerful friend is like a sunny day spreading brightness all around*".

In the peer group the adolescent learns to co-operate, to lead and follow, to think for a common cause and to adjust to the challenging social situation. The peer group satisfies various psychological needs of children like acceptance, affection, approval, belongings, fame, recognition, expression of thought and opinion etc. It is in this peer group the individual continues to formulate and revise his concept of *Self.*

NEEDS AND PROBLEMS OF ADOLESCENCE

An individual's needs and problems influence his development to a great extent. Adolescence is a crucial period in the life of an individual with its characteristic needs and problems of adjustment. Every adolescent has certain needs, the satisfaction of which is essential for his continued physical and others aspects of development. *A need is a tension within an organism which must be satisfied for the well being of the organism.* When a need is satisfied the tension is released and the individual experiences satisfaction. There are certain basic needs which are functioning in every individual. They are broadly classified into *Physiological needs and Psychological needs.*

Primary or Physiological Needs

The fulfillments of physiological needs are inevitable because they are concerned with the very existence of the individual. The need for oxygen, water and food, rest and sleep, sex gratification etc. are the important physiological needs.

Secondary or Socio-Psychological Needs

Needs that are associated with socio-cultural environment of an individual are called secondary needs. They are acquired through social learning and their satisfaction is necessary for the psychological well being of the individual. The important socio-psychological needs are as follows:

Needs for Security: The adolescent needs emotional, social and economic security in addition to physical security. The person who lacks the feeling of security may become maladjusted. The need for social security is associated with man's desire for gregariousness.

Need for Love: Affection or love is one of the most basic psychological needs of the adolescents. Adolescents have a strong desire to love and to be loved. The individual who is not loved will not develop proper attitudes and concepts concerning his own worth. Proper love will strengthen the individual's feeling of security.

Need for Approval: There is a craving for recognition in adolescents. His ego gets satisfaction when he is recognized and approved. The adolescent desire that he should be a centre of attraction for the opposite sex and his abilities, intelligence and capacities should be recognized by others. The teachers should find out the field in which the pupil can shine very well and which help him to earn admiration from others.

Need for Freedom and Independence: Adolescence is a time when the individual is striving to wean himself away from the control of parents and elders. He wants the right to give expression to his feelings, emotions and ideas. He feels annoyed and unpleasant when restriction is imposed on him.

Need for Self-expression and Achievement: Every adolescent has an inherent desire for the expression of his potentialities. He may have a poet, musician, painter etc. hidden within him for which he aspires to get adequate opportunity for the expression of his potentialities. He experiences satisfaction when he succeeded in them. Failure makes him depressed and disappointed. Hence the curriculum should be appropriate for every pupil so as to permit achievement for him.

PROBLEMS OF ADOLESCENTS WITH SPECIAL REFERENCE TO INDIAN CONTEXT

Any period of development is likely to be accompanied by many potential difficulties. Adolescence is a period of transition from childhood to adulthood that implies many development changes and associated problems. Some of the outstanding problems of Indian adolescence are the following:

Perplexity with regard to Somatic Variation: Every adolescent has more or less difficult task of adjusting to somatic variation which may occur in connection with puberty. The flow of blood during menstruation in girls and nocturnal emission in boys create worries and give birth to so many fears and anxieties. Since ours is a conservative society, youngsters are less informed about the physical changes that are occurring during puberty. Lack of scientific information about sex, hygiene and philosophy push them towards crude and perverted knowledge about sex related matters. It creates guilt and other serious complexes in the minds of the children which makes them introverted and secretive.

Problems Related with Intensification of Sex-consciousness: The sudden awakening of sex instinct during adolescence results in intensification of sex consciousness. Adolescents are curious to know about sex related topics and are seeking answers to their innumerable doubts in sexual matters. In our country most of the parents are illiterate and they do not have scientific knowledge of sex problems. Moreover, our social values are different from that of western countries, and hence parents hesitate to discuss sex problems with their children. So the adolescents resort socially unacceptable ways to quench their curiosity and satisfy their sexual needs. There is also the misguiding of the print and electronic media that finally results in sexual maladjustment in adolescents.

Adjustment Difficulties with Parents: Adolescents have a strong desire for freedom and independence. But often it is obstructed by parental oppositions. In Indian context, parental opposition may extend to such areas as choices of friends, education, recreational interests, dress, life-style, mode of behaviour time, schedule of going out and coming back to the house etc. The conflict between parental norms of behaviour and peer group often leads to friction in relationships and adolescents find it difficult to adjust to the needs and demands of parents. Failure to adjust with the parents may result in revolting against them and any other kind of authority.

Childhood-Adulthood Conflict: In our society, the adolescent is considered as neither a child nor an adult. He has to depend on his parents and elders for his physical and emotional needs. But at the same time he wants to hold independent views and opinions like an adult. He can very well manage his own affairs and resist any unnecessary interference from elders. He begins to feel ashamed and embarrassed for the protection and care shown by the parents. He is often treated in an ambiguous manner by parents and teachers. Sometimes they expect him to behave as an adult and at other times, they treat him as a child. The poor adolescent is caught between the role of the child and the adult, which pushes him towards confusion and tension.

Adjustment Difficulties with School Discipline: Most of the adolescents face a great problem in adjusting with school discipline. Sometimes schools expects too much from students who must submit to teachers who may be tyrannical sometimes. Schools should not implant habits of unquestioning obedience that inhibits the growth of young people towards true independence.

Adjustment Difficulties with Community: The adolescent is expected to find his place in a society marked by increasing social isolation and rapid technological changes. The rapidly changing world makes it difficult to anticipate and plan for adolescent life. They have difficulty in adjusting their capacity to the demands of the community. At this critical phase, most adolescents react by withdrawing into a non-demanding and non-working world of pleasure and satisfaction.

DEVELOPMENTAL CHARACTERISTICS OF ADOLESCENCE

Young people undergo many different changes as they go through adolescence and increasingly take on adult roles and responsibilities. These changes include physical changes, as well as changes in their thought processes and emotions (cognitive and emotional changes), sense of identity and values (psychological changes), relationships (social changes), and realistic aspirations for the future. All young people are unique and therefore the degree, rate and pace of specific physical, emotional and social changes vary with each young person. Adolescence is characterized by rapid change in several areas:

Physical and Motor Development

Physical development is often the most obvious change in a young persons as they grow and develop their adult physical characteristics. During adolescence the physical growth reaches its peak and body takes its final shape. The growth and functioning of organs reach their upper range and the glands become extremely active. There is a sudden shoot up in height, weight and size. The arms and legs developed to their final length. The size of the bones and muscles increase up to the greatest possible extent. Along with these somatic changes, motor activity also attains its maximum limit.

The respiratory, circulatory and digestive systems acquire their full development. Brain gets fully developed. Pimples may appear on the face. There occurs change in voice among both sexes. The voice of boys deepens and becomes harsher while the voice of girls becomes shrill and sweet during this period.

During adolescence the individual attains *biological maturation* which is accompanied by the appearance of *secondary sexual characteristics.* There is growth of hair under arms and around genital organs. Boys develop beard and moustaches on their faces and in girls the growth of breast and widening of pelvis are significant physical developments. The girls begin to menstruate every month and boys have nocturnal emission accompanied by erotic dreams.

Emotional Development

Adolescence is characterized by emotional instability and intensity. It is the period of heightening of all emotions like anxiety, fear, love, anger, etc. It is because of this fact the *adolescence is considered as a period of stress and strain.* Adolescents *are* not consistent in their emotional expression. Their emotions fluctuate very frequently and quickly. Sometimes they appear to be enthusiastic and sometimes moody.

With lots of changes in thinking comes a range of emotions that the young person may not have experienced previously. While developing own self identity the adolescent may experience more moodiness, irritability and frustration. Their ability to manage these fluctuating emotions becomes more advanced with further skill development. These changes also see the young person developing a greater sense of empathy and understanding from the experiences of others.

Self consciousness, self respect and personal pride is very strong in adolescents. He is often irritable, easily excited and explodes emotionally. His feelings are very strong, and reacts vigorously, he feels it very strongly. At no stage the individual is so restless and emotionally perturbed and touchy as in adolescence. He is too sensitive, inflammable and moody.

Intellectual Development

The concrete thinking of childhood begins to move to more complex abstract thinking. Skills such as planning, prioritizing, organizing thoughts, suppressing impulses, problem solving and weighing consequences are developing and influencing the decision making process in young people.

Adolescence is a period of great intellectual advancement. In this period functioning of the cognitive system develops to its maximum level. Intellectual powers like critical thinking, logical thinking and abstract reasoning also develop. The span of connection widens, depth of understanding increases, and functioning of memory sharpens.

The adolescent develops fine imagination. The improper channelization of imagination may lead an adolescent to day-dreaming. Writers, artists, poets, philosophers and inventors are all born in this period. The adolescent learns to reason and seek answer to everything scientifically. Ability to solve problems increases during this period. The areas of interest widen and his love for adventure reaches its climax. All adolescents have one or more hobbies and strong likes and dislikes.

Social Development

The most important characteristics of social development during adolescence is the increased influence of *peer group.* The individual develops a strong sense of loyalty towards this group. He wants to be accepted by the members of the group to which he belongs. The friends as well as the peer group selected by an adolescent shape his behaviour to a great extent. They develop a philosophy of life regarding values, beliefs, activities, conduct etc. with regards to the philosophy of the peer group.

While children generally see the family as an integral part of their life, many young people, while continuing to value the role of support of their family, begin to rely more heavily on the support and guidance provided by their friends. In addition, they may also begin to seek out intimate relationships.

Adolescence is the period of increased social conformity. The individual becomes self-conscious of his place in the society. They want to behave according to the norms of the society. They seek social status and look for approval in the society. They develop a feeling of social responsibility and are highly critical of social evils and injustice. During adolescence, boys and girls express a greater need for independence and strive for total social freedom from their parents. They make friendship with those who conform to their standard and emulate a personality trait they like. They do not tolerate the interference of others in selecting friends.

In the beginning of adolescence, the individual critically examines the moral code and asks a number of questions to establish his view points. Later he develops the ability to differentiate what is good and what is bad.

Psychological Development

Some of the most significant psychological changes relate to the development of autonomy and independent identity. This often leads to the challenging of decisions and actions that they may have previously accepted, and often the discovering of new boundaries as they work to create their own identity.

Sexual Development

The whole personality structure and behaviour of the adolescent is dominated by sex. During adolescence the individual becomes very conscious of sex. Contrary to the style of behaviour during childhood, the adolescent exhibits sexual trends in companionship. During this period the sexual development goes into three stages.

Stage of Auto-erotism: In the beginning sexual tendency manifests in self-love. Boys and girls fall in love with themselves. Self decoration and admiration before the mirror is a common practice. According to Freud this is the stage of ***narcissism***. [Narcissus, a Greek prince of almost unparalleled beauty, fell in love with himself] Self enjoyment by indulging in *masturbation* is prevalent at this stage.

Stage of Homo-sexuality: During the adolescence boys and girls are attracted to the members of their own sex. Persons of this age can often be seen roaming together, praising each other and finding other modes of expressing their mutual affection.

Stage of Hetrosexuality: During later adolescence, young men and women are seen attracted towards each other. They make to make friendship or even establish sexual relationships with the members of opposite sex.

PSYCHOLOGICAL CHARACTERISTICS OF ADOLESCENCE

The main psychological characteristics of adolescence are as follows:

- *Self-consciousness* is too much developed in adolescence.
- The adolescent is *intensely emotional*
- An adolescent is essentially a *hero-worshipper*
- Adolescent shows *interest in physical attractiveness* and good grooming
- *Sex-consciousness* becomes too intense at this time. They become interested in opposite sex and in extreme cases *homosexuality* is established.

- *Peer group relationship* is too much intense at this time.
- Adolescence is a period of *day-dreaming.*
- It is the *period of acquiring the attitudes and values* needed for effective participation in society.
- The Adolescent wants to free himself from bondage. There is a *tendency to revolt against authority.*
- Adolescents have strong *desire to achieve self-sufficiency* and make himself quite independent like an adult member of the society.

DEVELOPMENTAL THEORIES

Six primary classes of developmental theories are: biological, psychoanalytical, behavioural, cognitive, contextual and structural. They are discussed below:

1. Biological Theories

Biological theories cast human development as an *unfolding* process. Children proceed through a set sequence of invariant stages of development in roughly the same time. The environment provides opportunities for growth but exerts no direct influence; rather, development is overwhelmingly determined by genetics. A primary proponent was Arnold Gesell, who, together with his colleagues, published age-based norms for growth and behavioural changes. The Gesell norms provide general expectations and may be useful for identifying children who do not fit the age-based expectations (e.g., a child who displays excessive "baby" behaviour in the third grade). At the same time, the wide variation in developmental changes between children means that the norms have limited usefulness. When norms are misused and become criteria for learning readiness, they can retard educational progress. Although growth and behaviour are correlated with cognitive development, they are not valid reasons for assuming that children cannot learn.

Current biological work focuses on the extent that cognitive, behavioural and personality characteristics have genetic predispositions. Thus, the tendency for children to understand counting may be largely inherited and the capacity for language acquisition seems biologically predisposed. A long-standing debate concerns the extent that intelligence is inherited. Researchers continue to explore how genetics and environmental factors interact to influence development.

2. Psychoanalytic Theories

Psychoanalytic theories emphasize the fulfillment of *needs*, which differ as a function of developmental level. Development is viewed as progressive changes in personality, which emerges as children seek to satisfy their needs. Children pass through a series of stages, each of which is qualitatively different from preceding ones. Children interact with their environments to fulfill needs, and their successes in resolving conflicts associated with need fulfillment influence personality.

Two well-known psychoanalytic theorists were Sigmund Freud and Erik Erikson. Freud (1966) believed that the basic structure of a child's personality was established during the first five years of life. Erikson (1963), on the other

Table-9.1: Types of Developmental Theories

Type	*Key Developmental Processes*
Biological	Individuals proceed through an invariant sequence of stages; stage progression is largely determined by genetics.
Psychoanalytic	Development represents a series of changes in personality brought about by need satisfaction. Stages are qualitatively distinct.
Behavioral	Development represents changes in behaviors produced by conditioning; changes are continuous and quantitative.
Cognitive	Development represents changes in mental structures or processes that occur as individuals take in information and mentally construct understandings.
Contextual	Social and cultural factors affect development; changes in persons or situations interact with and influence other changes.
Structural	Development involves changes in cognitive structures or schemas.

hand, felt that development was a lifelong process and thus postulated developmental stages into old age. Psychoanalytic theories emphasize the role of innate factors in development. Needs are innate, and how they are resolved affects development. The role of learning in development is downplayed in favour of need resolution.

Psychoanalytic theories have their share of problems. As with other stage theories (e.g., Piaget's stage progression from child to child often is so uneven that using theories to explain development is difficult. Although the needs and conflicts described by psychoanalytic theories are well known to parents, caregivers and teachers, how they can be resolved successfully is left open. Consequently, how significant others in children's lives can best foster development is unclear. For example, should adults provide for all of children's needs or teach children self-regulation skills so they can begin to satisfy their own needs? Theories that offer clearer predictions about development and especially the role of learning have greater applicability to education.

3. Behavioural Theories

In contrast to biological and psychoanalytical theories that stress innate factors, behavioural theories—while acknowledging developmental capabilities—postulate that development can be explained by the same principles that explain other behaviours. The major developmental changes occur as a result of *conditioning*. Behavioural theories represent a continuity position: Small changes occur over time. Developmental changes are best viewed in quantitative terms: Children learn to do more in less time. The primary mechanism of learning is shaping of new behaviours through differential reinforcement of successive approximations to the target behaviours.

Behavioural theories do not specify critical periods in development. The capacity for learning continues throughout the life span. They also emphasize that the major changes in behaviour emanate from the environment, which provides the stimuli to which children respond and the reinforcement and punishment as consequences of their actions. Frank's comments in the opening vignette indicate a behavioural view of development. Behavioural theories downplay the role of personal factors associated with learners (e.g., thoughts, emotions) and the interaction between learners and their environments.

Consequently, these theories treat self-regulation largely as the establishment of self-reinforcement contingencies. Behavioural methods often are useful in teaching and learning, but explanations for learning and development based on conditioning are incomplete because they negate the role of personal influences.

4. Cognitive Theories

Beginning with the work of Piaget in the early 1960s, cognitive theories have gained ascendance in the field of human development. Cognitive theories focus on how children construct their understandings of themselves and of the world about them. Cognitive theories are constructivist; they postulate that understanding is not automatic. Others do not convey information that children process rotely; rather, children take in information and formulate their own knowledge. They are active seekers and processors of information. Cognitive theories are interactional because they explain development in terms of interactions between personal, behavioural, and environmental factors. Prominent cognitive theories are Piaget's, Bruner's, Vygotsky's, information processing and social cognitive theory.

5. Contextual Theories

These theories highlight the roles played by social and cultural factors. Evidence supporting this perspective comes from cross-cultural comparisons showing wide variability in developmental patterns, as well as from studies demonstrating that even within societies there is considerable variation in development (Meece, 2002). Societal practices clearly play a major role in development.

A well-known contextual model was formulated by Bronfenbrenner (1979), who postulated that the child's social world can be conceptualized as a set of concentric circles with the child at the common point of three intersecting circles: school, peers, and family. Outside of these is a larger circle containing neighbourhood, extended family, community, church, workplace, and mass media. The outermost circle contains such influences as laws, cultural values, political and economic systems, and social customs. The model assumes that changes in one level can affect other levels. Thus, physical changes in children can alter their social groups, which in turn are affected by cultural values. The model is highly interactional and is useful for understanding the complexity of influences on human development and its effects.

Cognitive and contextual theories stress that children are active constructors of knowledge and that development is a continuous process across the life span. Contextual theories emphasize the altered nature of social patterns and how these lead children into different interactions with peers and adults. Cognitive development occurs largely as a consequence of these interactions. In turn, children's behaviours alter environments. Thus, children may develop new interests that change the peer groups with which they closely associate. Some cognitive theories (e.g., Vygotsky's social cognitive) also are contextual in nature.

Contextual theories often are vague in their predictions of how changes in some aspects may affect development and vice versa. They also can be very complex, with a host of variables postulated to affect one another. This situation makes it difficult to conduct research. Despite these limitations, contextual theories call our attention to the need to study the many factors that are involved in human development.

6. Structural Theories

As mentioned earlier, the issue in the study of human development is whether it represents changes in cognitive structures or functions. Most contemporary views posit changes in functions, but structural theories have figured prominently in the discipline. Structural theories postulate that development involves changes in cognitive structures or *schemas.* Information that is learned (i.e. enters the structure) can help to alter the structure. These theories do not equate structures with physical locations in the brain; rather, structures are construed as constellations of capabilities or characteristic means of processing information. Two structural theories with relevance to learning are discussed below:

(i) Chomsky's (1957) Psycholinguistic Theory

Chomsky (1957, 1959) formulated a theory of language acquisition based on a system of *transformational grammar*. According to Chomsky, language can be differentiated into two levels: an overt *surface structure* that involves speech and syntax and a covert *deep structure* that includes meaning. A single deep structure can be represented by multiple surface structures. To illustrate this distinction, assume that Akram is playing basketball with Salman. The meaning as it might be represented as propositions in memory is:

Rhonda______playing basketball (with) — Salman

This meaning could be translated in various surface structures (utterances and sentences), such as:

- Akram is playing basketball with Salman.
- Salman is playing basketball with Akram.
- Akram? Playing basketball with Salman.
- Basketball is being played by Rhonda and Salman.

Chomsky's transformational grammar contains a number of rules that people presumably use to transform varying surface structures into the same meaning (deep structure). The deep structures are assumed to be part of the individual's genetic makeup. Language development, then, involves the progressive capability of mapping surface structures onto their corresponding deep structures.

(ii) Classical Information Processing Theory (Atkinson & Shiffrin, 1968)

Classical information processing theory provides another structural account of development. The Atkinson and Shiffrin (1968, 1971) model assumes that the computer is a useful metaphor for the operation of the human mind. The computer (with corresponding information processing) components are: input (sensory registers), immediate processing (working memory—WM), storage (long-term memory— LTM), output (response), and programming (executive, control processes).

The analogy between the structures of the mind and the computer is useful. Although the mind's structures do not necessarily correspond to physical locations (i.e., the operations performed may occur in multiple locations), structures are constrained in terms of what they do. Once information enters the system, it is processed in linear fashion (i.e., it follows a set path determined by its content) and little room exists for environmental impact (Zimmerman & Whitehurst, 1979). The operation of the structures is largely preprogrammed.

Developmental change occurs in the capacity and efficiency of processing. Through the use of strategies such as rehearsal and organization, older learners—compared with younger ones—are able to hold more information in WM. They relate it better to information in LTM, and have more extensive memory networks.

IMPORTANT POINTS FOR ADOLESCENTS

What adolescents can do?

- Avoid looking at your parents as the enemy. Chances are that they love you and have your best interests in mind, even if you don't necessarily agree with their way of showing that.
- Try to understand that your parents are human beings, with their own insecurities, needs, and feelings.
- Listen to your parents with an open mind, and try to see situations from their point of view.
- Share your feelings with your parents so that they can understand you better.
- Live up to your responsibilities at home and in school so that your parents will be more inclined to grant you the kind of independence you want and need.
- Bolster your criticisms of family, school, and government with suggestions for practical improvements.
- Be as courteous and considerate to your own parents as you would be to the parents of your friends.

HOW CAN PARENTS SUPPORT HEALTHY ADOLESCENT DEVELOPMENT?

The following guidelines may helpful for the parents:

- Give your undivided attention when your children want to talk. Don't read, watch television, or busy yourself with other tasks.
- Listen calmly and concentrate on hearing and understanding your children's point of view.
- Speak to your children as courteously and pleasantly as you would to a stranger. Your tone of voice can set the tone of a conversation.
- Understand your children's feelings, even if you don't always approve of their behaviour. Try not to make judgments. Keep the door open on any subject. Be an "open/approachable" parent.
- Avoid belittling and humiliating your children and laughing at what may seem to you to be naive or foolish questions and statements.
- Encourage your children to "test" new ideas in conversation by not judging their ideas and opinions, but instead by listening and then offering your

own views as plainly and honestly as possible. Love and mutual respect can coexist with differing points of view.

- Help your children build self-confidence by encouraging their participation in activities of their choice (not yours).
- Make an effort to commend your children frequently and appropriately. Too often, we take the good things for granted and focus on the bad, but everyone needs to be appreciated.
- Encourage your children to participate in family decision making and to work out family concerns together. Understand that your children need to challenge your opinions and your ways of doing things to achieve the separation from you that's essential for their own adult identity.

PIAGET'S THEORY OF COGNITIVE DEVELOPMENT

Piaget studied many children and this study led him to develop the theory that all children progress through four stages of cognitive development. While all children advance through the stages in the same order, some progress more rapidly than others. Piaget's stages of development are:

Sensorimotor Stage (age: birth to 2 years)

In this stage, a child's cognitive system is limited to his motor reflexes. Children in this stage learn from their caregivers, imitating what they see and hear, experimenting with sounds, and learning that they have some control of their movements. They begin to communicate and to learn actions with particular responses. During this stage children develop object permanence and build cognitive structures regarding how the world responds to them.

The sub-stages of sensorimotor stage are as follows:

Reflexes (0-1 month): The child uses only innate reflexes. For example, if a nipple or dummy is put into a baby's mouth, they will reflexively suck on it. If an object is placed in their palm, the hand will automatically grab it. These reflexes have the sole function of keeping the child alive.

Primary Circular Actions (1-4 months): The child now has a fixation with it's own body with regards to behaviour(what Piaget refers to as *primary* behaviour); they will perform actions repeatedly on themselves (like sucking their own hand). They also begin to refine reflexes here to form more complex versions of them.

Secondary Circular Reactions (4-8 months): At around 4 months, the child begins to take interest in their environment (their behaviour is *secondary*). They notice that they can actually influence events in their world, for example they can drop a teddy which bashes a ball on the floor. Although this occurs, the infant will not make conscious connections between what they do and the consequences, they merely observe that their actions have interesting effects.

Co-ordination of Secondary Circular Reactions (8-12 months): At this point, the child begins to engage in *goal-directed* behaviour; they begin to develop cause-effect relationships. So rather than crawl over to a teddy in a cart to pick it up, they might instead pull the cart over with the teddy to acquire it. The child effectively *knows* that their behaviour will have a certain consequence. At this stage, *object permanence* is acquired but I will explain this after these sub-stages.

Tertiary Circular Reactions (12-18 months): At this stage, children like to use creativity and flexibility with their previous behaviours, and the result of their experimentation often leads to different outcomes. So rather than grabbing a box, they might instead try to tilt or manipulate it.

Symbolic/Mental Representation (18-24 months): At this stage, the child develops *symbolic thought* and the ability to mentally represent objects in their head. Normally, the child would need to resort to trial-and-error to achieve a desired effect. Now, however, the child can 'plan' to some extent and mentally construct the consequences of an action in their head. Of course, predictions are not always accurate, but it is a step up from trial-and-error.

Pre-Operational Stage (ages 2 to 6 or 7 years)

For Piaget, this stage is one in which children are egocentric, seeing what happens around them only from their own point of view. Thinking is not logical at this stage, during which children begin to use language and mental imagery. Visual representation and hands-on experiences are necessary for children at this stage; they cannot form abstract ideas.

A major characteristic of this stage is *egocentrism*: perception of the world in relation to oneself only. Children struggle to perceive situations from another point of view or perspective, as shown by Piaget and Inhelder's Three Mountains Task (1956). In this study, children were asked what can be perceived from certain positions on a 3D model.

The child would have been asked, *"What view does Piaget have?"*. In the actual study though, they were shown around 8 cards of possible viewpoints rather than the three above. As you can imagine, the children struggled to decentralise and pick the correct picture.

Another feature of this stage is *conservation*. Children struggle to understand the difference in quantity and measurements in different situations. For example, suppose a child is shown a short, fat beaker full of water. When that water is transferred entirely to a tall, thin beaker—we would know the level of water is identical—only the beaker has changed. However, a child in this stage will conclude there is more water in the tall beaker, just because the level of water looks higher. Children in this stage also lack the required cognition to apply reversibility to situations; they cannot imagine objects or numbers reversed to their previous form. This will be explored in the next stage (where reversibility is present).

Concrete Operational Stage (ages 6 or 7 to 11)

During this stage children move from their egocentric point of view and are capable of taking another person's perspective and incorporating more than one view simultaneously. They can see and reason with concrete knowledge, but are unable to look at the abstract side of things and develop all the possible outcomes. Although they are increasing their ability to think abstractly, children at this age might work story problems but will deal with just the facts, not the abstract concepts. Logical and systematic thought patterns still dominate.

Formal Operational Stage (age 11 or 12 through adulthood)

During this stage a child is acquiring a knowledge base and cognitive structures that are similar to that of an adult. Logical, abstract, and theoretical thinking increases and children can use symbols related to abstract concepts in order to solve problems. At this stage, children are self-motivated and learn from reading and trying out new ideas and from friends and adults. Piaget believed children in this stage needed to revise their knowledge base but that not everyone reaches this stage of development.

Educational Implications of Different Stages of Cognitive Development

According to Piaget, children of a particular stage tend to reach a particular stage of cognitive development, therefore planning of curriculum and teaching method must be in tune with the cognitive development of that particular stage. This theory guides teachers and parents to provide suitable learning experiences according to the development level and cognitive functioning of their children. Therefore, the educational implications of different stages of cognitive development are as under:

The Sensorimotor Stage

- An experience of sensorimotor stage provides the foundation of cognitive development for later stages. During this stage, children actively use their body and senses. Parents may furnish some soft/hard toys and objects of different shapes. Through the bodily use and manipulation of these objects they may acquire some ideas about their environment.
- As the children try to suck the objects, push, pull, reach and drop them, through sensory and motor activity, they develop cognitively.

The Pre-operational Stage

- As the children at the pre-operational stage can imitate the activity which they have observed previously, the teacher may give instructions through actions.
- They may be encouraged to draw and to describe their drawings, as children's level of thinking is represented through their drawings.
- Parents and teachers should provide them a wide range of opportunities to talk with others to encourage their language development.
- Children may be asked to describe what they are seeing, hearing, tasting to foster their language ability.
- They may be given some cut out letters to build words or some simple tasks on arithmetic, to reveal their level of cognitive development.

The Concrete Operational Stage

- As children at the concrete operational stage are able to deal with concrete objects, teachers should use three dimensional objects and diagrams while teaching them subjects like Science, History, Geography etc.
- Teach complex ideas through familiar examples.
- Ask them to classify and group objects on the basis of single attribute.
- Present problems that stimulate analytical thinking.

The Formal Operational Stage

- Teachers should continue to provide concrete examples in a more sophisticated form.

- Encourage them to find out general principles.
- The activities should be challenging one but not so difficult.
- Ask them to explain how they arrive at solutions to problems.
- Guide them to reason scientifically and solve problems.
- Provide them some activities that encourage them to prepositional thinking.
- Give them the opportunities to gather as much information as possible, combine them and to form new propositions.

Educational Implications of Piaget's Theory of Cognitive Development

Piaget did not focus on how his theories could be applied within education, and some researchers have indicated that ambiguities in the theories themselves have made it difficult to apply them. Piaget did, however, advocate hands on learning, and these practices are often used in preschool and primary classrooms where children are encouraged to learn by discovery.

In general, all teachers as well as others who work with children can benefit from an awareness of these stages of development. Knowing when a child needs a practical application of an idea versus being able to use abstract reasoning can determine what information is presented and how it is presented. The use of symbols to represent an abstract idea, for instance, is not a skill that younger children will have. Therefore presenting information before a child is ready will result in frustration and an unwillingness to engage in an activity. Understanding these stages of development can aid the instructor or care-giver in planning age and developmentally appropriate activities and lessons that will keep children engaged and active in the classroom or playroom.

ERIKSON'S THEORY OF PSYCHOSOCIAL DEVELOPMENT

Erik Erikson, a German psychoanalyst heavily influenced by Sigmund Freud, explored three aspects of identity: the *ego identity* (self), *personal identity* (the personal idiosyncrasies) that distinguish a person from another, social/ cultural identity (the collection of social roles a person might play).

Erikson's psychosocial theory of development considers the impact of external factors, parents and society on personality development from childhood to adulthood. According to Erikson's theory, every person must pass through a series of eight interrelated stages over the entire life cycle:

1. Infant (*Hope*)—Basic Trust vs. Mistrust
2. Toddler (*Will*)—Autonomy vs. Shame
3. Preschooler (*Purpose*)—Initiative vs. Guilt
4. School-Age Child (*Competence*)—Industry vs Inferiority
5. Adolescent (*Fidelity*)—Identity vs Identity Diffusion
6. Young Adult (*Love*)—Intimacy vs Isolation
7. Middle-aged Adult (*Care*)—Generativity vs Self-absorption
8. Older Adult (*Wisdom*)—Integrity vs Despair

These eight stages, spanning from birth to death, are split in general age ranges.

1. Infancy: Birth-18 Months Old: Basic Trust vs Mistrust—Hope

During the first or second year of life, the major emphasis is on the mother and father's nurturing ability and care for a child, especially in terms of visual contact and touch. The child will develop optimism, trust, confidence, and security if properly cared for and handled. If a child does not experience trust, he or she may develop insecurity, worthlessness, and general mistrust towards the world.

2. Toddler/Early Childhood Years: 18 Months to 3 Years: Autonomy vs Shame—Will

The second stage occurs between 18 months and 3 years. At this point, the child has an opportunity to build self-esteem and autonomy as he or she learns new skills and right from wrong. The well-cared for child is sure of himself, carrying himself or herself with pride rather than shame. During this time of the "terrible twos", defiance, temper tantrums, and stubbornness can also appear. Children tend to be vulnerable during this stage, sometimes feeling shame and low self-esteem during an inability to learn certain skills.

3. Preschooler: 3 to 5 Years: Initiative vs Guilt—Purpose

During this period we experience a desire to copy the adults around us and take initiative in creating play situations. We make up stories with Barbie's and Ken's, toy phones and miniature cars, playing out roles in a trial universe, experimenting with the blueprint for what we believe it means to be an adult. We also begin to use that wonderful word for exploring the world—"WHY?"

While Erikson was influenced by Freud, he downplays biological sexuality in favour of the psychosocial features of conflict between child and parents. Nevertheless, he said that at this stage we usually become involved in the classic "Oedipal struggle" and resolve this struggle through "social role identification." If we are frustrated over natural desires and goals, we may easily experience guilt.

The most significant relationship is with the basic family.

4. School Age Child: 6 to 12 Years: Industry vs Inferiority—Competence

During this stage, often called the Latency, we are capable of learning, creating and accomplishing numerous new skills and knowledge, thus developing a sense of industry. This is also a very social stage of development and if we experience unresolved feelings of inadequacy and inferiority among our peers, we can have serious problems in terms of competence and self-esteem.

As the world expands a bit, our most significant relationship is with the school and neighbourhood. Parents are no longer the complete authorities they once were, although they are still important.

5. Adolescent: 12 to 18 Years: Identity vs. Role Confusion—Fidelity

In this fifth stage, development depends on what is done to a person. At this point, development now depends primarily upon what a person does. An adolescent must struggle to discover and find his or her own identity, while negotiating and struggling with social interactions and "fitting in", and developing a sense of morality and right from wrong.

Some attempt to delay entrance to adulthood and withdraw from responsibilities (moratorium). Those unsuccessful with this stage tend to experience role confusion and upheaval. Adolescents begin to develop a strong affiliation and devotion to ideals, causes, and friends.

6. Young adult: 18 to 35: Intimacy and Solidarity vs Isolation—Love

At the young adult stage, people tend to seek companionship and love. Some also begin to "settle down" and start families, although seems to have been pushed back farther in recent years.

Young adults seek deep intimacy and satisfying relationships, but if unsuccessful, isolation may occur. Significant relationships at this stage are with marital partners and friends.

7. Middle-aged Adult: 35 to 55 or 65: Generativity vs Self absorption or Stagnation—Care

Career and work are the most important things at this stage, along with family. Middle adulthood is also the time when people can take on greater responsibilities and control.

For this stage, working to establish stability and Erikson's idea of *generativity*—attempting to produce something that makes a difference to society. Inactivity and meaninglessness are common fears during this stage.

Major life shifts can occur during this stage. For example, children leave the household, careers can change, and so on. Some may struggle with finding purpose. Significant relationships are those within the family, workplace, local church and other communities.

8. Late Adult: 55 or 65 to Death: Integrity vs. Despair—Wisdom

Erikson believed that much of life is preparing for the middle adulthood stage and the last stage involves much reflection. As older adults, some can look back with a feeling of *integrity* — contentment and fulfillment, having led a meaningful life and valuable contribution to society. Others may have a sense of despair during this stage, reflecting upon their experiences and failures. They may fear death as they struggle to find a purpose to their lives, wondering "What was the point of life? Was it worth it?"

KOHLBERG'S THEORY OF MORAL DEVELOPMENT

Lawrence Kohlberg was one of the first to research the moral reasoning of adolescent boys and (later, college students) while at the University of Chicago in 1958 (Evans, 2010). He based his theory on Jean Piaget's three stages of moral development and identified three additional stages of development and revised Piaget's stages. To develop his theory he used a series of hypothetical dilemmas and focused on the process of how individuals make moral judgments and not the content of these decisions.

The theory is a six-stage sequence grouped into three levels. At level 1 (preconventional), individuals are judged by direct consequences and their perspective is on their own needs. At level 2 (conventional), individuals recognize the rules and expectations of others by comparing it to society's views. Level 3 (postconventional) is where individuals separate themselves from society's view and view rules as useful but interchangeable. The first stage of the preconventional level, (heteronomous morality stage) implies that the individual is obedient in order to avoid punishment. In the second stage (individualistic, instrumental morality) individuals follow rules in their own interest. At stage 3 (interpersonally normative morality), the conventional level is described as living up to what is expected by people and the need to be good in the eyes of others. At stage 4 (social system morality), individuals make moral decisions from the perspective of society as a whole. In stage 5 (human rights and social welfare morality) of the postconventional level, principles and values that emphasize basic rights become familiar. And at stage 6 (morality of unversalizable, reversible, and prescriptive general ethical principles) individuals believe in ideals as a rational person and follow self-chosen ethical principles.

There are three characteristics of Kohlberg's Stages: 1) Structure: individuals in any particular stage will display similar reasoning patterns of that stage regardless of the situation, 2) Sequential, advancement through stages is specific and in sequence, no skipping of stages: and 3) Hierarchical: each successive stage is more highly developed than the previous because it incorporates aspects of all earlier stages. Two factors facilitate moral development: exposure to others in higher stages of moral reasoning and disequilibrium, experiencing situations that cause internal moral conflict (Evans, 2010).

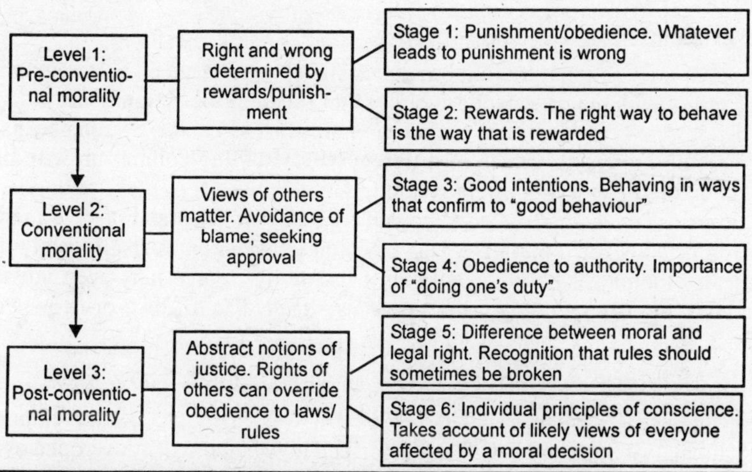

Retrieved from http://www.integratedsociopsychology.net/stages-moral_development.html

Figure-8.1: Levels and Stages of Kohlberg's Moral Development

LEVELS AND STAGES OF KOHLBERG'S MORAL DEVELOPMENT

Level 1: Pre-conventional Morality

The first level of morality, preconventional morality, can be further divided into two stages: obedience and punishment, and individualism and exchange.

Stage 1: Punishment- Obedience Orientation: Related to Skinner's Operational Conditioning, this stage includes the use of punishment so that the person refrains from doing the action and continues to obey the rules. For example, we follow the law because we do not want to go to jail.

Stage 2: Instrumental Relativist Orientation: In this stage, the person is said to judge the morality of an action based on how it satisfies the individual needs of the doer. For instance, a person steals money from another person because he needs that money to buy food for his hungry children. In Kohlberg's theory, the children tend to say that this action is morally right because of the serious need of the doer.

Level 2: Conventional Morality

The second level of morality involves the stages 3 and 4 of moral development. Conventional morality includes the society and societal roles in judging the morality of an action.

Stage 3: Good Boy-Nice Girl Orientation: In this stage, a person judges an action based on the societal roles and social expectations before him. This is also known as the "interpersonal relationships" phase. For example, a child gives away her lunch to a street peasant because she thinks doing so means being nice.

Stage 4: Law and Order Orientation: This stage includes respecting the authorities and following the rules, as well as doing a person's duty. The society is the main consideration of a person at this stage. For instance, a policeman refuses the money offered to him under the table and arrests the offender because he believes this is his duty as an officer of peace and order.

Level 3: Post-conventional Morality

The post-conventional morality includes stage 5 and stage 6. This is mainly concerned with the universal principles that relate to the action done.

Stage 5: Social Contract Orientation: In this stage, the person looks at various opinions and values of different people before coming up with the decision on the morality of the action.

Stage 6: Universal Ethical Principles Orientation: The final stage of moral reasoning, this orientation is when a person considers universally accepted ethical principles. The judgment may become innate and may even violate the laws and rules as the person becomes attached to his own principles of justice.

FREUD'S PSYCHOSEXUAL DEVELOPMENT THEORY

The theory of psychosexual development was proposed by the famous psychoanalyst Sigmund Freud and described how personality developed over the course of childhood. While the theory is well-known in psychology, it is also one of the most controversial.

Freud believed that personality developed through a series of childhood stages in which the pleasure-seeking energies of the Id become focused on certain erogenous areas. This psychosexual energy, or libido, was described as the driving force behind behaviour. Psychoanalytic theory suggested that personality is mostly established by the age of five. Early experiences play a large role in personality development and continue to influence behaviour later in life.

So what happens during each stage? What if a person fails to progress through a stage completely or favourably? If these psychosexual stages are completed successfully, it results in a healthy personality. If certain issues are not resolved at the appropriate stage, fixations can occur. A fixation is a persistent focus on an earlier psychosexual stage. Until this conflict is resolved, the individual will remain "stuck" in this stage. For example, a person who is fixated at the oral stage may be over-dependent on others and may seek oral stimulation through smoking, drinking, or eating.

Freud's Stages of Psychosexual Development

The Oral Stage *(Age Range: Birth to 1 Year):* Erogenous Zone: Mouth

During the oral stage, the infant's primary source of interaction occurs through the mouth. Therefore the rooting and sucking reflex is especially important. The mouth is vital for eating and the infant derives pleasure from oral stimulation through gratifying activities such as tasting and sucking. Because the infant is entirely dependent upon caretakers (who are responsible for feeding the child), the infant also develops a sense of trust and comfort through this oral stimulation.

The primary conflict at this stage is the weaning process—the child must become less dependent upon caretakers. If fixation occurs at this stage, Freud believed the individual would have issues with dependency or aggression. Oral fixation can result in problems with drinking, eating, smoking, or nail biting.

The Anal Stage (Age Range: 1 to 3 years): *Erogenous Zone: Bowel and Bladder Control*

During the anal stage, Freud believed that the primary focus of the libido was on controlling bladder and bowel movements. The major conflict at this stage is toilet training—the child has to learn to control his or her bodily needs. Developing this control leads to a sense of accomplishment and independence.

According to Freud, success at this stage is dependent upon the way in which parents approach toilet training. Parents who utilize praise and rewards for using the toilet at the appropriate time encourage positive outcomes and help children feel capable and productive. Freud believed that positive experiences during this stage served as the basis for people to become competent, productive and creative adults.

However, not all parents provide the support and encouragement that children need during this stage. Some parents instead punish, ridicule or shame a child for accidents. According to Freud, inappropriate parental responses can result in negative outcomes. If parents take an approach that is too lenient, Freud suggested that an *anal-expulsive personality* could develop in which the individual has a messy, wasteful or destructive personality. If parents are too strict or begin toilet training too early, Freud believed that an *anal-retentive personality* develops in which the individual is stringent, orderly, rigid, and obsessive.

The Phallic Stage (Age Range: 3 to 6 Years): *Erogenous Zone: Genitals*

During the phallic stage, the primary focus of the libido is on the genitals. At this age, children also begin to discover the differences between males and females. Freud also believed that boys begin to view their fathers as a rival for the mother's affection. The Oedipus complex describes these feelings of wanting to possess the mother and the desire to replace the father.

However, the child also fears that he will be punished by the father for these feelings, a fear Freud termed *castration anxiety*. The term Electra complex has been used to describe a similar set of feelings experienced by young girls. Freud, however, believed that girls instead experience *penis envy*. Eventually, the child begins to identify with the same-sex parent as a means of vicariously possessing the other parent. For girls, however, Freud believed that penis envy was never fully resolved and that all women remain somewhat fixated at this stage. Psychologists such as Karen Horney disputed this theory, calling it both inaccurate and demeaning to women. Instead, Horney proposed that men experience feelings of inferiority because they cannot give birth to children, a concept she referred to as *womb envy*.

The Latent Period (Age Range: 6 to Puberty): *Erogenous Zone: Sexual Feelings a Inactive*

During the latent period, the libido interests are suppressed. The development of the ego and superego contribute to this period of calm. The stage begins around the time that children enter into school and become more concerned with peer relationships, hobbies, and other interests.

The latent period is a time of exploration in which the sexual energy is still present, but it is directed into other areas such as intellectual pursuits and social interactions.

This stage is important in the development of social and communication skills and self-confidence.

The Genital Stage (Age Range: Puberty to Death): *Erogenous Zone: Maturing Sexual Interests*

During the final stage of psychosexual development, the individual develops a strong sexual interest in the opposite sex. This stage begins during puberty but lasts throughout the rest of a person's life.

Where in earlier stages the focus was solely on individual needs, interest in the welfare of others, grows during this stage. If the other stages have been completed successfully, the individual should now be well-balanced, warm, and caring. The goal of this stage is to establish a balance between the various life areas.

CHOMSKY'S THEORY OF LANGUAGE DEVELOPMENT

One of the greatest linguists of all times, Noam Chomsky asserts that language is innate. He wrote his famous book, *"Language and Mind"* in 1972, in which he proposed his famous theories on language acquisition. In this book Chomsky wrote, "*When we study human language, we are approaching what some might call the 'human essence,' the distinctive qualities of mind that are, so far as we know, unique to man.*" According to Chomsky, language is one characteristic that is unique to humans among all other living beings. Chomsky's theories have made it easier to understand the evolution and development of the languages.

Chomsky's theories on language are based upon the importance of linguistics in modern sciences. According to him, to study languages, it is important to study human nature that lies in human mind.

Chomsky on Language Acquisition

Noam Chomsky postulated that the mechanism of the language acquisition is derived from the innate processes. Innate is something which is already there in mind since birth. The theory proposed by Chomsky is proved by the children living in same linguistic community. Moreover, they are not influenced by the external experiences which bring about the comparable grammar. He thus proposed his theory on language acquisition in 1977 as *"all children share the same internal constraints which characterize narrowly the grammar they are going to construct."* He also proposed that all of us live in a biological world, and he viewed that mental world is no exception. He also believes that as there are stages of development for other parts of the body; language development can also be achieved up to a certain age.

Another postulate of Chomsky's language acquisition theory is the process of selecting the best grammar that matches with the data available. He related the structural linguistics with empiricist thoughts.

Chomsky: Language Acquisition Device

Noam Chomsky's work discusses the biological basis for language and claims that children have innate abilities to learn language. Chomsky terms this innate ability as the *"language acquisition device."* He believes children instinctively learn language without any formal instruction. He also believes children have a natural need to use language, and that in the absence of formal language children will develop a system of communication to meet their needs. He has observed that all children make the same type of language errors, regardless of the language they are taught. Chomsky also believes in the existence of a "universal grammar," which posits that there are certain grammatical rules all human languages share. However, his research does not identify areas of the brain or a genetic basis that enables humans' innate ability for language

Chomsky on Generative Grammar

When talking about generative grammar, his views are different from structuralist theory. According to Chomsky, generative grammar should *"render explicit the implicit knowledge of the speaker."* He proposed a set of well-defined rules to generate required sequence of words. Individuals instantly decipher that a certain combination of words make sense and different combination does not make sense. The explanatory theory of generative grammar is beautifully demonstrated by the rules of the English auxiliary system.

Chomsky on Semantics

According to Chomsky, the field of linguistics does not include the study of meaning and reference and the use of language. According to linguistic theory, the concepts of the grammar are not based upon semantics, but linguistic theory should provide an explanation to the semantic phenomenon.

THE ROLE OF TEACHER REGARDING LANGUAGE DEVELOPMENT

The teachers need to know the process of language development as this depends on desire to learn, changes to learn and guidance. Teachers need to act as a model, as with good model to imitate and with guidance in copying it, children will improve their pronunciation.

Students need support from other students and from the teacher to develop their speech. A teacher may encourage cooperative speech by asking children questions and answering their questions. Sometimes students may have speech problem, a teacher may guide by explanations, demonstrations and work with other students. This provides opportunities for cooperative learning.

According to Vygotsky, at any given point in development there are certain problems that a child is on the verge of being able to solve. The zone of proximal development is the area where the child cannot solve a problem alone but can be successful under adult guidance or in collaboration with more advanced peer. If the teacher is aware of this aspect, he may provide opportunity to work with someone who is just a bit better. He should encourage using language to organize their thinking and to talk about what they are trying to accomplish. Teacher can do much to help children improve their speech, as language plays a major role in learning, inside and outside the classroom.

HOWARD GARDNER'S MULTIPLE INTELLIGENCE (MI) THEORY

Howard Gardner, a professor of cognition and education at the Harvard Graduate School of Education, defined the theory of MI in his 1983 book Frames of Mind. This text names the first 7 of the intelligences that Gardner identified; he added the last two in his 1999 Intelligence Reframed.

Gardner's theory is based on his study of hundreds of people, which included brain research and interviews. From this research he has theorized that all humans possess all 9 intelligences in varying amounts, that each of us has a different intellectual composition, and that all of these 9 intelligences are located in different areas of the brain. The intelligences may work together or independently in the individual, and an understanding of these intelligences can have a profound impact on pedagogy. Gardner further theorizes that the intelligences can be strengthened or weakened by nurturing or ignoring them.

Gardner's Nine Intelligences

Gardner's theory identifies 9 areas of intelligence that exist in each human to varying degrees:

- Verbal-linguistic intelligence involves sensitivity to the sounds, rhythms, and meaning of words. People with high verbal-linguistic intelligence have well-developed verbal skills.
- Mathematical-logical intelligence is the ability to think abstractly and conceptually. Individuals with a larger degree of this intelligence are able to discern numeric or logical patterns.
- Musical intelligence is the ability to appreciate and produce pitch, timber, and rhythm.
- Visual-spatial intelligence is the ability to think in pictures and images and to visualize abstractly.
- Body-kinesthetic intelligence is the ability to skillfully handle objects and to control body movements.
- Interpersonal intelligence is the capacity to detect and respond to motivations, desires, and moods of others.

- Intrapersonal intelligence is the capacity for self-awareness and being "in tune" with inner feelings and thinking processes.
- Naturalistic intelligence is the ability to recognize and categorize animals, plants, and other objects in nature
- Existential intelligence is the capacity to take on deep questions about human existence.

How is MI Different from other Theories of Intelligence?

The theory of multiple intelligences has implications for both how intelligence is assessed and how students are taught. While traditional theories of intelligence rely on short-answer tests to evaluate IQ, MI theory holds that such assessments measure memorization and the ability to do well on tests. Some states have developed tests that value the process of problem solving instead of just the answers.

While traditional theories of intelligence hold that people are born with a certain amount of intelligence that remains static over one's lifetime, MI theory posits that humans have all of the 9 intelligences in their own unique combinations and that all types can be improved.

Educational Implications of Gardner's Multiple Intelligence Theory

Although Gardner's MI research is psychological in nature, the biggest impact it has had is on pedagogy. Educators have benefitted from the theory by being able to tailor instruction to various intelligences and to modify assignments so that students can work to their strengths. Offering a variety of ways in which learning objectives can be met helps students to choose the best way for them to approach as assignment.

Students who may not excel when traditional methods of instructions are used may "tune in" when a visual or kinesthetic teaching method is employed. Rather than teaching a topic or a subject, teachers who embrace the MI theory can structure learning activities around an issue or a question and allow students to approach the assignment in a way that demonstrates their unique understanding of the topic. Students may then become specialists in a particular topic, thereby bolstering their interest in the topic. When students are able to demonstrate and share their strengths, their investment in the learning process increases.

When students begin to understand how they learn and in what way they are intelligent, they are better able to direct their own learning and value their strengths. When teachers understand a student's intelligence, they can create opportunities for students to share their strengths with others. Students may exhibit their learning through portfolios, for instance, versus traditional exams. Students whose individual intelligence compositions are valued go on to become more balanced members of their culture, able to understand questions about notions such as what it means to achieve success or to have a good life. Teachers should take care not to label students as having one particular type of intelligence.

9
Constructivist Learning

Constructivism view of learning that is developed is based on Kelly's work (1950s) on personal construct and Ausubel (1960s) on learning based on what the learner knows. Furthermore, the earlier psychologist who focuses on children's thinking process is Jean Piaget. According to Piaget (1970), knowledge is constructed in learners' mind through their interaction with the environment. "Piaget believes that there was a biological inevitability as to how children developed". There are three concepts of Piaget's work which related to constructivist theory of knowledge which are assimilation, accommodation and equilibration. Therefore, Piaget's work had some insight which are: (1) children think differently related to their stage of development, (2) learning requires active involvement between children and environment, (3) children construct their own cognitive structures. Therefore, Piaget's work is important in the constructivist theory of learning.

Constructivist is different from the traditional view of learning in the sense of the view of the real world. The traditional view of knowledge is based on the common-sense belief that a real world exists regardless of whether we take interest in it or even notice it. The traditional knowledge implies that the knowledge is reality that will be replied in learners' mind. Furthermore, traditional education view focused on *"instructional goals such as recalling facts, generalization, defining concepts and performing procedures"*. Therefore, this view ignores the difference of pre-existing knowledge of individual. On the other hand, constructivist view learning as the product of interaction between existing understanding and new knowledge. There are three types of constructivism, which are personal constructivism, radical constructivism and social constructivism. Personal constructivism focuses on the prior knowledge of individual which can be constructed by individual. On the other hand, radical constructivism focuses on students' knowledge based on their experiences which recognize students' freedom to have their own ideas. Social constructivism focuses on individual who constructs the knowledge throughout the social process. However, in general, constructivists emphasize reasoning, critical thinking, social negotiation, self regulation and mindful reflection. They also view learning as an active process in which the learners actively construct knowledge as they try to comprehend their reality world.

According to Driver and Bell (1986) as cited in Parkinson (2004, p. 90), there are six characteristics of constructivist theory of learning:

- learning is not only dependent on the learning environment, but also on the knowledge of the learners,

- learning involves the construction of meaning,
- the construction of meaning is a continuous and active process,
- meanings, once constructed, are evaluated and can be accepted or rejected,
- learners have the final responsibility for their learning, and
- students construct the meaning between the experience with the physical world through natural language.

According to these six principles which are related to the Piaget's work, teacher could use this information to apply the teaching strategies using the constructivist theory of learning. Constructivism learning succeed to lead the new and meaningful learning for the students. The constructivist as theory of learning is very useful to apply in the classroom. One important aspect that can be developed through constructivist approach is that learners use active process to develop their own meaning and knowledge. As a result, learning process will be the meaningful experiences for the students.

PRINCIPLES OF CONSTRUCTIVIST LEARNING

Constructivism, a learning theory informed by cognitive psychology, educational research and neurological science, views learning as the product of experience and social discourse. Constructivists consider learning to be an individual and personal event. The following principles are based on the work of various constructivist theorists and are offered as a framework for this discussion.

Learners bring unique prior knowledge, experience and beliefs to a learning situation: Every learner has experiences that influence his or her understanding of the world. Those unique experiences are the foundation for learning; they provide opportunities for personal connections with new content.

Learning is internally controlled and mediated. Learners take in information, process it to fit their personal frameworks, and build new understanding. That knowledge construction occurs internally in the private domain of each individual.

Knowledge is constructed in multiple ways, through a variety of tools, resources, experiences, and contexts: Constructivist learning theory tells us that we learn in a variety of ways. The more opportunities we have, and the more actively engaged we are, the richer our understanding. Good teachers have always used experience as a valuable instructional tool; that is why we arrange field trips and hands-on projects. It is why an internship or apprenticeship is essential to the completion of most vocations, including teaching.

Learning is a process of accommodation, assimilation, or rejection to construct new conceptual structures, meaningful representations, or new mental models: Every person is surrounded by an infinite variety of images, ideas, information, and other stimuli that provide raw material for thought and understanding. If new information matches the learner's existing understanding, it is easily assimilated. If it does not match, the learner must determine how to accommodate it, either by forming new understanding, or rejecting the information.

Learning is both an active and reflective process: Learners combine experience (action) and thought (reflection) to build meaning. Both parts must be present to support the creation of new knowledge.

Social interaction introduces multiple perspectives through reflection, collaboration, negotiation, and shared meaning: In many situations, learning is enhanced by verbal representation of thoughts—it helps to speak about an idea to clarify procedures or float a theory to an audience. The exchange of different perceptions between learners enriches an individual's insight.

ADVANTAGES OF CONSTRUCTIVIST LEARNING

- The learner uses sensory input and does something with it, ultimately making meaning of it.
- Learning consists of both constructing meaning and constructing systems of meaning. Learning is layered.
- Learning occurs in the mind. Physical activity may be necessary, but is not sufficient alone.
- Learning involves language. Vygotsky believed that language and learning are inextricably intermeshed.
- Learning is a social activity.
- Learning is contextual. We do not isolate facts from the situations and environments in which they are relevant
- Knowledge is necessary for learning. It is the basis of structure and meaning-making. The more we know, the more we can learn.
- Learning takes time; it is not spontaneous. Learners go over information and ponder, practice or experiment with them.
- Motivation is a necessary component, because it causes the learner's sensory apparatus to be activated. Relevance, curiosity, fun, accomplishment, achievement, external rewards and other motivators facilitate ease of learning.

PRINCIPLES OF CONSTRUCTIVIST COURSE DESIGN

The main principles of constructivist course design are:

- Maintain a buffer between the learner and the potentially damaging effects of instructional practices. Emphasize the affective domain, make instruction relevant to the learner, help learners develop attitudes and beliefs that ill support both present learning and lifelong learning, and balance teacher-control with personal autonomy in the learning environment.
- Provide contexts for both autonomous learning and learning within relationships to other students—group discussion, projects, collaboration as well as independent.
- Provide reasons for learning within the learning activities themselves. Have students identify relevance and purpose.
- Promote and make conscious the skills and attitudes that enable a learner to assume responsibility for his/her cognitive and developmental processes.
- Use the strategic exploration of errors to strengthen the learners involvement with intentional learning processes and self-feedback.

CONSTRUCTIVIST LEARNING ENVIRONMENTS (CLEs)

Jonassen has proposed a model for developing constructivist learning environments (CLEs) around a specific learning goal. This goal may take one of several forms, from least to most complex:

- Question or issue
- Case study
- Long-term Project
- Problem (multiple cases and projects integrated at the curriculum level)

Jonassen recommends making the learning goals engaging and relevant but not overly structured.

In CLEs, learning is driven by the problem to be solved; students learn content and theory in order to solve the problem. This is different from traditional objectivist teaching where the theory would be presented first and problems would be used afterwards to practice theory. Depending on students' prior experiences, related cases and scaffolding may be necessary for support. Instructors also need to provide an authentic context for tasks and information resources, cognitive and collaborative tools.

Components of Constructivist Learning Environments:

Jonassen and Land (2002) suggest three components for constructivist learning environments:

- Context
- Construction
- Collaboration

Interactive learning environments (ILEs) have the following qualities:

Authentic activities: presenting authentic tasks that conceptualize rather than abstract information and provide real-world, case-based contexts, rather than pre-determined instructional sequences;

Construction: learners should be constructing artifacts and sharing them with their community;

Collaboration: to support collaborative construction of knowledge through social negotiation, as opposed to competition among learners for recognition;

Reflection: fostering reflective practice;

Situating the context: enable context and content dependent knowledge construction; and

Multi-modal interaction: providing multiple representations of reality, representing the natural complexity of the real world.

CONSTRUCTIVIST ASSUMPTIONS ABOUT LEARNING

- Constructivism is a view in which knowledge is believed to be constructed rather than acquired. It is not one theory but a multitude of approaches.
- Only the active learner is a successful learner. Learning by doing enables learners to achieve deep levels of understanding.
- Knowledge is constructed by learners as they attempt to make sense of their experiences.

- Learners are actively seeking meaning because learning with understanding is desired, as opposed to rote learning.
- Many constructivist theorists agree that there is a social component to learning, as learners test their own understandings against those of others, such as those of teachers or more advanced peers. Therefore, the social structure of a learning environment is important

CONSTRUCTIVIST LEARNING GOALS

- Emphasizes learning in context through meaningful activities.
- Focus on high-level thinking activities to develop cognitive flexibility.
- Constructivists are interested in having learners identify and pursue their own learning goals.
- Problem solving, reasoning, critical thinking and reflection constitute the goals of constructivist instruction.

CONSTRUCTIVIST CONDITIONS FOR LEARNING

- Focus on the process of learning, rather than the products of learning. This can be accomplished by embedding learning in complex, realistic and relevant environments.
- Simplifying tasks for learners will prevent them from learning how to solve the complex problems they will solve in real life by providing for social negotiation as an essential part of learning.
- Higher mental processes develop through social interaction. Students develop and defend individual perspectives while recognizing those of others and teachers support multiple perspectives and the use of multiple modes of representation.
- Viewing the same content through different sensory modes (such as visual, auditory, or tactile) enables different aspects of it to be seen and encourages ownership in learning.
- Students are actively involved in determining what their own learning needs are and how those needs can be satisfied, rather than being passive recipients of instruction that has been designed for them. Teachers share in the learning process rather than controlling it. It is imperative to nurture self-awareness of the knowledge construction process as the importance of metacognition and reflexivity is essential to the acquisition of goals such as reasoning, understanding multiple perspectives and articulating beliefs.

10
Introduction to Reflection

MEANING OF REFLECTION

Reflection is a mental process which, applied to the act of learning, challenges students to use critical thinking to examine presented information, question its validity, and draw conclusions based on the resulting ideas. This ongoing process allows the students to narrow possible solutions and eventually form a conclusion. The result of this struggle is achieving a better understanding of the concept. Without reflection, learning ends "well short of the re-organization of thinking that 'deep' learning requires" (Ewell, 1997, p. 9). Effective learning situations require time for thinking. Students also reflect on themselves as learners when they evaluate the thinking processes they used to determine which strategies worked best. They can then apply that information about how they learn as they approach learning in the future.

THE HISTORY OF REFLECTION

Historically, the root of reflective teaching began in the 1930s by Dewey who defined reflection as a proactive, ongoing examination of beliefs and practices elaborating on the ideas of previous philosophers and educationist as Plato, Aristotle, Confucius, Lao Tzu, Solomon and Buddha. Dewey (1933) identified three characteristics of reflective individuals that are quite important for teachers of today which are open-mindedness, responsibility and enthusiasm. This spark of reflection ended soon and the educational society never heard about the reflective teaching until the beginning of the 1980s and with the great efforts of Schön (1983, 1987) who built his work on the concept of practitioner-generated intuitive practice.

DEFINITION OF REFLECTION

> *"Reflection can be seen as the process of thinking carefully or deeply about a particular subject, typically involving past life and experiences. It usually also implies a deep or serious level of thought, especially within an academic context. Cottrell discusses this in practice, introducing reflection as follows"*

An interesting definition is offered by Richards (1994) who defines *"reflection as a process of learning from experience, in which self-inquiry is regarded as a key component of a learner's development."* There are many definitions for reflection. In reflective practice, practitioners engage in a continuous cycle of self-observation and evaluation, so they can comprehend their own actions and reactions. There are many definitions; however most can be restricted to two main views of reflective teaching, one that specifies reflection on the classroom while the second kind indicates reflection outside the classroom.

Reflection is the act of directing your thoughts to focus your attention on a subject or an experience. Reflection is an important part of learning through experience. By reflecting on our experiences, we maximize the potential of any new learning. This is particularly important when considering positives. They are often harder to recall than the bad elements of any experience.

DEWEY'S CRITERIA FOR REFLECTION

The famous educator John Dewey (1933) was one of the first to articulate the need for teachers to reflect on complex situations and to subsequently question what needs to be done to change and improve.

Nearly 100 years ago, John Dewey articulated his concept of how we think in a book by the same name (How We Think, 1910/1933). He identified several modes of thought, including belief, imagination and stream of consciousness but the mode he was most interested in was 'reflection'.

Dewey viewed reflective inquiry as **"***active, persistent, and careful consideration of any belief or supposed form of knowledge in the light of the grounds that support it and the further conclusions to which it tends [that] constitutes reflective thought***".** He encouraged teachers (and all citizens really) to make informed decisions about their teaching, and that these decisions be based on *systematic and conscious reflections* rather than fleeting thoughts about teaching.

According to John Dewey, *"Reflection involves not simply a sequence of ideas, but a consequence — a consecutive ordering in such a way that each determines the next as its proper outcome, while each in turn leans back on its predecessors. The successive portions of the reflective thought grow out of one another and support one another; they do not come and go in a medley. Each phase is a step from something to something — technically speaking, it is a term of thought. Each term leaves a deposit which is utilized in the next term. The stream or flow becomes a train, chain, or thread."*

John Dewey's four criteria for reflection are as follows:

- Reflection is a meaning making process that moves a learner from one experience into the next with deeper understanding of its relationships with and connections to other experiences and ideas. It is the thread that makes continuity of learning possible and ensures the progress of the individual and, ultimately, society. It is a means to essentially moral ends.
- Reflection is a systematic, rigorous, disciplined way of thinking, with its roots in scientific inquiry.
- Reflection needs to happen in community, in interaction with others.
- Reflection requires attitudes that value the personal and intellectual growth of onself and of others.

SCHON'S CRITERIA FOR REFLECTION

In 1983, Schon further expanded on the concept of reflective practice by elaborating on different types of reflective practice: Reflection-in-action and Reflection-on-action.

Reflection-in-action	Ability of professional 'experts' to think on their feet and to improvise.
Reflection-on-action	Actions are analysed and reframed after the event and potential solutions are developed.

ROGER'S CRITERIA FOR REFLECTION

Rogers outlines 4 criteria regarding reflection drawn from Dewey's writings:

- Reflection is a meaning-making process
- Reflection is a systematic, rigorous, disciplined way of thinking, with its roots in scientific inquiry.
- Reflection needs to happen in community, in interaction with others.
- Reflection requires attitudes that value the personal and intellectual growth of oneself and of others.

REFLECTION AND EDUCATION

Linguistically, the word *'reflection'* may be seen as a meditative form of looking at oneself, and as such may be seen as a form of experiential learning. Certainly, it is something that we do implicitly as part of being human, underpinning our identities through a process of negotiation between our sense of self and our experiences of others (Demetriou, 2000, p. 210). However, efforts to shift from the implicit to the explicit, pragmatic and measurable have been driven by subjective understandings of the term and its functions, and subsequently reflection as an educational process has remained a poorly defined concept.

This is not to say that it lacks a history of educational application. Within established educational models, such as Kolb (1984), reflection has been defined as central to the ways in which knowledge and learning can be driven through a cyclical process of identification, review, questioning and reconstruction. Here, *"Knowledge is continuously derived from and tested out in the experiences of the learner"* (Kolb, 1984, p. 27), and this can only take place where those experiences can be reviewed and analyzed retrospectively. Essentially, however, how one views reflection may be guided by the specific purpose through which it is approached, as can be seen within the work of the key reflective theorists.

Reflection is part of learning and thinking. We reflect in order to learn something or we learn as a result of reflecting and the term 'reflective learning' emphasizes the intention to learn from current or prior experience. As part of education, reflection as a process allows the student to establish connections between new and existing knowledge and experiences, to understand their own position within that relationship and to deepen the level at which they work with them at the academic, personal and professional levels.

Dewey—Reflection as Rationality

John Dewey saw reflection as a further dimension of thought, and as such in need of education; "while we cannot learn or be taught to think, we do have to learn to think well, especially acquire the general habit of reflection" (Dewey, 1933). For Dewey, reflection is a rational and purposeful act, an "active, persistent and careful consideration of any belief or supposed form of knowledge in the light of the grounds that support it, and further conclusions to which it leads... it includes a conscious and voluntary effort to establish belief upon a firm basis of evidence and rationality" (Dewey, 1933). Interestingly, from a modern educational perspective, Dewey's reference to different forms of belief and knowledge may reveal his willingness to apply objective rationality to more affective and emotional concerns.

Schön—Reflection and the Professional

Schön, however, concentrated on the use of rational reflection within the understanding and development of professional practice. Schön argued that the application of theory within practice is driven by reflection, the use of such a process ultimately leading to a state of expertise. His goal was therefore to make the tacit knowledge which epitomizes expertise explicit so that it could be considered and improved, and that reflection-on-action, the retrospective analysis of experience, would drive that process. Interestingly, Schön also proposed a form of reflection-in-action, in which reflection is seen as part of active thought.

Boud and Walker—Reflection as Holistic Act

Interestingly, while Dewey only mentions emotions implicitly and Schön avoids them through his focus on professional expertise, Boud & Walker (1998) specifically question the appropriateness of a reflective process in which personal emotional subjectivity is avoided, highlighting the need to explore a wider range of experiential dimensions. Boud and Walker seek to avoid the dehumanization of the reflective process by offering "the challenge of incorporating ideas about reflection, which in some cases are only partially understood, into teaching contexts which are not conducive to the questioning of experience—that is, situations which do not allow learners to explore 'a state of perplexity, hesitation, doubt (Dewey 1933), 'inner discomforts' (Brookfield, 1987), 'distorting dilemmas' (Mezirow, 1990), uncertainties, discrepancies and dissatisfactions which precipitate, and are central to, any notion of reflection" (Boud & Walker, 1998, p. 192).

THE PROCESS OF REFLECTION

Reflection is not only a description of *'what you've seen'* or *'what you've done'*, but rather it is a process of drawing comparisons with what happened, what you already know, relating this experience to the theories you have been introduced to and modifying your own ideas and professional practice in light of this reflection.

A scaffold for this process is the 4 Rs. The steps below are based on Bain (2002). This 4Rs process is based on the Reflection-on-action described earlier by Dewey, Schon and Van Manen. The process is designed to encourage you to address your ongoing learning from a number of standpoints (practical, cognitive, emotional; your values, your beliefs, your ethics and the political imperatives placed upon you). It is intended that this framework will assist you to address many of the problems and dilemmas that you will face in your teaching.

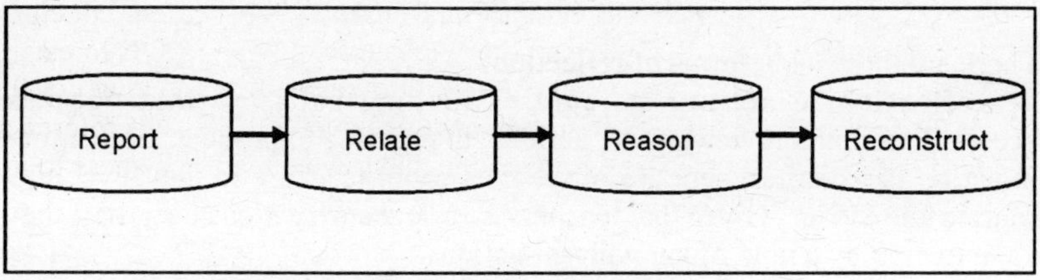

Figure 10.1: The Process of Reflection

Report: At this stage you describe, report or re-tell the key elements of what you have learnt, seen or experienced. Why is it relevant? Respond to the incident or issue by making observations, expressing your opinion, or asking questions.

Relate: You should draw a relationship between your *current* personal or theoretical understandings and identify aspects of the observation which have personal meaning or connect with your experience. Relate or make a connection between the incident or issue and your own skills, professional experience, or discipline knowledge. Have I seen this before? Were the conditions the same or different? Do I have the skills and knowledge to deal with this?

Reason: You should explore the relationship between theory and practice and seek a deep understanding of why something has happened. You can explore or analyze a concept, event or experience by asking questions and looking for answers, reviewing the literature, considering alternatives and multiple perspectives. Highlight in detail significant factors underlying the incident or issue. How would a knowledgeable and/or experienced person perceive/handle this? What are the ethics involved?

Reconstruct: Discuss improvements which could be made or identify something you need or plan to do or change. You should be able to generalize and/or apply your learning to other contexts and future professional practice. This may involve developing general principles, formulating personal theories of teaching or taking a stand or position on an issue. How would I deal with this next time? What might work and why? Are there different options? What might happen if....? Can I make changes which will benefit others?

Critical Reflection: The idea of critical reflection is a development of Habermas's (1974) *critical social science*. It is based on the assumption that self-reflection will be almost inevitably distorted by the social context and personal history of the reflector. According to Silverman & Casazza (2000 - *"Critical reflection entails a challenge to the hidden assumptions of both the reflector and those of the surrounding social context. Critical reflection goes beyond mere reflection, which could be simply a review of actions in the light of accepted precepts, in that it requires the reflector to "deconstruct long-held habits of behaviour by looking beyond the behaviour itself to their own self-image and examining why they do what they do"*. In other words, when engaging in critical reflection, you should *make explicit* and *challenge* (as in review) your own basic assumptions and those of the community (society) in which you work.

FORMS OF REFLECTION

There are three main forms of reflection:

Reflection-in-action: It requires looking back on what one has accomplished and reviewing the actions, thoughts, and product. Reflection-in-action is when teachers are in the classroom teaching in their everyday routine knowledge. Given that teachers carry out such actions everyday, they have to employ a kind of knowing-in-action.

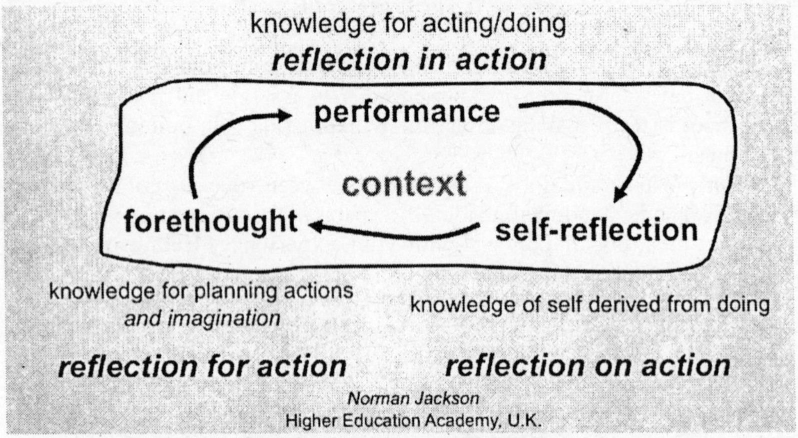

Figure 10.2: Forms of Reflection

Reflection-on-action: The second form of reflection is *reflection-in-action.* In this activity, the individual is responsible for reflecting while in the act of carrying out the task. If, for example, the student is writing a story and has left out the setting, reflection-in-action could guide the correction of a major component of the story writing. Reflection-on-action is less problematic since it is viewed as teachers' thoughts and retrospective study of their presentation

Reflection-for-action: Reflection-for-action is different from the other two types since it is proactive in nature. The final reflective form centers on *reflection-for-action.* This reflection form expects the participant to review what has been accomplished and identify constructive guidelines to follow to succeed in the given task in the future.

BENEFITS OF REFLECTION

Reflection is integral to the service-learning experience in the following ways:

- Reflection transforms experience into genuine learning about individual values and goals and about larger social issues.
- Reflection challenges students to connect service activities to course objectives and to develop higher-level thinking and problem solving.
- Reflection works against the perpetuation of stereotypes by raising students' awareness of the social structures surrounding service environments.
- By fostering a sense of connection to the community and a deeper awareness of community needs, reflection increases the likelihood that students will remain committed to service beyond the term of the course.

REFLECTIVE PRACTICE MODELS (MODELS FOR REFLECTION)

Various experts have produced Reflective Practice models to help people use Reflective Practice more deliberately, proactively, and effectively. These models also help beginners to remember the process of reflecting from events/ experiences for effective learning, and can also restrict (unhelpful) 'creative narrative reflections', in which we develop subjective thinking into fanciful or fearful imaginings. There are a number of models for reflection. These models often have three common elements:

(i) Description (ii) Analysis
(iii) Action ('so what' or 'reflexivity') element

The models can provide the frameworks for asking questions; they can also prompt to think more deeply about the whole process of reflection and becoming a reflective practitioner. However, the process of reflection remains a personal one; only one can decide what works for your own reflective practice.

KOLB'S LEARNING CYCLE (1984)

David A. Kolb created a learning cycle to incorporate reflection as a key process. It incorporates four key elements—concrete experience, observation and reflection, the ability to form new abstract concepts and the ability to test those in new situations. The learning cycle begins at any one of these points. In essence, where a person carries out an action they can then both observe and reflect upon its underlying processes and possible consequences. Subsequently, the action becomes open to conceptualization as a type of action with generalizable outcomes, a concept that can then be further tested through new experiences in order to both validate them and develop them further.

Kolb's Learning Cycle is a well-known theory which argues we learn from our experiences of life, even on an everyday basis. It also treats reflection as an integral part of such learning. According to Kolb (1984), the process of learning follows a pattern or cycle consisting of four stages, one of which involves what Kolb refers to as 'reflective observation'. The stages are illustrated and summarized below:

THE FOUR STAGE LEARNING CYCLE

Kolb proposed that an individual learner moves through a spiral of immediate experience which leads to observations and reflections on the experience. These reflections are then absorbed and linked with previous knowledge and translated into abstract concepts or theories, which result in new ways and actions to adjust to the experience that can be tested and explored. Kolb described the four stages in the cycle of experiential learning as:

1. Concrete Experience - (CE)
2. Reflective Observation - (RO)
3. Abstract Conceptualization - (AC)
4. Active Experimentation - (AE)

Stage 1: Experience (Kolb's "Concrete experiences")

Life is full of experiences we can learn from. Whether at home or at work or out and about, there are countless opportunities for us to 'kick-start' the learning cycle. This stage of the learning cycle emphasizes personal involvement with

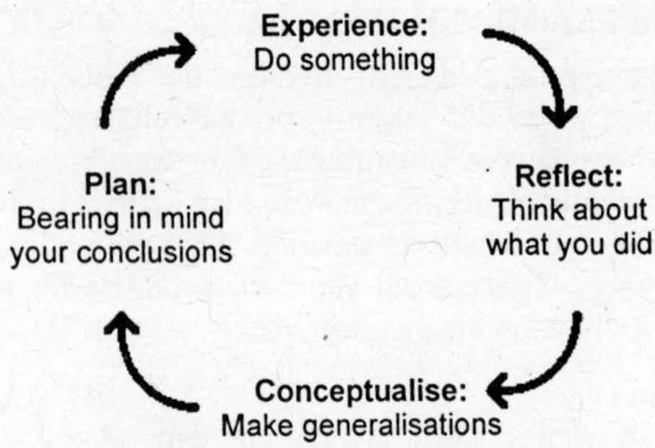

Figure 10.3: Kolb's Learning Cycle

people in everyday situations. In this stage, the learner would tend to rely more on feelings than on a systematic approach to problems and situations. In a learning situation, the learner relies on the ability to be open-minded and adaptability to change. For example, a student performs an initial interview for the first time.

Stage 2: Reflect (Kolb's "Reflective Observation")

Reflection involves thinking about what we have done and experienced. Some people are naturally good at this. Others train themselves to be more deliberate about reviewing their experiences and recording them.

In this stage of the learning cycle, people understand ideas and situations from different points of view. In a learning situation the learner would rely on patience, objectivity, and careful judgment but would not necessarily take any action. The learner would rely on their own thoughts and feelings in forming opinions. In the example, after finishing the student reflects on what they did, makes observations and discusses how they went with their educator.

Stage 3: Conceptualize (Kolb's "Abstract Conceptualization")

When we pass from thinking about our experiences to interpreting them, we enter into the realm of what Kolb termed 'conceptualization'. To conceptualize is to generate a hypothesis about the meaning of our experiences.

In the active experimentation stage of the learning cycle we effectively 'test' the hypotheses we have adopted. Our new experiences will either support or challenge these hypotheses. In this stage, learning involves using theories, logic and ideas, rather than feelings, to understand problems or situations. Typically, the learner relies on systematic planning and develops theories and ideas to solve problems. In the example, the student then thinks about the interview process and their performance and tries to make links between previous experience of interviewing, the client and what they heard, and any theories or knowledge they can apply.

Stage 4: Plan (Kolb's "Active Experimentation")

To learn from our experiences it is not sufficient just to have them. This will only take us into stage 1 of the cycle. Rather, any experience has the potential to yield learning, but only if we pass through all Kolb's stages by reflecting on our experiences, interpreting them and testing our interpretations.

Active Experimentation (AE)

Learning in this stage takes an active form - experimenting with changing situations. The learner would take a practical approach and be concerned with what really works, as opposed to simply watching a situation. In the example, the student considers ways to improve, and tries out methods and strategies based on the previous stages of the cycle.

Summing up, learning from our experiences involves the key element of reflection. Obviously, most people don't theorize about their learning in this way, but in their learning follow Kolb's cycle without knowing it.

GIBBS REFLECTIVE CYCLE MODEL (1988)

Gibbs' (1998) reflective cycle guides us through six stages of reflection. The Gibbs' reflective cycle, inspired partly by Kolb's learning cycle, enables us to focus especially on our own and others' feelings, views and perceptions. This relates strongly to ideas about empathy. The process is essentially a cycle or loop, containing the following elements:

- *Description:* What happened?
- *Feelings:* What were you thinking and feeling?
- *Evaluation:* What was good and bad about the experience?
- *Analysis:* What sense can you make of the situation?
- *Conclusion:* What else could you have done?
- *Action Plan:* If it arose again what would you do? (back to 1 Description)

The description of six stages is as follows:

Description: what happened?: What, where and when? Who did/said what, what did you do/read/see hear? In what order did things happen? What were the circumstances? What were you responsible for?

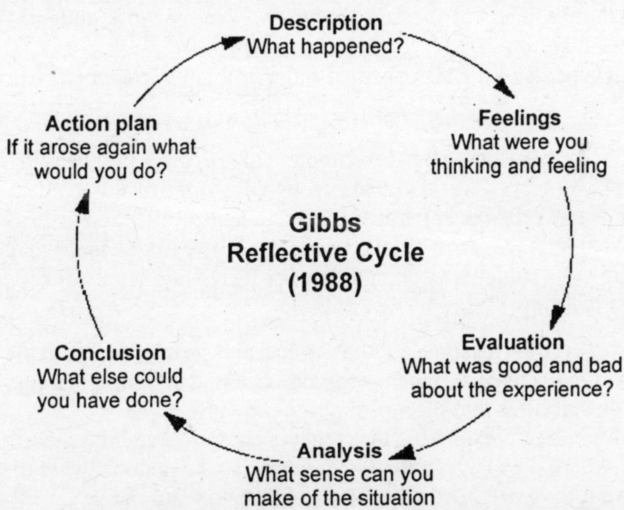

Figure 10.4: Diagram: Gibbs G [1988] Learning by Doing: A guide to teaching and learning methods. Further Education Unit. Oxford Polytechnic: Oxford. [Brookes.ac.uk])

Feelings: what were you thinking about?: What was your initial gut reaction, and what does this tell you? Did your feelings change? What were you thinking?

Evaluation: what was good or bad about the experience?: What pleased, interested or was important to you? What made you unhappy? What difficulties were there? Who/what was unhelpful? Why? What needs improvement?

Analysis: what sense can you make of the situation?: Compare theory and practice. What similarities or differences are there between this experience and other experiences? Think about what actually happened. What choices did you make and what effect did they have?

Conclusion: what else could you have done?: What have you learnt for the future? What else could you have done?

Action Plan: what will you do next time?: If a similar situation arose again, what would you do?

REFLECTING ON STUDENTS' WORK

One way that we as teachers can be reflective is to look critically at the assessment tasks. We should think about the following points related to 'Reflection-on-action':

- Have they understood the nature of the task?
- Did they see it as relevant to their learning?
- Were they able to structure their responses in an appropriate way?
- What were the misconceptions about the task that some students had?
- Did the students' final products indicate a level of mastery over the knowledge and skills?
- Are there evident gaps in their knowledge or skills?
- Are there clear areas which need more explicit teaching?
- Were there aspects of the task that the student or most students managed successfully?
- Which aspects of the task seemed most problematic or misconstrued?

ENCOURAGING REFLECTION IN STUDENTS

We have been focusing on the development of reflective practices in ourselves as teachers, however we also need to be cognizant of the need to develop those very same reflective practices in our students. Reflection in the classroom can occur at any age. As a teacher there are many things that you can do to encourage your students to engage in ever increasing levels of reflection on their own learning:

- Structure your lessons so that there are points where reflection is encouraged. This may mean stepping back and stopping activity.
- Include activities that prompt inquiry and curiosity.
- Develop reflective thinking tasks that encourage students to stop and think about where they have come from, what they have done, what they learnt, and what they will need to do in the future to learn more.

11
Learning In and Out of School in Diverse Environments

The changes around the world caused by globalization and worldwide immigration are significantly influencing education. Students educated in one nation must compete for jobs with people educated in other nations. Technology enables companies to outsource jobs from wealth nations to poorer nations. Globalization moves jobs, people, products, and ideas across nations. Although nationalism is strong and national borders are as tight as ever, globalization challenges national borders because of its influence on trade, technology, jobs, and the rights of people who participate in global population movements

Globalization, global job competition, and the digital world in which students are socialized make it imperative for educators to rethink the conventional aims and means of education for all students, including those from majority and minority groups. Theoretical and empirical evidence indicates that there is a significant lag between education in the public schools and the digital technology and culture in which students today are deeply involved. The schools are not keeping up with the digital age in which students live and participate. Most of the learning that occurs across the life span takes places in informal environments. People spend the majority of their time from infancy to adulthood in informal learning settings

LIFE-LONG, LIFE-WIDE AND LIFE-DEEP LEARNING

The meaning of life-long, life-wide and life-deep learning is given below

Life-Long Learning

Life-long learning refers to the acquisition of fundamental behaviours (e.g., walking and recognizing faces) and real-world information (e.g., objects fall when dropped, steeper inclines require more exertion than gradual ones). Learning that extends from our childhood into old age includes all the ways we manage interpersonal sociability, reflect our belief systems, and orient to new experiences. Most of the time, such learning is intuited, "picked up," and unconscious.

Life-long learning may conjure up specific kinds of information that relate primarily to career choices and the practical needs of daily living. As learners have gained all these sorts of information, they have also developed particular skills on which effective and satisfying performance depends. Generally, learners prefer to seek out information and acquire ways of doing things because they are motivated to do so by their interests, curiosity, pleasure, and sense that they have talents to support a move toward certain kinds of tasks and challenges. Whether learning to play the banjo, build wooden boats, or whip up a perfect chocolate cake, learners take in information and techniques through observing, trying, testing, and finding satisfaction. Orientation toward these efforts begins in infancy and continues into old age.

Life-Wide Learning

Life-wide learning involves a breadth of experiences, guides, and locations and includes core issues such as adversity, comfort, and support in our lives. It takes in everything from knowing as a seven year old how to say no to chocolate cake at a friend's birthday party without explaining your allergy to learning how to predict traffic patterns on a busy freeway. It tells an individual where an open parking space might be in a crowded town center and helps her figure out how to regroup if her wallet is stolen during a vacation in an unfamiliar city. This learning carries individuals through adaptation to new situations, ranging from unfamiliar terms and instructions on tax forms to relocation from one apartment complex to another.

Life-Deep Learning

Life-deep learning embraces religious, moral, ethical, and social values that guide what people believe, how they act, and how they judge themselves and others. Fundamental in such learning is language. The symbol making and processing capacity of humans is one of the most remarkable of human traits, underlying what they think and do and many of the ways they learn. People have to learn how to use all that comes with the gift of language in their roles: as child, parent, religious instructor or mentor, tenant, neighbour, employee, and public citizen. Each of these roles requires more than a single way of talking or a single medium of presentation.

MEANING OF OUT-OF-SCHOOL LEARNING

Out-of-school learning is an educational concept first proposed by *Lauren Resnick* in the 1987 presidential address consisting of curricular and non curricular learning experiences for pupils and students outside the school environment. The point of out-of-school learning is to overcome learning disabilities, development of talents, strengthen communities and increase interest in education by creating extra learning opportunities in the real world. Out-of-school learning increases the interest in education and school itself.

Out-of-school learning is typically not coordinated by the school itself. Out-of-school experiences are organized with community partners such as museums, sport facilities, charity initiatives and more. Out-of-school experiences can range from service learning to summer school and expeditions or more commonly occur in day to day experiences at afterschool with creative ventures such as arts courses and even sports. Some other examples of out-of-school learning are:

- homework and homework clubs
- study clubs—extending curriculum

- mentoring—by other pupils and by adults, including parents
- learning about learning
- community service and citizenship
- residential activities—study weeks or weekends

It has been found in research that out-of-school learning can be a great opportunity to discover and develop talents, especially if a professional organization develops a learning environment that guides groups of pupils/ students in their co-operation in creating a professional and publicly visible product, presentation or performance. Educational institutions can offer valuable out-of-school learning experiences.

Benefits of Outdoor Learning and Experience

The benefits of outdoor learning and experience are as follows:

- The benefits of outdoor education can include learning about nature, society, nature-society interactions and oneself.
- Outdoor education can involve working with others, developing new skills, undertaking practical conservation and influencing society.
- The intended outcomes of such experiences can encompass knowledge and understanding, attitudes and feelings, values and beliefs, activities or behaviours, personal development and social development.
- Outdoor learning outcomes as changes in thinking, feeling and/or behaviour resulting directly or indirectly from outdoor education.
- Outdoor learning supports academic achievement as well as the development of 'soft' skills and social skills.
- It can take place on school trips, on visits in the local community or in the school grounds
- Education outside the classroom is of significant benefit to students. Academic fieldwork clearly enhances the teaching of science and geography, but other subjects such as history, art and design and citizenship can also be brought to life by high quality educational visits. Group activities, which may include adventurous expeditions, can develop social skills and give self-confidence. Furthermore, outdoor education has a key role to play in the social inclusion agenda, offering children who may not otherwise have the opportunity or the simple chance to experience the countryside, or other parts of our heritage that many others take for granted.

Teaching Outside the Classroom

Teaching and learning can become inherently spontaneous and student-centered when moved from the confines of the classroom into the world at large. From the collaborative learning atmosphere that results from the unique relationships developed outside the classroom to the deep learning that occurs when students must put into practice "in the real world" what they have theorized about from behind a desk, field experiences are unmatched in their learning potential. Field experiences early in a student's career can be formative and can inspire students to continue in a field.

Learning experiences outside the classroom are inherently interdisciplinary.

When we go out into the world, we encounter it as a whole and are forced to engage multiple modalities, no matter which pair of disciplinary "lenses" we intended to wear. Therefore, scientists and humanists alike do well to consider the ways in which other disciplines might enrich their own disciplinary approach to their field.

What is the Outdoor Classroom?

Outdoor classroom are those spaces where students can experience familiar and unfamiliar phenomena beyond the normal confines of the classroom.

Objectives of Learning Outside the Classroom

Learning outside the classroom can be teacher-centered and expository or it can be more enquiry-based and student-centered. This choice depends on the nature and objectives of the lesson. A great range of objectives can be achieved through learning outside the classroom, including:

- The formation of attitudes and the development of an aesthetic awareness
- The development of understanding and knowledge
- The development of skills.

Although the teacher holds the ultimate responsibility for what happens in any lesson, the experience of learning outside the classroom can help students develop a greater sense of their own responsibilities towards each other and the tasks on which they are working.

When planning learning outside the classroom, it is necessary to match the activities selected with the objectives and purposes of the fieldwork. The selection of objectives will depend to some extent upon the timing of the fieldwork within the sequence of learning activities:

- Early in the learning sequence, learning outside the classroom may be used for basic information gathering and increasing the motivation of students.
- Towards the end of a unit of work, learning outside the classroom may be used to draw a number of themes together.
- Integrated throughout a unit of work, learning outside the classroom can develop student understanding of concepts, generalizations and principles.

PRINCIPLES OF IN AND OUT OF SCHOOL LEARNING

The principles related to in and out of school learning are:

- Learning is situated in broad socio-economic and historical contexts and is mediated by local cultural practices and perspectives.
- Learning takes place not only in school but also in the multiple contexts and valued practices of everyday lives across the life span.
- All learners need multiple sources of support from a variety of institutions to promote their personal and intellectual development.
- Learning is facilitated when learners are encouraged to use their home and community language resources as a basis for expanding their linguistic repertoires.

LEARNING THEORIES SUPPORTING OUTDOOR CLASSROOM LEARNING

Different theories of learning provide empirically based accounts of the variables, factors and contexts which influence the learning process in the outdoor classroom, and provide explanations of the ways in which that influence occurs. The theories illustrate fundamentally different assumptions about how learning might occur in an outdoor setting, and identify key features and pedagogical approaches associated with each of three perspectives: the associative (strengthening behavioural associations), the constructive (making meaning from experiences), and the situative (engaging in acceptable social practices).

FOCI AND OUTCOMES OF OUTDOOR LEARNING

Table 11.1 shows a number of possible foci for outdoor education set against possible outcomes:

Table 11.1 Foci and possible outcomes for outdoor education

Foci of outdoor education can include	Intended outcomes of such experiences can include
• learning about *nature*, for example, in an ecological or horticultural study	• knowledge and understanding of, for example, geographical processes, ecology or food growing techniques
• learning about *society*, for example, in community-based gardening initiatives or conservation projects	• attitudes and feelings, for example, towards intensive stock rearing, access to the countryside or fair trade
• learning about *nature-society interactions*, for example, in visits to outdoor nature centers or areas of outstanding natural beauty	• values and beliefs, for example, about the value of the environment, one's relationship to it, or biodiversity loss
• learning about *oneself*, for example, in personal fulfillment through challenging adventure education or working with animals	• personal development, for example, self-confidence, knowing fact from value, enhancing personal effectiveness
• learning about *working with others*, for example, in small-group fieldwork or residential experience	• activities and behaviours, for example, pro-environment actions, coping strategies or making a personal commitment
• learning *new skills*, for example, through fieldwork or practical activities in school grounds	• skills, for example, identification of species with a key or map-reading
• learning about *practical conservation*, for example, through focused activities in the countryside or in city farms	• skills, for example, in clearing undergrowth or removing invasive alien species
• learning about *influencing society*, for example, by campaigning on controversial issues or working with disadvantaged groups	• social development, for example, working with others, promoting democratic social change or reducing racism
• learning *research skills*, for example, through action research on field or school grounds work	• enhanced capacity to carry out systematic enquiry on one's own or other's work with children

PERSONAL AND SOCIAL BENEFITS OF PURPOSEFUL EDUCATIONAL ACTIVITIES IN THE OUTDOOR CLASSROOM

The personal and social benefits of purposeful educational activities in the outdoor classroom can be listed in the table given below:

	Developing Understanding of Transactions Between People and Environment
A	• Treating animals with care and sensitivity, caring for animals, giving them food water, and keeping them clean • Learning to respect the natural world • Feeling a sense of belonging in the countryside and that this is a place they can return too • Being part of various groups and communities, urban and rural • Understanding how whole communities work and the link between urban and rural within their own community • Providing new role models for children (for example, the male farmer helping to birth lambs)
	Encouraging Personal Responsibility; Engendering Confidence
B	• Learning to have a go • Building confidence and self esteem • Taking pride in what you have done • Being able to organise themselves • Children who are often difficult in the classroom find new ways to shine
	Facilitating Self-discovery
C	• Being taken outside the comfort zone • Learning about themselves and who they are • Enjoying something they didn't think they would enjoy • Fuzzy science – (learning about) a world which is not black and white • Learning to touch living creatures; overcoming fear • Overcoming their fear of wilderness
	Developing Interpersonal Skills; Challenging Stereotypes
D	• Working together as a team • Working with others on a problem • Arguing things out • Appreciating other perspectives • Learning to live together • Changing power relations with their peers • Learning that different environments can alter the balance of power and show different sides to people • Breaking down stereotypes about people living and working in the countryside.

THE RANGE AND EFFECTIVENESS OF APPROACHES TO OUTDOOR EDUCATION

Five different types of educational emphasis related to outdoor education have been identified: the experience, the outdoor context, pedagogy, and integrating idea and learning. The types (presented in the diagram below), whilst not necessarily fully discrete, can all make important and distinctive contributions to the totality of the learning experience. These different types remind stakeholders of differing possibilities about both priority and process, and allow them to map these in relation to the productive interaction needed in using the outdoor classroom for learning.

The above typology highlights four important features for supporting learning in the outdoor classroom:

- Contextualization: acknowledging the realities of the educational setting;
- Promoting good learning design: supporting well informed approaches to the use of outdoor classroom;
- Promoting professional learning: enabling individuals or groups to do something new or differently by learning from experience; and
- Working with communities of learners and practitioners: supporting learning and change.

APPROACHES TO LEARNING OUTSIDE THE CLASSROOM

Three common approaches to learning outside the classroom are:

Field Teaching

This is the traditional approach to teaching and learning outside the classroom. It involves taking students to a field location and delivering a mini-lecture from which students are expected to take notes. Little opportunity exists for student input and reaction. When done well, this approach can involve students in the careful observation and description of a scene or activity and in suggesting possible explanations based on previously acquired information.

This approach is useful if students are inexperienced in making their own observations or if they lack confidence in their ability to solve problems. This approach provides a structured way for them to find their own examples as an integral part of the learning experience.

Field Research

This approach represents an inductive approach to learning. It involves observation, description and explanation but with a problem solving focus. Students often use techniques similar to those used in historical enquiry, geographical research or scientific explanation. This is the inductive approach to fieldwork.

Guided Field Research

Guided Field Research is a synthesis of Field Teaching and Field Research. It combines the teacher guidance and structure of Field Teaching with the independent research focus of Field Research. Guided Field Research is an adapted form of field research for young students or students inexperienced in learning outdoors.

METHODS OF LEARNING OUTSIDE THE CLASSROOM/SCHOOL

There are many ways to make learning extend outside the classroom:

Field Trips Method

Field trips can take a variety of forms that meet a variety of needs and can enhance deep, active learning. Along with the engagement with concepts that is required by these experiences, the student bonding that occurs on field trips enhances the learning experience and creates a learning community as students continue onward in a discipline. Teaching in the field also gives teachers the opportunity to get to know their students in greater depth in terms of how the students see the world differently than the instructor. This insight into student' world-view can help the instructor to better communicate the concepts of the course.

Service Learning and Community Engagement Method

One way to escape the confines of the classroom and to afford students opportunities to grow is to encourage students to learn from and to serve the surrounding community. In its simplest form, this may involve field trips into a community where students will have occasions to have discussions with community members or local experts on an issue related to course content. Even greater learning potentials and community benefits rest in more intensive forms of community engagement in the form of service learning projects. These projects, typically designed by both faculty and community partners, allow for students to learn in highly effective ways while helping a community address its needs. In all of these experiences, student growth can be extensive, whether it is through improved critical thinking and problem solving skills, greater personal efficacy and leadership development, or enhanced social responsibility and career opportunities.

Models of Community Engagement Teaching

What does community engaged teaching look like in practice? There are many variations and each have their usefulness for different applications. According to Kerissa Heffernan, there are six general models.

1. Discipline-Based Model: In this model, students are expected to have a presence in the community throughout the semester and reflect on their experiences regularly. In these reflections, they use course content as a basis for their analysis and understanding of the key theoretical, methodological and applied issues at hand.

2. Problem-Based Model: Students relate to the community much as "consultants" working for a "client." Students work with community members to understand a particular community problem or need. This model presumes that the students have or will develop capacities with which to help communities solve a problem. For example, architecture students might design a park; business students might develop a web site; botany students might identify non-native plants and suggest eradication methods.

3. Capstone Course Model: These courses are generally designed for majors and minors in a given discipline and are offered almost exclusively to students in their final year. Capstone courses ask students to draw upon the knowledge they have obtained throughout their course work and combine it with relevant service work in the community. The goal of capstone courses is usually either exploring a new topic or synthesizing students' understanding of their discipline.

4. Service Internship Model: This approach asks students to work as many as 10 to 20 hours a week in a community setting. As in traditional internships, students are charged with producing a body of work that is of value to the community or site. However, unlike traditional internships, service internships have on-going faculty-guided reflection to challenge the students to analyze their new experiences using discipline-based theories. Service internships focus on reciprocity: the idea that the community and the student benefit equally from the experience.

5. Action Research Model: Community-based action research is similar to an independent study option for the student who is highly experienced in community work. This approach can be effective with small classes or groups of students. In this model, students work closely with faculty members to learn research methodology while serving as advocates for communities. This model assumes that students are or can be trained to be competent in time management and can negotiate diverse communities.

6. Directed Study Additional/Extra Credit Model: Students can register for up to three additional/extra credits in a course by making special arrangements with the instructor to complete an added community-based project. The course instructor serves as the advisor for the directed study option. Such arrangements require departmental approval and formal student registration.

7. Action Research Projects: This type of class involves students in research within the community. The results of the research are communicated to the agency so that it can be used to address community needs. Action research and participatory action research take a significant amount of time to build relationships of trust in the community and identify common research agendas; however, community research projects can support the ongoing research of faculty. Extending this type of research beyond the confines of a semester may be best for all involved.

8. Disciplinary Capstone Projects: Community engagement is an excellent way to build upon students' cumulative knowledge in a specific discipline and to demonstrate the integration of that knowledge with real life issues. Upper class students can explore ways their disciplinary expertise and competencies translate into addressing community needs. Other community-based classes within the department can prepare the student for this more extensive community-based class.

9. Multiple Course Projects: Community engagement projects with one or more partners may span different courses in the same semester or multiple courses over a year or longer. These projects must be broad enough to meet the learning goals of multiple courses over time, and because of this they may have a cumulative impact on both student learning and community development that is robust. Such projects may be particularly suited to course clusters or learning communities within or across disciplines, or course sequences, e.g., within a major that build student capacity towards advanced learning and community action goals.

Study Abroad Method

There are several models for study-abroad programmes. In some, participants enroll in foreign universities as visiting, non-matriculated students. In other programmes, the sending institution retains more control over the curriculum, duration, faculty selection and experience. Increasingly, schools are internationalizing their curriculum by offering short-term, faculty-led, study abroad programmes.

Technology Outside the Classroom Method

Today's smart phones and tablet devices (iPads and such) make it relatively easy for students to bring digital technology with them when they leave the classroom. Once in the field, students can use mobile devices—including ones they already own—to engage in learning activities. Below are some examples to help a student to start thinking about how to use technology outside the classroom.

Place-Based Learning Method

Places have both natural and cultural histories, which therefore lend themselves to examination by all disciplines. Field experiences and research are at the core of many of the natural and social sciences. The sciences have something to teach the humanities because field experiences are such a core component of their methodology. In the humanities field, experiences might be working in archives, collecting oral histories, performing one's art for a public audience, but it could also include visiting important historical sites and place-based experiences including using places for inspiration.

PLANNING FOR LEARNING OUTSIDE THE CLASSROOM

Generally there are three stages to effective learning outside the classroom:

- Preparation in class (pre-field stage);
- The fieldwork itself (field stage); and
- Follow-up in class (post-field stage).

A key step in planning effective learning outside the classroom is identifying the tasks to be completed at above three stages of the learning process. The following points should be remembered:

- List the things that the students would have to know before the work outside the classroom began.
- List the skills that the students would have used in their work outside the classroom.
- What follow-up activities were done in class?

PREPARATION OF LEARNING OUTSIDE THE CLASSROOM

Taking students outside the school grounds involves a wide range of preparatory administrative, safety and legal responsibilities as well as educational plans. These preparatory tasks include:

- Familiarize yourself with the appropriate school and system policies for conducting learning experiences beyond the school grounds.
- Pre-visit the site(s).
- Develop clear objectives for the study.
- Decide how you can build on previous learning experiences.

- Plan pre-field study learning experiences and prepare students to see fieldwork as active learning.
- Prepare fieldwork activities and resources.
- Decide how much time is required for the tasks and for travel to and from the site.
- Identify appropriate student/adult ratio. Parents and other community helpers may need to be invited and briefed to assist teachers with supervision.
- Prepare background information for other staff and parent/community helpers.
- Be aware of any possible distractions to the students at the site.
- Identify all possible risks and manage them appropriately, i.e. think through possible risks and how you will address them.
- Organize the following:
  - ➢ Consent form for parents
  - ➢ Food requirements
  - ➢ Permission to visit the site
  - ➢ Toilet facilities
  - ➢ Finance
  - ➢ Departure and arrival times
  - ➢ Transportation
  - ➢ Insurance issues
  - ➢ Clothing and equipment

12
Understanding Teaching

Teaching is an important part of the process of education. Its special function is to impart knowledge, develop understanding and skill. Teaching is usually associated with 3 R's i.e. Reading, Writing and Arithmetic—imparting knowledge of school subjects. Education, on the other hand, has a wider connotation in terms of 7 R's i.e. Reading, Writing, Arithmetic (Denoting school subjects) and Rights, Responsibilities, Relationships and Recreation (new requirements and ideals of democratic set up). In teaching, we limit our outlook, omitting those more important means of education which are involved in the school as a systematically organized social community, including its tone or general moral atmosphere, its government and discipline, and that potent influence—the personality of the teacher. James Welton thinks, *"We treat of teaching by itself, because it is an aspect of school life which can be singled out in thought, though it cannot be separated, in reality, from the whole of which it forms a part and because it covers a fairly consistent body of doctrine. It is true that the value and success of all school teaching depends on those wider and deeper elements of school life—tone, discipline, etc.—which are omitting But, it is also true that whilst the latter may be excellent, the former may be of poor quality."*

MEANING OF TEACHING

Teaching is a relationship which is established among three focal points in education—the teacher, the student and the subject matter. Teaching is the process by which the teacher brings the student and the subject matter together. The teacher and the taught are active, the former in teaching and the latter in learning. Modern teaching is not a mechanical process. It is exacting and intricate as well. Teaching is not *'telling and testing'*. Teaching is the complex art of guiding students through a variety of selected experiences towards the attainment of appropriate teaching-learning goals.

TEACHING AS A TRI-POLAR PROCESS

Teaching is a tri-polar process involving the source of teaching (human and material), students and set of activities designed and manipulated primarily to bring suitable changes in the behaviour of the students.

DEFINITIONS OF TEACHING

Some important definitions of teaching are as follows:

1. *Albert Einstein* (A Swiss Physicist: 1879—1950) – "The supreme art of teaching is to awaken joy in creative expression and knowledge."

2. *American Educational Research Association* Commission in 'Handbook of Research on Teaching' (1962)—"Teaching is a form of interpersonal influence aimed at changing the behaviour potential of another person."

3. *Amidon and Hunter* (1967)—"Teaching is an interactive process, primarily involving classroom talk, which takes place between teacher and pupils and occurs during certain definable activities."

4. *Anatole France* (French Novelist: 1844-1924)—"The whole art of teaching is only the art of awakening the natural curiosity of young minds for the purpose of satisfying it afterwards."

5. *B.O. Smith* (1963)—"Teaching is a system of actions involving an agent, an end in view, and a situation including two sets of factors—those over which the agent has no control (class size, size of classroom, physical characteristics of pupils etc.) and those that he can be modify (ways of asking questions, almost instruction and way of structuring information or ideas gleaned.)"

6. *Burton*—"Teaching is the stimulation, guidance, direction and encouragement of learning."

7. *Clarke* (1970), "Teaching refers to activities that are designed and performed to produce change in student (pupil) behaviour."

8. *Floyd Well*, "Children are notoriously curious about everything except the things people want them to know. It then remains for us to refrain from forcing any kind of knowledge upon them and they will be curious about everything."

9. *Galileo* (Italian Astronomer (1564—1642), "You cannot teach a man anything, you can only help him to find it himself."

10. *H.C. Morrison* (1934), "Teaching is an intimate contact between a more mature personality and less mature one which is designed to further the education of the latter.

11. *Israel Sheffler*: Teaching may be characterised as an activity aimed at the achievement of learning, and practised in such a manner as to respect the student's intellectual integrity and capacity for independent judgment."

12. *John Dewey* (1859-1952), "One might as well say he has sold when no one has bought, as to say he has taught when no one has learned."

13. Teaching has been defined by *Wells, G.* (1982) as "cluster of activities that are noted about teachers such as explaining, deducing, questioning, motivating, taking attendance, keeping record of works, students' progress and students' background information. The range of professional duties performed by teachers is wide and extensive. At the heart of a teacher's role is the promotion of learning for all pupils."

14. *John Dewey*, "Teaching is a system of action involving an agent, an end in view and a situation including two sets of factors—those over which the agent has no control (class size, size of classroom, physical characteristics of pupils etc.) and those that he can modify such as ways of asking question about instructions and ways of structuring information or ideas gleaned."

15. *John Brubacher* (1939), "Teaching is an arrangement and manipulation of a situation in which there are gaps and obstructions which an individual will seek to overcome and from which he will learn in the course of doing so."

16. *John Chapman*, "The gift of teaching is a peculiar talent, and it implies a need and craving in the teacher himself."

17. *Joyce and Well* (1972), "Teaching is a process by which teacher and students create a shared environment including set of values and beliefs (agreement about what is improvement) which in turn colour their view of reality."

18. *J. Welton*, "To know where the pupils are and where they should try to be, are the first two essentials of good teaching."

19. *Michael Oakeshort*, "Teaching is two-fold activity of communicating information and communicating judgement."

20. *N.L. Gage* (1962), "Teaching is a form of interpersonal influence aimed at changing the behaviour potential of another personnel."

21. *Ned. A. Flanders*, "Teaching is an interaction process. Interaction means participation of both teacher and students and both are benefitted by this. This interaction takes place for achieving desired objectives."

22. *Paul Goodman*, "A good teacher feels his way, looking for response."

23. *Thomas P. Green* (1971), "Teaching is the task of a teacher which is performed for the development of a child."

24. *W.R. Ryburn*, "Teaching includes the training of emotions of the child. It is one of the means of giving right feeling to the children."

25. *William Lyon*, "In my mind teaching is not merely a life work, a profession, an occupation, a struggle. It is a passion. I love to teach, as a painter loves to paint, as a musician loves to play, as a singer loves to sing, as a strongman rejoices to run a race."

26. *Yoakm and Simpson*, "Teaching is a means whereby society trains the young in a selected environment as quickly as possible to adjust themselves to the world in which they live."

In the type of teaching as mentioned by Morrison, teaching is reduced to what the teacher does. There is interaction but the flow of instruction is from the teacher. In this type of teaching, the learners may become passive listeners. Brubacher's definition of teaching assigns more places to the learner. This approach tends to be child or learner-centered. B.O. Smith seems to be more pragmatic in his approach to teaching. He accepts certain limitations of the learner in the teaching-learning process.

OBJECTIVES OF TEACHING

Teaching is a continuous process and it is a purposeful process. It lacks entity in the absence of objective. Hence, objectives are essential for a successful teaching process. Some main objectives of teaching are as follows:

- The main objective of teaching is helping the pupils so that they can understand the realities properly and may adjust in a better way.
- Enabling the pupils to establish the contact with truth and to take the decisions by teaching.
- Another objective of the teaching is that it should make a pupil the best worker and the best thinker.
- There is another objective of teaching. It is to help one or the other everyday

so that the new experiences are gained and that pupil may perform some constructive task.

NATURE OF TEACHING

The main characteristics of teaching are listed below:

- Teaching is a tri-polar process.
- Teaching is an interactive process.
- Teaching is an art as well as a science.
- Teaching is both formal and informal—inside the class and outside the class.
- Teaching is a conscious as well as an unconscious process.
- Teaching takes place in some social set up.
- Teaching is dynamic. It is related to time and place.
- Teaching is dominated by the communication skills.
- Teaching is task oriented.
- Teaching is telling, showing and doing.
- Teaching is a face to face encounter.
- Teaching is a system of actions which are varied in form and are related to content and pupil behaviour.
- Teaching facilities learning.
- Teaching is observable through teacher-behaviour or public-teacher action.
- Teaching is therapy of learners.
- Teaching is encouraging, expressing, balancing and harmonising learning.
- Teaching is measurable and quantifiable by observational techniques.
- Teaching is continuum form training to indoctrination.
- Teaching is modifiable by the use of mechanism of feed-back devices.
- Teaching is helping the child to respond to his environment.
- Teaching is stimulating the child.
- Teaching is training the emotions of the child.
- Teaching is guiding the child.
- Teaching is amenable to scientific observation and analysis.
- Teaching is a profession in which a teacher instructs and educates.
- Teaching can be analysed in the following ways:
  - ➢ Types of teacher-activity.
  - ➢ Types of educational objectives.
  - ➢ Types of learning conditions or structure.
  - ➢ Types of learning components.
  - ➢ Types of pupil-activity.

IMPORTANT ASPECTS OF TEACHING

A review of the definitions given above points to us the significance of the following aspects of teaching:

Who is to Teach?: A teacher is to teach. He should, therefore, present a good model of teaching.

Whom to Teach?: A child is to be taught. Therefore, while teaching, his abilities and interests must be taken care of. He should be kept active.

Why to Teach?: Teaching is not for storing information but to enabling the child to develop his various faculties.

What to Teach?: Those experiences and activities are to be provided which enable the learner acquire desirable knowledge, skills and attitudes.

How to Teach?: This implies that the teacher must be well versed in the use of teaching technology.

When to Teach?: Teaching situations should be such as they develop motivation in the students to learn.

Where to Teach?: Classroom, library, laboratory, workshops and play-ground etc, are the various places to carry on teaching. Of course, the relative importance of each depends on the type of activity of experience to be provided to the learner.

FUNCTIONS OF TEACHING

The main functions of teaching are as follows:

- Creating learning situations.
- Motivating the child to learn.
- Arranging for conditions which assist in the growth and development of the child's mind and body.
- Utilizing the initiative and play urges of the children to facilitate learning.
- Turning the children into creative beings.
- Inspiring children with the nobility of thoughts, feelings and actions.
- Giving information and explaining it.
- Diagnosing learning problems.
- Making curricular material.
- Evaluating, recording and reporting.

WHAT IS EFFECTIVE TEACHING?

Effective teaching is the teaching that successfully achieves the learning objectives by the pupils as identified by the teacher. The most effective teaching is that which results in the most effective learning. In addition, the learning is a process not the product, it involves all those experiences and training through teaching of an individual, which helps to change the behaviour and prepares to take necessary adjustment and adaptation in changed situation. There are essentially two simple elements to effective teaching:

- The teacher must have a clear idea of what learning is to be nurtured
- The teacher sets up and provides a learning experience that enables this to happen.

The root of effective teaching is evolved in the following tenets:

- Pupils learn best in a positive and nurturing environment established by teachers who believe that every pupil is capable of learning.
- All pupils have areas of strengths and interests that can be useful in advancing pupil learning. Effective teachers establish an instructional environment that will draw on these strengths.
- Teachers take into account the *whole pupil*; in other words, they attend to the cognitive, affective, social, and physical dimensions when developing an instructional programme.

- Active engagement and interaction facilitate pupil learning.
- New learning is built upon previously learned information. Learning is enhanced when prior knowledge and cultural and social experiences are valued, acknowledged and leveraged throughout the curriculum.
- Pupil learning is both individually and socially constructed; it is influenced by cultural, familial and social context.
- Meaningful assessment is both formative and summative; it relies on multiple measures, including informal observations.

Characteristics of Teaching

The main characteristics of teaching are as follows:

Teaching is an Interactive Process: One of the main characteristics of good teaching is that it should be interactive process. It is with the help of this interaction that the learners too become active in any learning process. We attain and achieve specific purposes and objectives that may be the academic growth of the learner, his physical improvement and making him economically sound, so that he may resist and exist well in the present conditions of life due to the blessings of proper interaction.

Teaching is both Formal and Informal: Another characteristic feature of teaching is that it may occur formally or informally. Formal means where we have an organized system with a definite purpose. It is planned, systematic, definite and deliberate. Informal system means unorganized system and it is unplanned, unsystematic, incidental and indefinite. For example, in the classroom, the teacher and the students meet in a formal way and teaching takes place. Outside the classroom also, the teacher and the students meet where teaching does take place, which is informal teaching. Both formal and informal ways helps us in achieving the desired goals.

Teaching is both Art as well Science: Teaching is both art as well as science. Silverman (1966) explains it in these words, *"To be sure—teaching like the practice of medicine—is very much an art, which is to say, it calls for exercise of talent and creativity. But like medicine, it is also a science, for it involves a repertoire of techniques, procedures and skills that can be systematically studied, described and improved. A good teacher, like a great doctor is one who adds creativity and inspiration to the basic repertoire."* Teaching is not everybody`s cup of tea. It is an art, which is favourite of the selected few. As Rabinder Nath Tagore has said, *"Teacher can never teach unless he is learning himself"*, so it is the profession which requires blood, sweat and tears. For those, it is not profession but a mission and have craze for it.

Teaching is Not One Sided: Any teaching, whether, formal or informal in which only the teacher remains active and learners simply silent spectators is not good teaching at all. In autocratic system of teaching, the teacher is the only leader of the group. No one can criticize him, even if he disseminates wrong information. He only remains active and students indulge in day-dreaming. This type of teaching is not good because it does not give any opportunity to a learner to show his capacities, capabilities, interests etc. and the result is unsatisfactory i.e. all in vain. The main feature of good teaching is that in it both the teacher and the learner have to be fully active, face to face with each other and this interaction makes teaching-learning process an effective and successful one.

Teaching is Not an Independent Activity: Man is a social animal. He cannot survive in vacuum. He has to establish relationships with other members of his society in order to survive, to fulfill his needs etc. Teaching too is a social process. It takes place in some social set up, where the teacher aims at improving the behaviour of the individual or some social group. Good teaching always prepares the individuals to become cultured, socially acceptable, morally, intellectually, physically fit in order to render good service to whole humanity. In this process of an all round growth and development of the social beings, the teacher also comes out to be a far better individual with his knowledge updated and enriched.

Teaching is a Planned Activity: Good teaching is well planned and well prepared activity. It is organized in a systematic way. Before teaching takes place, a teacher prepares and plans his lesson in advance. He collects all information from different sources like books, journals, references etc. in order to make his teaching a successful one. A lot of thinking is done on it in advance, once teaching is started by the teacher in the classroom. He thinks of different methods, audio-visual aids, charts, maps etc. in order to make his teaching more and more effective. When he plans the lesson in advance, the teaching then goes on systematically and smoothly.

Teaching is Diagnostic and Remedial: Good teaching is diagnostic and remedial in the sense that the teacher first knows exactly the abilities, capacities and interests of his pupils. He knows the individual differences of the learners in order to select suitable teaching materials, methods, audio-visual aids, and academic environment to be involved in the teaching process. He uses the diagnostic technique in order to know the difficulties and problems of learners and then accordingly he suggests suitable remedial measures in order to remedy those difficulties.

Teaching is Dominated by Communication Skills: Good teaching depends on the communication skills. The better the communication, the better is the process of teaching. The learners of any class will receive anything from the sender, if they will be in a position to understand that. For example, if a teacher is teaching to class V students in Uttar Pradesh (UP), if he uses the Bengali language in order to disseminate information, the pupils will not gain anything because they do not understand the said language (Bangala) and should use mother tongue as medium of instructions.

Teaching is Worthy of Analysis and Interpretation: Good teaching can be observed, analyzed and assessed. The analysis and assessment may provide essential feedback for bringing desirable improvement in the process of teaching. The improvement can be brought about in the teacher, in the learner or in the teaching-learning process. For example, a new innovation in teacher training programme viz. microteaching is a technique through which we observe analyze and asses the teachers and their teaching through different skills and prepares them to become good and effective teachers.

Good Teaching is Democratic: Good teaching is always democratic in its attitude. It attempts to create a democratic environment in which every individual is respected in all matters. In this environment, every individual is entitled to equal rights with every other individual in the class and that he is subject to the same rules with respect to social equality as other pupil. No one is discriminated on the basis of caste, colour, creed or religion; everyone is given equal status according to good teaching.

Teaching Causes Motivation: The activity of teaching causes motivation that results into learning, for example when pupil-teachers go for practice teaching, it is the teaching which motivates those pupil-teachers in order to plan their lessons and during this planning, they themselves learn more and more about the content.

Teaching is Professional in Character: Teaching is an activity, which is carried out by professionals. Every activity requires a person who is professional. For example in medicine, a carpenter will not come out as successful because he has no knowledge of that specific field viz. medical profession. It requires only those who have already received training in this field. Same is the case with teaching profession. It demands those persons who are skilled and have gone through different teacher-training courses. This activity involves the teacher and the learner and as a result of it, there occurs development of both teachers and students.

PRINCIPLES OF TEACHING

Successful teaching necessitates that the teacher comes down to the level of the pupils and at the same time assists them in rising above it. To a great extent, the principles of teaching to be followed depend upon the age of the pupils, the subjects and topic of the lesson. However, there are certain general principles, which should underline the teaching of all subjects:

Principle of Activity

Children are active by nature and any process or method that is not based upon the student activity is not in accord with the progressive educational theories. Rousseau considers the child as a 'Hero' in the drama of education and therefore he must be allowed to play the dominant role. So, the first principle is to keep the class active.

Principle of Definite Goals or Objectives

Destination or goals of teaching-learning process must be clear to the teachers and students. Goals and objectives keep the teachers and students on the right track. Definiteness of goals helps in planning, executing and evaluating every step, phase or act of the teaching-learning process.

Principle of Child Centeredness

The entire teaching endeavour is for the child. Therefore, it is essential that teaching strategies should cater to the aptitude, interest and abilities of the students. In the drama of education, child should be assigned the role of 'hero'.

Principle of Individual Differences

No two children are alike. Teaching must cater to the individual differences of the children

Principle of Linking with Life

Teaching can never be performed in a vacuum. It is always in a social context. In the teaching of all the school subjects, examples from everyday life should be given their due place.

Principle of Correlation

Knowledge is one 'whole'. Various ideas and events are interrelated. There exist links among various subjects. Correlation of the present events can be made with the past. Similarly, future can be visualized on the basis of the present happenings or state of affairs. Gandhiji propounded his system of Basic education with correlation as its cornerstone—correlation with the craft, correlation with the physical environment and correlation with social environment.

Principle of Active Involvement and Participation of Students

Teaching-learning is a two-way process. Traditional teaching was almost teacher-centred. There was very little scope for the involvement of the students. The teacher taught and the students listened to him passively. The new teaching emphasizes that the students must actively participate in all the stages and steps of teaching-learning.

Principle of Cooperation

Classroom environment becomes lively when the teacher and the taught work in unison, helping each other in carrying out the task of teaching and learning. All the participants have the same common interest. Naturally, they must co-operate with teacher.

Principle of Remedial Teaching

All students do not learn with the same speed and accomplishment. Some lag behind and need extra coaching. The teacher has to find out where the fault lies and think for positive measures. He may have to arrange for remedial or compensatory or extra teaching for any particular group of students for removing their specific difficulties.

Principle of Creating Conducive Environment

Physical as well as social environment of the classroom plays a vital role in motivating the learners. Arrangement of light and furniture etc. should be properly attended to. There should be proper discipline and order. The teacher should be sympathetic but firm.

Principle of Planning

Planning determines the quality or success of any task. Planning in teaching involves the preparation of the lesson notes, provision of teaching aids and working out strategies to be adopted in the delivery of the lesson.

Principle of Effective Strategies

Teaching process to be effective must adopt proper means, strategies and tactics. A teaching strategy is a generalized plan for a lesson, which includes structure, desired learning behaviour in terms of goals of instruction and an outline of planned tactics necessary to implement the strategy.

Principle of Flexibility

Strategies should serve as guides for effective teaching. Strategies may have to be changed if the classroom situations, so warrant. Teaching is a complex task and a live phenomenon. The possibilities of alternation in planned strategies cannot be ruled out at the execution stage. A teacher must be quite imaginative and resourceful for adapting himself and his teaching of the requirements of the teaching-learning environment.

Principle of Variety

A variety of teaching aids and strategies should be adopted to motivate and sustain the interests of the students. Variety serves as great tonic for creating fresh environment and checking boredom and lethargy.

Following are some of the important principals of teaching:

- Principle of using the experience already acquired.
- Principle of knowledge and skills are of use in daily life.
- Principal of providing for individual differences.
- Principle of readiness.
- Principle of meaningfulness.
- Principle of defining specifically objectives of the lesson.
- Principle of following the psychological principles which have been developed by great educators. The important principles are:
  - Proceed from simple to complex.
  - Proceed from concrete to abstract.
  - Proceed from general to complex.
  - Proceed from known to unknown.
  - Proceed from induction to deduction or vice versa.
  - Arrange for frequent reinforcement.

TEACHING AS A COMPLEX TASK

Teaching results in learning. This 'teaching behaviour' when analyzed will explain the concepts of teaching and learning. The following components involved in the teaching task will reveal to you that teaching is a complex task:

Teaching is a System of Activities: Teaching is not just one activity but a series of logical activities like explaining, demonstrating, asking questions, defining, describing, classifying, answering, reacting, directing, giving pauses, praising, encouraging, and rebuking. These specific activities go into making the teaching activity.

Teaching is an Interaction of Elements: We know that teaching is a process that involves the elements, namely the teacher, the subject and the learner. Of the three mentioned, the teacher and the pupil being characteristically social, the entire process of teaching becomes social with the intention of bringing about learning.

Teaching is a Constant Shaping-up Process: Teaching is an interaction of elements. This being so, there is every possibility that this process of teaching has every scope of improvement with experience and efforts on the part of the teacher.

Teaching is Goal Oriented: Teaching is always with a purpose, the major one that of bringing about a desirable change in behaviour. You know that this change is effected due to learning. We could therefore logically conclude that teaching is goal-oriented, the goal being specific with reference to the needs and objectives of teaching-learning.

Teaching is an Influence Directed Activity: In a teaching-learning activity, there is an influence exerted by the teacher on the learner. It is only on very rare occasions that the learner influences the teacher. Thus you can conveniently conclude that teaching-learning activity is an influence-directional activity.

Teaching has a Logical and Linguistic Dimension: Teaching activities like defining, describing, classifying etc. are logical and at the same time possess a linguistic dimension. These two aspects namely logic and language are inseparable from the act of teaching. Language is the basis for all teaching interactions and without logic; a teacher cannot succeed in classifying, comparing or contrast. Teaching is thus logic and language based.

Teaching is a Family of Activities: Teaching is a conglomeration of activities like conditioning, indoctrinating, informing, training and instructing. The structure of teaching concept could be described by analyzing these activities. These activities are related to each other and there is a gradual transition from one to the next. Therefore, teaching can be said to be a family of activities that are interrelated.

Teaching is a Complex Skill: Teaching is a complex skill that has many sub-skills. These sub-skills are those that when analyzed and identified reveal the complexity of the skill of teaching.

The above points very well show that teaching is a complex activity involving the various elements, activities and components mentioned therein.

MAXIMS OF TEACHING

Every teacher wants to make maximum involvement and participation of the learners in the learning process. He sets the classroom in such a way that it becomes attractive for them. He adopts different methods, rules, principles etc. in order to make his lesson effective and purposeful. He uses general rule or formula and applies it to particular example in order to make teaching-learning process easy and up to the understandable level of students.

These settled principles, tenets, working rules or general truths through which teaching becomes interesting, easy and effective are called the maxims of teaching. They have universal significance. Every person who is expected to enter into the teaching profession has to familiarize himself with the maxims of teaching. Their knowledge helps him to proceed systematically.

The different maxims of teaching are briefly explained below. The teacher should always proceed keeping them in view.

From Known to Unknown

When a child enters into school, he possesses some knowledge and it is the duty of teacher to enlarge his previous knowledge. Whatever he possesses should be linked with the new knowledge. If we link new knowledge with the old knowledge, our teaching becomes clearer and more definite.

This maxim facilitates the learning process and economizes the efforts of the teacher and the taught. For example, in teaching English to the children, he is to teach the word 'water.' He reminds them the Kashmiri word 'Aab' which they already know and then tells them that in English we say 'water.' This helps the learners to understand things fully. Also that, the teaching becomes definite, clearer and more fruitful.

From Simple to Complex

The main objective of teaching for teacher and the learners is to learn something. In the process of teaching and learning, simple or easy things should be first presented to the students and gradually he should proceed towards complex or difficult things. The presentation of simple material makes the learners interested, confident and encouraged. As they will show interest towards simple material, gradually they become receptive to the complex matter. On the other hand, if complex matter is presented first, the learner becomes upset, feels bored and finds himself in a challenging situation. For example in Mathematics, we first present the idea +, –, x and then division.

From Concrete to Abstract

Concrete things are solid things and they can be visualized but abstract things are only imaginative things. The child understands more easily when taught through its senses and never forgets that material. On the other hand, if abstract things or ideas are presented, he is likely to forget it soon. As Frobel said, *"Our lessons ought to start in the concrete and end in the abstract"*. For example, when we teach the solar system, we first visualize the sun through our senses and give the concept of eight planets, galaxies, meteorites etc. Through this process, the learners understand the materials more easily. Some power of imagination also develops in them. But, if we reverse the situation, it will become difficult for learners to understand anything. Another example, when we teach counting to the students, we should first take the help of concrete objects like bread, stones etc. And then proceed to digits and numbers.

From Analysis to Synthesis

When we divide a thing into easy parts or separate elements in order to understand it easily, it is called analysis. It is the process which helps in understanding the hidden elements of a thing or the cause of some incident of behaviour. For instance, in order to tell about the structure or functions of heart, the parts of the heart are shown separately and knowledge of every part is given. After it, the students are made to understand the structure or system of working of the heart. In this way, even a very difficult thing can be easily understood. Synthesis is just opposite of analysis. All parts are shown as a whole. The process of analysis is easier than synthesis for understanding a thing. This process develops the analytical power of the students. It is the best method of starting the teaching process. For example, while teaching digestive system, we should first analyse the different parts of digestive system one-by-one and then give the synthesis view of it. Hence, a good teacher always proceeds from analysis to synthesis.

From Particular to General

A teacher should always proceed from particular to general statements. General facts, principles and ideas are difficult to understand and hence, the teacher should always first present particular things and then lead to general things. Suppose, the teacher is teaching continuous tense, while teaching English, he should first of all give few examples, and then on the basis of those make them generalize that this tense is used to denote an action that is going on at the time of speaking. Hence, a teacher should proceed from particular to general.

From Empirical to Rational

Empirical knowledge is that which is based on observation and experience and for which no reasoning is needed at all. It is concrete, particular and simple. We can feel and experience it. On the other hand, rational knowledge is based upon arguments and explanations. For example, suppose the students are to be taught that water boils on heating. They should first be made to heat the water and see it boiling. Then the teacher should explain that when water is heated, the molecules gain kinetic energy and there is thermal agitation of the molecules which make the water boils. This maxim is an extension of some of the previous maims, namely proceed from simple to complex, concrete to abstract and from particular to general.

From Induction to Deduction

The process of deriving general laws, rules or formulae from particular examples is called induction. If a statement is true in a special situation, it will also be true in other similar situations. It means drawing a conclusion from set of examples. For example, when hydrogen reacts with boron, it gives Boron hydride, when potassium reacts with hydrogen, it gives potassium hydride. Thus, we come to the conclusion that when all elements react with hydrogen they form hydrides. While using this process in teaching, a teacher has to present particular examples or experiences and tell about similarity of their attributes. Deduction is just opposite of induction. In it, we derive a certain particular conclusion from general laws, rules or principles. For example, in language teaching, before giving the definition of noun, the students are acquainted with the example of noun like Man, Chair, Delhi etc. and then they are led to general definition of noun. So, a good teacher always proceeds from induction and finishes at deduction.

From Psychological to Logical

Modern education gives more emphases on psychology of the child. The child's psychological development is of utmost important than any other thing. A teacher while teaching should follow this maxim viz. from psychological to logical. Psychological approach takes into consideration the pupil, his interests, abilities, aptitudes, development level, needs and reactions. The teacher should keep in mind the psychological selection of the subject matter to be presented before the pupils. Logical approach considers the arrangement of the chosen content into logical order and steps. For example, a teacher tells the story of a poem to students when they are not interested in reading. With this a teacher proceeds from psychological to logical sequence.

From Actual to Representative

First hand experiences make learning more vivid and efficient than to give them representative ones. A teacher while selecting the content for presentation should make all efforts possible to present it through actual, natural or real objects than from their improvised representative ones like pictures, models etc. For example, to teach about 'Golden Temple of Amritsar', a teacher should ideally visit the actual place which will make the learning more vivid and the pupils will retain it for a long time in spite of teaching through sketches, model or a picture. Representative forms should be used in the higher classes than in lower ones.

From Whole to Parts

This maxim is the offshoot of Gestalt theory of learning whose main emphasis was to perceive things or objects as whole and not in the form of parts. Whole is more understandable, motivating and effective than the parts. In teaching, the teacher should first give a synoptic view of lesson and then analyze it into different parts. For example, the teacher while teaching about the pollination in plants, should first take the flower and analyze it into different parts; give detailed information about each and every part like the sepals, petals, androceium, gynoceium etc. In this way, maximum learning is possible. It is actually the reverse of the maxim "analysis to synthesis".

From Definite to Indefinite

A teacher should always start from definite, because definiteness has its limited boundaries and jurisdiction than indefinite things. We always have confidence on definite and tested things. We learn easily indefinite things on the basis of definite things. Hence, a teacher while teaching any content should first present definite things, ideas and then students can learn indefinite thing easily. Definite things, definite rules of grammar help the learner to have good knowledge. Gradually, he can be taught about indefinite things.

DIFFERENCE BETWEEN TEACHING, LEARNING, INSTRUCTION, TRAINING AND CONDITIONING

In order to understand the real meaning of teaching, it is essential to understand the difference between (i) teaching, (ii) instruction, and (iii) learning. Hence, we are clarifying the differences in these three terms in the following lines:

Teaching

In teaching, an interaction occurs between the teacher and the pupils. As a result of which the pupils are diverted towards the objectives. In other words, the main element of teaching is the mutual relationship or the interaction between the teacher and the pupils that advances the pupils towards objectives.

Learning

Learning means—(a) activities, and (b) experience. Both teaching and instruction influence learning through various activities and experiences. Hence, the learning and teaching mean the modification of pupils' behaviour through activities and experiences.

Training

Training is concerned with a little higher level of teaching than conditioning. It helps in shaping conduct and teaching various skills. A worker may be trained to perform certain tasks requiring very specific skills. He may do a number of jobs on some machine skillfully without knowing its basic structure and operation, the utility of his output and similar other questions. While less intelligent or simple behaviour may be produced through training, the complicated behaviour requiring more intelligence need a higher mode of teaching.

Instruction

The instruction does not involve an interaction between the teacher and the pupil. Still the instruction can divert the pupils towards objectives. The main difference between teaching and instruction is that the teaching includes instruction but the instruction does not include teaching. Hence, the teaching is instruction but the instruction is not teaching. In spite of this, all the three cognitive, affective and psychomotor aspects of the pupils can be developed by teaching, while by instruction only cognitive aspect can be developed. Hence, no instruction can replace the teaching. In short, instruction is that process which diverts the pupils towards the objectives of cognitive aspects.

Conditioning

Conditioning is the lowest level or mode of teaching. A dog may be conditioned to lift his paw when it hears a bell. Similarly, many of the animals and human beings may be taught to respond to signals, alarms, signs and warnings through conditioning. Most of our desirable and undesirable behaviours and habits are the creation of the process of conditioning.

RELATIONSHIP BETWEEN TEACHING AND LEARNING

It is essential to establish the relationship between teaching and learning. The understanding of the relationship between the teaching and the learning requires the understanding of meaning of these two.

The meaning of learning can be explained by various definitions. According to Woodworth, *"The process of acquiring new knowledge and new responses is the process of learning."*

Crow & Crow have considered that the *"learning is the acquisition of habits, knowledge and attitude."*

J.P. Guilford has accepted learning as any change in behaviour as a result of behaviour.

Pavlov's view is that the learning is habit formation resulting from conditioning.

The main function of the teaching remains focused on learning. Whenever there is teaching, it will be followed by learning too. But B.O. Smith contradicts this view. According to him, it is not essential that the learning is induced by teaching. He considers both as different from each other. According to Smith, *"Teaching is a system of actions intended to produce learning"*.

Thomas Green has explained that learning cannot be possible without teaching, but without learning, teaching ispossible. Gates has also explained about learning that "It is modification of behaviour, through experiences and activity."

It is very much clearer from various definitions of learning that the modification of behaviour and formation of habits is called learning. Hence, a relationship of teaching and learning is clear from the meaning of learning.

13
Variables of Teaching

A good teaching has been explained as having a provision of learning experiences so that the teaching objectives may be achieved as a result of desired modifications in the behaviour of pupils. For this, the knowledge of various aspects and activities of teaching is necessary for a teacher. Hence, in this unit, by explaining the various aspects of teaching and variables therein, we are throwing light on various teaching activities in detail. John Brubacher rightly says: *"Teaching is an arrangement and manipulation of a situation in which there are gaps and obstructions which an individual will seek to overcome and from which he will learn in the course of doing so."*

MEANING OF VARIABLES

A variable has been defined as *'Any response or behaviour which can take different degrees'*. For example, effects of various amounts of study on school performance. A teaching process has three variables:

The Teacher: The first variable of teaching is 'the teacher'. The teacher is said to be an *'independent variable'*. The teaching organization, planning and its organization is carried on by the teacher.

The Pupil: The second variable of teaching-process is 'The pupil'. The pupil is considered as the *'dependent variable'* because the teaching has to be active in accordance with the planning, organization and presentation.

The Content and Teaching Methods: It is the third variable of the teaching. It has been termed as *'Intervening variable'*. Interaction between pupil and the teacher, teaching method and the nature of teaching material intervene in the responses of the pupils.

TYPES OF VARIABLES

The variables are mainly of three types which are as follows:

Independent Variable: An independent variable is that variable in which the experimenter can bring changes and that variable brings a change in the dependent variable. We can manage the independent variable according to our will.

Dependent Variable: The dependent variable is that variable which acquires changes as a result of changes occurred in some other dependent variable.

Intervening Variable: A variable located or active in between an independent and a dependent variable is an intervening variable. For Example, in the teaching process, the teacher is an independent variable, the pupil is a dependent variable and the methods to be used in teaching, motivation techniques, contents etc. are all examples of intervening variables.

FUNCTIONS OF VARIABLES

In the teaching process, the following are the functions of variables:

Diagnostic Function

The diagnostic function is the first aspect of the process. In this, the teacher decides about the pupil's entering-behaviour on the basis of which the teaching objective can be achieved. Hence, the teacher considers only two things under the diagnostic function. These are: (i) the pupil, and (ii) the content.

He, first of all, determines the previous knowledge or entering behaviour of the pupil. Then, he arranges the elements of the contents to be taught in a sequence by analyzing them logically so that the teaching activity may be performed in a psychological sequence. In this way, the diagnostic function is the foundation of the remedial aspect of the teaching.

This function is performed in accordance with the pre-active phase. In this function, the teacher takes decisions considering the following variables:

Analysis of Teaching Problem: The first variable of diagnostic aspect is the analysis of the teaching problem. Hence, the teacher should decide about the entering behaviour of the pupils while giving a thought to the problem related to that content with far-sightedness and depth which is to be studied by the pupils. It is also to be decided whether that content is according to their capacity or not. In other words, the teacher should take the decision concerning the pupils and the content so that the desired objectives may be attained. It should be kept in mind that the decision taken by the teacher as stated proves fruitful for the remedial aspect or the inter-active phase of the teaching.

Determining the Entering Behaviour of Student: The second variable of the diagnostic aspect is to determine clearly the entering behaviours of the pupils. After this, the teacher should present the new knowledge to the pupils. Its advantages are that after presenting the new knowledge, the information of changes in the behaviour of the pupils will be easy to acquire. Hence, for determining the entering behaviours of the pupils, the teacher should prepare and use such evaluative question, keeping in view the contents, which should be reliable and valid.

Individual Differences: The third variable of the diagnostic aspect is the consideration of individual differences of the pupils. The principle of individual differences means that every pupil has different interests, attitudes, capacities, abilities and needs. Keeping in view the individual differences of the pupils, the teacher should perform the teaching task at the average level on one hand, and should guide sympathetically the talented and backward pupils on the other hand, which can lead the teaching to the attainment of the objectives with a success.

Task Analysis: The fourth variable of diagnostic aspect is the task analysis. The teacher should analyze carefully the learning activities related to the contents. Its reason is that the success or the failure of the lesson depends upon the task-analysis. The readers are requested to study the task analysis chapter in this book.

Analysis of Content in view of Types of Learning: The last variable of the diagnostic aspect is the analysis of the content with regard to the type of learning. The teacher should know the nature of learning. Also, he should know the tactics and principles to be used in the various situations so that teaching may become easy, clear, effective, understandable and scientific.

Remedial Function

In the remedial aspects, an effort is made to bring the desired changes in the behaviours of the pupils. Hence, the teacher should make decision regarding the use of teaching methods, strategies and tactics and mutual relationships between various variables, keeping in view the individual differences of the pupils. In this aspect, assistance must be sought for action research in order to solve the various problems which arise during the teaching. Thus, in remedial aspect, the teacher should manage the teaching variables in such a way that the maximum teaching objectives are attained by deciding the teaching techniques and tactics. This aspect has the following variables:

Selection of Teaching Strategies and Tactics: The first variable of teaching strategies and tactics is their selection. It should be remembered that the success of teaching and learning depends upon the appropriate selection and use of teaching strategies and tactics. The teacher should perform this important function in accordance with his ability and experience at the time of planning the teaching, so that the teaching objectives may be achieved while presenting the content, using the selected strategies and tactics and by making the lesson easy and clear.

Arrangement of Feedback Devices: The second important variable of diagnostic aspect is the arrangement of feedback devices. Here, it is essential to state that the feedback is the soul of successful teaching. Its reason is that the feedback provides reinforcement to the pupils which in turn, provides motivation and encouragement for learning. Hence, while teaching, the teacher should provide necessary feedback by using praise and blame techniques for motivating and encouraging the pupils so that the teaching objectives may be achieved by producing maximum learning experiences and desired behavioural changes in the pupils.

Evaluative Function

The evaluation is the third important variable of teaching. In this aspect, the diagnostic aspect is evaluated. It should be remembered that the criterion of evaluation is the achievement of the objectives. If the objectives are achieved, the remedy by the teacher is correct, otherwise it is defective.

In other words, if the teaching objectives are not achieved, the teacher should not blame pupils for his failure. He should change the variables of the diagnostic aspect so that the objectives may be achieved. It should be remembered that this aspect is in accordance with the post-active phase. This aspect has the following important variables:

Construction of Criterion Test: The first variable of evaluation aspect is the construction of criterion test which provides clear information regarding the changes brought in the behaviour of the pupil by remedial teaching. The main characteristic of the criterion test is its objectivity. In other words, this test is reliable and valid. Its aim is to evaluate the determined objectives. Hence, the teacher should construct the criterion test with great care.

Evaluation of Behavioural Changes: The second variable of the evaluation aspect is the evaluation of pupils' behavioural changes. The teacher should perform this function on the basis of criterion test.

Diagnostic Phase: The last variable of evaluation aspect is the diagnostic phase. This diagnostic phase means to know by evaluation, the extent of the success of teaching. If it is not successful, then there is need to think about the type of modification that may be required. The diagnostic phase means to know the evaluation, the extent to which the teaching objectives have been achieved as a result of using the methods or strategies or tactics at the time of teaching.

If the teaching objectives have not been achieved as a result of their use, then the planning organization, leading and controlling of the teaching process should be repeated.

Diagnostic Function	*Remedial Function*	*Evaluative Function*
Analysis of Teaching problem.	Selection of teaching Strategies and Tactics.	Construction of Criterion test.
Determining Entering behaviour of pupils.	Arranging feedback devices.	Evaluation of Behavioural changes.
Individual differences.		
Analysis of Task-elements		Diagnostic phase
Analysis of Content		

14
Phases of Teaching

Teaching is quite a complex process designed in a social setup. Therefore, in order to make it a successful mission and up to the understandable level of students. It needs to be designed in such a way that it becomes effective. It has to be done in systematic steps. The different steps constituting the teaching process are called the phases or operations or stages of teaching. Jackson divides the teaching into three stages or phases as:

- Pre- active or planning phase of teaching
- Interactive or implementation phase of teaching
- Post active or evaluative phase of teaching

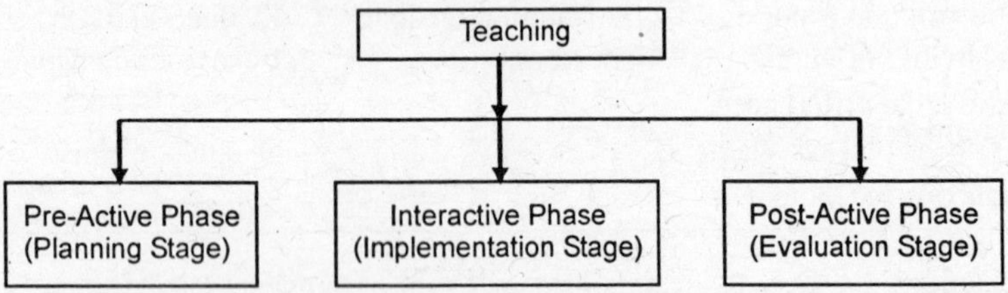

Figutre 14.1: Phases of Teaching

Now we will discuss these steps one by one as given below:

PRE-ACTIVE PHASE OF TEACHING

It is also called as planning stage or phase of teaching. The whole planning regarding the lesson is carried out in this phase. It includes all those activities, which a teacher performs before classroom teaching in order to make his lesson more easy and effective. At this stage, he plans the lesson, how it should be introduced, how to motivate the learners, which method and technique should be used. Different audio-visual materials too are taken into consideration. The whole planning is done only to make the learning material easy and understandable. The following activities are included in this stage of teaching:

Formulation of the Objectives

At first, the teacher determines (formulates) the teaching objectives, which he has to achieve in the form of behavioural changes of the students. These objectives serve as an instrument through which he brings change in the students' entering behaviour. He divides these objectives into two type viz. entering behaviour and the terminal behaviour of the students.

Decision Making about the Subject Content

When the teacher fixes the objectives, he makes decision about the content, which he has to present before the pupils and through which he desires to bring change in their behaviours. When the teacher selects the content for presentation before students, he keeps in mind the following important points:

- Need of the curriculum prescribed for the students.
- The entering behaviour of the students.
- The terminal behaviour of the students.
- Level of motivation that will be effective for the students.
- Different methods and techniques suitable to content.

Sequencing of Content for Presentation

When the teacher chooses the content which he has to present before students, he arranges the content in to logical and psychological sequence, so that the learners comprehend the subject-matter easily.

Decision about Strategies of Teaching

After the teacher has made a logical and psychological sequence of the content material, he decides about the suitable teaching methods, proper strategies and tactics in order to make the content easy and reachable to their brains. He selects the different methods and strategies keeping in view the level of students and objectives of teaching.

Distribution of Teaching Strategies

The only decision about the different strategies and tactics for presenting the content to the students is not sufficient. The teacher has also to decide how and when he needs to make use of these strategies during the classroom teaching. For example, if the teacher has to present before the students on the content *functions of heart*, he has to decide when and where he will show the model of the heart, its different parts and how they function.

INTERACTIVE PHASE OF TEACHING

All those activities which a teacher carries over right from entering the classroom till the presentation of the content are included under this phase. It is the implementation of pre-active phase of teaching. Pre-active stage acts as its base where everything is planned, so that during presentation, the teacher accomplishes his task. According to P. Jackson, *"The teacher provides pupils verbal stimulation of various kinds, makes explanations, ask questions, listens to students' responses and provides guidance."* It is the stage of explanations of technical terms, removing of doubts and gaining of new information. The following activities are included in the inter-active phase of teaching:

Sizing up of the Class

After planning the whole lesson, the teacher now enters into the classroom. As he enters, he perceives the size of the class. He does this activity in a few seconds. He analyses the chemistry of the whole classroom. He comes to know the pupils who can help him in his teaching and those who can create problem for him. In the same way, the pupils perceive the personality of the teacher in a moment. Hence, the teacher should possess all those qualities, which are necessary for this profession.

Diagnosis of Learners

When the teacher perceives the class size, he immediately checks the worth of pupils by means of different techniques. He tries to diagnose the achievement levels of pupils by assessing their abilities, aptitudes, interests and academic background.

Action and Reaction (Achievement)

After diagnosing the learners, the teacher initiates to present his content before the students. As soon as he presents the content material, two types of activities occur in this process viz. initiation and response. Both these activities occur between the teacher and the students. Both verbal and nonverbal interaction occurs during this sub-stage. In other words, when the teacher performs some activities, the pupils react to those actions or when pupils perform some activities, the teacher reacts to those activities and thus the interaction goes on in the teaching-learning process. For example, when a teacher starts delivering his lecture, he initiates the process and when students respond either in the form of questions, which arise in the form of doubts or in the form of technical terms not explained in the form of response, it creates an interaction in the classroom. We can present this interaction of the teaching by the following diagram:

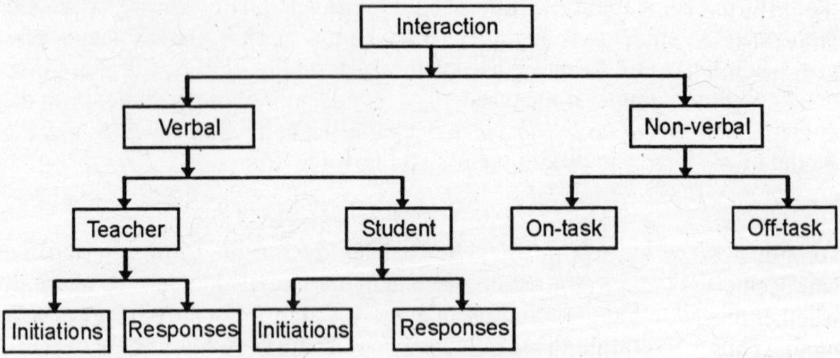

Figure 14.2: Interaction of the Teaching

The teacher performs the following activities in order to analyze the nature of verbal and non-verbal activities of this interaction:

Selection of Stimuli

The presentation of new knowledge before the students is the motto of teaching. The presentation of new knowledge acts as stimuli and can be verbal or non-verbal. The teacher should present those stimuli, which will be effective to create desirable situations for the teaching process and control the undesirable stimuli only for effectiveness of this process.

Presentation of Stimuli

When the teacher selects the stimuli for presentation before the students, he should present those one's which will create an interest among learners towards learning. During such presentation of stimuli, the teacher keeps in mind how these stimuli should be presented, so that proper motivation may be provided to them. The presentation should also be relevant for objectives and should be presented in logical and psychological sequence, so that proper rapport develops between teacher and pupils. In other words, teacher has to keep in mind the form, context and order of the stimuli.

Reinforcement

When the teacher presents the stimuli (content materials) in the form of verbal and non-verbal cues, he has to use that mechanism through which the students rate of responds increases or he has to use reinforcement. Reinforcement is a condition, which increases the possibility of occurrence of a particular response. It is two types viz. positive and negative reinforcement. The teacher sometimes uses positive and other times negative reinforcement in order to strengthen their rate of responding, modifying or correcting the response.

Deployment of Strategies

At the time of interaction, which goes on between the teacher and the pupils, the teacher produces such activities and conditions by the reinforcement strategies, which affect the activities of the pupils. As soon as the teaching process starts, he uses verbal and non-verbal behaviours, so that the content should be impressive and effective. In the deployment of the teaching strategies, three areas should be considered viz. presentation of subject matter, levels of learning and level of learners, so that proper interaction occurs between them.

POST-ACTIVE OR EVALUATION PHASE OF TEACHING

As the inter-active stage of teaching sums up, the teacher checks whether the presentation of content takes the form of success and effectiveness. He checks the effectiveness by means of different techniques like asking some questions verbally or in written form. He measures their behaviours, whether a change had occurred in their terminal behaviour or not. He evaluates them to check whether the said objectives formulated at planning stage have been achieved or not. Thus, evaluation stage includes all those activities, which can evaluate the achievements and attainment of the pupils. It includes the following activities:

Defining the Exact Dimensions of Changes Caused by Teaching: As the teaching task sums up, teacher now tries to see the changes occurred in the behaviour of the learners through teaching. He defines exactly the changes that occurred in the dimensions of behaviour, which is called criterion behaviour. He compares the entering behaviour of pupils with the terminating behaviour. If he notices that the desired changes had occurred in the behaviour of maximum number of students, he concludes that the different teaching strategies and tactics have worked effectively with the help of which teaching objectives have been achieved.

Selecting Appropriate Testing Devices and Techniques: The teacher selects the different testing devices and techniques in order to measure the behavioural changes of the students. He selects those techniques, which are reliable and valid.

Changing the Strategies in terms of Evidence Gathered: The teacher gathers evidence in support of different techniques, instructional procedures, methods and the strategies used during inter-active phase of teaching. This evidence serves as the best tool to know whether modifications have occurred in the students' behaviour and how successfully the objectives have been achieved. These evidences not only check the progress of students but also of teacher, whether he diagnosed the learners correctly or he has to bring changes in the different strategies and tactics adopted by him.

15
Levels of Teaching

Teaching is a purposeful process which has close relationship with learning. Therefore, in the modern age, teaching-learning are accepted as one concept. Remember that the content has its own nature by which various learning levels can be affected with the acquisition of various teaching objectives. It is to be observed that a teacher can present the content at three levels, from thoughtless to thoughtful situations. These levels are:

1. Memory level
2. Understanding level
3. Reflective level.

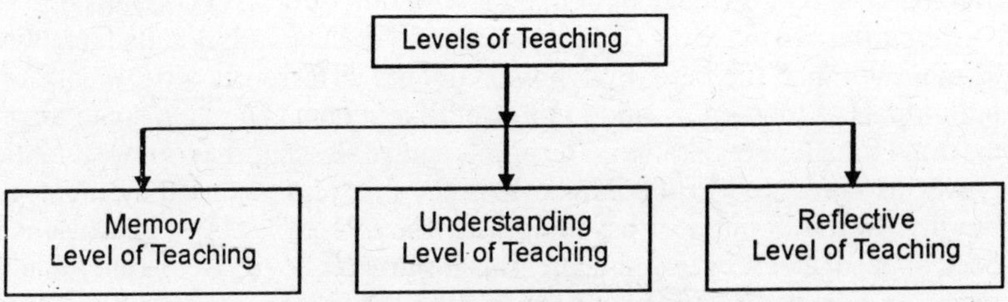

Figutre 15.1: Levels of Teaching

It depends upon the teacher's competency that to what extent he succeeds in reaching up to reflective level starting from memory level on the basis of his efficiency and experiences. It is a common observation that the normal teaching corresponds to the memory level teaching. Such learned and efficient teachers who succeed in upgrading their teaching from memory level to reflective level-teaching are lacking.

MEMORY LEVEL OF TEACHING

Meaning of Memory

Memory is a mental process which occurs essentially in some quantity in every living being. Actually, when a person sees some object, thing or place, then the engrams of the object, thing or a place are formed in his mind. To memorize these engrams or pre-learnt things is called memory. We recall these accumulated past experiences when required and we recognize them by bringing them into our conscious mind, then that is called memory.

Definition of Memory

Ideas of following scholars make clear the meaning of memory:

1. Woodworth, *"Memory is the direct use of what is learned."*
2. J.S. Ross, *"A memory is a new experience determined by the dispositions laid down by a previous experience, the relation between the two being clearly apprehended."*
3. Mcdougall, *"Memory implies imagining of events as experienced in the past and recognizing them to one's own past experience."*
4. Stout, *"Memory is the ideal revival in which the objects of past experience reinstate as far as possible in the order and manner of the original occurrence."*

Phases of Memory

The following are the phases of memory:

Learning: Memory depends upon the engrams of experiences. Hence, the first phase of memory is the learning of some facts. Learning task is done by the conscious mind. In this phase, the life-experiences get engrammed in the brain in the form of mental impressions and these can be made conscious as and when needed. Hence, the pupils should acquire direct knowledge. Repeat it again and again. They should search out the meaning of that knowledge. Memorize that knowledge by linking it with other objects or subjects.

Retention: To make the contents permanent in the minds is called retention. Remember that the retention power occurs differently in the different individuals. A memory is said to be good if a person can retain something in his mind for a longer duration. The pupils and adolescents have more retention power as compared to the adults. It is for this reason that they memorize rapidly. In the opinion of psychologists, the retention power reaches at its peak at the age of 25 years and after this it starts reducing. Remember that the retention power depends mainly upon four conditions, which are: (i) brain, (ii) health, (iii) interest, and (iv) thinking. Every experience learns impressions in the brain. Our brain not only protects these impressions, but also arranges them in a sequence. Retention power is also closely related to the structure of the brain. Due to the differences in the structure of the brain of every person, variations in the retention power occur.

Physical health is also deeply related to the retention power. Our nervous tissues function very conveniently when we have sound health. Consequently, we learn anything very easily. It is the reason that in the morning, i.e. with complete sound health, when we learn something, it gets memorized very rapidly. It is the only reason that our nervous tissues don't work properly when we have ill-health. Hence, our retention power lowers down. Retention power is also related to the interest and thinking. We remember rapidly in which we have interest. Due to our interest, we think about that thing again and again and we establish relationship with other things resulting in our rapid learning.

Recall: The learnt experiences when brought to conscious mind are called recall. Recalling of past experiences is responsible for a person's good or bad memory. If he fails to recall when needed all goes in vain even in spite of his superb learning. When a person fails to recall the retained material, that enhances the chances of forgetting. Psychologists have emphasized on certain laws in order to bring learnt material at the conscious level. These laws are:

- Law of Contiguity
- Law of Similarity
- Law of Contrast
- Law of Continuity of Interest
- Law of Primacy
- Law of Recency
- Law of Frequency
- Law of Vividness

Recognition: If we see an object or a person and we can say that we have seen before that object or a person is termed as recognition. In other words, recognition is that mental process by which we can tell, by coming in contact with an object or a person what a thing is, who is the person and when we were introduced? Remember that the recall and recognition have the similar relationship as that of brain and the body. Recalling becomes difficult when the association among objects does not occur and consequently we are unable to remember them. Contrary to this, we recognize them quickly when our association among those objects and persons becomes strong.

Characteristics of Good Memory

Characteristics of good memory are as follows:

Rapidity in Learning: The first characteristic of good characteristic is its rapidity and simplicity in learning. Hence, the memory of those pupils can be said as good who learn rapidly.

Stability of Retention: Another characteristic of good memory is retention of learnt material for a longer duration. The pupils are said to have a good memory if they retain for a longer time what they have learnt.

Rapidity in Recall: In addition to rapid learning and stability of retention, the third characteristic of good memory is rapidity in recall. Those pupils are said to have good memory who can bring anything to their conscious level very rapidly. Only those pupils are said to have good memory who can recall anything according to the needs and at proper time.

Serviceableness: The fourth characteristic of good memory is its score ability at some occasion. There are some pupils who possess much but when needed, they remember only irrelevant material. Contrary to this, there is no dearth of the pupils who bring only desirable at the conscious level. Only those pupils are said to have good memory who can recall the appropriate material according to the need.

Forgetting Irrelevant Things: A good memory requires forgetting of irrelevant things. The recalling of irrelevant things at the time of examination does not benefit the pupils. Similarly, recalling the painful events of life struggle does not prove advantageous in any way.

Classification of Memory

Persons differ in ability to memorize. Some persons don't forget after a single reading. Contrary to this, people forget frequently even after repeated learning. On the basis of their different abilities memory can be classified as follows:

1. *Immediate Memory:* Immediate memory is that when a person recall immediately after learning something. This type of memory has the following two characteristics:

- It is temporary. It is possible that the learnt material may not retain for a longer period,
- Its development occurs along with age.

In an infancy period, the development of the pupil is slow and somewhat faster during childhood. During adolescence, this rate of development acquires its maximum limits.

2. *Personal Memory:* While recalling past experiences, we remember our personal past experiences.

3. *Permanent Memory:* The recalling of learnt material for a longer time is known as permanent memory. In other words, the things with which our association is strong are remembered for a longer duration.

4. *Logical Memory:* To learn something by using intellect and its recalling when needed is called logical memory. Burgson has termed this memory as true memory.

5. *Rote Memory:* Rote memory is that memory in which the facts are crammed without any understanding. Such type of memory is very sharp during childhood. It is the reason that counting and tables etc. are crammed very rapidly. However, the memory is not considered as very good memory.

6. *Mechanical Memory:* Mechanical memory is also known as physical memory. When our body becomes habitual of doing any task repeatedly, then our body has no need to recall that task again and again. For example, a swimmer swims without any major recalling.

7. *Active Memory:* The recalling of past experiences needs some efforts, for example the candidates sitting in examination hall have to make efforts to recall the answer to the questions again and again.

8. *Passive Memory:* In passive memory, we recall the past experiences without any effort.

9. *Impressional Memory:* The recalling of the material learnt from the books and companions is called imperssional memory. There is no place of personal experiences in such types of memories.

MEMORY LEVEL OF TEACHING

Remember that the memory level teaching is thoughtless. In this level of teaching, emphasis is laid on the presentation of facts and information and its cramming. It is a matter of observation that the cramming of facts of the contents has no relation with intelligence. Its reason is that the mentally handicapped children can also cram. Yes, it is something else that if the content is purposeful, then it can be crammed very conveniently and also can be retained for a longer duration. Hence, memory level teaching lacks insight. Almost all the pupils cram the contents unwillingly. They succeed in the school examination on the basis of scores secured by cramming but they seem to fail in the lengthy examination of the life. In short, memory level is the level of cramming. In reality, there is a definite pattern of memory level teaching. In this type of teaching, the teacher is like a dictator who suppresses the independence, interests, attitudes and competencies of the pupils and tries to impose the facts and information upon the pupils. Hence, in this level of teaching, the teacher remains active but the pupils go on learning by heart in strict discipline as a passive listener.

In short, no inter-action occurs between the teacher and the pupils. In the memory level teaching, signal learning, chain learning and stimulus-response learning are emphasized. In the end, both essay type and objective type examinations are used to evaluate the learnt contents. The above description shows that the memory level teaching is teacher-centred. Pupils have secondary place in this level of teaching. As a result, the teacher goes on imposing facts and information externally by keeping them in the strict discipline in order to develop the pupils mentally, neglecting their interest, attitudes, abilities and needs. This makes the pupils as crammers but they cannot be an intelligent learned person. The teaching of this level has the maximum level of motivation.

The evaluation of the acquired knowledge is done by traditional methods. In spite of many drawbacks, the memory level of teaching has some special importance. Its reason is that the teaching at understanding and reflective levels can be successful only when the teaching at memory level occurs. In other words, understanding and reflective level teaching cannot take place unless and until memory level teaching has not been managed.

Model of Memory Level of Teaching

Herbart is considered exponent of memory-level teaching. He has described the following steps while presenting the model of memory level teaching:

(a) Focus

According to Herbart, the focus of memory level teaching is the emphasis on cramming of facts and development of the following capacities:

- Training of mental aspects.
- Providing knowledge of facts.
- Retaining the learnt facts.
- Recalling and re-presenting the learnt facts.

(b) Syntax

Herbart has divided the memory level-teaching into five steps which are known as Herbart's Five Formula Steps. By following these five steps, the teacher can create learning situations for memory-level teaching. The following is the sequence of Herbart's five steps:

(i) (a) Preparation: Preparation is the first step of teaching method. In this step, some questions are asked to test the previous knowledge of pupils so that the curiosity to learn new knowledge may be aroused in them. In other words, in this step, the pupils are prepared to acquire new knowledge by testing their previous knowledge.

(b) Statement of Aim: This step is the part of the first step. Here the topic becomes clearer to the pupils and the teacher himself writes the topic on the black-board.

(ii) Presentation: In this step, the lesson is developed with the help of the

pupils. In other words, by stimulating their mental activity, the pupils are provided with opportunities for self-learning. The teacher tries to derive most of the information from the pupils so that a relationship may be established between the new and the previous knowledge.

(iii) Comparison and Association: Herbart has named this step as association. Here, the mutual relationship is established among facts, events and experiments by comparisons which clarify the learning material in the minds of the pupils. Hence, the teacher should establish a relationship between two subjects and between the facts and events of one subject and other facts and events of the same subject and make their comparison so that the new knowledge may be clarified and made permanent in the minds of the pupils.

(iv) Generalization: Herbart named this step as a system. After explaining the basic lesson, the pupils are given the opportunities to think in this lesson. After this, they formulate some such principles and laws which can be used in the future life situations.

(v) Application: It is the last step of teaching. In this step it is observed whether the new learnt knowledge can be used in new situations or not. This can be verified by the principle through questioning or he can provide new opportunities to make use of learnt knowledge. This makes the knowledge permanent and the laws can be verified.

(c) Social System

The process of teaching is social and professional. The members of this social system are: (i) pupil, and (ii) the teacher. At this level, the behaviour of the teacher is dominating based upon the dictatorial and authoritarian tendencies. As a result of this, the pupil functions as a passive listener. Hence, the function of the teacher is—(i) presenting the contents, (ii) controlling the pupils' activities, and (iii) providing motivation to them. All the activities are performed by the teacher and the pupils follow considering them ideal.

(d) Support System

In the examination system of memory-level teaching, cramming is stressed. Hence, while evaluating the teaching of this level, both oral and written examinations are used. Remember that while the teaching of this level is evaluated, essay type examination is considered more useful, but the steps like recall and recognition are also used successfully through the objective type examination.

Guidelines for Memory Level of Teaching

Memory level teaching provides help to the teaching at understanding and reflective levels on one side while it provides basis for the success of these two. Hence, the following suggestions are being given to make the memory-level teaching effective:

- The teacher should try to achieve the cognitive objective.
- The content to be presented should be purposeful.
- The teaching points should be presented as a whole or in total.
- The content should be presented in a sequence.

- There should be no teaching when the pupils are tired.
- Only whole-method should be used.
- A definite reinforcement system should be used.
- Recall should be grown through practice.
- Recapitulation should be done in a rhythm.

UNDERSTANDING LEVEL OF TEACHING

In understanding level of teaching, the teacher tries to present his instructions and stresses to make understand to the pupils the generalizations, principles and facts. It results in turning the teaching thoughtful. In other words, in understanding-level teaching, the teacher tries to provide more and more opportunities to develop the intellectual behaviours of the pupils. This develops the essential competencies for generalizations, insight and solving the problems. In this way, both pupils and teachers participate in developing the lesson while teaching occurs at the understanding level.

Model of Understanding Level of Teaching

The model of understanding-level teaching was indoctrinated by Morrison. Hence, it is named as Morrison's Teaching Model. Morrison has described the structure of this model in the following four steps:

(a) Focus

According to Morrison, the focus or objective of the understanding-level teaching model is that the pupil should achieve the mastery of the concept. In other words, the teacher stresses upon the mastery of the content so that a desirable change may occur in the personality of the pupils.

(b) Syntax

Morrison has divided the syntax of understanding-level teaching in to five steps and a teacher can create teaching and learning situations following them. The order of five steps of this model is as follows:

(i) *Exploration:* Morrison has included the following activities under this step:

- Previous knowledge testing by questioning.
- Analyzing the contents, the elements are arranged in a logical sequence from psychological point of view.
- Determining how the units of contents or new knowledge should be presented.

(ii) *Presentation:* At this stage, the teacher remains more active. He performs the following activities for the presentation of the contents:

- The teacher presents the content in small units. Also, he tries to maintain the sequence of these units and a relationship with the pupils establishes.
- While presenting the contents, the teacher also diagnoses whether the contents have been understood by the pupils or not. If not, how many pupils could not acquire this understanding?
- The teacher recapitulates the contents till most of the pupils acquire the understanding.

(iii) *Assimilation:* After presenting the contents, the teacher reaches at the conclusion that most of the pupils have gained the new knowledge, he provides pupils opportunities for assimilation. It has the following characteristics:

- The pupils are provided with occasions for generalization through assimilation so that they get the mastery of the concept.
- Assimilation-opportunities are provided in order to stress upon the depth of the content.
- At the time of assimilation, every pupil studies in accordance with his requirement. Hence, the teacher should provide maximum opportunities of performing individual activities.
- In assimilation, the pupils work themselves in laboratories and libraries. Hence, home assignments are also given.
- In the assimilation period, supervised study occurs. During this period, both pupils and the teachers remain active. The pupils perform individual activities and the teachers guide them according to the need during supervision.
- During the assimilation period, the teacher tests whether the pupils have achieved mastery over the contents or not. If this does not happen, the teacher should provide re-opportunities for assimilation after observing precautions during supervision.

(iv) *Organization*: The period of assimilation is of mastery test. After succeeding in the mastery test, the pupils enter the period of organization or recitation according to the nature of contents. According to Morrison, during organization, the pupils are provided with the occasions for re-presentation. All the pupils write contents in their own language. From this, the teacher comes to the conclusion whether the pupils can write the contents without anybody's help or not. Hence, the pupils enter into recitation rather to the organization.

(v) *Recitation*: Recitation is the last step of understanding level teaching. During this period, the pupils present the contents orally before the teacher and his mates.

(c) Social System

In the understanding level of teaching, the various steps of social system go on changing. In presentation, the teacher controls the behaviour of the pupils like memory-level by keeping himself more active and he also provides necessary motivation. In assimilation-period, both pupils and the teacher remain active. The teacher imparts necessary instructions to the pupils they work themselves with full involvement.

(d) Support System

In understanding-level teaching, the support system does not remain static, but it goes on changing. The pupils have to pass the examination of presentation in order to perform experiment in assimilation. Similarly, they have to pass assimilation test essentially for their entry into organization and recitation. At the end of organization period, a written test takes place. Similarly, recitation is followed by an oral test. Hence, both oral and written tests (essay type and objective type) occur during the various steps of understanding-level of teaching.

Features of Teaching at Understanding Level

The following are the limitations and characteristics of understanding-level model given by Morrison:

- The main problem of this teaching system is its stress upon the mastery of the content. Human behaviour is over-looked.
- Morrison has considered teacher's involvement in the content as motivation for the pupils, while psychological motivation can prove more effective.
- Mastery of the contents restricts the development to the cognitive aspect only and it does not help in developing affective and psychomotor aspects.
- Psychologically, this model of teaching given by Morrison is considered more effective.
- With the teaching model, a deep study of the contents can be carried out by the pupils. Hence, this model causes complete learning.

Guidelines for Understanding Level of Teaching

Morrison has provided the following suggestions to make the understanding level of teaching more effective:

- The pupils should be allowed to enter the understanding level of teaching unless and until they pass out the tests of memory-level teaching.
- Every step of understanding level of teaching should be followed in a proper sequence.
- The pupils should be promoted to the new step unless they pass the tests of previous stage. For example, pupils should be allowed to enter assimilation when they pass the tests of presentation.
- The teacher should provide psychological motivation from time to time in spite of his involvement in the content. Also he should raise the aspiration level of the pupils.
- The teacher should make efforts for solving the problems related to understanding level of teaching.

REFLECTIVE LEVEL OF TEACHING

Reflective-level teaching means 'problem-centered' teaching. In this, the classroom environment is open sufficiently. The teacher creates such a problem before the pupils which arouses so much mental tension in the pupils that they start solving their problems by formulating and testing their hypothesis as a result of their own motivation and activeness. At last, a time comes when the problem is solved.

In short, the teaching of reflective level cooperates in developing creative capacities by providing pupils with the opportunities of developing intellectual behaviour. The real situation is that the human life is a struggle. He has to do his best for achieving his aims of life. Sometimes, the achievement of the aims occurs, without any obstruction, in a natural way. But, sometime, human beings have to face numerous obstacles in order to achieve his aims. From this point of view, the provision of the teaching of reflective level is essential for the pupils. It is this teaching level which develops the reflective power of the pupils. As this power develops when they grow up, they can solve their problems of life by reasoning, logic and imagination and they can lead a successful and happy life.

M.L. Bigge has rightly written about reflective level of teaching while clarifying it, *"Reflective-level of teaching tends to develop the class-room atmosphere which is more alive and exciting, more critical and penetrating and more open to fresh and original thinking. Furthermore, the type of enquiry pursued by a reflective class tends to be more rigorous and work producing than pursued at an understanding learning situation."*

Model of Reflective Level of Teaching

The credit goes to Hunt for developing reflective level of teaching. Therefore, this teaching model is named as Hunt's Model of Teaching. Hunt has described the structure of reflective level model in the following steps:

(a) Focus

The reflective level of teaching has the following three objectives:

- To develop problem-solving competency among the pupils.
- To develop critical and constructive thinking among pupils.
- To develop independent and original thinking power among the pupils.

(b) Syntax

The syntax of reflective level teaching is designed in the following four steps, keeping in mind the individual and social nature:

- In the first step, the teacher creates a problematic situation before the pupils.
- In the second step, pupils formulate hypotheses for testing. Remember that more than one hypothesis may be formulated for the solution of a problem.
- In the third step, to verify the hypotheses, pupils collect data. On the basis of these collected data, it is decided whether these hypotheses may help in the solution of the problem or not.
- In the fourth step, hypotheses are tested. Results are derived on the basis of these tests which are original ideas of the pupils.

(c) Social System

In the reflective level of teaching, the classroom environment is open and independent. In such environment, the pupil occupies primary places and the teacher's place is secondary. At this stage, the teacher has three main functions:

- To present some problem before the pupils.
- To use discussion and seminar during teaching.
- To raise the level of aspiration of the pupils. All the pupils become active and sensitive for solving the problem. Hence, at this level, both self-motivation of the pupil and the social motivation have importance.

(d) Support System

For reflective level of teaching, objective type tests are not useful. The proper evaluation of the pupils' competencies can be done correctly by easy type tests. While examining reflecting level:

- the attitudes and beliefs of the pupils should be evaluated
- their involvement in the learning activities should be evaluated
- it should be evaluated that how much development of the critical and creative competencies of the pupils have taken place.

Features of Reflective Level of Teaching

The following are the limitations and characteristics of reflective level of teaching as described by Hunt:

- In reflective level of teaching, no definite programme is followed as in the case of memory and understanding levels of teaching.
- This level of teaching is required for the pupils of higher classes. It is because this level of teaching carries much importance for age and maturation.
- The teaching at reflective level is problem-centred.
- In this level of teaching, only group-discussion method is considered effective.
- Reflective level of teaching cannot be restricted only to the curriculum, contents and text-books.
- In the reflective level of teaching, pupils can criticize their teachers openly.

Guidelines for Reflective Level of Teaching

Hunt has presented the following suggestions to make the reflective level of teaching more effective:

- Teacher should allow those pupils' entry into the reflective level of teaching who succeed in the tests of memory and understanding levels of teaching.
- In the reflective level of teaching, the teacher should follow all the four steps of his level observing the precautions.
- The teacher should raise the level of aspiration of the pupils to make the teaching at reflective level a success.
- In order to eliminate the weaknesses of the teacher, cognitive field psychology should be stressed.
- The teacher should create such problematic situations before the pupils in which original and creative thinking may develop in them.
- At the time of teaching, there should be a free and open environment so that the pupils may participate actively in discussion in order to solve the problem.
- The teacher should present the problem before the pupils so that they may formulate the hypotheses after realizing the problem.

16
Models of Teaching

Teaching means helping students to learn well. Powerful learners have a wide range of strategies for acquiring knowledge. Models of Teaching were designed to impart to learners such strategies, which will help learners to think clearly and wisely and build social skills and commitment. They help students to acquire information, ideas, skills, values, and ways of thinking and means of expressing themselves in a nutshell. They are taught how to learn. Models of Teaching include many but not all of the major philosophical and psychological orientations towards teaching and learning. Each of them has coherent theoretical bases (Joyce and Weil, 1972).

The models approach to teaching was first described by *Joyce* and *Weil* (1972), who defined a model as "a pattern or plan which can be used to shape a curriculum or course to select instructional material and to guide teacher's action." In the words of Bruce Joyce "Models of Teaching are really models of learning. As we help students acquire information, ideas, skills, values, way of thinking and means of expressing themselves; we are also teaching them how to learn. In fact the most important long-term outcome of instruction may be the students increased capabilities to learn more easily and effectively in the future, both because of the knowledge and skills they have acquired and because they have mastered learning process". According to Dewey (1916)—"The core of the process of teaching is the arrangement of environments within which the student can interact."

For achieving the Educational objectives, the first and foremost step is a suitable instructional strategy. There is no single best way or teaching strategy that can be employed in all situations since the number of teaching goals is large and diverse in nature. This led researchers to explore various methods and techniques for the development of cognitive, affective and psychomotor domains. The best strategy of effective teaching is the one that is most reading towards a particular goal in a given situation. This is the philosophy behind the Models of Teaching.

MEANING OF MODELS OF TEACHING

Joyce and Weil (1972) says, "*A model of teaching is a plan or pattern that we can use to design face-to-face teaching in class-rooms or tutorial settings and to shape instructional materials - including books, films, tapes, computer mediated programmes and curricula (long term courses of study). Each model guides us as we design instruction to help students achieve various objectives*". These models also teach students how to learn.

Effective learners gain information, ideas and wisdom from their teachers and use learning resources effectively. Successful teachers present powerful cognitive and social tasks to their students and teach the students how to make productive use of them. Fundamental purpose of Models of Teaching is to enhance the ability of students to achieve various objectives of learning.

Models of teaching afford a lively and provocative introduction to the complexity of teaching (Joyce and Weil, 1972). A Teaching Model can be considered as a type of blue-print for teaching. It provides structure and direction for teaching. It provides guidelines for designing educational activities and environments for developing a teacher's repertoire of instructional approaches to meet a range of objectives. But Models of teaching are not cure—alls or applicable to all teaching situations. With the help of the Models of Teaching teachers teach more effectively by making the teaching act more systematic and efficient.

Models of Teaching are a tool to help good teachers teach more effectively by making their teaching more systematic. A model of teaching consists of guidelines for designing educational activities and environment. It specifies ways of teaching and learning that are intended to achieve certain kinds of goals. The use of models requires an ability to identify different types of instructional goals so that specific model can be selected to match a particular goal. A teaching model can be considered as a type of blue print for teaching.

DEFINITIONS OF MODELS OF TEACHING

Some of the definitions of models of teaching are given below:

1. *Joyce* and *Weil* (1972): "Teaching models are just instructional designs. They describe the process of specifying and producing particular environmental situations which cause the students to interact in such a way that specific change occurs in his behaviour."
2. *Joyce* and *Weil* (1972): "Teaching model is a pattern or plan which can be used to shape a curriculum or course, to select instructional materials and to guide a teacher's actions."
3. *Weil* and *Joyce* (1978): "A model of teaching consists of guidelines for designing educational activities and environments. It specifies ways of teaching and learning that are intended to achieve certain kinds of goals."
4. *N. K. Jangira* and *Ajit Singh* (1983): "A model of teaching is a set of inter-related components arranged in a sequence which provides guidelines to realize specific goal. It helps in designing instructional activities and environmental facilities, carrying out of these activities and realization of the stipulated objectives."
5. *Paul D. Eggen et al.* (1979): "Models are prescriptive teaching strategies designed to accomplish particular instructional goals".
6. *Allen and Ryan* (1969); "Modeling is an individual demonstrating particular pattern which the trainee through imitation."
7. *B.K. Passi L.C. Singh* and *D.N. Sansanwal* (1991); "A model of teaching consist of guidelines for designing educational activities and environments. Model of teaching is a plan that can also be utilized to shape courses of studies, to design instructional material and to guide instruction."

In conclusion, teaching models may be described as some sort of guidelines, plans, techniques or strategies designed to achieve specific educational objectives. They differ from general teaching objectives in the sense that they are designed to meet specific objectives or goals.

PECULIARITIES OF MODELS OF TEACHING

The main peculiarities of Models of Teaching are mentioned as follows:

- All Models of Teaching specify the learning outcomes in detail on observable student performance.
- Every Model of Teaching specifies in definite terms the environmental conditions under which a student's response should be observed.
- A Model of Teaching is not a combination of facts but on the other hand it is systematic procedure to modify the behaviour of the learners.
- All Models of Teaching denotes mechanism that provide for students reaction and interaction with the environment.
- A Model describes the criteria of acceptable performance, which is expected from the students.

MAIN CHARACTERISTICS OF MODELS OF TEACHING

The main characteristics of models of teaching are as under:

- Specification of learning outcomes; A models of teaching specify what the students should perform after completing an instructional sequence.
- Specification on environment; A models of teaching specifies in definite terms the environmental condition under which a student's response should be observed.
- Specification of criterion of performance; A models of teaching specifies the criterion for performance which is expected from the students.
- Specification of operation; A models of teaching specifies the mechanism that provides for the reaction of students and interaction with the environment.
- Scientific procedure; A models of teaching is based on a systematic procedure to modify the behaviour of the learner. It is not a haphazard combination of facts.

MERITS OF MODELS OF TEACHING

The merits of models of teaching are as follows:

- It is a natural way of teaching and learning.
- It is helpful in developing the power of imagination of the students.
- It helps in the developments of reasoning power of the students.
- It helps the students to analyze things systematically.
- It keeps students actively engaged in the classroom activity.
- It helps in making the students good observers.
- It keeps the students busy in the classroom work.

LIMITATIONS OF MODELS OF TEACHING

The limitations of models of teaching are:

- It makes high demands on the students as well as teachers.
- All the students of the class may not be able to participate in the teaching-learning process.

- Some students, on account of their shyness, fail to derive the requisite advantage of this model.

FUNCTIONS OF MODELS OF TEACHING

The main functions of models of teaching are as follows:

- They help in guiding the teacher to select appropriate teaching techniques, strategies and methods for the effective utilization of the teaching situation and material for realizing the objectives.
- They help in bringing about desirable changes in the behaviour of the learners.
- They help in finding out ways and means of creating favourable environmental situation for carrying out teaching process.
- They help in achieving desirable teacher-pupil interaction during teaching.
- They help in the construction of a curriculum or contents of a course.
- They help in the proper selection of instruction material for teaching the prepared course or the curriculum.
- They help in designing appropriate educational activities.
- They assist procedure of material to create interesting and effective materials and learning sources.
- They stimulate the development of new educational innovations.
- They help in the formation of theory of teaching.
- They help to establish teaching and learning relationship empirically.

Main functions of the Models of Teaching are explained in the Figure 16.1 given below:

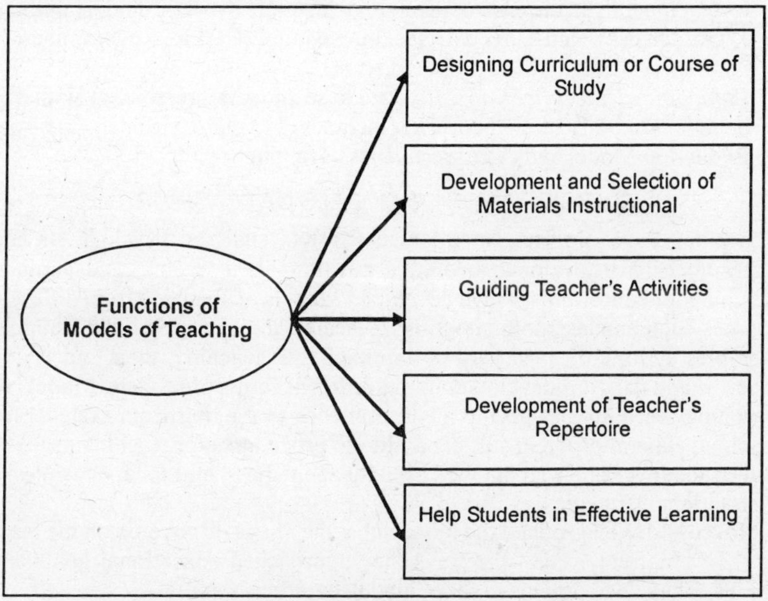

Figure 16.1: The Diagrammatic Representation of the Functions of Models of Teaching

TYPES OF TEACHING MODELS

Every teaching model has its specific objective. In order to achieve the objective of a teaching model, the teacher has to choose right type of model for achieving the particular objective. The teaching models have been classified into three main types:

Philosophical Teaching Models: Israel Saffer had mentioned such types of models. These include (1) The Insight Model (Plato) and (2) The Impression Model of Teaching (John Locke).

Psychological Teaching Model: John P. Dececco had mentioned such types of models. It includes (1) A Basic Teaching Model (Robert Glaser) and (2) An Interaction Model of Teaching (N.A. Flander).

Modern Teaching Models: Bruce R. Joyce has divided all the teaching models under the title "Modern teaching models" in the following four categories:

- *Social Interaction Model:* The social aspects of human beings are kept in view and their social development is more emphasized. It includes (1) Social Inquiry Model (Byron, Mossilas and Cox), (2) Group Investigation Model (Herbert, Thelen and John Dewey) and (3) Classroom Meeting Model (William Glaser).
- *Information Processing Models:* The models of this type are concerned with the intellectual development of the individual and help to develop the method of processing information from the environment. It includes (1) Concept Attainment Model (J. Bruner) (2) Advance Organizer Model (David P. Ausubel) and (3) Inductive Thinking Model (Hilda Taba).
- *Personal Development Models:* These types of models help an individual to develop fully in the environment. It includes (1) Synectic model (William J. Gordon) (2) Non-Directive Teaching Model (Carl R. Rogers) and (3) Awareness Training Model (David Hunt).
- *Behavioural Modification Model:* These models are related with the behaviour modification theories. It includes (1) Training Model, (2) Stress Reduction Model and (3) Assertiveness Training.

CLASSIFICATION OF MODELS OF TEACHING

Educators, Psychologists, Sociologists, System analysts, Psychiatrists and many others have developed theoretical positions about teaching and learning. A number or educationists have developed Models of Teaching from different sources such as classroom situations, research in psychology and training, therapies and theories. Variety of approaches of teaching, their underlying theories and uses are developed in the different forms of models. Models of Teaching are built around the mental process as ranging from systems for teaching general problem solving ability to procedures for teaching process. But Bruce Joyce and Marsha Weil brought about the revolutionary changes in Instructional strategies.

Joyce and Weil grouped the models that they have discovered on the basis of their chief emphasis—the ways they approached educational goals and means. They have organized these models into four families:

1. The Information Processing Family

2. The Social Family
3. The Personal Family
4. The Behavioural Systems Family

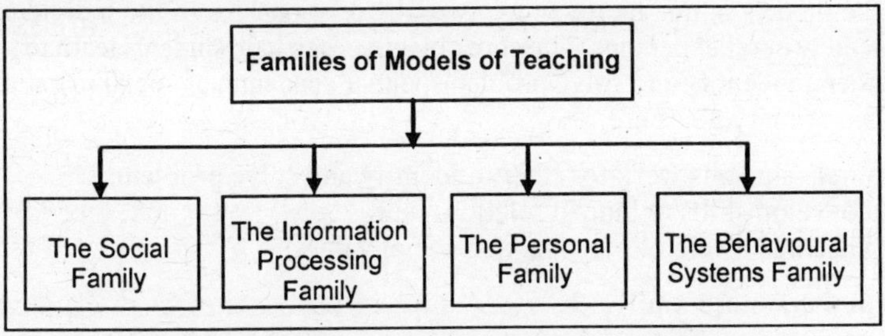

Figure 16.2: Classification of Models of Teaching

1. The Information Processing Family

The models in this family are designed to teach students the skills of learning through thinking. They aim at increasing student's ability to seek and master information, organize it, build and test hypotheses, apply what they are learning in their independent reading and writing and their exploration of themselves and the world around them.

Information Processing Models increase student's ability to seek and master information, organize it and apply it with test and learn by their independent reading and writing. It helps students in the mastery of methods of inquiry; mastery of academic concepts and facts; development of general intellectual skills such as the ability to think more logically.

These models focus on intellectual capacity. They are concerned with the ability of the learner to observe, organize data, understand information, form concepts, employ verbal and nonverbal symbols and solve problems. The primary purposes are:

- The mastery of methods of inquiry
- The mastery of academic concepts and facts
- The development of general intellectual skills such as the ability to reason and think more logically

2. The Social Family

Man is a social creature. The models under Social Family range from the simplest processes of organizing students to work together to elaborate models that teach democratic social organization, analysis of major social problems and critical social values and issues. The models in this family emphasize the relationship of the individual with the society or other person.

The core objective is to help students learn to work together, to identify and solve problems, either academic or social in nature. Consequently, with respect to goals, models from this orientation, give priority to the improvement of the individual's ability to relate others, the improvement of democratic processes and the improvement of the society (Joyce and Weil 1978).

The main aims of this category is to help students work together to identify and solve problems; to develop skills in human relations,: to become aware of personal and social values. These models emphasize the democratic social organization and the analysis of major social problems and critical social values and issues.

The models in this family emphasize the relationships of the individual to the society or other persons. The core objective is to help students learn to work together. to identify and solve problems, either academic or social in nature.

The primary goals are:

- to help students work together to identify and solve problems
- to develop skills to human relations, and
- to become aware of personal and social values.

3. The Personal Family

The models in this family focus on the individual and give emphasize on the development of integrated feeling, thinking self—the personal identity. They shape the environment around the capacity for self-education and the need to develop self-awareness and understanding. Models belonging to this family, share an orientation towards the individual and the development of selfhood. The emphasis of this model is on developing an individual into an integrated confident and competent personality. They attempt to help students understand themselves and their goal, and to develop the means for educating themselves.

The main focus is to increase the students' sense of self-worth; to help students understand themselves more fully; to help students recognize their emotions and become more aware of the way emotions affect other aspects of their behaviour; to help them develop goals for learning; to help students develop plans for increasing their competence; to increase the students' creativity and playfulness and to increase the students' openness to new experience. These models shape the environment around the capacity for self-education and the need to develop self awareness and understanding.

Models which belong to this family deal with the individual and the development of self hood. The emphasis of these models is on developing an individual into an integrated, confident and competent personality. They attempt to help students understand themselves and their goals, and to develop the means for educating themselves. Many of the personal models of teaching have been developed by counsellors, therapists and other persons interested in stimulating individual's creativity and self expression.

The primary goals are:

- to increase the student's self worth,
- to help students understand themselves more fully.
- to help students recognize their emotions and become more aware of the
- way emotions effect other aspects of their behaviour,
- to help them develop goals for learning,
- to help students develop plans for increasing their competence,
- to increase the students' creativity and playfulness,
- to increase the students' openness to new experience.

4. The Behavioural Systems Family

The models in this family are developed taking into consideration the human beings ability to modify behaviour in response to tasks and feedback. These models are used in a wide variety of application from teaching information, concepts and skills, to increasing comfort and relaxation, decreasing phobias, changing habits, and learning to control one's behaviour. These models are evolved from attempts to develop efficient systems for sequencing learning tasks and shaping behaviour of the learner and describe them in terms of visible behaviour rather than understanding an unobservable behaviour.

The main focus is to change the behaviour of the learner; to transmit culture by teaching skills and knowledge. These models are used in the wide variety of applications, from teaching information, concepts and skills, increasing comfort and relaxation and decreasing phobias, changing habits and learning to control one's behaviour.

The sample synoptic view of these four categories is give below in Table 16.1.

Table 16.1: Families of Models of Teaching

S. No.	*Family of Model*	*Examples of Model*
1.	Social Family	1. Group Investigation Model 2. Social Inquiry Model 3. Role Playing Model 4. Jurisprudential Inquiry Model 5. Cooperative Learning Model 6. Group Investigation Model 7. Laboratory Training Model 8. Social Simulation Model
2.	Information Processing Family	1. Inquiry Training Model 2. Concept Attainment Model 3. Advance Organizer Model 4. Biological Science Inquiry Model 5. Cognitive Development Model 6. Synectics Model (to develop creativity) 7. General Inductive Model 8. Taba Inductive Thinking Model 9. General Deductive Model 10. Suchman's Inquiry Model 11. Memory Model 12. Cognitive Growth Model
3.	Personal Family	1. Non Directive Teaching Model 2. Awareness Training Model 3. Classroom Meeting Model
4.	Behavioural Systems Family	1. Contingency Management Model 2. Self Control Model 3. Assertiveness Training Model 4. Direct Instruction Model 5. Mastery Learning 7. Learning from Simulations 8. Training Model 9. Stress Reduction Model 10. Desensitization Model 11. Assertiveness Training Model

COMPONENTS OF A TEACHING MODEL

According to Joyce and Weil (1972) the components of a teaching model are as follows:

Focus

Focus is the central intent of the model. Focal components revolve around the main objective of the model. Is it the focus of the learning event to encourage learning by manipulating thought or types of thinking; growth in learning through external stimuli or rewards; social learning, or social and emotional growth through interaction; or increased levels of self-achievement and personal growth through personally directed choices? Models are usually developed with a focus, an end-game, or specific intention in mind. For instance, Madeline Hunter's very popular Mastery Teaching concept focuses on presenting materials in a tightly controlled, very repetitive way so that learners have optimal opportunities to get content, concepts, or processes right the first time. Another example—in cooperative learning models the focus is on the importance of social interchange and peer support in learning new things. Therefore models differ one from the other in terms of their primary objective or focal point of their intended outcomes.

Syntax

The syntax describes the terms of sequences of activities called phases; Each model has a distinct flow of phases. Syntax describes the model's structure and includes the sequence of steps involved in the organization of the model. It includes the major components and the phases of unfolding, or the sequencing of steps, and describes how the model progresses. Obviously the syntax can be quite different for each model.

Social System

The social system describes student and teacher role and relationships and the kind of norms that are encouraged. The Social System describes the interactions between students and teacher as each model is viewed as if it were a mini society. Since every teaching model is different, each model will have its own social system and rules of engagement. This portion concerns the interactive roles and relationships between the teacher and the student, expected norms, and which student behaviours should be rewarded. These may be overtly described or simply inferred. Depending on the philosophical orientation of the model, in some models the role of the teachers is dominant, while in others his or her role is passive. In some models the roles center on the teacher, and in others the concentration is on the students. There are still other models that require shared roles whereby teachers and students share roles equally. In this segment both motivational strategies and tactics for engaging students could be discussed too.

Principle of Reaction

Principle of reaction tells the teacher how to regard the learner and how to respond to what the learner does. Principles of Reaction tell the teacher how to regard the learner and how to respond to what the learner does during the use of the model. Often responses in using a designated model should be appropriate and selectively specific. This element is concerned with the teacher's reactions to the students' responses. This portion of the model alerts the teacher on how to react to the responses of the students. It is here that the teacher learns whether the learners have been actively involved in the model's processes and steps.

Support System

Support system refers to additional requirements beyond the usual human skills, capacities and technical facilities necessary to implement a Model. Support system defines the supporting conditions required to implement the model successfully. 'Support' refers to any additional requirements, beyond the usual general human skills and capabilities, that are needed to implement the model. This component relates to any additional requirements beyond those generally possessed by teachers or found in schools. What requirements are needed to make this model work? Are special skills or knowledge needed; or is there special equipment, media, or learning environment requirements that need to be accessed in using this model? This support would also include special books, films, laboratory kits, reference materials, permissions, facilities, etc.

Instructional and Nurturant Effects

The instructional effects are those directly achieved by leading the learner in certain directions. The nurturant effects come from experiencing the environment created by the model. Application is the utility of the model as it can be transferred to other situations. Each model attempts to implement some change in learners and influence their thinking, feelings, social interactions, or physical movements in some way so that those changes can be transferred to other situations and experiences.

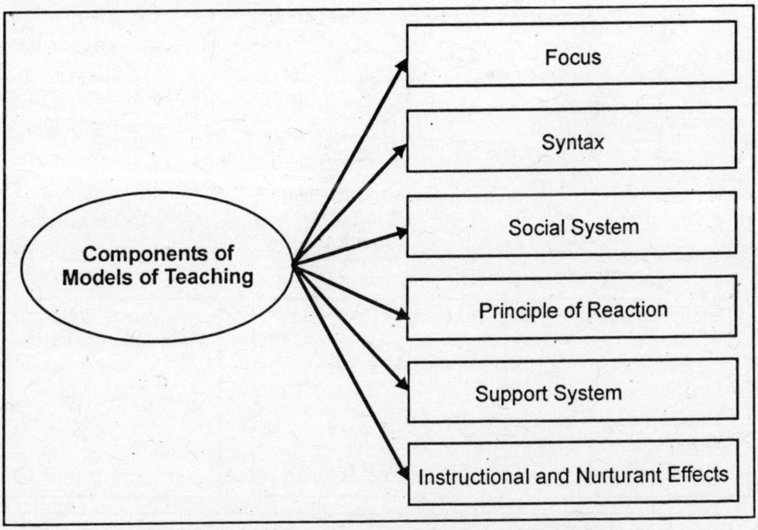

Figure 16.3: Components of Models of Teaching

ADVANCE ORGANIZER MODEL

Advance Organizer Model is given by *'David Ausubel'* who is one of the educational psychologists. This theory of meaningful verbal learning deals with three concerns:

- How knowledge (curriculum content) is organized;
- How the mind works to process new information (learning); and
- How teacher can apply these ideas about curriculum and learning when they present new material to students (instruction). This model is designed to strengthen student's cognitive structure.

His ideas are unique in the sense that while most modern educationist condemn the method of teacher presentation in the class room. He thought to improve the technique of presentation in such a way as to ensure meaningful learning. He stresses mastery of academic material as an important goal of class room teaching.

In order to explain his ideas, he introduces the term meaningful verbal learning. Verbal learning became inferior when it changes to rote learning instead of meaningful learning. How the latter type of learning could be assured. According to him:

- Organization of knowledge or the curriculum content.
- Guiding learning in accordance with the principle by which human mind possess new information,
- Careful application of these principles by the teacher, at the time of presentation.

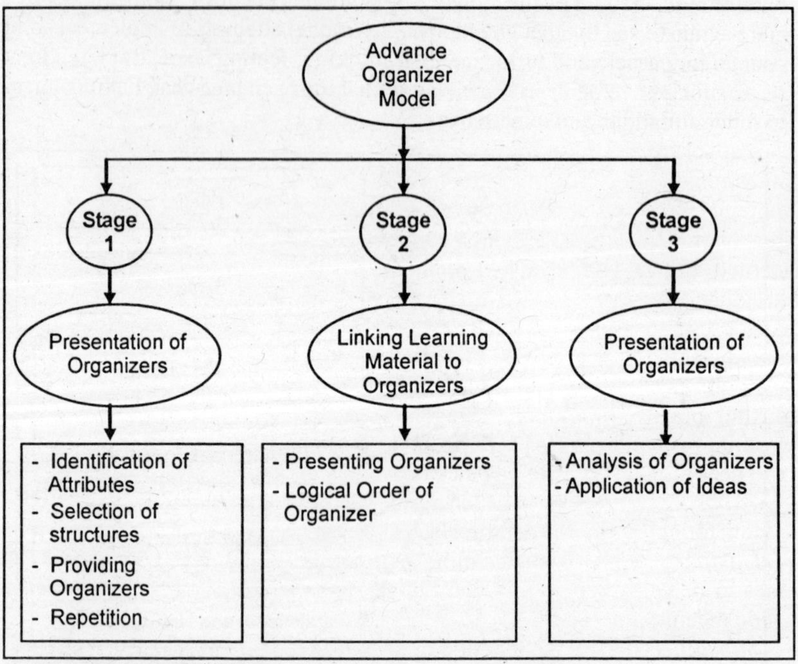

Figure 16.4: A Diagrammatic Representation of Strategies of AOM

To him effective education is one in which teachers are able to convey minimum information in a meaningful manner. This is more so in the higher classes where the teacher play the role of the lecturer.

In this model, teacher plays the role of organizer of subject matter and presents information through lectures, readings and providing tasks to the learner to integrate what has been learned. In this approach, teacher is responsible for organizing and presenting what is to be learned. The learner's primary role is to master ideas and information. The Advance Organizers provide concepts and principles to the students directly.

Important Concepts Related to Advance Organizer Model

Important key concepts related to advance organizer model are as under:

Students Existing Cognitive Structure: At a given time and with the respect to given subject matter, cognitive structure refer to a student's knowledge of that matter with special reference to how much he knows, how well he knows and how effectively the knowledge is structured. According to him, how meaningfully a student can learn new material can depends on his cognitive structure. Hence, before new knowledge is presented, the teacher should ensure the clarity and sufficiency of the existing cognitive structure. It is the absence of this verbal learning degenerate to rote learning.

Meaningful Learning Set: This is a condition in which connections could easily be established between the new material to be learnt and the related material that already exist in the cognitive structure. Such a mental set makes the learner ready to receive the new knowledge.

Structure of Concept: Each discipline has a structure of concept, hierarchically organized. While organizing the knowledge in a cognitive structure, human mind has the tendency to follow the same hierarchical order.

Advance Organizer: This include the material presented in advance as introduction to the new materials to be presented. This are so called because they are presented to the learner in advance as the primary means of organizing and strengthening cognitive structure. Advance organizer will be border and more abstract in nature than the new task, but will act as a container for the new ones. This will include in a general way all the new item that are to be learned afresh. The advanced organizer will include item to the cognitive structure of the learner with which a new material can be linked when they are later presented. This can include terms, concept, facts, propositions, etc.. already familiar to the learner, and also can be supplemented with illustrations, analogies etc. Through an organizer will be familiar to the learner, it need further clarifications and re teaching to ensure that the new item are meaningfully linked. This is to be linked with the aims of the lesson in mind.

There are two types of advance organizers:

Expository: are those in which a general class relationship is exposed with a view to include more specific classes.

Comparative: As the name indicate those that contain concepts similar to ones to be presented so that familiar relations are established and learning made meaningful.

Subsumer: This is the function of the advanced organizer. An organizer is helpful to subsume the specific concept involved in a broader concept.

Progressive Differentiation: Ausubel thinks that the hierarchical order in the processing of information is from the border and more general to the specific once. It is the process of maintaining this gradation by which specific items and gradually presented by one in the hierarchical order that is known as progressive differentiation.

Integrative Re-conciliation: This is the term that explains the conscious effort to relate new items to previously learnt content in such a way as to make the cognitive structure an integrated whole. This would help the learner to adjust with or reconcile with the newness in the learning. This naturally follows progressive differentiation if it is systematically done in relation to the advance organizer.

COMPONENTS OF ADVANCE ORGANIZER MODEL

The components of advance organizer model are as follows:

Syntax

The Advance Organizer Model has three phases of activity given below:

Phase-1: Presentation of the Advance Organizer

The aim of the lesson is made clear and then the organizer is presented. The concept etc. that have to act as the subsume have to be clarified and illustrated. The teacher should ensure the required cognitive structure by discussion, questioning and feedback.

Phase-2: Presentation of the Learning Task or Material

Present the minor concept in the order using the principle of progressive differentiation. A variety of tools and techniques can be adopted for this. Use of pictures, aids; films could be helpful for making learning meaningful.

Phase-3: Strengthening Cognitive Organization

Phase three tests the relationship of the learning material to existing ideas to bring about an active learning process. This is done by adopting the principle

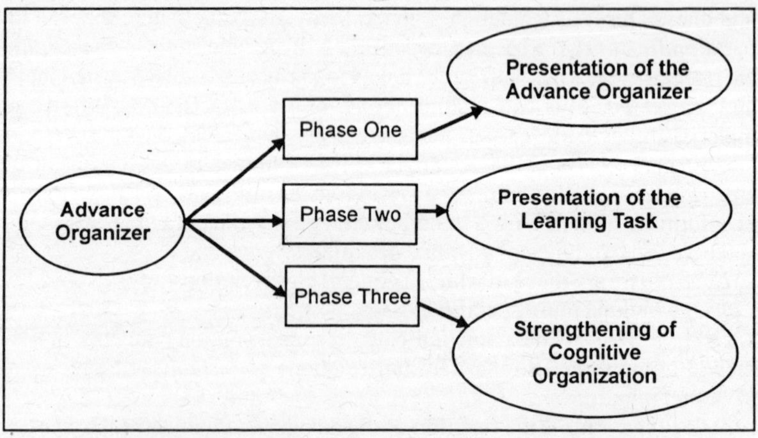

Figure 16.5: Syntax of the Advance Organizer Model

Table-16.2: Phases of Advance Organizer Model

Phase	Outline	Activity
Phase one	Presentation of Advance Organizer	1. Clarify aims of the lesson. 2. Present organizer a. Identify defining attributes b. Give examples c. Provide context d. Repeat
		3. Prompt awareness of learner's relevant knowledge and experience.
Phase two	Presentation of learning Task or Material	1. Present material. 2. Maintain attention. 3. Make organization explicit. 4. Make logical order of learning material explicit.
Phase three	Strengthening Cognitive organization	1. Use principles of integrative reconciliation.
		2. Promote active reception learning. 3. Elicit critical approach to subject matter. 4. Clarify.

of integrative reconciliation. By this, the teacher ensure meaningful reception and then reinforces this by a critical approach and further clarification of the doubts raised by the pupils.

Social System: In Advance Organizer Model the teacher retains control of the intellectual structure, to relate the learning material to the organizers and to help students differentiate new material from previously leads to the successful acquisition of material.

Principles of Reaction: Negotiation of meaning and responses between the teacher and the learner clarifies the meaning of the new learning material with existing knowledge of the students. Mutual interaction between teacher and learner responsively connect organizers and learning material.

Support System: The effectiveness of the advance organizer depends on an integral and appropriate relationship between the conceptual organizer and the content. This model provides guidelines for recognizing structural materials.

Instructional and Nurturant Effects: The instrumental values of this model are—the ideas themselves that are used as the organizer are learned, as well as information presented to the students (Fig. 16.6).

CONCEPT ATTAINMENT MODEL

Concept Attainment Model is given by Jerome Bruner. This model requires a student to figure out the attributes of a category that is already formed in another person's mind by comparing and contrasting example (called exemplars) that contains the characteristics (called attributes) of the concepts with examples that do not contain those attributes.

Examplars

The examplars are a subset of a collection of data or data sets. The category is the subset or collection of examples that share one or more characteristics that are missing in the others. It is by comparing the positive examplars and contrasting them with the negative ones that the concept or category is learned.

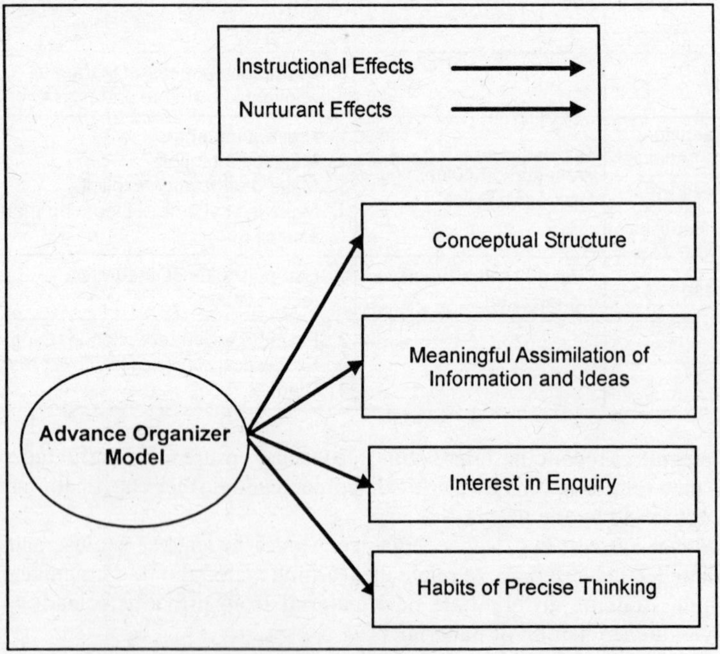

Figure 16.6: Instructional and Nurturant Effects of AOM

Components of Concept Attainment Model

The main components of concept attainment model are shown in Fig. 16.7:

Syntax

In Concept Attainment Model, phase one involves presenting data to the learner. Each unit of data is a separate example or non-example of the concept. The units are presented in pairs. The data may be events, people, objects, stories, pictures or any other discriminable units. In phase two, the students test their attainment of the concept, first by correctly identifying additional unlabeled examples of the concept and then by generating their own examples. In phase three, students begin to analyze the strategies by which they attain concepts (Fig. 16.8).

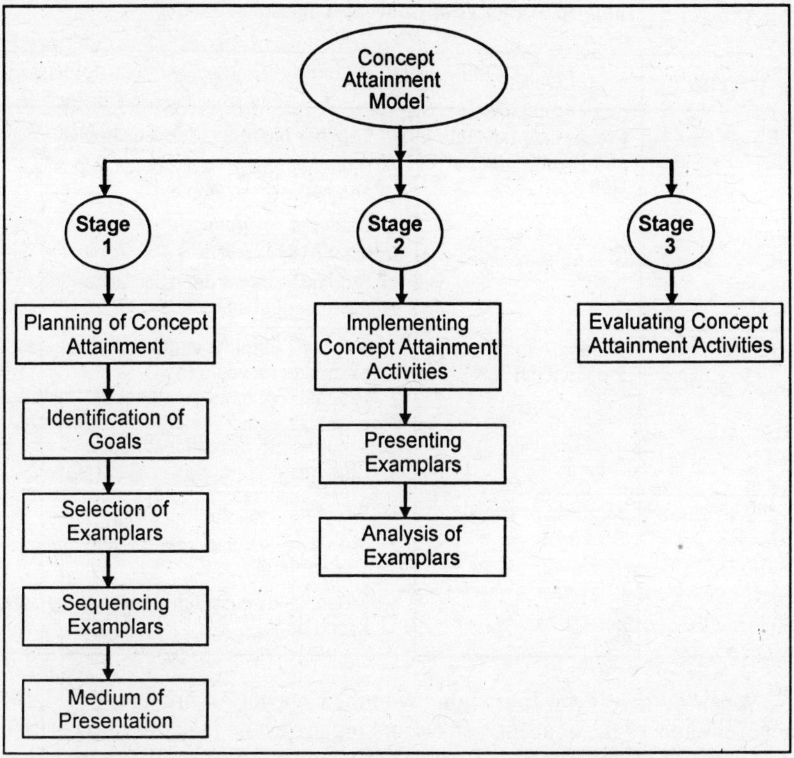

Figure 16.7: A Diagrammatic Representation of Strategies of CAM

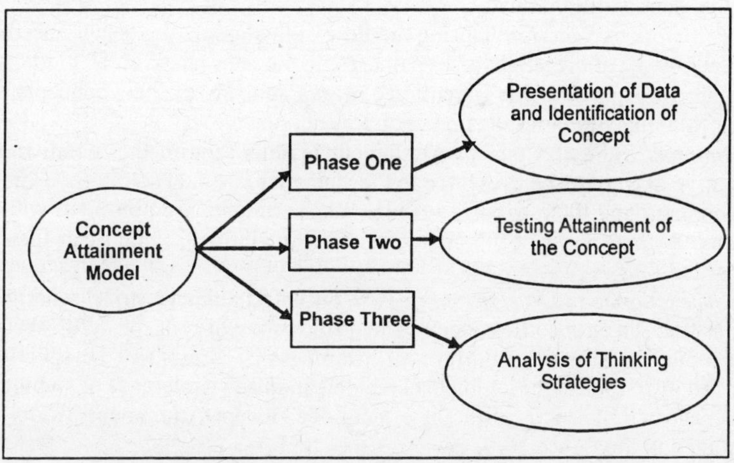

Figure 16.8: Syntax of the Concept Attainment Model

Table 16.3: Phases of Concept Attainment Model

Phase	*Outline*	*Activity*
Phase One	Presentation of Data and Identification of Concept	1. Teacher present labeled examples. 2. Students compare attributes in positive and negative example. 3. Students generate and test hypotheses. 4. Students state a definition according to the essential attributes.
Phase Two	Testing Attainment of the Concept	1. Students identify additional unlabeled examples as yes or no. 2. Teacher confirms hypotheses, names concepts and re-states definitions according to essential attributes. 3. Students generate examples.
Phase Three	Analysis of Thinking Strategies	1. Students describe thoughts. 2. Students discuss role of hypotheses and attributes. 3. Students discuss type and number of hypotheses.

Social System: Prior to teaching with the Concept Attainment Model, the teacher chooses the concept, selects and organizes the material into positive and negative examples and sequences the example. The three major functions of the teacher during concept attainment activity are to record, prompt (cue) and present additional data.

Principle of Reaction: During the flow of the lesson, the teacher needs to be supportive of the students' hypotheses. In the later phase of the model, the teacher turn the students' attention towards analysis of their concepts and their thinking strategies, again being very supportive.

Support System: Concept Attainment lessons require that positive and negative examplars be presented to the students. The data sources are known beforehand and the attributes visible. When students are presented with an example, they describe its characteristics (attributes), which can then be recorded.

Instructional and Nurturant Effects: Concept Attainment Model is designed for instruction on specific concepts and on the nature of concepts. With abstract concepts, the strategies nurture an awareness of alternative perspectives, sensitivity to logical reasoning in communication and a tolerance of ambiguity. The instructional and nurturant effects of Concept Attainment Model are depicted in the figure 16.9.

INQUIRY TRAINING MODEL OR RICHARD SUCHMAN INQUIRY MODEL

The inquiry model, developed by Richard Suchman, is based on the premise that the intellectual strategies used by scientists to solve problems and inquire

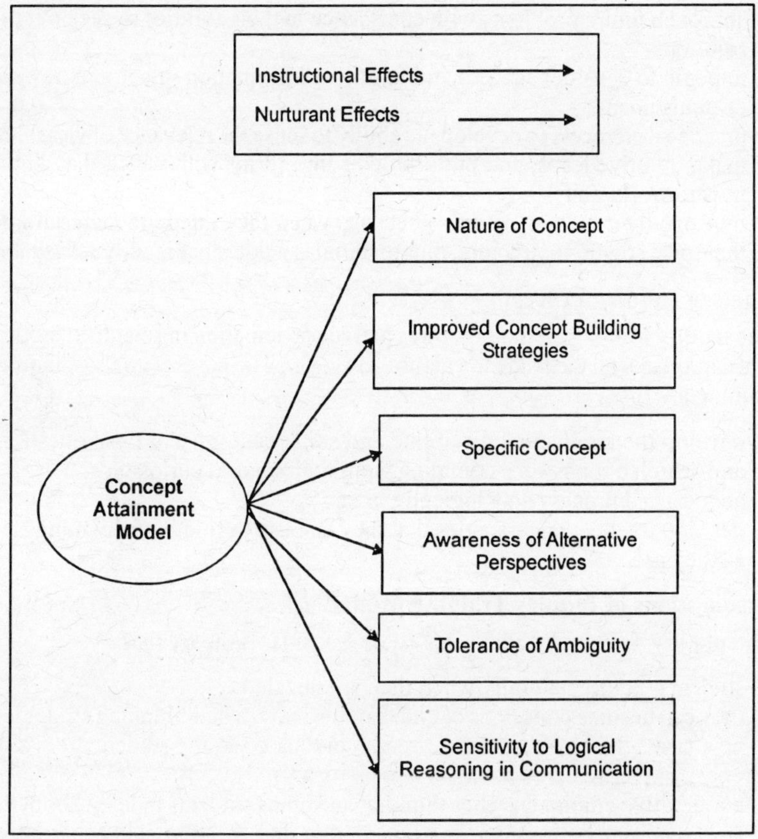

Figure 16.9: Instructional and Nurturant Effects of CAM

into the unknown can be taught to students. Using the natural curiosity of students, they can be trained and disciplined in the procedures of inquiry. The model was developed from analyzing the methods used in creative research personnel. The elements of their inquiry process were identified and these were built into an instructional model called inquiry training.

Inquiry training is designed to bring students directly into the scientific process through exercises that compress the scientific process intosmall periods of time. The training has resulted in an increased understanding of science, more creative thinking, and skills for obtaining and analyzing information as students establish facts, build concepts, and then generate and test explanations or theories. The students are active learners involved in exploration, questioning, problem solving, inductive reasoning, invention, labeling, and discovery.

Importance of Inquiry Process for Students

The inquiry process will help students:

- approach future problems with confidence in their abilities to seek out the solution
- to begin to consider success and failure as information rather than reward or punishment;
- practice the process to develop the ability to sense the relevance of variables, make intuitive leaps, and put problems into forms with which they know how to work; and
- improve their memory process because when they integrate material into their own cognitive structure, thus material is made more readily retrievable

Goals of Inquiry Process

The inquiry training method requires active participation in scientific inquiry and capitalizes on the student's natural curiosity. The general goals of inquiry training are to:

- develop the intellectual discipline and skills necessary to raise questions and search out answers stemming from their natural curiosity;
- acquire and process data logically' and
- develop intellectual strategies that they can use to find out why things are as they are.

Assumptions of Inquiry Training Model

The Inquiry Training Model is based on Suchman's theory that:

- students inquire naturally when they are puzzled;
- they can become conscious of and learn to analyze their thinking strategies;
- new strategies can be taught directly and added to the students' existing ones; and
- cooperative inquiry enriches thinking and helps students to learn about the tentative, emergent nature of knowledge and to appreciate alternative explanations.

Phases of Inquiry Training Model

Inquiry training has five phases given below:

- The first phase is the student's confrontation with the puzzling situation.
- Phases two and three are the data-gathering operations of verification and experimentation. In the data-gathering phases, the students ask a series of question that the teacher answers with a yes or no, and they conduct a series of experiments of the problem situation.
- In the fourth phase, the students organize the information obtained during the data-gathering phases and try to explain the discrepancy.
- In the last phase, students analyze the problem-solving strategies they used during the inquiry.

Role of Teacher in Inquiry Training Model

The teacher's role is to construct the problem situation, to referee the inquiry procedures, to respond to students' inquiry probes with the necessary information, to help students establish a focus in their, and to facilitate discussion of the problem situation among the students.

Components of Inquiry Training Model

The components of inquiry training model are as follows:

Syntax

The Inquiry Training Model has five phases of activity given below:

Phase-I: Encounter with the Problem.

The inquiry session actually begins with the presentation of a discrepant event. The distinguishing feature of discrepancy is that it involves an illogical phenomenon that conflicts with the notions of reality. Anything that is mysterious, unexpected or unknown, suits for a discrepant event. Suchman believes that individuals have a natural tendency to inquire. Hence he deliberately selects episodes that have sufficiently surprising outcome to make it difficult to encounter. The learners cannot remain indifferent to the encounter. The learners cannot dismiss the solutions as obvious. They have to work to explain the situation and the product of that work may be a new insight into the phenomenon, new concepts, and new theories.

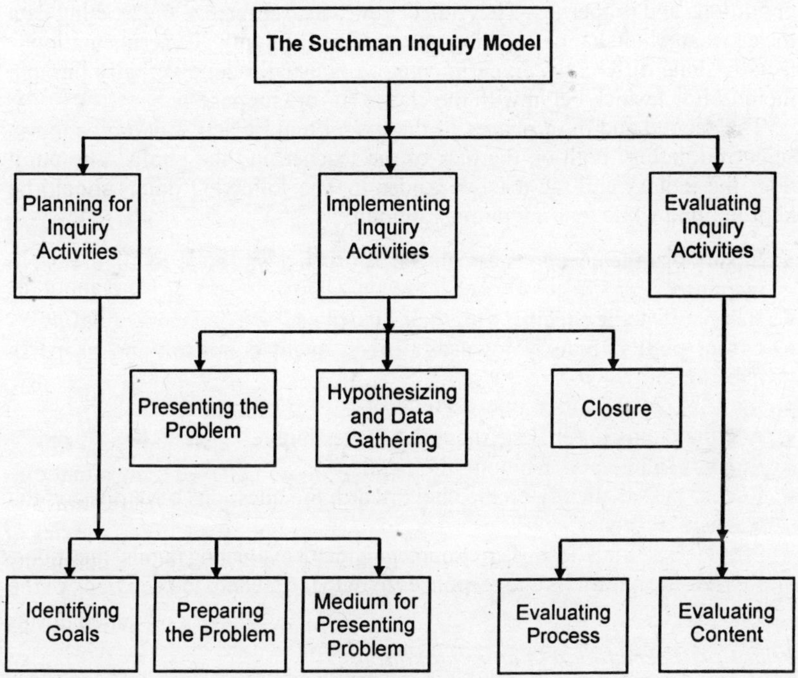

Figure 16.10

Phase- II: Data Gathering-Verification

When students have noted the discrepancy in the puzzling event they proceed to ask questions keeping the rules of the game in mind. This is the second phase of the model -the data gathering -verification. Verification is the process whereby students gather information about an event they see or experience. Verification questions are those which verify the facts related to the situation - the nature and identity of the subject, the events and conditions surrounding the puzzling event, the property of the object etc. These questions attempt to verify 'what is'.

Four types of questions may be asked by the students to verify the data

- Object questions - verify the nature of the objects involved in the problem situation.
- Event questions - verify the occurrence and nature of an action
- Condition questions - verify the state of objects or events at a particular time.
- Property questions - verify the generalized behaviour of the object under specified conditions

Phase- III: Date Gathering-Experimentation

As students become aware of the properties of the data, hypotheses come to their minds which guide further inquiry. This is the third phase of the model which involves experimentation, using the verified data about objects; events conditions and properties. They select new data, reorganize the existing data to see what would happen if things were done differently. Experimentation is usually done differently. Experimentation is usually done verbally through the questions which begin with the clause 'if' or 'suppose'.

The second and third phases of the model require active participation in scientific inquiry both on the part of the teacher and the pupils. The pupil does the inquiry and the teacher guides it. The following points should be kept in mind while guiding pupils to inquire:

- Ensure that the questions are phrased in such a way so as to elicit Yes/No response.
- Ask pupils to be specific with their questions.
- Direct pupils' inquiry towards object, event condition and property questions.
- Invite experimentation questions.
- Ask the pupils to rephrase the invalid questions.
- Encourage interaction among the pupils.
- Record systematically on the chalk board, the questions of pupils and the teachers' response.
- Provide a free intellectual environment without evaluating pupils' questions.
- Review the questions and responses to help the student to keep track of the process.

Phase-IV: Formulation of an Explanation

After developing several causal relationships and testing them with the help of experimentation questions, students may ultimately arrive at the fourth phase of - the model - formulating and explaining the theory. A theory may be built at four different levels:

- ***Simple Linear Causation:*** At this level students state that 'X' causes 'Y'. Where 'X' and 'Y' are related to cause and effect.

- ***Theory of Properties:*** By analyzing the generalized property of objects of concern, students build a higher level of theory. In other words, based on the property questions, students find an answer why 'X' causes 'Y'.
- ***Drawing Analogies:*** An analogy is a partial likeness or agreement between two things. It is a comparison made with reference to the theory formulated. Drawing analogies helps in better understanding of the theory formulated.
- ***Citing Application:*** The fourth level of theory building is citing applications. How a theory can be applied to different situations is stated by the students. Two types of applications may be cited:
  - ➢ Applications which are already known
  - ➢ Probable application

While giving applications students actually think in the lines of scientists and inventors.

It is quite easy to identify simple linear causation theory during an inquiry training session. By verification and experimentation questions students can easily be guided to find out that 'X" causes 'Y". However building the theory of properties by finding how and why 'X' causes 'Y' needs a complex approach. Apart from the teacher guiding the pupils to think about properties that are causing this particular relationship, he may need to provide reference material in the form of books, journals, experimental kits etc.

The Inquiry session ends with the analysis of the inquiry process, which constitutes the final phase. There are two stages in this phase.

- Recapitulation of the steps of the model
- Analysis of the strategies of inquiry

Phase-V: Analysis of the Inquiry Process

Recapitulation of the steps is necessary in the first few lessons for the pupils to learn and remember the procedure. When pupils are familiar with the steps of the inquiry, this stage may be omitted.

The fifth stage viz. analysis of the inquiry procedure is an important step from the point of view of the development of inquiry strategies among students. During this phase the content or explanation of the discrepant event is not important but the process by which students arrive at the explanation of the event is important. Therefore this model is more process oriented than product oriented. Due to the inclusion of this phase, inquiry becomes a conscious and a systematic process to the inquirer.

This step determines the questions that were most effective, the lines of questioning that were productive and those that were not, or the type of information the students needed and did not obtain. Hence this phase is essential if we are to make the inquiry process a conscious one and systematically try to improve it.

Principles of Reaction

The Inquiry Training Model is unique in the sense that the principles of reaction in this model are quite different from those in other Models of Teaching. The most important reactions of the teacher take place during the second and third phase. The teacher has to help the students to inquire, but not do the inquiry for them. The teacher can if necessary keep the inquiry moving by making new information available to the group and by focusing on particular problem events or by raising questions. During the last phase the teacher's task is to keep the inquiry directed towards the process of investigation itself.

Social System (Role of the Teacher and the Students)

The teacher selects or designs the puzzling situations and presents it to the students. However during the inquiry session teacher and students, both participated as equals. As the students iearn the principles of inquiry the teacher guides them to use the resource material and performs cxperiments and conducts discussions with other students.

Support System

The support that can be used in this model comprises a set of confronting materials, a teacher who understands the intellectual process and strategies of inquiry, and other resource material in the form of books, films, self instructional material, maps diagrams etc. to verify the data, form hypothesis and build the theory of properties.

Instructional and Nurturant effects

The major outcomes of the models are:

- development of scientific process skills viz., observing, collecting and organizing data,
- identifying and controlling variables,
- making and testing hypothesis,
- formulating explanations and
- drawing inference.

17
Teaching Skills

Teaching is an essential part of education. Its special function is to impart knowledge, develop understanding and skills. It is usually associated with the imparting of 3 Rs- reading, writing, arithmetic. The teachers play a vital role in imparting knowledge to the learners. "to know how to teach is the great art of teaching"

A teacher makes use of number of methods and techniques to bring about effective learning. The techniques include, motivating the students, explaining, questioning, writing on the blackboard, using teaching aids and so on. The teacher could also make use of nonverbal behaviours such as smiling, nodding and gesturing. These groups of activities are called skills. A teaching skill is a group of teaching acts/behaviours intended to facilitate pupils' learning directly or indirectly. If the teacher trainees are conscious and aware of teaching skills, they will be able to concentrate on each of these skills and gain masterly over the skill. Microteaching introduces the teacher trainee to a wide range of teaching skills and allows the teacher trainee to practice each skill one at a time until he or she becomes proficient in the skill. Later on, the teacher trainee will be able to link many such skills to achieve the desirable outcome.

MEANING OF TEACHING SKILLS

Teaching is not a single skill but a composite one. Various skills are required by the teacher to make his teaching effective. Teaching is a complex process because it deals with human behaviour which is in itself very dynamic in nature. The teaching process becomes complex when a teacher desires to be an effective and the whole process of teaching and learning result oriented. To achieve this teacher needs to inculcate abilities and skills which will make his teaching effective. The complex process of teaching can be divided into various components that are simple and defined. These components are called teaching skills which can be identified, practiced, evaluated, controlled and acquired through training.

A skill is a specific behaviour or activity, which requires doing on particular work of job or t ask. The performance of the concerned activity is automatically improved through its learning and practice. Teaching activity involves different skills, and which are essential to teach effectively.

Teaching constitutes a number of verbal and non-verbal acts. A set of related behaviours on teaching acts aim at specific objectives. These may be called as a teaching skill. All these teaching skill contribute to good teaching. These skills can be defined, observed, measured and controlled by means of practice.

Definitions of Teaching Skills

Some important definitions of teaching skills are:

1. According to Passi (1976), "*Teaching skill is a group of teaching acts or behaviours intended to facilitate pupil's learning directly or indirectly.*"
2. "A teaching skill is that behaviour of the teacher which facilitates pupils' learning directly or indirectly."
3. *"A teaching skill includes all arts and behaviour of the teacher which maximizes pupils' learning."*
4. *"A teaching skill is that art of the teacher which makes communication between the teacher and pupils sufficiently."*
5. "A teaching skill is that behaviour of the teacher which facilitates pupils' learning directly or indirectly."
6. "A teaching skill includes all arts and behaviour of the teacher which maximizes pupils' learning."
7. "A teaching skill is that art of the teacher which makes communication between the teacher and pupils sufficiently."
8. "A teaching skill is defined as a set of behaviours associated with the teaching of the subject matter which are especially effective in bringing about desirable changes in the teacher or the trainee who Makes practice of the skill."
9. According to Gage (1968), *"Teaching skills are specific instructional activities and procedures that a teacher may use in his classroom. These are related to the various stages of teaching or in the continuous flow of teacher performance."*

Characteristics of Teaching Skills

The main characteristics of teaching skills are as follows:

- *Identifiable:* Teaching skills can be identified by analyzing teaching behaviours. Allen & Ryan (1969) identified 14 skills of teaching.
- *Observable:* Teaching skills can be observed and this is the reason they have been identified.
- *Trainable:* We can train pupil teachers in using these skills which can be developed through instruction and training.
- *Measurable:* Teaching skills can be measured by simple observation, by making observation schedule and check list.
- *Perception:* cognition and action are three basic components of teaching skills.

NATURE OF TEACHING SKILL

The following is the nature of teaching skill:

- A teaching skill is a set of strictly overt or observable behaviours.
- Purely cognitive skills such as problem-solving are not considered a teaching skill.
- Teaching skills have three basic components, viz. perception, cognition and action.
- Teaching skills have three dimensions: (1) non-verbal behaviour, (2) openness, and (3) nature of moves in teaching to which the skill belongs

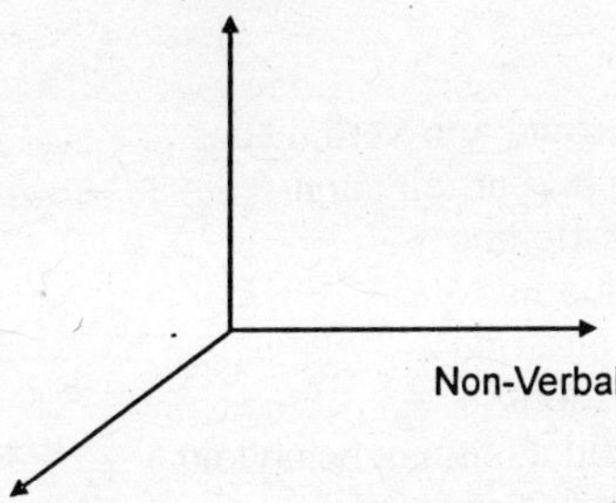

Figure 17.1: Three Dimensional Structure of Teaching Skill

A large number of teaching skills have been identified. The first effort in this direction was made by Allen and Ryan resulted in identifying 'Fourteen Teaching Skills'.

COMPONENTS OF TEACHING SKILLS

Teaching skills have essentially three components:

Perception: Teaching skills have a perceptual component for observing and receiving feedback. The teacher observes and selects appropriate teaching skill to be acquired by him.

Cognition: It refers to the behaviour or experience of knowing in which there is some degree of awareness as in thinking and problem-solving. Skills are thus cognitive strategies that allow the teachers to complete their assigned tasks i.e. teaching-learning activities which they lear through education and training.

Action: Teaching skills demand every teacher to actually practice his perceived and acquired knowledge in an effective way in the classroom.

While using difficult methodology, the teacher can use different skills as explaining, illustrations, narration etc. to make his teaching learning process more effective. The effective teacher must not only posses a good repertoire of skills but also understand when and why nto use certain skills. A skillful teacher understands that educational objectives require different teaching skills and behaviours.

WHY DO WE NEED TO HAVE SKILLS IN TEACHING

We need skills in teaching"

- To ensure competency in teaching.
- To make the class interesting.
- To enable the teacher to develop confidence in teaching.
- To avoid confusion
- To enable the teacher to understand individual differences in learning.

TYPES OF TEACHING SKILLS

Attempts have been made to list teaching skills. Allen and Ryan listed the following teaching skills at Stanford University in the U.S.A.:

1. Stimulus Variation
2. Set induction
3. Closure
4. Teacher silence and non-verbal cues
5. Reinforcing pupil participation
6. Fluency in questioning
7. Probing questioning
8. Use of higher questions
9. Divergent questions
10. Recognizing and attending behaviour
11. Illustrating and use of examples
12. Lecturing
13. Planned repetition
14. Completeness of communication

B.K. Passi has given the following list of Teaching Skills in his book *"Becoming Better Teacher; Micro-teaching Approach"*:

1. Writing instructional objectives
2. Introducing a lesson
3. Fluency in questioning
4. Probing questioning
5. Explaining
6. Illustrating with examples
7. Stimulus variation
8. Silence and non-verbal cues
9. Reinforcement
10. Increasing pupil participation
11. Using black board
12. Achieving Closure
13. Recognizing attending behaviour

NCERT (National Council of Educational Research and Training) in its publication *"Core Teaching Skills"* (1982) has laid stress on the following teaching skills:

1. Writing instructional objectives
2. Organizing the content
3. Creating set for introducing the lesson
4. Introducing a lesson
5. Structuring classroom questions
6. Question delivery and its distribution
7. Response management
8. Explaining
9. Illustrating with examples
10. Using teaching aids
11. Stimulus variation
12. Pacing of the lesson
13. Promoting pupil participation

14. Use of blackboard
15. Achieving closure of the lesson
16. Giving assignments
17. Evaluating the pupil's progress
18. Diagnosing pupil learning difficulties and taking remedial measures
19. Management of the class

CORE TEACHING SKILLS

It is not possible to train all the pupil-teachers in all these skills in any training programme because of the constraints of time and funds. Therefore a set of teaching skills, which cuts across the subject areas, has been identified. They have been found very useful for every teacher. The set of these skills are known as core teaching skills.

Core Teaching Skills are:

1. Skill of Probing Questions
2. Skill of Explaining
3. Skill of illustrating With Examples
4. Skill of Stimulus Variation
5. Skill of reinforcement
6. Skill of Questioning
7. Skill of Using Blackboard
8. Skill of Introducing a Lesson

CLASSIFICATION OF TEACHING SKILLS

Teaching skills can be classified according to the stage of the lesson as given in Table 17.1.

CORE TEACHING SKILLS AND THEIR COMPONENTS

Below is the brief discussion of core teaching skills with their major components:

Skill of Introducing a Lesson or Set Induction

Introduction skill is the skill required to begin the teaching—learning process.

Objectives of Skill of Introduction a Lesson

The objectives of the skill of introduction a lesson are to:

- Get students attention & their readiness for learning
- Arouse student's motivation
- Clearly indicate the learning experience to be provided
- Suggest ways & means of the approaching activity to be done
- Review previous experiences/knowledge & makes its link to the present content/task

Components of Introduction Skill

The components of Introduction Skill are given in table 17.2:

Table 17.1: Teaching Skills Related to Different Stages of Lesson

Stage of Lesson	*Related Teaching Skill*
1. Planning Stage	1. Writing Instructional Objectives 2. Selecting the Content 3. Organizing the Content 4. Selection of the Audio-Visual Material
2. Introductory Stage	5. Creating Set for Introducing the Lesson 6. Introducing the Lesson
3. Presentation Stage	7. Structured Classroom Questions 8. Fluency in Questioning 9. Probing Questions 10. Questions-Delivery and Distribution 11. Use of Higher Order Questions 12. Divergent Questions 13. Response Management 14. Pacing the Lesson 15. Lecturing 16. Explaining 17. Discussing 18. Demonstrating 19. Illustrating with Examples 20. Using Teaching Aids 21. Using Blackboard 22. Stimulus Variation 23. Silence and Non-verbal Cues 24. Reinforcement 25. Promoting Pupils Participation 26. Reorganizing Attending Behaviour 27. Management of the Class
4. Closing Stage	28. Achieving Closure 29. Planned Repetition 30. Giving Assignments 31. Evaluating the Pupil's Progress 32. Diagnosing the Pupil's Learning Difficulties and Taking Remedial Measures

Table 17.2: Components of Introduction Skill

Skill Components	*How to use them*
Gaining Attention	By using voice, gesture & eye contact. Use of audio-visual aids. Changing the pattern of teacher-pupil interaction.
Use of Previous Knowledge	Previous knowledge refers to the learner's level of achievements before instruction begins. Use of previous knowledge is a must, because it helps to establish integration between the pre-existing knowledge of the learner and the new knowledge that the teacher wants to impart him.
Use of Appropriate Device	In order to motivate the learner, the teacher should make use of appropriate devices or techniques while introducing a lesson. For example- dramatization, models, audio-visual aids etc.

Skill of Stimulus Variation

If the class room environment becomes monotonous, then it puts a negative impact on the teaching and learning process. It is therefore, essential to make the class room environment challenging and interesting such that the teaching –learning process becomes lively, interesting, pleasant and a thought provoking experience. This process of bringing variation in the overall interactive environment of the class with the help of stimuli change is called stimulus variation.

It is very important for a teacher to ensure and sustain pupil's attention. For this purpose the teacher uses some gestures, body movements, makes certain verbal statements etc. all these behaviours are related to stimulus variation. The skill of stimulus variation can be defined as deliberate change in the attention drawing behaviours of the teacher in order to secure and sustain pupil's attention towards the lesson.

Objectives of Skill of Stimulus Variation

The objectives of the skill of stimulus variation are to:

- Break monotony of the class
- Bring variation in presentation
- Bring and maintain attention of pupils
- Make teaching attractive & interesting
- Make teaching effective by using various senses
- Involve students in the teaching-learning process

Components of Stimulus Variation Skill

The components of Stimulus Variation Skill are given in table 17.3:

Table 17.3: Components of Stimulus Variation Skill

Teacher Movement	The teacher should not be static, he should be moving around the lecture table so that he and the students remain active.
Teacher Gesture	The body language & the facial expression of the teacher should be pleasant, relevant to explain the concepts & make teaching a live experience. It should be varied time to time & according to the need.
Change in Interaction Style	The class room interaction pattern must be changed constantly to make the class lively and everybody participate in the learning process. There may be four types of interaction pattern: a) Teacher to whole class b) Teacher to group of students c) Teacher to individual student d) Student to student
Change in Speech Pattern	The teacher should vary his speech pattern depending on the relevance of the concept and to break monotony of the class. It also helps in gaining and maintaining students attention & in reflecting the importance of the

(Contd.)

	concept being expressed. The following three speech pattern may be used for this purpose: a) Pausing b) Low pitch c) High pitch
Oral – Visual Switching	According to the need of the topic, it becomes necessary to shift sensory channels of students. It can be done in the following ways: a) Verbal to visual b) Verbal to verbal-visual c) Visual to verbal d) Visual to verbal-visual
Pupil Activity	Students should be involved in organizing activity based learning.
Change in Sensory Focus	Focusing implies drawing the attention of the learners towards a particular point which the teacher wishes to emphasize. Such technique involves verbal focusing, gestural focusing, or verbal-gestural focusing. Focusing pupils attention on particular point or concept by using (1) verbal statement like 'look at the blackboard', 'see the figure in the chart' etc. (2) gestures and (3) both verbal statements and non-verbal cues. Making use of the different senses like hearing, seeing, touching and so on.

Skill of Using Blackboard

Blackboard (BB) is one of the most important tools in classroom teaching. Effective use of BB increases the effectiveness of teaching.

Objectives of Skill of Using Blackboard

The objectives of the skill of using blackboard are to serves the following purposes:

- Effective visual aid
- Provides clarity in understanding concepts
- Draws attention of students at relevant points
- Presents holistic picture of the content

Components of Using Blackboard Skill

The components of Using Blackboard Skill are given in table 17.4:

Table 17.4: Components of Using Blackboard Skill

Legibility of Hand Writing	Distinct difference between letters Adequate space between letters Adequate space between words Slant of the letter nearly vertical All letters of the same size Size of the letters large enough to be read Thickness of the line uniform

(Contd.)

Neatness	Adequate spacing between lines Lines parallel to the base of the black board No over writing Focusing the relevant matter
Appropriateness	Continuity in the points Simplicity Proper use of color chalk Appropriate presentation of illustrations and diagrams Underlining only the important points
Organization of Blackboard Work	Systematic planning of space Spacing to exhibit the sequence of the items being presented Adjustment of space for presenting related items in totality

Questioning Skill

Questions are the most important tool of thinking, reasoning, learning and teaching. Questions are used at every stage of teaching, i.e., pre-active, interactive and post-active stages.

Objectives of Questioning Skill

The objectives of questioning skill to:

- Finding out previous knowledge
- Revising the topic
- Stimulating thought process
- Encouraging discussion
- Getting students participation

Questioning Approaches

The questioning approaches are:

Targeting Questions - a list of questions is put to a particular student or a group of student. After which it is rotated in the class from one student to another.

Delivery - in this type of approach all participants have to consider the questions. Students are given time to think about the answers after teacher calls individual students and asks them to give answers.

Acknowledging the answers - sometimes teacher put questions to acknowledge the answer of the previous question & to reinforce their positive response.

Level or Order of Question

Depending on the complexity of questions, there are three levels of questions; lower order, middle order and higher order questions. The teacher uses any of these levels of questions depending on student aptitude, nature of content, purpose of questioning and levels of teaching.

Types of Questions

Open questions—those questions for which there is not a single definite answer.

Closed questions—these are the questions which have only one correct answer.

Rhetorical/dramatic questions—these are the questions for which there are no easy answers. These are higher order thinking questions.

Components of Questioning Skill

The components of Questioning Skill are given in table 17.5:

Table 17.5: Components of Questioning Skill

Structure	Grammatical correctness and lucidity Conciseness Relevance Specificity
Process	Speed Voice Pause Style
Product	

Reinforcement Skill

Reinforcement is a skill which a teacher uses to increase the frequency of positive or desirable behaviour of the learner or to decrease the negative or undesirable behaviour of the learner.

Reinforcement is strengthening the connection between a stimulus and a response. There are two types of reinforcement's i.e. positive reinforcement and negative reinforcement. Positive reinforcement provides pleasant experience or a feeling of satisfaction which contributes towards strengthening of desirable responses or behaviours. The negative reinforcement results in unpleasant experiences, which help in weakening the occurrence of undesirable responses or behaviours.

The skill of reinforcement can increase the students' involvement in learning in a number of ways. The skill is used when the teacher reinforces correct responses with a smile, when the teacher praises a good response or encourages a slow learner. Such positive reinforces strengthen desirable responses whereas negative reinforces such as scolding, punishing the students, sarcastic remarks etc. weaken the undesirable response. However, the use of more and more positive reinforcers maximizes pupils' involvement of learning rather than the use of negative reinforcers. Therefore, the skills of reinforcement involve the teacher to use more and more positive reinforcers and to decrease the use of negative reinforcers so that the pupils' participation is maximized.

Objectives of Reinforcement Skill

The objectives of reinforcement skill are to:

- Attract and retain attention of the class
- Encourage pupils for positive behaviour
- Discourage pupils for negative behaviour
- Increase students confidence level

Components of Reinforcement Skill

The components of Reinforcement Skill are given in table-17.6:

Table 17.6: Components of Reinforcement Skill

Verbal	a) Positive – repeating students answer & praising them b) Negative – scolding & telling students to improve
Non-verbal	a) Positive – Smile, positive head movement etc. b) Negative – anger, negative head movement etc.
Contact Reinforcement	Patting the back, hand shaking & putting hands on the students head.
Proximity Reinforcement	Going nearer to the pupils & making them more involved & interested in learning
Activity Reinforcement	Giving a task, a project, home work, assignment, etc.
Token Reinforcement	Awarding marks, grades, good, excellent, etc. on pupils note book.
Inappropriate Use of Reinforcement	This is the situation when the teacher does not encourage the pupil with respect to quality of his response. He uses same type of comment for every response.
Denial Reinforcement	This is the situation, where the teacher does not give reinforcement when the situation is demanding encouragement.

Explaining Skill

A teacher is said to be explaining when he is describing 'how', 'why' and sometimes 'what' of a concept, phenomenon, event, action or condition. It can be described as an activity to bring about an understanding in the learning about a concept; principle etc. While explaining, the teacher gives:

- Causes for some phenomena, event or action
- Reason for some phenomena, event or action
- Steps involved in arriving at a result or
- Various events that have resulted in phenomena

Explaining bridges the gap in understanding the new knowledge by relating it to the past experience. Thus explaining depends upon the type of the past experience, the type of the new knowledge and the type of the relationship between them. Explanations can be made more effective by using simple and clear language for clarity, examples and illustration materials for better understanding and appropriate link words for relating the concepts.

This is the skill required to develop understanding and higher order thinking among students. This skill is one of the most important attributes a good teacher must possess.

Objectives of Explaining Skill

The objectives of explaining skill are to:

- Clarify an issue
- Describe process, structures and procedures
- State reasons of events and phenomena

Components of Explaining Skill

The components of explaining Skill are given in table 17.7:

Table 17.7: Components of Explaining Skill

Use of Beginning Statements	Before starting any explanation, the teacher should make the pupils aware of what he is to teach on that day through a clear beginning statement.
Use of Explaining Links	This technique is used primarily to explain the links in statements with 'so', 'therefore', 'because', 'due to', 'as a result of', 'in order to' etc.
Clarity	State concepts clearly Define new terms and concepts; use simple language, maintain logical sequence. Use suitable examples and illustration Voice modulation to emphasis Develop the explanation from: Known to unknown. Examples to rule.
Use of Concluding Statement	This is the statement made at the end of the explanation. It includes the summary of all the main results of the explanation.
Questions to Test Pupils Under-standings	These are short questions put to the pupils to test their understanding of the concept after the explanation. The main purpose is simply to judge whether the pupils have understood or not.
Fluency	Use simple language / easy flow of ideas / use appropriate vocabulary
Use of Link Words	Use linking words and phrases. Example : therefore, similarly, that is, since, that is why, because, in order to, hence ... etc.
Stimulating Questions	Check the understanding by questioning. Stimulate and channelize the students thinking by thought provoking questions like how, why type.

Precautions for Explaining Skill

At the time of using explaining skill, the following points should be remember in mind:

- It should be in simple language.
- It should not be given the shape of an advice.
- The thoughts included in it should be in a sequence.

- Irrelevant things should not be included in it.
- It should be according to the age, experience and mental level of the pupils.

Probing Question Skill

Probing questions are those which help the pupils to think in depth about the various aspects of the problem. By asking such questions again, the teacher makes the pupils more thoughtful. He enables the pupils to understand the subject deeply.

Components of Probing Question Skill

The components of Probing Question Skill are given in Table 17.8:

Table 17.8: Components of Probing Question Skill

Prompting	When a pupil expresses his inability to answer some question in the class or his answer is incomplete, the teacher can ask such questions which prompt the pupils in solving the already asked questions.
Seeking Further Information	When the pupils answer correctly in the class but the teacher wants more information and further clarification from the learner by putting 'how' and 'why' of correct part the response.
Refocusing	When the teacher ask the same question from other pupil for comparison. This is known as Refocusing.
Redirecting Questions	Questions which are directed to more than one learner to answer are called redirected questions.
Increasing Critical Awareness	This technique is used when the pupil's response is correct. The teacher puts higher order questions to stimulate the pupil to think beyond what the pupil knows. This involves the 'how' and 'why' and sometimes 'what' type of questions on the point under discussion.

Skill of Illustration with Examples

When a teacher finds difficult in making students understand an abstract idea, concept or principle despite the best explanation, he or she then resorts to the use of illustrations. The teacher uses his experience to illustrate the concept with the help of examples. The clearer the examples are, the more learning will be taking place.

Components of Skill of Illustration with Examples

The components of Skill of Illustration with Examples are given in table 17.9:

Table 17.9: Components of Skill of Illustration with Examples

Formulating Simple Examples	A simple example is one which is related to the previous knowledge of pupils. It should be according to the age level, grade level and the background of pupils.
Formulating Relevant Examples	An example is relevant to the concept, when the concept or the rule can be applied to it. This means to say that the rule is explained by the example.
Formulating Interesting Examples	An example is interesting if it can arouse curiosity and interest of pupils. This can be judged by the attending behavior of students. If the pupils keenly attend to the example, it is really interesting.
Use of Appropriate Media for Examples	Appropriateness of media refers to its suitability to age level, grade level, maturity and to the unit taught. The decision about the nature of media, whether verbal or non verbal depends on the nature of concept.
Use of Inductive and Deductive Approach for Example	This involves the teacher giving examples relating to the concept or rule to clarify it. The pupils on the basis of the examples given, formulate the rule. After this the teacher asks the pupils to give examples to test whether the pupils have rightly understood the concept or not.

18
Micro-Teaching

The main objective of teacher-training institutions is to mould the behaviour of both pre-service and in-service teachers. They are trained in these institutions by providing them proper training. It has changed the old saying that teachers are born not produced, now we use that teachers are made, not born. It is the micro-teaching which has revolutionized the whole teaching-programme by providing training to both pre-service and in-service teachers. It is a training concept which is scaled down in terms of class, size and time in order to minimize the complexities of the normal teaching encounter. The length and scope of the lesson is reduced, only one skill is practiced at a time.

ORIGIN AND DEVELOPMENT OF MICRO-TEACHING

The term micro-teaching was first coined by Dwight Allen of Stanford University, USA in 1963, when an Experimental Project on the identification of teaching skills was in progress under the guidance and supervision of the faculty members (Bush, Allen, McDonald Acheson and many others). This project was aided by Ford Foundation and Kettering Foundation. The team of experts was assigned the development of testing and evaluation tools to measure the attainment of teaching skills. At this juncture Keath Acheson, a research worker was investigating the utility of video tape recorder in the development of technical teaching skills. This instrument could be used for recording the class interaction and the behaviours of the trainee vividly and accurately. This led to the development of a systematic and accurate method of giving feedback to the teacher trainee.

All the steps of micro-teaching technique Teach → Feedback → Re-plan → Re-teach → Re-feedback were formulated. Thus, the name of micro-teaching was coined for this method of developing teaching skills in 1963. Since then this technique of teacher training has been widely used in almost all Colleges and Universities of Europe and Asia. In India, it is being used with great emphasis in all the teacher training programmes of developing teaching skills and competencies among teacher trainees.

MEANING OF MICRO-TEACHING

Micro teaching is a procedure in which a student teacher practices teaching with a reduce number of pupils in a reduced period of time with emphasis on a narrow and specific teaching skill.

A teaching skill is a group of teaching acts/behaviours intended to facilitate pupils' learning directly or indirectly. If the teacher trainees are conscious and aware of teaching skills, they will be able to concentrate on each of these skills and gain masterly over the skill. Microteaching introduces the teacher trainee to a wide range of teaching skills and allows the teacher trainee to practice each skill one at a time until he or she becomes proficient in the skill. Later on, the teacher trainee will be able to link many such skills to achieve the desirable outcome.

DEFINITIONS OF MICRO-TEACHING

Some of the definitions which will enable us to understand the meaning of micro-teaching are as:

1. *D.W. Allen* (1966), "Micro-Teaching is a scaled down teaching encounter in class size and class-time".
2. *Allen, D.W.* and *Eve, A.W.* (1968), "Micro-teaching is a system of controlled practice that makes it possible to concentrate on specified teaching behaviour and to practice teaching under controlled conditions"
3. *R.N. Bush* (1968), "Micro-Teaching is a teacher education technique which allows teachers to apply well defined teaching skills to a carefully prepared lesson in a planned series of five to ten minutes encounter with a small group of real classroom students, often with an opportunity to observe the performance on video-tape".
4. *Mc. Alease* and *Unwin* (1971), "Micro-Teaching is most often applied to the use of closed circuit television to give immediate feedback to a trainee-teacher's performance in a simplified environment".
5. *B.K. Passi* and *M.S. Lalita* (1976), "Micro-Teaching is a training technique which requires student teachers to teach a single concept using specified teaching skill to a small number of pupils in a short duration of time"
6. *Encyclopedia of Education (Ed. Deighton, L.C. 1971)*, "Micro-Teaching is a real, constructed, scaled down teaching encounter, which is used for teacher training, curriculum development and research."
7. *N.K. Jangira* and *Singh Ajit* (1982), "Micro-Teaching is a training setting for the student teacher where complexities of the normal classroom teaching are reduced by practising one component skill at a time, limiting the content to a single concept, reducing the size to 5 to 10 pupils and reducing the duration of the lesson to 5 to 10 minutes."
8. *Kuma R.* (1996), "Micro-Teaching is a technique of training in which one learns the skills of teaching through a scaled down process of teaching learning."
9. *L.C. Singh* (1977), "Microteaching is a scaled down teaching encounter in which a teacher teaches a small unit to a group of five pupils for a small period of 5 to 20 minutes."
10. *Flamders, Ned. A.* (1960), "Micro—teaching programme is organized to expose the trainees to an organized curriculum of miniature teaching encounters, moving from the complex to the more complex."
11. *Clift, J. C. and Others* (1976), "Micro-teaching is a teacher training programme which reduces the teaching situation to a simpler and more controlled encounter achieved by limiting the practice teaching to a specific skill and reducing time and class size."

From the above stated definitions a more comprehensive definition of microteaching can be stated as follows. Microteaching is a teacher training technique where the complexities of the normal classroom teaching are reduced by:

- Practicing one teaching skill at a time
- Limiting the content to a single concept
- Reducing the class size to 5 to 7 and
- Reducing the duration of the lesson to 5 to 7 minutes.

OBJECTIVES OF MICRO-TEACHING

The main objectives of micro-teaching are:

- To enable teacher trainees to learn and assimilate new teaching skills under controlled conditions.
- To enable teacher trainees to master a number of teaching skills
- To enable teacher trainees to gain confidence in teaching.

NATURE OF MICRO-TEACHING

From the above definitions, the following points highlight the nature of micro-teaching:

Training Technique: Micro-Teaching is a training technique and not a teaching technique. It makes them to learn the art of teaching. The teachers are provided training through training institutions in order to mould their behaviour and to challenge the dictum "teachers are born not made".

Miniaturized Teaching: It is micro or miniaturized teaching in the sense that it reduced the complexities of real teaching by practising one skill at a time, reducing class size to 5 to 10 pupils, reducing duration of the lesson to 5 to 10 minutes, limiting the content in its scope and length.

New Innovation: It is relatively a new technique or new experiment in the field of teacher education more specifically in student teaching.

Individualized Device: It is a highly individualized training device. Each trainee has to practise the different skills one by one until he gains mastery over all the skills and then use the integrated skills in a normal classroom.

Feedback Device: It gives immediate knowledge of results or feedback to the trainees about their performances immediately after completing their lessons. This feedback is provided either through videotape recorder or by the method master with the help of ratings.

One Skill at a Time: The normal classroom teaching uses integrated skills and through this traditional approach of teaching all the skills cannot be mastered. Micro-teaching provides opportunity to select one skill at a time and practice it through its scaled down encounter and then take other skills in a similar manner.

In conclusion, we can say that micro-teaching is a technique or device of imparting training to the inexperienced or experienced one's for learning the art of teaching by practising specific teaching skills through scaled down teaching encounter, i.e.; reducing the complexities of teaching in terms of size, time and context.

MAIN PROPOSITIONS/ASSUMPTIONS OF MICRO-TEACHING

Allen and Ryan (1969) mentioned the following main propositions of micro-teaching:

- Micro-teaching is a teaching technique, which is based on construction of a teaching situation in which the student teacher and pupils work together in a practice situation. Bonafide teaching does take place.
- It lessens the complexities of normal classroom teaching, i.e, class size, scope of lesson and time are reduced.
- It focuses on training for the accomplishment of the specific tasks. These tasks may be the practice of instructional skills, the practice of techniques of teaching, the mastery of certain circular material or the demonstration of teaching models.
- It allows for the increased level of practice. In a micro-teaching setting the time, number of pupils, methods of feedback and supervision etc; may be manipulated.
- It greatly expands the normal knowledge of results or feedback dimensions in teaching. Immediately after teaching a brief micro-lesson, the trainee is engaged in a critique of his performance. All this feedback can be immediately translated into his practice when the trainee re-teaches shortly after the critique conference.

ADVANTAGES OF MICRO-TEACHING

The main advantages of micro-teaching are as follows:

- Microteaching is an effective feedback device for the modification of teacher-behaviour.
- Microteaching is useful for developing teaching efficiently in pre-service and in-service teacher education Programme.
- It can be done either in real classroom conditions or in stimulated conditions.
- It is a training device for improving teaching practice and to prepare effective teachers.
- The knowledge of practice and teaching skill can be given by the use of microteaching.
- The specific teaching skills are developed by the microteaching experiences-e.g. Reinforcement skills, Probing questions etc.
- It lessens the complexities of the normal classroom teaching by scaled down teaching.
- The training of teachers becomes individualized. Each trainee makes progress in developing teaching skills at his own rating dependent upon his ability.
- The mechanism of feedback device can be combined with other devices such as simulated social skill training (SSST) and interaction analysis device which provide continuous reinforcement to the trainee performances.
- It permits increased control and regulated teaching practice.
- It is an economical device and use of videotape enables the trainee to analyze his own teaching performances.
- It focuses attention on teaching behaviour to modify and improve in a desired direction.

- It makes trainees familiar with various teaching styles e.g. Black-board writing, Use of aids, Asking questions etc,
- It is a real teaching. It focuses on developing teaching skills and competencies.
- It is an analytical approach to training.
- It is a relatively new innovation in the field of teacher effective education.
- It is a highly individualized training device to prepare effective teachers.
- It produces adequate feedback for trainee's performance.
- It is a scaled down teaching.
- It reduces the class size up to 5 to 10 pupils.
- It reduces the duration of period 5 to 10 minutes.
- It reduces the size of the topic.
- It reduces the teaching skill. A single skill is practiced.
- Use of video—tape and closed circuit television makes observation very objective.
- The teacher—trainees are enabling to gain confidence in teaching and to master a number of skills by dealing with a small group of pupils.
- The teacher-trainees are enabled to learn and assimilate new teaching skills under controlled conditions
- It helps to develop and master important teaching skills.
- It helps to accomplish specific teacher competencies.
- It caters the need of individual differences in the teacher training.
- It is more effective in modifying teacher behaviour.
- It is an individualized training technique.
- It employs real teaching situation for developing skills.
- It reduces the complexity of teaching process as it is a scaled down teaching.
- It helps to get deeper knowledge regarding the art of teaching.

USES OF MICRO-TEACHING

The main uses of micro-teaching are as under:

- Helps in reducing the complexities of the normal class room teaching.
- Helps the teacher trainee gain more confidence in real teaching,
- It creates among the teacher trainees an awareness of various skills of which teaching is composed of.
- It simulates the class room scene and gives the teacher trainee an experience of real teaching.
- It helps in systematic and objective analysis of the pattern of class room communication through specific observation schedule.
- It is more effective in modifying teacher behaviour.
- It is an effective technique for transfer of teaching competencies to the class room.
- It helps in getting acquainted with class room manners to a certain extent.
- Feedback enables the teacher trainee to consciously concentrate on specific behavioural modification.
- It helps the teacher-trainees in better understanding of the meaning and concept of the term teaching.

DISADVANTAGES OF MICRO -TEACHING

Following are the disadvantages of microteaching:

- Microteaching tends to reduce creativity of teachers.
- For successful implementation, microteaching requires competent and suitably trained teacher educators.
- Microteaching can be carried on successfully in a controlled environment only.
- Microteaching is very time consuming.
- The application of microteaching to new teaching practices is limited.
- Microteaching alone may not be adequate. It needs to be supplemented and integrated with other teaching techniques.
- Micro teaching is skill oriented and not content oriented.
- It covers only a few specific skills.
- The question of integrating the skill is quite challenging.
- Teaching is not just a summation of teaching skills.
- A large number of trainees cannot be given the opportunity for re-teaching and re-planning.
- It requires special classroom setting.
- It covers only a few specific skills.
- It deviates from normal classroom teaching.
- It may raise administrative problem while arranging micro lessons

PHASES OF MICRO-TEACHING

The three phases of micro-teaching are as follows:

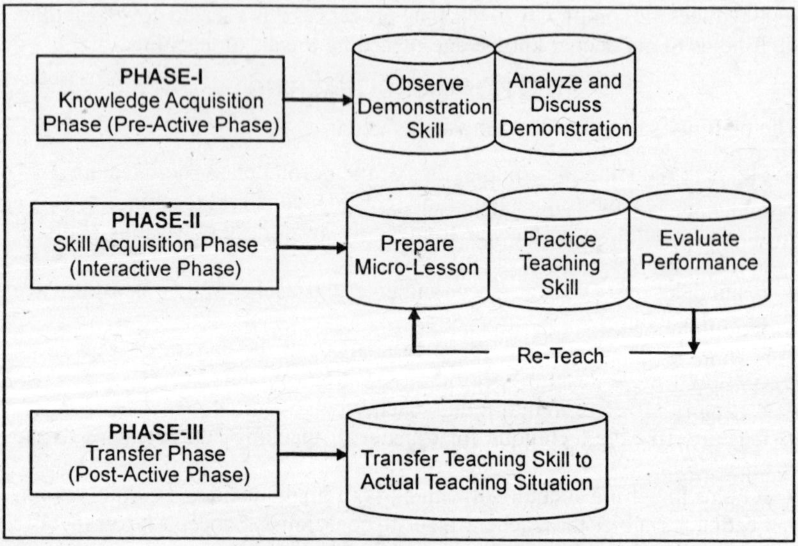

Figure 18.1: Phases of Micro Teaching

I: Knowledge Acquisition Phase: In this phase, the concept of micro-teaching along with its various components is discussed. The knowledge about the different skills is provided. The method master delivers a skill lesson and the trainee observes this demonstration lesson. By observing the lesson, they discuss it with the method master, analyze its weak and strong points with a view to identify and discriminate the component behaviour of the skills. By observing this model lesson, they get training in both theoretical as well as practical aspects of that skill.

II: Skill Acquisition Phase: After the trainee has received the theoretical background of the skill and a model lesson by the method master, the actual phase of acquiring the skill starts. The trainees now prepare their own micro lessons on a particular skill which is scaled down in all aspects. They now teach the particular micro-lesson to a particular group of students. This teach session is observed by the supervisor who gives immediate feedback to the trainee about his performance. After receiving the feedback, he again re-plans the lesson according to suggestions provided by supervisor and re-teaches his lesson to same group or another group of students. This is followed by a re-feedback session based on ratings of supervisor, students and if available by video-tape recording. This cycle is repeated till he gains mastery over the skill and in similar way, he practises all the skills one by one till he gains mastery over all the skills. He now prepares an integrated skill lesson and delivers it in front of trainees.

III: Transfer Phase: After gaining mastery over all the skills in the second phase, the trainees are now given an opportunity to face the normal classroom. Here size, time and context are not limited but his lesson is of 40 or 50 minute's duration including its size and scope. Instead of artificial situations, he teaches in the real classroom where he utilizes all the skills during presentation of one particular content.

STEPS OF MICRO-TEACHING

In micro-teaching, the trainee should follow the following steps in a systematic manner to achieve the required skills:

Orientation: In the beginning, necessary theoretical background is given about micro-teaching regarding its various aspects viz. concept of micro-teaching, procedure of micro-teaching, advantage, limitations and requirements and setting for adopting micro-teaching technique.

Discussion and Selection of Teaching Skill: After giving the necessary orientation regarding micro-teaching, the discussion about the different skills and their components takes place. The skills are thoroughly analyzed and discussed in order to provide the knowledge and awareness of teaching skills. A particular skill is selected for practice.

Demonstration: After selecting a particular skill for practice, a demonstration or model lesson is presented before the trainees by teacher educator or supervisor. It is also called as modeling i.e.; demonstration of the desired behaviours relating to a skill for imitation by the observers.

Observation of Model Lesson and Criticism: The demonstration lesson delivered by teacher educator or supervisor is carefully viewed, listened and observed by the trainees. This demonstration lesson is observed through different devices or observation schedules only to analyze the weak and strong points of the lesson in order to provide feedback to the person giving the model lesson.

Planning the Micro-Lesson: The student teacher now plans his own micro-lesson with the help of his supervisor and preceding steps.

The Indian model of micro-teaching developed by NCERT gives the following settings for planning the micro-lesson:

- Number of students 5 to 10.
- Types of students, real students or preferably peers.
- Type of supervisor: teacher-educators or peers.
- Time duration of 5 to 10 minutes.
- Time duration of micro-teaching cycle 36 minutes.

Practicing the Skill (Teach-session): Under this step, the trainee teacher teaches his prepared micro-lesson for 6 minutes in a micro class. The lesson is observed by the teacher educator or supervisor or peers with the help of appropriate devices observation schedules.

Feedback Session: The teach session is followed by feedback session. The trainee teacher is provided the feedback of his performance about the lesson he delivered in a micro-class. He is given suggestions for improvement in order to gain mastery over the particular skill. The feedback session lasts for 6 minutes where the trainees and supervisor discuss about his teaching behaviour.

Re-planning: After receiving the feedback, the trainee teacher re-plans his micro-lesson keeping in view the suggestion got from different sources like peers or supervisor. This session lasts for 12 minutes. If the video-tape is available for feedback, he himself watches the use of different components of a skill and where the weakness lies.

Re-teach: The re-planned lesson is now re-taught to another group of students for the same duration to practise the same skill. Again the supervisor or teacher educator observes his re-taught lesson by using appropriate devices or observation schedules. This session lasts for 6 minutes.

Re-feedback: The re-teach session is followed by re-feedback which is of 6 minutes duration. The student teacher is again given feedback of his performance during micro-lesson.

Repeating the Cycle: The micro-cycle is repeated again and again till the student teacher gains mastery over the skill.

MICRO-TEACHING CYCLE

The six steps that generally involved in micro-teaching cycle are - Plan, Teach, Feedback, Re-plan, Re-teach, Re-feedback. There can be variations as per requirement of the objective of practice session. These steps are diagrammatically represented in the following figure 18.2.

Plan: This involves the selection of the topic and related content of such a nature in which the use of components of the skill under practice may be made easily and conveniently. The topic is analyzed into different activities of the teacher and the pupils. The activities are planned in such a logical sequence where maximum application of the components of a skill is possible.

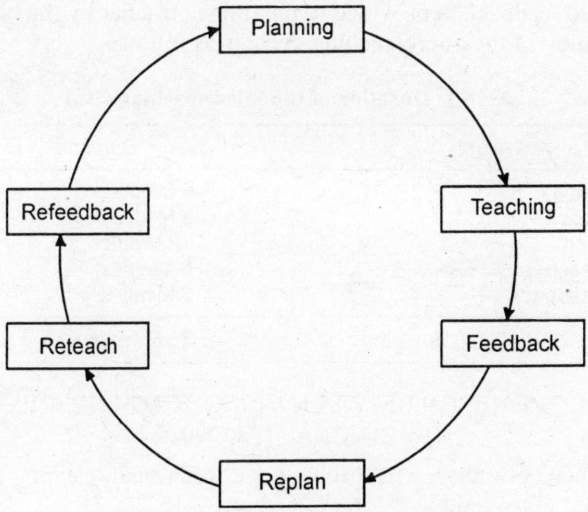

Figure 18.2: Micro-Teaching Cycle

Teach: This involves the attempts of the teacher trainee to use the components of the skill in suitable situations coming up in the process of teaching-learning as per his/her planning of activities. If the situation is different and not as visualized (in the planning of the activities, the teacher should modify his/her behaviour as per the demand of the situation in the class. He should have the courage and confidence to handle the situation arising in the class effectively.

Feedback: This term refers to giving information to the teacher trainee about his performance. The information includes the points of strength as well as weakness relating to his/her performance. This helps the teacher trainee to improve upon his/her performance in the desired direction.

Re-plan: The teacher trainee re-plans his lesson incorporating the points of strength and removing the points not skillfully handled during teaching in the previous attempt either on the same topic or on another topic suiting to the teacher trainee for improvement.

Re-teach: This involves teaching to the same group of pupils if the topic is changed or to a different group of pupils if the topic is the same. This is done to remove boredom or monotony of the pupil. The teacher trainee teaches the class with renewed courage and confidence to perform better than the previous attempt.

Re-feedback: This is the most important component of Micro-teaching for behaviour modification of teacher trainee in the desired direction in each and every skill practice.

INDIAN MODEL OF MICROTEACHING

The Indian model of microteaching has the following salient features:

1. The micro-lesson is taught/demonstrated under normal conditions with minimum electronic gadgetry. Available infrastructure (space, material and equipments) is used as the microteaching laboratory.

2. Immediate feedback is provided to the trainee teacher by the observers.
3. The duration of the microteaching cycle is as follows:

Table 18.1: Duration of the Microteaching Cycle

Activities	*Duration*
Teaching	6 Minutes
Feedback	6 Minutes
Re-Plan	12 Minutes
Re-Teach	6 Minutes
Re-Feedback	6 Minutes
Total	**36 Minutes**

COMPARISON BETWEEN MICRO-TEACHING AND TRADITIONAL TEACHING

The difference between micro-teaching and traditional teaching is given in the table 18.2 given below:

Table 18.2: Difference between Micro-Teaching and Traditional Teaching

Micro-Teaching	*Traditional Teaching*
1. Objectives are specified in behavioural terms.	1. Objectives are general and not specified in behavioural terms.
2. Class consists of small group of 5-10 students.	2. Class consists of 40-60 students.
3. The teacher takes up one skill at a time.	3. The teacher practices several skills at a time.
4. Duration time for teaching is 5-10 minutes.	4. The duration is 40-50 minutes.
5. There is immediate feed-back.	5. Immediate feed-back is not available.
6. Teaching is carried on under controlled situation.	6. There is no control over situation.
7. Teaching is relatively simple.	7. Teaching become complex.
8. The role of supervisor is specific and well defined to improve teaching.	8. The role of the supervisor is vague.
9. Patterns of class room interaction can be studied objectively.	9. Patterns of classroom interactions cannot be studied objectively.
10. Students gains confidence in teaching	10. Students usually tensed and scared
11. Provision for re-teaching	11. No provision for re- teaching

19
Practising Teaching Skills through Micro-Teaching

The major premise underlying the concept of micro-teaching is that the complex teaching act or behaviour can be split into teaching component skills; each simple, well-defined and limited. These skills can be identified, practiced, evaluated, controlled and acquired through proper training.

A teaching skill has been defined in various ways. A few definitions will clarify the meaning of the term. McIntyre, *et al.* (1977) define teaching skill as *"a set of related teaching behaviours whichn is specified types of classroom interaction situations tend to facilitate the achievement of specified types of educational objectives"*

Some of the important teaching skills are discussed below:

INTRODUCING A LESSON OR SET INDUCTION SKILL

Success of teaching a lesson depends on its introduction. The attention of the students towards learning the matter starts with the introduction of the lesson. In this the new knowledge may be properly linked with the existing knowledge of pupils. The introductory questions should be based on the previous knowledge related to the present content and the teacher has to proceed from known to unknown. The skill of introducing a lesson establishes rapport with the learners and facilitates concentration on his teaching. Effectiveness of introducing a lesson depends on the maximum use of previous knowledge and attention gaining of the learners, adopting appropriate devices, continuity, and relevant questions or statements pertaining to the content.

COMPONENTS OF INTRODUCING A LESSON OR SET INDUCTION SKILL

Introducing a lesson significantly influences the learning of a new lesson. The various components of the skill involved in introduction of a lesson are:

Use of Previous Knowledge (UPK)

Previous knowledge of students refers to the level of achievements from previous experiences. Testing the previous knowledge of students helps the teacher to establish integration between the pre-existing knowledge of the student and the new knowledge that the teacher wants to impart. Through this skill, the teacher knows the status of motivation, intellectual abilities and socio-cultural background of the student.

Preliminary Attention Gaining (PAG)

In the beginning of a lesson, the students may not be in an attentive mood being mentally unprepared for learning. The teacher's duty is to create desire for learning among the students. The teacher attracts the students towards his teaching by doing some attractive activity and creating curiosity. To gain attention at the preliminary stage interest or curiosity should be aroused among the students. The teacher can employ different attention attracting activities such as telling a story, recalling the previous experiences etc.

Use of Appropriate Device (UAD)

The teacher should make use of appropriate devices or techniques while introducing a lesson to motivate the students. The teacher creates such a situation by use of different types of devices such as:

- Questioning
- Use of examples, analogies, similarities
- Storytelling, describing related instances
- Lecturing, describing, narrating
- Use of A.V. aids
- Role-playing, dramatization
- Demonstration, experimentation etc.

In order to motivate the learners, the use of such devices should be suitable to the age, experience, maturity, etc. of the learner. The devices could be relevant only if they are related to the aims of the lesson/content. Unrelated devices confuse the learners and do not contribute towards establishing a healthy rapport with them.

Arousing Motivation (AM)

The teacher should link the required previous knowledge of the present knowledge with motivation of the present knowledge with motivation in introducing a lesson. The teacher should use the questions or activities to motivate the students towards the current topic or concept before declaring the topic or lesson.

Relevance and Continuity or Sequencing of questions and Statements (RC)

The teacher should use relevant and sequence questions to recall previous knowledge, to generate motivation towards the lesson and attract attention of the students.

Topic Declaration (TD)

The teacher should declare the topic or lesson after introducing the lesson. It indicates the beginning of presentation of the lesson. By this topic declaration, the students understand what they are going to be learning in that period.

MICRO-LESSON PLAN

Skill: Induction/Introduction **Subject:** Economics
Class: 10+2
Topic: Factor of Green Revolution

Sl. No.	*Teacher's Activity*	*Pupils' Activity*
1	Where the most population of our country lives?	In the villages
2	What is the main occupation of villagers?	Agriculture
3	Which crops the farmers grow in their fields?	Wheat, Rice, cotton, sugar-cane etc.
4	What we call to the sudden growth in Production of rice and wheat in 1966-67 in Punjab?	Green Revolution
5	What are the major factors behind green revolution?	No Response

Announcement of the Topic: After getting the satisfactory or unsatisfactory response of the students. Pupil Teacher will announce the topic by saying, "Well students, today we shall study about '**Factors of Green Revolution**".

Rating Scale

Topic: Factor of Green Revolution

Components of Skill	*Grading*					*Supervisor Remarks*
Use of Previous Knowledge (UPK)	A	B	C	D	E	
Preliminary Attention Gaining (PAG)	A	B	C	D	E	
Use of Appropriate Device (UAD)	A	B	C	D	E	
Arousing Motivation (AM)	A	B	C	D	E	
Relevance and Continuity or Sequencing of questions and Statements (RC)	A	B	C	D	E	
Topic Declaration (TD)	A	B	C	D	E	

Note:
"A" means 95 to 100 per cent correct use of component.
"B" means 85 to 94 per cent correct use of component.
"C" means 75 to 84 per cent correct use of component.
"D" means 65 to 74 per cent correct use of component.
"E" means below 65 per cent correct use of component.

Pupil Teacher Signature **Supervisor Signature**

QUESTIONING SKILL

According to Alice Wellington Rollins—*"The test of a good teacher is not how many questions he can ask his pupils that they will answer readily, but how many questions he inspires them to ask him which he finds it hard to answer."*

A question is any sentence, which has an interrogative form or function. In classroom settings, teacher questions are defined as instructional cues or stimuli that convey to students the content elements to be learned and directions for what they are to do and how they are to do it. Effective questioning is a real compliment to the instructional skills. It shows the ability to understand the student's real needs. It shows that for meaning that's deeper than the spoken message. Effective questioning is a powerful learned skill.

Questioning skill may be defined as *"a teaching skill helpful in putting the desired meaningful, clear and concise, grammatically correct, simple and quite straightforward questions to the students in a classroom teaching-learning situation for the purpose of drawing their attention on one or the other teaching points, making them active and alert to the ongoing teaching-learning process, testing their understanding and comprehension at the various stages of the lesson and motivating as well as providing them opportunity for the proper expression of their thoughts, imagination, recall and recognition and creative and constructive faculties."*

Purposes of Questioning

Questioning is useful to teachers for effectively planning class participation activities, for designing homework assignments and for writing exams. It also helps the teacher to match their goals or objectives for an assignment with the actual components of the assignment What are the purposes of teachers' classroom questions? A variety of purposes emerges, including:

- To develop interest and motivate students to become actively involved in lessons.
- To help students learn to construct meaning, to relate concepts, to guide thinking
- To evaluate students' preparation and check on homework or seatwork completion
- To develop critical thinking skills and inquiring attitude to understand how students form concepts
- To review and summarize previous lessons and, to summarize information
- To nurture insights by exposing new relationships, and to gain insight about students' interests
- To reveal prior misconception, to diagnose strengths and weaknesses, and to help students set realistic expectations by providing feedback
- To evaluate, to assess achievement of instructional goals and objectives
- To stimulate students to pursue knowledge on their own and, to help students develop the habit of reflection, to increase students' incentive to inquire, to discipline, manage, or control
- To encourage involvement of passive learner's, and to give listening clues.
- To determine what students know and don't know
- To develop critical and creative thinking skills

- To provide a review of material and content
- To prepare students for what is to be learned
- To check for comprehension or level of understanding
- To attract student attention
- To practice life-long learning skills
- To have fun learning
- To engage students in discussion
- To teach students to ask questions

Levels of Questions

There are three levels of questions on the basis of Bloom's Taxonomy of Educational Objectives. These three levels of questions are:

Low Level Questions or Low Order Questions

Low-level questions refer to questions that require one to recall information that has been registered in memory. Low-level questions operate on the level of knowledge, drawing from one's knowledge base of a subject.

Knowledge: Questions related to this desire the students recall or recognize the already learned facts, generalization, definitions, values and skills. Such questions do not ensure understanding of the knowledge.

Recall: Define the term 'Natural Environment'.

Recognition: Distinguish between four major components of environments.

Middle Level Questions or Middle Order Questions

These questions stimulate mental process in students and they are related to the understanding of the concept, facts, knowledge etc. of the student.

Translation: It indicates seeking a change of medium or mode of expression used to describe an object, concept or generalization.

Q1: Define the term 'Natural Resources' in your own words.
Q2: What does this model represent?

Interpretation: It involves comparison and explaining relationships between ideas, concepts, generalizations, definitions, values and skills.

Q1: Explain the meaning of skill of stimulus of variation.
Q2: Compare between biosphere and lithosphere.

Application: It refers to the use of the acquired knowledge in one situation to the solution of some specific problem in another situation.

Q1: What is the significance of hydrosphere for human being on earth?
Q2: What would be the time in America when the time in New Delhi is 12 noon?

Higher Level Questions or Higher Order Questions

The High-level questions encompass questions that require one to process information rather than simply recall it. High-level questions operate on one's ability to comprehend, apply, analyze, synthesize, and evaluate information. These questions develop creative ability of the students. They stimulate the highest level of mental process in students

Analysis: It involves inductive and deductive reasoning. It refers to examining materials, situations or environments with a view to separate them in to their components parts.

Q1: What are the general characteristics of hydrosphere and lithosphere?

Q2: Does the evidence support the generalization that farmers in India are in debt?

Synthesis: It refers to unique and original interpretation of facts, concepts and generalizations.

Q1: What sort of life do you expect without printed material?

Evaluation: It means to judge a position in the perspective of appropriate standards and values.

Q1: Do you favour the parliamentary form of govt. and why?

Q2: Why do you think that the private enterprises are better than public enterprises?

Division of Questioning

Questioning can be put into two divisions: Open-Ended Questions and Closed-Ended Questions.

Open-Ended Questions

Open-ended questions are questions without a fixed limit. An open question is likely to receive a long answer. They encourage continued conversation and help you get more information. They often provide opportunities to gain insight into the other person's feelings. Open-ended questions draw out more information. Open-ended questions start with who, what, where, why, when, and how.

Characteristics of Open-Ended Questions: Open questions have the following characteristics:

- They ask the respondent to think and reflect.
- They will give you opinions and feelings.
- They hand control of the conversation to the respondent.
- Open questions begin with such as: what, why, how, describe.
- Using open questions can be scary, as they seem to hand the baton of control over to the other person. However, well-placed questions do leave you in control as you steer their interest and engage them where you want them.
- When opening conversations, a good balance is around three closed questions to one open question. The closed questions start the conversation and summarize progress, whilst the open question gets the other person thinking and continuing to give you useful information about them.

Closed-Ended Questions

Closed-ended questions have a fixed limit. A closed question can be answered with either a single word or a short phrase. They are often answered with a yes or no, or with a simple statement of fact. Closed-ended questions are used to direct the conversation. They usually get specific information or confirm facts.

Characteristics of Closed-Ended Questions: Closed questions have the following characteristics:

- They give you facts.
- They are easy to answer.
- They are quick to answer.
- They keep control of the conversation with the questioner.

We use the open-ended questions to get more information and the closed-ended questions to focus in on one area.

Types of questions

There are 5 basic types of questions: *factual*, *convergent*, *divergent*, *evaluative* and *combination*.

Factual

Factual questions solicit reasonably simple, straightforward answers based on obvious facts or awareness. They are usually at the lowest level of cognitive or affective processes. Answers are frequently either right or wrong.

Q1: *What is the name the Shakespeare plays about the Prince of Denmark?*

Convergent

Answers to convergent questions are usually within a very finite range of acceptable accuracy. These may be at several different levels of cognition (comprehension, application, analysis) or the answerer may have to make inferences or conjectures based on personal awareness, or on material read, presented or known.

Q1: *On reflecting on the entirety of the play* Hamlet, *what were the main reasons why Ophelia went mad?* (This is not specifically stated in one direct statement in the text of Hamlet. Here the reader must make simple inferences as to why Ophelia committed suicide.)

Divergent

Divergent questions allow students to explore different avenues and create many different variations and alternative answers or scenarios. Correctness may be:

- based on logical projections
- contextual, or
- arrived at through basic knowledge, conjecture, inference, projection, creation, intuition, or imagination.

Divergent questions often require students to analyze, synthesize, or evaluate a knowledge base and then project or predict different outcomes. Frequently the intention of these types of divergent questions is to stimulate imaginative and creative thought, or investigate cause-and-effect relationships, or provoke deeper thought or extensive investigations. Be prepared for the fact that there may not be right or definitely correct answers to these questions.

Q1: *In the love relationship between Hamlet and Ophelia, what might have happened to their relationship and their lives if Hamlet had not been so obsessed with the revenge of his father's death?*

Evaluative

Evaluative questions usually require sophisticated levels of cognitive and/or emotional or affective judgment. In attempting to answer evaluative questions, students may be combining multiple logical and/or affective thinking processes, or comparative frameworks. Often an answer is analyzed at multiple levels and from different perspectives before the answerer arrives at newly synthesized information or conclusions.

Q1: *What are the similarities and differences between the deaths of Ophelia and Juliet?*

Q2: *What are the similarities and differences between Roman gladiatorial games and modern football?*

Rhetorical

The rhetorical question is usually defined as any question asked for a purpose other than to obtain the information the question asks. A rhetorical question is a figure of speech in the form of a question posed for its persuasive effect without the expectation of a reply. Rhetorical questions encourage the listener to think about what the (often obvious) answer to the question must be. When a speaker states, *"How much longer must our people suffer with this wide spread corruption?"* no formal answer is expected. Rather, it is a rhetorical device used by the speaker to assert or deny something. While sometimes amusing and even humorous, rhetorical questions are rarely meant for pure, comedic effect.

Overhead

This type of question is not directed at any particular individual, but is asked of the entire class... "over their heads." The ask-pause-call technique is used in asking overhead questions allows every students in the class to profit from the thinking involved in the formulation of an answer. The overhead questioning technique is encouraged because your lead-off questions will start discussions

Direct

A direct question is asked of one person whom you call by name before asking the question. Direct questions are especially effective when you suspect an individual's attention is wandering.

Relay

The relay technique places the teacher in the position of a moderator. The teacher accepts a question from a trainee, and then turns it over to another trainee to answer. This technique is very effective in promoting trainee participation and class discussion. Before doing this, bear in mind that you must be able to answer the question. This is not a duplicate. The fact that the mechanism for solving the problem is identical doesn't matter, because it would be different use cases that would cause people to ask the question. So the people who want the "top down" approach would not be searching with the "sub site" question. So they would not be able to find the question.

Probing Questions

A probing question is open-ended question, but it is a follow-up. It is narrower. It asks about one area. Probing questions are valuable in getting to the heart of the matter.

The Echo Question

It is a good technique for getting more information. The teacher can use this like a probing question. The idea is to use the last part of a phrase the teacher said. Slightly raise the tone of your voice at the end of the phrase to convert it to a question. Then pause and use silence. An echo question repeats part of the phrase that the student used, using voice inflection to convert it to a question. Some people call it mirroring or reflecting. Others call it parroting. It is a valuable technique to use.

Leading Questions

Many things can be good or bad. Leading questions can also be good or bad. Leading questions, if used improperly, can be manipulative because the teacher leading the student to give the answer he wants. Leading questions often end with suggestive nudges toward the desired answer. Some ending phrases would be, "Don't you?", "Shouldn't you?", "Won't you?", "Haven't you?", and "Right

Socratic Questioning

Socratic questioning is at the heart of critical thinking. Six types of Socratic questions are:

- Questions for clarification
- Questions that probe assumptions
- Questions that probe reasons and evidence
- Questions about Viewpoints and Perspectives
- Questions that probe implications and consequences
- Questions about the question

Components of the Questioning Skill

Broadly, there are mainly two components of questioning skill namely: framing of the questions and presentation of the questions in the class.

Framing of Questions

Questions can serve their purpose well when they are framed with necessary care and preparation on the part of a teacher by taking cognition of the following things:

1. *Relevancy:* Framed questions should be quite relevant to the topic being taught.
2. *Clarity:* The questions should be framed ion a simple and clear language. Ambiguity of any kind may kill the very purpose of putting questions.
3. *Precision or Conciseness:* While framing the questions, due care should be taken for keeping them as precise and brief as possible.

4. *Specificity:* The questions should be quite specific and to the point related to the content material presented to the students, the demand of the specific stage of the lesson or the purpose to be served by it.
5. *Grammatically Correctness:* It should be duly cared that the framed questions should be grammatically correct.

Presentation of Questions in the Class

While presenting questions in the classroom, the following components must be kept in mind:

1. *Voice of the Teacher:* Teachers should try to present the questions in a quite clear and audible voice being properly heard by all the students. He should also be careful about the proper accent, tone, pitch and rhythm of the voice along with the accompanying gestures and other non-verbal expressions while asking any question.

2. *Speed and Pause:* Due care should be taken for the maintenance of proper speed in the asking of the questions on the part of a teacher. He should give enough time to a student or the class for responding to the question asked by him on a simple logic that the rate or speed of thinking and responding on the part of the students tends to be slower than the speed of asking questions.

3. *Distribution of Questions:* Question should be addressed the whole class rather than its being put to an individual student. Out of the raised hands of the students who are willing to answer the question, teacher may now provide opportunity to any one of them or may choose from the group of the students who have not raised their hands for answer the question. The distribution of the questions must be quite fair and even all along the corners of the class. Every student of the class must feel that teacher may be asked to respond to a question any time during the course of the lesson, therefore, he must remain quite alert and attentive to things going on in the classroom.

4. *Prompting and Cuing:* Prompting consists of helping the students to provide the correct answer. A series of prompts, followed by encouragement, help students to gain confidence in giving replies. This is done by building up on the partial answer given by a student leading towards the correct answer. For instance, a teacher may say, 'well probably you were meaning to say this (orienting the answer to the proper direction), now can you further elaborate on this.' Cuing consists of giving hints by the teacher to help the students to find the answer. In a lesson teacher may ask 'Can you tell the effect of force on a body?' If no response is obtained, he may demonstrate by pushing the duster on the table with finger and ask what has happened to the duster when pushed. The usual response will be it moves and gradually with further cues the correct response that the position of a body is changed under the effect of force will be reached. Cues provided should be relevant to the question and designed such that these lead the students towards the correct answer.

5. *Teacher Behaviour:* Teacher must demonstrate a quite spontaneous and natural behaviour while asking questions in the class. He must possess a necessary degree of patience, restraint and sweetness in his voice and style of asking questions as well as responding to the responses of the students. He should also try to bring variety, novelty and change in the mode and style of his asking questions.

STIMULUS VARIATION SKILL

Continuous use of the same stimulus for a long period reduces the attention in that activity. The teacher behaviours influence pupil's attention. Variation in stimulus secures more attention among the students.

Any external force that disturbs the equilibrium is known as stimulus. So by stimulus variation, we mean the change n the intensity of the external force by a teacher while teaching. The skill of stimulus variation in other words means the regulation of stimuli by the teacher while teaching. Thus skill of stimulus variation may be defined as a set of observations for bringing desirable change or variation in the stimuli used to secure and sustain pupil's attention towards class room activities.

It has been generally observed that children especially up to the age of 10 years are not able to attend to one thing for a long period. The effectiveness of the teaching learning process in such a situation depends to a great extent on the stimulus variation used by the teacher behaviour. Some of the common teacher behaviours in the class room which fall under variation are:

Movement of the Teacher in the Class: This component of the skill helps in capturing and sustaining the attention of the class while teaching. Therefore the movement of the teacher in the class is of essential. But only meaningful movements are to be made. Thus a teacher while practicing the skill of stimulus variation should learn to make well planned meaningful movements for securing as sustaining the attention of students.

Gestures of the Teacher in the Class: Gestures are non-verbal clues which enhance the value of the message. They are usually made with the help of the movement of the eye, hand, head, body, facial expressions, like extending the hands in a typical shape to indicate how big or small one object is.

Change of Voice by the Teacher: It involves the variation in the tone, pitch or speed of his or her voice, to pay special attention to a particular point or sentence or paragraph while teaching. Variation of voice by the teacher is directly noted by the students and it has direct influence in capturing the attention of the students.

Focusing by the Teacher: The component of focusing of the skill of stimulus variation refers to the behaviours that help in focusing pupil's attention on a particular object word, idea, rule, concept, method, formula or generalization during teaching.

To exercise the component of focusing by the teacher the following methodology is followed.

- The use of verbal statements "look here in the map", "it is important to note"
- The use of gestures
- The use of both verbal statements and non-verbal gestures.

Change in Interaction Styles by the Teacher

- The process of teaching learning involves interaction. Change in interaction style means the change in the process of teaching learning. There are three main styles of interaction such as:

- Teacher pupils or teacher group interaction (teacher coveys or gets responses from the class or groups as a whole)
- Teacher pupil interaction (here teacher communicates with an individual pupil.)
- Pupil-pupil interaction here a teacher employs many pupils in a dialogue without doing direct discussion.

Pausing by the Teacher: Pausing refers to the behaviour related wit h introducing silence during teaching. A pause of approximately of 3 or 4 seconds is regarded as quite effective in securing and sustaining the pupils attention in the class while teaching.

Aural-Visual Switching: This behaviour refers to the introduction of the change or variation in the use of medium, from aural to visual, from visual to aural or a combination of aural and visual.

Physical Involvement of Students: This component of the skill of stimulus variation refers to the introduction of the change or variation in the types, forms and styles of the physical involvement of the pupil in the class. Sometimes they may be engaged in dramatizing and other times in writing on the blackboard, participating in the demonstration or handling some instrument or aid material etc.

COMPONENTS OF STIMULUS VARIATION SKILL

The following components of the skill, stimulus variation, influence the teaching-learning process effectively:

Teacher's Movement (TM): The teacher should move from one place to another on the teaching dais and towards all the students to attract attention of the entire class and to focus the attention of students the teacher. The movement of the teacher secures and maintains attention of the students.

Pupil's Movement (PM): A pupil moves from one place to another. The physical participation holds pupil's interest and attention in this task in which they are engaged physical participation can be in the form of handling apparatus, dramatization and writing on the blackboard.

Teacher's Gesture (TG): Expression of feelings and emotions involving non- verbal behaviours are called gestures. Gestures consists of hand and hand movements, eye movements, facial expressions, etc,. use of gestures increase the effectiveness of verbal communication. Gestures: Eyes movement, facial expression, body movements and movement of hands and legs.

Change in Voice (CV): The teacher's voice dominates the entire class. Voice modulation pitch, tone, and speed play a vital role in the class room. Communication constant use of the same level of pitch, tone, and speed by the teacher makes his communication dull, inactive and has an adverse effect. So, the teachers should modulate their voice.

Sensory Focus (SF): The movements, gestures and change in the voice of teacher secure pupil's attention. The verbal statements and gestures together are known as verbal-cum- gesture focusing. Verbal-cum-gesture focusing is termed as sensory focus. The sensory focus influences the attention of the students.

- Verbal Statement: Excellent
- Gesture : Nodding of head
- Verbal-cum-gesture: Excellent and nodding of head at a time.

Change in Interaction Pattern (CIP): The interactive act of teaching is constantly communication between the teacher and pupils as an initiatory or responsive act. The interaction is broadly of two types: Verbal and Non-verbal. This interaction is nothing but communication, when the teacher or pupils communicate in verbally, interaction operation through gestures without talking. The main patterns of interaction between teacher and pupils are teacher-pupil interaction, teacher- group interaction, pupil-pupil interaction, and teacher-whole class interaction. The teacher should introduce variation in the interaction patterns to secure and maintain pupil attention.

Pausing (P): Pausing is silence for some seconds. The silence indicates pause during talk. Silence has a meaning of its own and if it is used effectively, it helps in securing and sustaining pupil attention. A short pause before saying something important is an effective way of attracting pupil attention. A pause of 3 seconds duration is considered appropriate for this purpose. If the pause is unduly long, it loses its effectiveness in serving pupil attention.

Audio—Visual Switching (AVS): Visual medium can be in the form of showing a chart, pictures, graph, map, and model in the form of drawing pictures, figures and graphs on the black board. But, the audio in the form of speech only. Only audio medium or only visual medium creates boredom in the class. A teacher while imparting knowledge to his pupils uses either audio or visual medium. A teacher should vary his medium in order to secure and sustain attention i.e. from audio to visual or visual to audio.

BLACK BOARD SKILL

Black board is the powerful teaching aid to teach from KG to PG. Black board; the visual aids is widely use in all sections of education and training. The development of information and communication technology is reducing the chalkboard work. Still it is the most suitable for giving a holistic picture of the lesson. A good black board work brings clearness in perception and it can be suitably used for displaying notes and diagrams during a lesson and for working through calculations in a classroom situation.

Components of Black Board Skill

The components of the skill of use of black board are:

Legibility (L): Legible handwriting of the teacher on the blackboard draws the attention of the learners and encourages them to improve their handwriting. Illegible hand writing irritates the learners and results in maximum mistakes. The teacher should see that a clear distinction is ensured between every letter. Adequate space is maintained between individual letters and words etc, to make handwritings more eligible.

Size and Alignment (SA): In black board writhing the size and alignment of the letters is very important. The size of the letters on the black board should not only be uniform but also the size of the letters should be large enough to be read by the students in the last row. The size of the capital letters should be as nearly vertical as possible without being diverged from a line.

Highlighting Main Points (HMP): The teacher should underline to highlight the main points or words on the black board. Coloured chalks should be used suitably to draw the learner's attention on the main points.

Utilization of the Space (US): For the proper utilization of the space important words or statements should be written on the board. Overwriting on the letters should be avoided as it makes the black board work untidy. Only essential material should be retained on the black board and unnecessary words should be rubbed off.

Correctness (C): The teacher should be careful about correct spelling, punctuation, grammar etc,. in constructing sentences on the blackboard. While writing on the black board, inadequate knowledge of English grammar or mistakes done by the teacher reduces the attentiveness of the learners in the classroom.

Position of the Teacher (PT): At the time of writing, the teacher should stand on one side of the blackboard with an angle of 45 degrees, so that the written work is visible to the learners on the black board. This means the teacher's position should not be in between the learners and the black board.

Eye Contact with Pupils (ECP): The teacher should maintain eye contact with his learners at the time of writing on the board. This controlling interaction maintains discipline and sustains the attention of the learners. Too much or too less eye contact will be counter production in the classroom.

Cleaning Of Black Board (CB): Teacher should clean the blackboard from top to bottom and not spread dust in the room. He should rub the points on the black board after the student notes them down. After completion of the lesson, the teacher should clean the entire blackboard leaving the classroom.

DEMONSTRATION SKILL

Demonstration is an activity or process of teaching involving the showing of specimens or experiments or devices to explain and describe the concerned concept, idea, teaching point etc., in the teaching-learning process. That process makes the subject matter concrete with real life situation. The demonstration in teaching makes learning simpler and meaningful to the learner.

Components of Demonstration Skill

The components of demonstration skill are:

Appropriate Topic, Concepts, Ideas and Teaching Points (A): The demonstration should be appropriate to the topic, concept, idea and teaching point. The appropriate specimens, experiments, or devices should be related to the topic, concept and teaching point in the demonstration to make teaching effective.

Sequence Order of Presentation (SOP): The presentation material such as specimens or experiments or devices should be arranged in sequence order and presented in a systematic way. The sequential procedure in presentation of material indicates better preparation of the teaching learning activity.

Adequacy of Manipulative Skill (AMS): In the demonstration of experimentation, the instruments or equipment should be repeatedly displayed in the teaching—learning process. Adequate manipulative or manual skills would certainly result in creating interest in the minds of the learners.

Creation of Appropriate Situation (CAS): In the demonstration process appropriate physical situation with proper aids, instruments, diagrams, gestures, movements etc. should convey the idea appropriately. The demonstration arouses the curiosity of the learner.

Generalization (G): Whenever the demonstration comes to an end, the teacher should conclude the theory and frame a rule or a principle. The teacher performs the demonstration to consolidate the learned points with the help of the learners.

REINFORCEMENT SKILL

All pupils generally need social approval of their behaviour. When they answer a question, they are eager to know whether their answers are correct or not. When they are appreciated for the correct answers they are eager to continue their responses in future also. This increases their participation. The appreciation for correct responses is positive reinforcement. The positive reinforcement are use for strengthening the responses or behaviours of individuals. On the other hand, if the pupils are scolded of not encouraged for their responses, they never participate in future. This kind of disencouraging activity of the teacher's called negative reinforcement. The negative reinforcements are used for weakening of eliminating the undesirable responses or behaviours. These reinforcements are in the form of verbal and non-verbal.

Reinforcement constitutes one of the essential conditions of learning. Hence every teacher has to master the skill for adopting appropriate strategies for reinforcing the learners. This skill has to be exhibited by teachers in the manner in which they respond to the responses and actions of pupils. Reinforcement results in response modification and is based on the principle of feedback followed by immediate rewarding of desirable or correct responses and actions. Encouraging reactions of a teacher would strengthen and discouraging reaction would weaken pupils responses involved in the learning process. Hence teacher should manage his reactions to pupil response with skill.

The stimuli that provide or contribute to the pleasant experience are called positive reinforcement or desirable behaviours. While the stimuli providing unpleasant experience can be termed as negative reinforces. Thus in the class room teaching positive reinforces are used for strengthening the desirable responses of learners and negative reinforces for weakening or eliminating the undesirable responses or behaviours.

Components of Reinforcement Skill

The components of reinforcement skill are given below.

Positive Verbal Reinforcement (PVR): The verbal behaviour (statement) of teacher accepts student feelings, repeats, rephrases student responses, surroundings student ideas etc., Using responses words such as—excellent, fantastic, splendid, right, yes, correct, fine, continue, go-ahead, carryon, well done, etc., and extra verbal expressions such as 'uh-uh', 'hm-hm' etc., are positive verbal reinforcements.

Positive Non-Verbal Reinforcement (PNVR): Using extra verbal cues like 'um-um', aha to encourage pupils while answering, writing the responses in the board, teacher's gestures, conveying pleasant feelings, approval of student responses such as smiling, nodding of head, delighted laugh, clapping, keeping eyes on the responding student and giving ear to the student indicate positive non-verbal reinforcements.

Negative Verbal Reinforcements (NVR): Teacher's statements such as the use of discouraging words like, 'no' wrong, incorrect, stop it, non—sense, try something else, remark in a sarcastic way, I don't like what you are doing, do not do like this, that is not good, etc., correspond to negative verbal reinforcements.

Negative Non- Verbal Reinforcements (NNVR): The teacher demonstrates his disapproval to indicate non-verbal expression of a student's in appropriate behaviour or incorrect response to his questions. Frowning, raising the eye brows, staring, disapproval by hands, negative reinforcements.

The first two PVR and PNVR indicate the skill of desirable reinforcements where as NVR and NNVR indicate the skill of undesirable reinforcements. Trainee should be encouraged to participate reinforces to increase pupil's participation. The undesirable reinforcements, which affect students learning adversely, should be avoided as far as possible. The teacher can with draw the negative reinforcements in classroom interaction by practicing the reinforcement skill in microteaching.

PROBING QUESTIONING SKILL

Probing questioning: The skill of probing questioning involves going deep into student responses through step by step questioning with a view to eliciting the required responses. Each question is followed by a variety of student responses, such as to no response, wrong response, partially correct response, incomplete response and correct response. Let us consider the five response situations one by one:

No Response Situation: No response situation may be there due to a student's inability to understand the questions, to structured response, or due to the lack of requisite facts, concepts, generalizations needed for the purpose of responding or the failure to recall the related facts.

Wrong Response Situation: Wrong responses to a question indicate the lack of knowledge of facts, concepts and generalizations on the part of the student.

Partially Correct Response Situation: It represents the response parts, which are similar to the criterion or correct responses. The respondent has a partial knowledge, facts, concepts and generalizations on the part of the students.

Incomplete Responses Situation: Some times when an incomplete response situation occurs, we infer that either the student is not having the necessary facts, concepts or generalization in his memory or it may be due to he is inability to understand or structure a response to the question.

Correct Response Situation: Correct response situation refers to the statements expressed by the student, which completely satisfy the response.

These specific sets of behaviour (student response situation) are out lined in the ensuing skill components.

COMPONENTS OF PROBING QUESTIONING SKILL

The skill of probing questioning comprises component behaviours of seeking further information, redirecting, refocusing and developing critical awareness. The components are:

Prompting: Giving hints or clues to lead the students from no response or wrong response to correct response. sometimes the initial questions may be too difficult for children to answer. In such cases, instead of abandoning the questions, they can be modified possibly by breaking it down into parts giving clues or hints. Prompting question: what is the sum of the angles of a triangle?

Seeking Further Information (SFI) or Seeking Clarification (SC): Dealing with an incomplete response situation and partially corresponsive situation consists of eliciting additional information from the responding pupil to bring the initial response to the expected response in more complex ad novel situations.

The teacher may ask the student for more clarification or information, by saying: *"What, exactly, do you mean?"*, *"Please rephrase that statement."*, *"Could you elaborate on that point?"*, *"What do you mean by the term...?"*etc.

Re Focusing (RF): To deal with 'correct response situation' the teacher re focuses pupil responses and wants the pupil to relax it to some area already learnt or requires the pupil to consider the implications of the given response in more complex and novel situations.

If a student has given a satisfactory response, it might seem unnecessary to probe it. However, the teacher could use this opportunity to refocus on a related issue. For example *"If this is true, what are the implications for...?"*, *"How does Sumit's answer relate to...?"*, *"Can you relate this to...?"*, *"Let's analyze that answer/comment."*

Re Directing (RD): For more students' involvement and to deal with 'no response', 'incomplete response' and partially correct response, the same question is redirected to more students for response.

Developing Critical Awareness (DCA) or Increasing Students' Critical Awareness (ISCA): This involves asking *'why'* and *'how'* of the correct response. The teacher expects the pupil to justify his response or explain its rationale. This process develops his critical awareness

Teacher wants the student to justify her/his response. e.g. *"What are you assuming?"*. *"What are your reasons for thinking that is so?"*, *"Is there more to it?"*, *"How would an opponent of this view respond?"*

Situations for Use of Probing Question

- When a pupil expresses his inability to answer some question in the class or his answer is incomplete, the teacher can ask such questions which ***"Prompt"*** the pupils in solving the already asked questions.
- This technique is known as ***'Seeking further information'*** technique, when

the pupils answer correctly in the class, but the teacher wants to seek more information.

- Sometimes, the teacher can ask probing questions to ***concentrate the attention*** of the pupils. Similarly, for the very same purpose, the teacher may ask the same question from other pupil. This is known as ***'Refocusing'***.
- In classroom, if the teacher wants to introduce the pupils with various aspects of the problem, then he can ask the **same *question after slight changes in the language***. This is known as ***'Redirection'.***
- In class, the teacher can ask questions bearing '**why**' in order ***to develop the reasoning power*** of the pupils. By getting motivated from such questions, pupils involve themselves in the process of reasoning. This is known as ***'Critical Awareness Technique'***.

Prompting Technique

This technique means to go deep into the pupil's response when it is incorrect or no response. Then a series of hints or prompts are given to pupil through step by step questioning in order to lead the pupil to the desired correct response. Let us take the following example:

Example-1

Teacher: What are the functions of Money?
Pupil: No response.
Teacher: What you pay purchase a chocolate?
Pupil: Money or Rupees or Paisa.

Seeking Further Information:

This technique is used when the response of pupil is incomplete or partially correct. The teacher helps the pupil to clarify or elaborate or explain his initial response by asking more small questions or creating situation in which the pupil is made to think and respond.

Example-2:

Teacher: What are the functions of Money?
Pupil: No response.
Teacher: What you pay purchase a chocolate?
Pupil: Money or Rupees or Paisa.
Teacher: What are the other functions of Money?

Redirection:

This technique involves asking the same question from another pupil. The main purpose of this technique is to increase more and more pupil participation. When the situation is of no response or incorrect response prompting should be preferred to redirection.

Example-3

Teacher: What are the characteristic of Money?

Imran: No response
Akram: It is transferable (Redırection)
Mohan: It act as Medium of Exchange (Redirection)
Krihsan: It is act as store of Value (Redirection)
Sohail: It is helpful in deferred payments(Redirection)

Refocusing:

It is used when the pupil's response is correct. This involves comparing the phenomena in his response with other phenomena either for similarity/ difference or relationship between the two situations. How one thing in point is different from the other thing? How one response of the pupil is related to any other point? How one thing is similar to another thing? Such types of questions are put to the pupil.

Example-4

Teacher: What is difference in act of Medium of Exchange and deferred payments (**Refocusing**)
Teacher: How act of store of Value is difference form act of Medium of Exchange **(Refocusing)**

Increasing Critical Awareness:

This technique is used when the pupil's response is correct. The teacher puts higher order questions to stimulate the pupil to think beyond what the pupil knows. This involves the 'how' and 'why' and sometimes 'what' type of questions on the point under discussion.

Example-5

1. What are secondary functions of money?
2. How money is helpful in Capital formation? etc.

Now you have understood the skill and its components. How to practice these components has been illustrated by the following micro-lesson plan.

MICRO-LESSON PLAN-2

Skill: Skill of Probing Question
Subject: Economics
Class: 10+2
Topic: Functions of Money

Sl. No.	*Teacher's Activity*	*Pupils' Activity*	*Components of Skill*
1	What are the functions of Money?	No Response	
2	What you pay purchase a chocolate?	Money or Rupee	**Prompt**

(Contd.)

Sl. No.	*Teacher's Activity*	*Pupils' Activity*	*Components of Skill*
3	What are the other functions of Money?	Pay Loans, Help in saving Capital formation	**Seeking Further Information**
4	What are the characteristic of Money?	Ram: No response Sohan: It is transferable (Redirection) Mohan: It act as Medium of Exchange (Redirection) Krihsan: It is act as store of Value (Redirection) Gopal: It is helpful in deferred payments (Redirection)	**Redirecting**
5	What is difference in act of Medium of Exchange and deferred payments?		**(Refocusing)**
6	1. What are secondary function of money? 2. How money is helpful in Capital formation?		**Increasing Critical Awareness**

Rating Scale

Topic: Functions of Money

Components of Skill	*Grading*					*Supervisor Remarks*
Prompting	A	B	C	D	E	
Seeking Further Information (SFI) or Seeking Clarification (SC)	A	B	C	D	E	
Re Focusing (RF)	A	B	C	D	E	
Re Directing (RD)	A	B	C	D	E	
Developing Critical Awareness (DCA) or Increasing Students' Critical Awareness (ISCA)	A	B	C	D	E	
	A	B	C	D	E	

NOTE:

"A" means 95 to 100 per cent correct use of component.
"B" means 85 to 94 per cent correct use of component.
"C" means 75 to 84 per cent correct use of component.
"D" means 65 to 74 per cent correct use of component.
"E" means below 65 per cent correct use of component.

Pupil Teacher Signature **Supervisor Signature**

SKILL OF CLOSURE

In closure or recapitulation, the teacher can consolidate the main points by putting a few questions based on the topic taught. The questions should be logically liked to cover the whole lesson as summary of the lesson. He may use charts, models, diagrams etc. for consolidation of the lesson. The questions may be oral or/and written by using nonverbal media including experimentation. The students can use this situation of what they have learnt during the lesson in solving the problems in a new situation or in different situations. The teacher can review the past knowledge of the students, both provide for future learning in the form of homework or assignment.

Components of Closure of Skill

The various components of the skill closure/Recapitulation are:

Consolidation of Major Points (CMP): The teacher should consolidate the major points of his presented content matter at the closure or recapitulation process. It helps in remembering important points of the lesson.

Providing Opportunity to Apply New Knowledge to New Situation or Indifferent Situations (OP): Whatever the students gain new knowledge in the lesson taught, they apply their knowledge in a new situation or different situations in the recapitulation. That opportunity is felt at the closure of a lesson. Without providing this opportunity, the students are unable to apply their gained knowledge to new or different situations.

Linking Previous Knowledge to New Knowledge and New Knowledge to Future Knowledge of the Students (LK): The teacher establishes a link from the previous knowledge to new knowledge and from the new knowledge to future knowledge by taking different examples.

Home Work or Assignment (HW): Home work or Assignment is an important task in closure. At the end of his teaching, the teacher provides homework or assignment to recall or to apply or to learn different situations.

EXPLAINING SKILL

Explaining skill: Explaining skill makes the pupils to understand ideas, concepts and principles, a teacher has to explain vividly. Explanation is a set of inter—relation statements made by the teacher related to an idea or phenomenon. In order to be a good listener the teacher trainee has to develop the following components.

Components of Explaining Skill: The main components of explaining skill are as under:

Cognitive Link (CL): While introducing a new concept, the teacher is to follow the principle of 'known to unknown' establishing a link between the old (already known) and the new one. A new concept, if it is complex, can be introducing and developed only through a series of sub concepts. A new concept all sub-concepts must be linked with one another logically.

Use of Illustration (ILL): A new concept is to be adequately illustrated in terms of vital situations or life experiences. Illustrations also include citing example and non example (if needed and if possible) illustrations must serve the purpose of concretizing the abstract concepts concerned.

Comparing and Contrasting (CC): Some concepts are often so closely interrelated that the pupils may find it difficult to discriminate between them. These may bring effectively to the attention of the learner. This component serves the purpose of discriminating between two related but different concepts.

Meaningful Repetition (MR): By repeating a brief description of a concept, a term or a definition at regular intervals, the ideas get fixed in the minds of the learners. Repletion must be purposive, deliberative, meaningful and relevant. Over – repetition creates boredom to the learners. As such over-repetition should not be used.

INTEGRATION OF TEACHING SKILLS (LINK PRACTICE)

When mastery has been attained in various skills, the teacher trainee is allowed to teach the skills together. This separate training programme to integrate various isolated skills is known as *'Link Practice'*

In microteaching technique, teaching skills are practiced one by one separately. At a time, only one skill can be practiced. While practicing one skill, the use of that particular skill is maximized and other related skills may also occur taking indirect role. Skills practiced in isolation have no meaning unless they are integrated in teaching.

Hence, after attaining mastery in various skills, opportunity should be given to the teacher trainees to teach in real situations integrating the skills mastered already. So, separate training programme is necessary for this purpose. This programme is called *Link practice.*

Link practice is a bridge between microteaching and full-class teaching where microteaching skills are effectively integrated and transferred. There is a big contrast between microteaching and full class teaching. In microteaching, there is a scaled down process in terms of class room size, skills, scope of the lesson, time etc. Micro teaching is practiced under stimulated conditions. In macro teaching in addition to the existence of macro elements, there are also class room management problems. In link practice, the trainees are given chance of teaching real pupils.

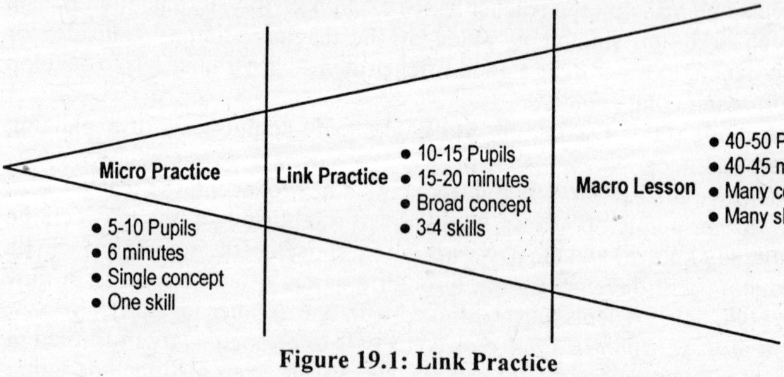

Figure 19.1: Link Practice

There are many methods for link practice. One of the method is that after practicing three sub skills separately, the trainee may combine all the three sub skills in a lesson of 10 minutes. He then practices another three sub skills separately and links them. He then combines all the six sub skills in a single lesson of 15 minutes. And so on till the entire sub skills are combined in a macro lesson of 40 minutes and teaching a full class.

Link practice sessions are arranged with about 20 pupils for about the normal class period i.e. 20 minutes. The trainee prepares a series of eight short lessons on single unit and teaches each lesson for 20 minutes using appropriate skills particular to the content. The number of lessons used in link practice is flexible but selected topic should be adequately covered. The teaching skills namely 'Set Induction' and Closure cannot be practiced in microteaching session in isolation. So, in link practice, the trainees include these skills also. At the end of each lesson, the trainee should get feedback about the lessons.

Advantages of Integration of Teaching Skills

The main advantages of Link Practice (Integration of Teaching Skills) are as under:

- It helps the trainee to transfer effectively all the skills learnt in the micro-teaching sessions.
- It helps to bridge the gap between training in isolated teaching skills and the real teaching situation faced by a student teacher.
- Desirable Number of Pupils:15-20
- Preferable Duration: 20 minutes.
- Desirable Number of Skills:3-4 Skills

Methods of Link Practice (Integration of Teaching Skills)

Link practice or integration of skills can be done in two ways:

1. Integration in Parts: In this type of method, 3 or 4 teaching skills are integrated and transferred them into a lesson of 15-20 minutes duration. And again 3 or 4 skills are integrated and are transferred all the skills to one lesson.

2. Integration as a Whole: In this type of method, student teacher integrates all the individual teaching skills by taking them as a whole and transferred them into a real teaching situation.

20
Traditional and Constructivist Lesson Planning

A lesson plan is the systematic preparation done in a scientific manner. Effective and successful teaching mainly depends on perfect lesson planning. A lesson plan represents a single teaching unit meant for a class period. Generally a lesson plan is teacher's mental and emotional visualization of classroom activities.

TYPES OF LESSON PLANS

Based on the *B. S. Bloom taxonomy of Educational objectives*, lesson plans can be classified in the following types:

Knowledge Lesson

Here the learner's cognitive aspect of his mental activity is more active which result an increase in his knowledge. Knowledge lesson are those which cause an increase in the knowledge of various facts and events through the knowledge lesson such as the lessons of History, Geography, Economics, Civics, Mathematics, Science and Grammar.

Application Lesson

These are based on the affective aspect of learner's activity. These give aesthetic inspiration to the pupils and develop their appreciation. They take interest in studying these lessons. Poetry lessons are good example of this type.

Skill Lesson

In skill lessons, the psycho-motor aspect of the learner's mental activity is more active. Skill lessons make the pupils efficient in doing some task, while the teacher provides some guidance to the pupils in the beginning. Following the teacher's or guidelines all the pupils get involved in accomplishing the task. This provides man opportunities for experimenting and practice. The creative power of the pupils is more active in skill lessons. Painting, handicraft, gardening and agriculture etc. are examples of skill lesson.

LESSON PLANNING

Good lesson planning is the key to successful teaching. Lesson planning in advance has a futuristic implication which permits a teacher to anticipate pupils' reactions and by using these reactions to prepare adequately in order to avoid foreseeable difficulties. It helps a teacher manage his/her class time effectively.

DEFINITION OF LESSON PLANNING

1. Good defines a lesson plan as an *"Outline of the important points of a*

lesson arranged in the order in which they are to be presented to students by the teacher".

2. *"Lesson plan is the title given to a statement of the achievement to be realized and the specific means by which these are to be attained as a result of the activities engaged in during the period."*
3. According to Bossing, *"Daily lesson planning involves defining the objectives, selecting and arranging the subject matter and determining the method and procedure".*

CHARACTERISTICS OF GOOD LESSON PLAN

The following are the main characteristics of lesson plan:

Objective Based: The lesson plan must be based on one or the other objective. While writing this, objectives should be written and defined clearly because its main objective is to achieve some goal.

Decision about Appropriate Material Aids: The material aid is an important means of the teacher. Hence correct decision regarding the charts, graphs, pictures, diagrams and maps should be taken while preparing ideal lesson plan and these should be marked at proper places which a teacher is to use them while teaching.

Based Previous Knowledge: An ideal lesson plan should be based on the previous knowledge of the pupils. This will avoid difficulty in acquiring new knowledge by the pupils.

Division of Lesson Plan in Units: Lessons are of three types (a) knowledge lesson (b) skill lesson (c) appreciation lesson. In an ideal lesson plan all the relevant steps of these three types of lesson plan should be determined. Each lesson should be divided into suitable units so that the pupils may understand the lesson gradually.

Simplicity of Activities: In an ideal lesson plan, the simplicity of the lesson plan and clarity of thoughts should be according to the mental level of the pupils.

Determination of Activities: In an ideal lesson plan, the activities of a teacher and the pupils should be determined before-hand.

Home Work: There should a provision of home work in an ideal lesson plan. This will enable the pupils to learn the appreciation of the acquired knowledge.

Self-evaluation: A good lesson plan must have a suitable plan for self-criticism. The teacher should put some questions to him and find out the answer and there by judge the effectiveness of the lesson writing.

Use of Illustration: Examples should be used which have relevance with the daily life of the peoples.

Use of Blackboard: The blackboard summary of each and every unit should be written on the blackboard.

NEEDS OF LESSON PLANNING

The lesson plan does not allow the teacher to deviate and its keep him on the way. In the process of teaching, lesson plan is needed due to the following reasons:

- Through lesson plan, the teacher regularly achieves the teaching objectives and process in the form of complex objectives and processes.
- A lesson plan develops the possibilities of adjustment in the classroom situation which makes the teaching effective.
- A lesson plan helps in calling every step of curriculum unit.
- A lesson plan helps in planning the process of teaching on the basis of class control, motivation and individual differences.

IMPORTANCE OF LESSON PLANNING

Planning is essential for every aspect of human activities, but for a planned teaching more planning is required. The discussion about the importance of lesson planning is as follows:

Suitable Environment: In a lesson plan objectives are fixed and the teaching strategies, techniques and material aid etc. are decided beforehand. When a proper teaching environment is created, the teaching task goes in a much planned way.

Based on Previous Knowledge: In preparing lesson plans, the teacher presents new knowledge as the basis of previous knowledge of the pupils. This enables the pupils to gain the knowledge very conveniently on one side; the teacher succeeds in acquiring his objective on the other side.

Psychological Teaching: The teacher uses proper teaching strategies, techniques and instruments keeping in mind the interests, aptitudes, needs, capacities and abilities of the pupils for teaching them when the lesson plans are prepared. This makes the teaching more psychological.

Limitation of Subject Matter: In a lesson plan, the subject matter becomes limited. This enables the teacher to give up irrelevant things. He only remembers definite and limited matter and its presentation before the pupils become easy. The pupils also receive the knowledge in a systematic and organized way.

Determination of Activities: In a lesson plan, the teachers and pupils activities are pre-decided according to the class level. This makes the teaching activities meaningful and purposeful.

Preparation of Material Aids: At the time of preparing a lesson plan, the teacher decides what facts are to be clarified by what strategies, techniques and instruments and what aid is to be used at what time. This prepares the necessary and effective aids before starting the teaching task.

Developing of Teaching Skill: The lesson plan acts as an important means for developing teaching skills in the pupil-teacher.

Teaching with Confidence: The preparation of a lesson plan makes the subject and other allied subjects more clearly to the teachers. This arouses self confidence among them. When a teacher gets developed the feeling of self-confidence, then he presents the new knowledge to the pupils with more enthusiasm and pleasure.

Discipline in Class: By preparing lesson plan, the teacher becomes aware of what, when and how much is to be done in the class. This absorbs all the pupils in their respective tasks. Hence, it results in appreciable classroom discipline.

Time Sense: Lesson plan is prepared allotting to the duration of the periods.

Teaching from Memory Level to Reflective Level: In an ideal lesson plan, development and thought provoking questions should be asked. Also there should be an effort to stretch the teaching from memory level to reflective level.

Advantages of Lesson Planning

The main advantages of Lesson Planning are as under:

- Lesson planning makes the work regular, well-organized and systematic.
- It enhances the self-confidence and self-reliance of the teacher.
- It facilitates appropriate use of teaching aids at appropriate places.
- It is economical in terms of time, as every step has been planned with forethought.
- The students' interest can be retained by planning suitable activities and assignments, according to the mental level of the students.
- It establishes the correlation between teaching and learning.
- It helps the teacher to select appropriate methodology for teaching according to the subject matter.
- It helps the teacher to make the best planning for learning activities during the teaching.
- While keeping in mind the individual differences in the class, the teacher becomes able to organize the classroom activities.
- It helps the teacher in modifying student's attitude, aptitude, interest and capabilities in right and desired direction.

CRITERIA OF A GOOD LESSON PLAN

The important features of what a lesson plan should contain are:

- *Why* should this lesson be taught (Objectives)?
- *What* should be taught (Content)?
- *How* should it be taught (Method)?

TRADITIONAL APPROACHES TO LESSON PLANNING

For planning the lesson and writing it, various traditional approaches are used. Some of the important traditional approaches to lesson planning are as follows:

- Herbartian Approach
- Morrison's or Unit Approach
- Bloom's Approach
- RCEM Approach

Herbartian Approach to Lesson Planning

Generally known as *Herbartian Formal Five Steps Approach*, it is the product of the Herbartian School of Pedagogy propagated by J. F. Herbart (1776-1841). The formal steps involved in the Herbartian Approach are as follows:

Preparation or Introduction

This step is concerned with the task of preparing the students for receiving new knowledge. In preparation, nothing new is taught to students. Relevant to the topic in hand he teacher should make himself sure of what the pupils already know, by putting a few questions, based on the pupils previous knowledge. In general, with the help of this step, the teacher can check the students entering behaviour before he starts teaching the lesson. Thus, testing previous knowledge, developing interest in the minds of students and maintaining curiosity of the students can be achieved with the help of this step.

The following activities involved in this step:

- The assumption about the previous knowledge of the students in relevance to the lesson
- The testing of the previous knowledge
- Utilizing the previous knowledge for introducing the lesson
- Motivating the students for studying the present lesson

Presentation

It is the key step and only through which the actual process of teaching is going to take place. Here the aims of the lesson should be stated clearly and the heading should be written on the blackboard. We have to provide situation for both the teacher and the students to participate in the process of teaching and learning. Our ultimate aim of the presentation is to make the concepts understandable to the students. Therefore simple language is used. Appropriate and specific examples and illustrations of the concepts will make the understanding better. The interest of the students on the subject matter should be maintained continuously by the way of asking questions from time to time in this stage. The teacher should carefully and skillfully arrange his material so that his pupils may clearly and readily grasp it. The teacher should make proper use of questions, charts, graphs, pictures, models and other illustrative for demonstration and explanation. At the end of each section a few questions concerning that section only should be asked to whether the pupils are now ready for the acquisition of new knowledge.

Comparison of Association

More importance should be given in this stage to compare the facts observed by the students with another concept by way of giving examples. By making use of this comparison, the students can derive definitions or theories. The students are encouraged to give new suitable examples for the concept instead of the examples given in the book to make them think in an innovative manner.

Generalization

This step is concerned with arriving at some general ideas or drawing out the necessary conclusions by the students on the basis of the different comparisons, contracts and associated observed in the learning material present by the teacher. As far as possible the task of formulation should be left to students. The teacher at this stage should try to remain in the background for providing only necessary guidance and correction.

Application

In this stage, the teacher makes the students to use the understood knowledge in an unfamiliar situation. Unless the knowledge of science is applied in new situations or in our day-to-day life, the study of science will become meaningless. This application of scientific principles will strengthen learning and will make the learning permanent.

Merits of Herbartian Lesson Planning Approach

The following are the advantages of the Herbartian lesson planning approach:

It follows logical and psychological aspects and therefore incorporate the basic principles of learning

- It is an easy and simple approach of lesson planning
- Content matter is given utmost importance
- It employs deductive thinking in learning
- It is the method that can be used to teach any subject of the school-science subjects, social studies and languages.
- It uses previous knowledge of the students to impart the new knowledge
- This approach can be used to any size of the class or organization

Demerits of Herbartian Lesson Planning Approach

Although the Herbartian lesson plan is the most widely used approach in lesson planning, it has some demerits. They are as follows:

- It mainly emphasizes on the content matter
- It confines teaching only to memory level
- It ignores the attitudes and requirements of the students
- It helps in achieving only cognitive objectives where as it can not be employed to achieve the effective and psychomotor objectives
- This approach is highly dominated by the teacher
- It does not provide for the opportunities of the students creativity and originality as it is highly structured.
- Emphasis is given presentation.

DIFFERENCE BETWEEN THE TRADITIONAL (BEHAVIOURIST) AND CONSTRUCTIVIST LESSON PLANNING

The difference between the Behaviourist and Constructivist Lesson Planning is as under:

Behaviourist Lesson Planning

- In the behaviourist lesson plan format everything is virtually structured.
- There is a set format and everyone adhere to this strict format with little or no room for variation.
- Learning is similar to a set time frame and an event occurs in a series of sequences.
- The teacher's role is one that is centered on structured experiences.
- Lesson is given with guided facts outlined.
- The teacher is basically the only lead person in this format. In other words one could say that the teacher is the leader and the students are not active followers.
- Student role is a recipient with little or no input.

- Information and knowledge is given and that individual only receives the facts.
- Everyone is expected to be learning at the same time and at the same pace.
- All students are given the same lesson materials and work independently.
- The mood of the classroom setting is set or planned and focus is the key.
- The activities are set based on seatwork, testing, lectures, and discussions.
- Testing is based on written information. In this type of format one can see that everything is systematically placed together.

Constructivist Lesson Planning

- Constructivist lesson plan format is one that goes beyond structure and more hands on approach. Although there are guidelines there is still room for deviation.
- Learning is not set on specified time fame.
- The teacher and the students interact. Mainly the focus shifts from teacher to student in an effort to enhance thinking.
- Information is given based on facts. Then an exploration takes place where prior knowledge is discussed and all information is gathered.
- There is a bridge that is set to enhance the learning process.
- Students play an active role as well in this type of format.
- The teacher is the leader but the students are active participants.
- Everyone is not isolated. Students can work as groups and individually. In this setting grouping and hands on is the key. In other words one may say that this format is not as strict.

When compared side by side on can see that there is a difference between the behaviourist and the constructivist lesson format and they are not the same. Students still learn regardless of the format use and the teacher is still in control. Facts are given but the format of how the information is displayed is different. As one can see the learning process varies and the guidelines used to bring about learning varies as well. Regardless of the format used as long as the information is given correctly everyone can benefit from using a lesson plan format.

Elements of Constructivist Lesson Plan

The constructivist lesson plan uses six basic elements to come up with a strategy of how the learning process will occur. It is based on scientific theory and observation. It details and contains the elements of learning. Through this process we formulate our own ideas and thoughts. Once this happens, everything is developed and learning occurs. The elements that are used to gauge this process consist of situation, grouping, bridge, question, exhibit and reflection.

Situation

In the situation phase, a manner of how order is addressed is dealt with for the student to sort out. There must be a title, problem solving, answering of questions, conclusion drawing and goal setting is stated all centered around how the student is going to come up with their own understanding.

Grouping

Next is grouping of team, individually or together. Then the other part deals with materials and how they are going to be for explanation and event. These are the two headings under grouping.

Bridge

Then a bridge is formed so prior understanding is worked into what will be taught. This could be explored through a game.

Question

Then the question phase which is used also as prompts to continue engaging.

Exhibit

Also there is the exhibit phase similar to a show and tell.

Reflection

Finally, there is reflection where thinking and thoughts are emphasized; here one can look back on what was learned.

In the constructivist lesson plan there is always active sharing of information and everyone is involved in the learning process. The teacher is merely guiding the thought of the student to bring about learning and understanding. There are always suggestions being made in this lesson plan for the student to engage into. In this lesson plan the student's opinion is taken into consideration and everything is relevant in this process. Concepts of learning is addressed and taught with the student in mind.

Student knowledge to learning ration is displayed in this form of lesson plan. Encouragement, engagement and active participation are all essential in the constructivist lesson plan. In the constructivist lesson plan the role of the student and teacher are always changing to bring about learning. One could say that with this lesson plan thinking is a criterion. All of these concepts are taken into consideration when formulating a constructivist lesson plan and learning is continual.

5 E's Model of Constructivistic Lesson Planning

Careful lesson planning can help to insure the successful running of courses. Incorporating best practices in teaching and learning into the design process will help students meet learning objectives for course.

Constructivism is a theory of learning stating that learners construct new ideas or concepts based upon their current/past knowledge. It is a very open type of planning. Teachers can design instructions around a learning objective, gather resources and provide students with an opportunity to explore build and demonstrate their learning. It shifts the learning environment from one which is very instructor-centered to one that is very learner-centered.

The 5E's model of constructivism is given by Roger W. Bybee and Joseph A. Taylor. The steps of 5 E's Lesson Planning Model based on constructivist learning design are given below:

Engage

In the stage *Engage*, the students first encounter and identify the instructional task. Here, they make connections between past and present learning experiences, lay the organizational ground work for the activities ahead and stimulate their involvement in the anticipation of these activities. Asking a question, defining a problem, showing a surprising event and acting out a problematic situation are all ways to engage the students and focus them on the instructional tasks.

Explore

In the *Exploration* stage, the students have the opportunity to get directly involved with phenomena and materials. Involving themselves in these activities they develop a grounding of experience with the phenomenon. As they work together in teams, students build a base of common experience which assists them in the process of sharing and communicating. The teacher acts as a facilitator, providing materials and guiding the students' focus. The students' inquiry process drives the instruction during an exploration.

Explain

The third stage, *Explain*, is the point at which the learner begins to put the abstract experience through which she/he has gone/into a communicable form. Language provides motivation for sequencing events into a logical format. Communication occurs between peers, the facilitator, or within the learner himself. Working in groups, learners support each other's understanding as they articulate their observations, ideas, questions and hypotheses. Language provides a tool of communicable labels. These labels, applied to elements of abstract exploration, give the learner a means of sharing these explorations. Explanations from the facilitator can provide names that correspond to historical and standard language, for student findings and events. For example a child, through her exploration, may state they have noticed that a magnet has a tendency to *"stick"* to a certain metallic object. The facilitator, in her discussion with the child, might at this stage introduce terminology referring to *"an attracting force"*. Introducing labels, after the child has had a direct experience, is far more meaningful than before that experience. The experiential base she has built offers the student an attachment place for the label. Common language enhances the sharing and communication between facilitator and students. The facilitator can determine levels of understanding and possible misconceptions. Created works such as writing, drawing, video, or tape recordings are communications that provide recorded evidence of the learner's development, progress and growth.

Elaborate

In *Elaborate stage*, the students expand on the concepts they have learned, make connections to other related concepts, and apply their understandings to the world around them. For example, while exploring light phenomena, a learner constructs an understanding of the path light travels through space. Examining a lamp post, she may notice that the shadow of the post changes its location as the day grows later. This observation can lead to further inquiry as to possible connections between the shadow's changing location and the changes in direction of the light source, the Sun. Applications to real world events, such as where to plant flowers so that they receive sunlight most of the day, or how to prop up a beach umbrella for shade from the Sun, are both extensions and applications of the concept that light travels in a straight path. These connections often lead to further inquiry and new understandings.

Evaluate

Evaluate, the fifth "E", is an on-going diagnostic process that allows the teacher to determine if the learner has attained understanding of concepts and knowledge. Evaluation and assessment can occur at all points along the continuum of the instructional process. Some of the tools that assist in this diagnostic process are: rubrics (quantified and prioritized outcome expectations) determined hand-in-hand with the lesson design, teacher observation structured by checklists, student interviews, portfolios designed with specific purposes, project and problem-based learning products, and embedded assessments. Concrete evidence of the learning proceed is most valuable in communications between students, teachers, parents and administrators. Displays of attainment and progress enhance understanding for all parties involved in the educational process, and can become jumping off points for further enrichment of the students' education. These evidences of learning serve to guide the teacher in further lesson planning and may signal the need for modification and change of direction. For example, if a teacher perceives clear evidence of misconception, then he/she can revisit the concept to enhance clearer understanding. If the students show profound interest in a branching direction of inquiry, the teacher can consider refocusing the investigation to take advantage of this high level of interest.

Viewing the evaluation process as a continuous one gives the constructivistic philosophy a kind of cyclical structure. The learning process is open-ended and open to change. There is an ongoing loop where questions lead to answers but more questions and instruction is driven by both predetermined lesson design and the inquiry process.

Model Constructivist Lesson Plan

A sample lesson plan for the topic 'Angles' in class five Mathematics is given below.

Specific Objectives of the Lesson

At the end of this lesson students will be able to:

- recognize angles in complex situations
- draw an angle of given measure and
- measure a given angle

Engage

Provide each student with two sticks and ask them to join the sticks using any adhesive material. Let students move about to observe what the others have done. Let the teacher classify these creations depending on where the sticks are joined. All those joined at one of the two ends of the sticks are put together.

If the sticks have been joined anywhere in the middle, those creations are put in a separate group (See Figure 20.1).

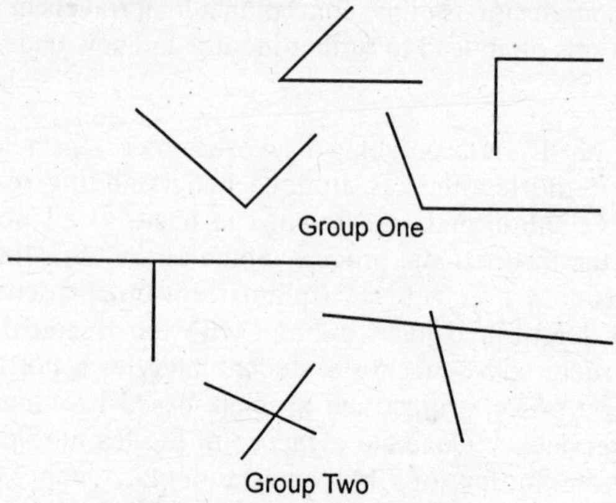

Figure 20.1: Group of Sticks

Let students find reasons for such a grouping. This will lead them to the concept of angles. The teacher will have to introduce the term 'angle'. However, the concept that an angle is the union of two non-collinear rays will be derived by the students. Do not expect the students to use any technical terms that they are unfamiliar with. Insist on the formation of the concept. (Inform students that group two contains more than one angle. The teacher may use these figures later when the concept of angle is well formed.)

Explore

Let the students explore the classroom and make a list of all the places where they see angles. Provide initial guidance if they face any difficulty. This activity can be done in small groups of three or four. Let students list on a chart paper places where they found angles. It would be a good idea to have them sketch their observations. The next step in the Explore stage would be to help them measure angles. At this stage perhaps the teacher's demonstration would be effective as emphasis on the right way to use a protractor could be stressed on. Distribute sheets with angles to be measured. To introduce the students to types of angles, an activity could be arranged, where angles of different measures are put in three boxes labelled acute angle, right angle and obtuse angle. Have students measure the angles in each box and conclude the basis for classification.

Explain

Let students explain what acute angles, right angles and obtuse angles are. Let them justify their answers.

Elaborate

This stage requires the students to extrapolate their knowledge to new situations. Have them measure angles in various polygons and classify them. Have them create acute angles, right angles and obtuse angles with the right movements of their elbows. Identify angles in the letters of the alphabet. Show them architectural designs and have them identify various angles. Include structures like the Leaning tower of Pisa. Let students read about why it inclines. Draw a circle to represent the earth and show how a place on say 20 degree North latitude makes an angle of 20 degrees with the centre of the earth. Let them provide examples from their P.T. exercises where angles are involved. The whole focus is to be aware that angles pervade so many different spheres of daily life.

Evaluate

The step of evaluation could be in the form of a test, a quiz or even a craft project where the students create an object and identify and measure the angles in the craft article.

21
Identification and Formulation of Teaching or Instructional Objectives

The teaching objectives are identified after analyzing the content to be taught because teaching is a meaningful and purposeful activity. The teaching objectives are determined in the planning stage. The teacher can identify his teaching or instructional objectives with the help of his knowledge and understanding of educational objectives. The educational objectives imply the change that we try to produce in the child.

The educational objectives are given in the statement form. These are broad and philosophical in nature. The teaching objectives are specific and psychological in nature. The teaching strategies and tactics are selected on the basis of teaching-learning objectives.

B. S. Bloom said *"Educational objectives are not only the goals towards which the curriculum is shaped and towards which instruction is guided but they also the goals that provide the detailed specification of the construction and use of evaluative technique."*

USES OF EDUCATIONAL OBJECTIVES

The main uses of educational objectives are:

- Educational objectives provide the direction to the teaching and learning activities which are designed for achieving an ultimate goal.
- Educational objectives help for planned change.
- Educational objectives provide the basis for organizing teaching and learning activities.

Dr. B.S. Bloom believes that education is a tri-polar process (Fig. 21.1).

The learning experiences are provided by teaching activities to achieve educational objectives and change of behaviour is evaluated in terms of educational objectives. Thus, educational objectives are the basis of teaching activities and evaluation techniques.

DIFFERENCE BETWEEN GOAL, AIMS AND OBJECTIVES

The difference between goal, aims and objectives is given below.

Goal

It is the ultimate target that an individual wishes to achieve in his or her life. It is very broad, long term and takes years to achieve.

Aims

They are more specific than goals and help in achieving the set goal. They can be middle to long term.

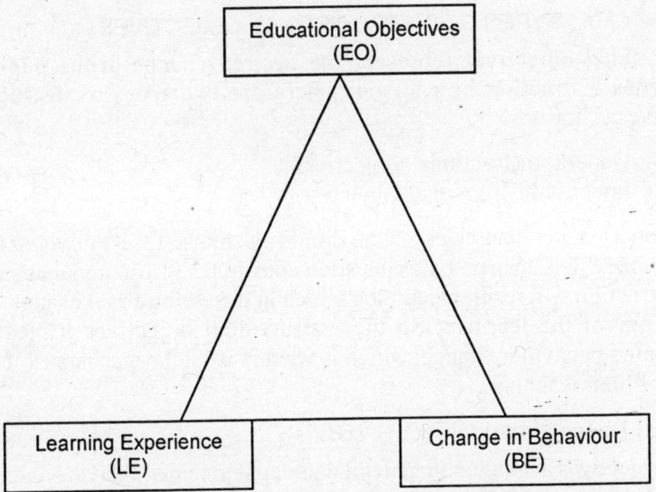

Figure 21.1: Relationship between Educational Objectives, Learning Experiences and Change in Behaviour

Objectives

These are short term targets, which are specific in nature and can be achieved in less time. Which help in achieving the aims in an effective way.

Types of Objectives

Mainly the objectives are of three types:

1. Aims or General Objectives or Educational Objectives

These objectives related to the subject.

2. Specific Objectives or Teaching Objectives

These objectives pertain to a particular topic in a particular time period. These can further be divided into the following categories:

- Knowledge
- Understanding
- Application
- Creativity

3. Behavioural Objectives

These objectives indicate the expected behavioural outcome or changes that can occur in the students e.g. the students will be able to define a fact or draw an outline of the fact.

MEANING AND IMPORTANCE OF TEACHING OBJECTIVES

The teaching objectives are achieved in terms of change of behaviour of the learners. These are specific, direct and practical in nature, therefore, these are most useful for teachers. The teaching objectives are related to learning outcome or change of behaviour of the learners.

TYPES OF INSTRUCTIONAL OBJECTIVES

Instructional objectives represent the desired change in the pupil who undergoes instruction in a lesson. There are two types of instructional objectives. They are:

(i) General Instructional Objectives
(ii) Specific Instructional Objectives

When a teacher plans a lesson, he should ask himself, *"Why should I teach this lesson?"* The answer to this question constitutes Instructional objectives. All instruction will result in learning which in turn bring about changes in the behaviour of the learners. So the instructional objectives it means the anticipated behaviour change, which is what is what the teachers expect as a result of their teaching.

General Instructional Objective (GIOs)

If the objectives are stated in general and vague manner, then they are called general objectives. They contain non-behavioural verb i.e. they contain non-action verb.

For example:

- The learner acquires knowledge of the various branches of science.
- The learner develops skill in manipulating apparatus.

Here the verbs *'acquires'* and *'develops'* are non-action verbs which are cannot measure or observe directly, because they are in the form of inner development or passive aspect of mental activity. For Example:

The pupil:

- Acquires knowledge of friction
- Understands various types of friction
- Applies knowledge of friction in relevant unfamiliar situation
- Develops skill in doing experiments
- Develops interest in experimenting

Specific Instructional Objectives (SIOs)

If the objectives are stated in specific, then they are called specific objectives. They contain behavioural verb i.e. they contain 'action' verb. The observable and measurable behavioural changes as a result of realizing an objective is termed as specific instructional objectives or specification. For example:

The learner defines friction. Here defines is the active verb. The statement of specification should contain two parts:

- Modification Part (MP)
- Content Part (CP)

Example;

The learner defines (MP) friction (CP)

The table 21.1 shows illustrative examples of specifications with specified behavioural part and content part from physical science.

Table 21.1: Illustrative Examples of Specifications

Level	*Specific Objective/Specifications*	
	Behavioural Part	**Content Part**
Knowledge	Recalls Recognizes	The branches of science
Understanding	Distinguishes	between metals and non-metals
	Identifies	the physical properties of metals
	Selects	colored salts from the salts
	Compares	velocity and acceleration
	Classifies	primary, secondary and tertiary alcohol
	Identifies	between rest and motion
	relationships	for first order lever
	Give examples	the preparation of Iron
	Describes	the function of generator
	Explains	the ideas of input devices
	Generalizes	
Application	Gives reason	Why sky appears blue?
	Infers	The result obtained in the experiment
	Computes	The normality of the liquid
	Analyses	Analyses situations
	Establishes relationships	Establishes relationship between metals and non-metals
	Suggests	Improvisation to apparatus
	Selects	Apparatus with purpose
	Detects	Detects errors
	Give new illustrations	For friction
Skill	Draws	The diagram of screw gauge
	Labels	The part of a generator
	Doing experiments	Of simple pendulum
	Participates	In a science quiz
Interest	Collects	Picture of scientists, some machines etc.
	Prepares	Posters on water pollution
	Writes	An article on 'Globalization' for school magazine
	Organizes	Organizes science exhibition on ICT in Science Education

TAXONOMY OF INSTRUCTIONAL OBJECTIVES

Taxonomy means a system of classification and in this sense; a taxonomy like Bloom's Taxonomy presents a system of classification of the teaching objectives. Benjamin Bloom and his associates (In 1956) divided teaching objectives into three domains Cognitive (about knowing), Affective (about feeling, attitude, interests, values and believes) and Psychomotor (about doing). The taxonomy related to cognitive domain has been presented by Bloom and his associates (Bloom *et al.*, 1956), the second related to affective domain by Krathwohl, Bloom and Masia (Krathwohl *et al.*, 1964) and the third related to psychomotor domain by Harrow (1972) and Simpson (1966).

Cognitive Domain (Bloom, 1956)

- It represents the intellectual component of mental life.
- This domain includes those objectives which deal with knowing, thinking and problem solving.
- This domain is divided into six major classes of objectives.

1. Knowledge

Knowledge is the lowest level of cognitive domain. Knowledge represents memory and constitutes recall and recognition of various facts, concepts, principles, theories and laws.

1.0 Knowledge Levels
1.10 Knowledge of specifics
1.11 Knowledge of terminology
1.12 Knowledge of specific facts
1.20 Knowledge of ways and means of dealing with specifics
1.21 Knowledge of conventions
1.22 Knowledge of trends and sequences
1.23 Knowledge of classifications and categories
1.24 Knowledge of criteria
1.25 Knowledge of methodology
1.30 Knowledge of universals and abstractions in a field
1.31 Knowledge of principles and generalizations
1.32 Knowledge of theories and structures

2. Understanding or Comprehension

It is the second level of cognitive domain, and develops only after the development of knowledge in any particular area of study. The individual become capable of doing, summarize or define the acquired knowledge in his own words, interpret the acquired information, classify various objects into groups based on some criteria. The individual relates two or more events, describes and explain events.

2.0 Comprehension Levels
2.1 Translation
2.2 Interpretation
2.3 Extrapolation

3. Application

After having developed knowledge & comprehension of any concept, the individual is able to apply them in his day to day life. By applying the acquired knowledge and comprehension of various contents, the individual can solve many problems of daily life, of concrete and abstract situations.

3.0 Application Levels
3.1 Use of rules
3.2 Use of methods
3.3 Use of concepts

4. Analysis

It is the next higher level of cognitive ability. The individual develops the potential to break the whole into its various components and detect the relationship & organization of various parts. Students develop the ability to break a theory into its various inherent facts, concepts & principles.

4.0 Analysis Levels
4.1 Analysis of elements
4.2 Analysis of relationships
4.3 Analysis of organizational principles

5. Synthesis

It is the process of putting together various elements to make a whole. It is a complex ability at higher level of cognition which involves the creation of a new pattern or structure by manipulating various constituents. It has the elements of creativity in it.

5.0 Synthesis Levels
5.1 Production of a unique communication
5.2 Production of a plan, or proposed set of operations
5.3 Derivation of a set of abstract relations

6. Evaluation

It is the highest and the most complex cognitive ability, which involves all the five abilities. It is the process of judging the worth or value of a thing. It is both a qualitative and quantitative process. It develops decision making ability in the individual.

6.0 Evaluation Levels
6.1 Evaluation in terms of internal evidence
6.2 Judgments in terms of external criteria

Affective Domain (Krathwohl, Bloom, Masia, 1964)

This domain includes the development of feelings, interest, appreciation, attitudes and values. This domain is divided into five major classes of objectives.

1. Receiving

This is the ability of an individual to receive information. It includes attention, awareness, and willingness of an individual towards something. Receiving develops readiness towards listening, seeing and any kind of activity.

1.0 Receiving Levels

1.1 Awareness
1.2 Willingness to receive
1.3 Controlled or selected attention

2. Responding

This is the second level objective. Regularity and punctuality in attention and motivation lead to responding. Receiving and responding form a two way communication process and thus facilitate teaching and learning.

2.0 Responding Levels

2.1 Acquiescence in responding
2.2 Willingness to respond
2.3 Satisfaction in response

3. Valuing

During the process of receiving and responding, an individual is naturally inclined towards making value judgment about the things he is concerned with. It may be an object, an event, an idea, a rule or modern aspects of our culture. An individual sets guidelines for controlling his own behaviour. Valuing is based on the internalization of a set of specified values.

3.0 Valuing Levels

3.1 Acceptance of a value
3.2 Preference for a value
3.3 Commitment

4. Organization

Through the process of valuing the individual imbibes various values from time to time. He analyses different imbibed values and finally constructs relatively enduring value system by organizing and synthesizing them. This leads to the formation of philosophy of life in the individual.

4.0 Organization Levels

4.1 Conceptualization of a value
4.2 Organization of a value system

5. Characterization

It is the highest level of objectives under affective domain. At this stage, the individual develops a set of values, attitudes and beliefs for himself that helps in building his character and gives shape to his philosophy and total personality. The behaviour is pervasive, consistent, and predictable.

5.0 Characterization Levels

5.1 Generalized set
5.2 Characterization of value

Psychomotor Domain (Dave, 1975)

This domain includes those objectives of education which deals with manual and motor skills. The action abilities are classified under this domain. The psychomotor domain includes physical movement, coordination, and use of the motor-skill areas. Five categories are found under this domain.

1. Imitation

Imitation means observing and patterning behaviour after someone else. Performance may be of low quality.

1.0 Imitation Levels

1.1 Impulsion
1.2 Over repetition

2. Manipulation

It means being able to perform certain actions by following instructions and practicing. Manipulation of an act includes differentiating among various movements, and selecting the proper one.

2.0 Manipulation Levels

2.1 Following direction
2.2 Selection
2.3 fixations

3. Precisionm

Refining, becoming more exact. Few errors are apparent.

3.0 Precision Levels

3.1 Reproduction
3.2 control

4. Articulation

It means coordinating in a series of actions, achieving harmony and internal consistency.

4.0 Articulation Levels

4.1 Sequence
4.2 Harmony

5. Naturalization

In naturalization, high level performance become natural, without needing to think much about it.

5.0 Naturalization Levels

5.1 Automatism
5.2 Interiorisation

Revised Bloom's Taxonomy

In 1956, Benjamin Bloom headed a group of educational psychologists who developed a classification of levels of intellectual behaviour important in learning. During the 1990's a new group of cognitive psychologist, lead by Lorin Anderson (a former student of Bloom's), updated the taxonomy reflecting relevance to 21st century work.

Change in Terms

- The names of six major categories were changed from *noun* to *verb* forms.
- As the taxonomy reflects different forms of thinking and thinking is an *active* process verbs were used rather than nouns.
- The subcategories of the six major categories were also replaced by verbs and some subcategories were reorganized.
- The knowledge category was renamed. Knowledge is an outcome or product of thinking not a form of thinking. Consequently, the word knowledge was inappropriate to describe a category of thinking and was replaced with the word *remembering* instead.
- Comprehension and synthesis were re-titled to *understanding* and *creating* respectively, in order to better reflect the nature of the thinking defined in each category.
- From One Dimension to Two Dimensions (1. The Knowledge dimension-kind of knowledge to be learned (factual, conceptual, procedural, meta-cognitive. 2. Cognitive process dimension—process used to learn (remember, understand, apply, analyze, evaluate, create)

THE COGNITIVE DIMENSION PROCESS

Table 21.2: Level 1

Categories and Cognitive Processes	*Alternative Names*	*Definition*
Remember		Retrieve knowledge from long-term memory
Recognizing	Identifying	Locating knowledge in long-term memory that is consistent with presented material
Recalling	Retrieving	Retrieving relevant knowledge from long-term memory

Table 21.3: Level 2

Categories and Cognitive Processes	*Alternative Names*	*Definition*
Understand		Construct meaning from instructional messages, including oral, written, and graphic communication

(Contd.)

Categories and Cognitive Processes	*Alternative Names*	*Definition*
Interpreting	Clarifying Paraphrasing Representing Translating	Changing from one form of representation to another
Exemplifying	Illustrating Instantiating	Finding a specific example or illustration of a concept or principle
Classifying	Categorizing Subsuming	Determining that something belongs to a category
Summarizing	Abstracting Generalizing	Abstracting a general theme or major point(s)
Inferring	Concluding Extrapolating Interpolating Predicting	Drawing a logical conclusion from presented information
Comparing	Contrasting Mapping Matching	Detecting correspondences between two ideas, objects, and the like
Explaining	Constructing models	Constructing a cause and effect model of a system

Table 21.4: Level 3

Categories and Cognitive Processes	*Alternative Names*	*Definition*
Apply		Applying a procedure to a familiar task
Executing	Carrying out	Applying a procedure to a familiar task
Implementing	Using	Applying a procedure to an unfamiliar task

Table 21.5: Level 4

Categories and Cognitive Processes	*Alternative Names*	*Definition*
Analyze		Break material into its constituent parts and determine how the parts relate to one another and to an overall structure or purpose
Differentiating	Discriminating Distinguishing Focusing Selecting	Distinguishing relevant from irrelevant parts or important from unimportant parts of presented material
Organizing	Finding coherence Integrating Outlining Parsing Structuring	Determining how elements fit or function within a structure
Attributing	Deconstructing	Determine a point of view, bias, values, or intent underlying presented material

Table 21.6: Level 5

Categories and Cognitive Processes	*Alternative Names*	*Definition*
Evaluate		Make judgments based on criteria and standards
Checking	Coordinating Detecting Monitoring Testing	Detecting inconsistencies or fallacies within a process or product; determining whether a process or product has internal consistency; detecting the effectiveness of a procedure as it is being implemented
Critiquing	Judging	Detecting inconsistencies between a product and external criteria; determining whether a product has external consistency; detecting the appropriateness of a procedure for a given problem

Table 21.7: Level 6

Categories and Cognitive Processes	*Alternative Names*	*Definition*
Create		Put elements together to form a coherent or functional whole; reorganize elements into a new pattern or structure
Generating	Hypothesizing	Coming up with alternative hypotheses based on criteria
Planning	Designing	Devising a procedure for accomplishing some task
Producing	Constructing	Inventing a product

Table 21.8: Structure of the Knowledge Dimension of the Revised Taxonomy

Dimension	*Definition*
A. **Factual Knowledge** 1. Knowledge of terminology 2. Knowledge of specific details and elements	The basic elements students must know to be acquainted with a discipline or solve problems in it
B. **Conceptual Knowledge** 1. Knowledge of classifications and categories 2. Knowledge of principles and generalizations 3. Knowledge of theories, models, and structures	The interrelationships among the basic elements within a larger structure that enable them to function together
C. **Procedural Knowledge** 1. Knowledge of subject-specific skills and algorithms 2. Knowledge of subject-specific techniques and methods 3. Knowledge of criteria for determining when to use appropriate procedures	How to do something, methods of inquiry, and criteria for using skills, algorithms, techniques, and methods

Dimension	*Definition*
D. Metacognitive Knowledge 1. Strategic knowledge 2. Knowledge about cognitive tasks, including appropriate contextual and conditional knowledge 3. Self-knowledge	Knowledge of cognition in general as well as awareness and knowledge of one's own cognition

The Taxonomy Table

In the revised Taxonomy, the fact that any objective would be represented in two dimensions immediately suggested the possibility of constructing a two-dimensional table, which we termed the Taxonomy Table. The Knowledge dimension would form the vertical axis of the table, whereas the Cognitive Process dimension would form the horizontal axis. The intersections of the knowledge and cognitive process categories would form the cells. Consequently, any objective could be classified in the Taxonomy Table in one or more cells that correspond with the intersection of the column(s) appropriate for categorizing the verb(s) and the row(s) appropriate for categorizing the noun(s) or noun phrase(s).

Using the Table to classify objectives, activities, and assessments provides a clear, concise, visual representation of a particular course or unit. Once completed, the entries in the Taxonomy Table can be used to examine relative emphasis, curriculum alignment, and missed educational opportunities. Based on this examination, teachers can decide where and how to improve the planning of curriculum and the delivery of instruction.

Table 21.9: The Cognitive Process Dimension

The Knowledge Dimension	*Remember*	*Understand*	*Apply*	*Analyze*	*Evaluate*	*Create*
Factual Knowledge						
Conceptual Knowledge						
Procedural Knowledge						
Metacognitive Knowledge						

WRITING OBJECTIVES IN BEHAVIOURAL TERMS

There are several approaches of writing objectives in behavioural terms. The most important approaches are given below:

Robert Mager's Approach

According to Robert Mager (1962), instructional objectives are best described in terms of the terminal behaviour expected from the learners. He recommends the following things for the writing of the objectives:

- Identification of the terminal behaviour or performance and its naming.
- Description of the important conditions under which the behaviour is expected to occur.
- Specification of the criteria of acceptable performance (desired terminal behaviour) by describing how good a learner's performance must be for being acceptable.

Robert Miller's Approach

Robert Mager, in his approach neglected the conative domain or psychomotor aspect of behaviour. Robert Miller (1962) for meeting the requirement of writing psychomotor objectives put forward his scheme based on skill analysis by outlining the following procedure:

- Description of the indicator, indicating the relevant activity.
- Description of the indication or stimulus that calls for a response.
- Controlling of the object that is to be activated.
- Description of the activity to be performed.
- The indication of the adequacy of responses or feedback.

RCEM Approach

Both Mager's and Miller's approach have remained unsuccessful in the task of writing all instructional objectives belonging to all the three domains of behaviour. While Mager's approach serves the purpose of cognitive and affective objectives, Miller's approach is meant for psychomotor objectives.

RCEM approach makes use of mental process or mental abilities in place of action verbs in the writing of instructional objectives. It makes use of its own taxonomy of objectives, known as RCEM taxonomy of objectives, a modified form of the Bloom's taxonomy. The four categories of objectives, as may be evident from the table, have been divided into seventeen mental processes or abilities. These processes or abilities are used for writing the instructional objectives in behavioural terms. For this purpose, RCEM approach lays down the necessary outline of the seventeen frames or statements as follows:

1. Knowledge Objectives
   1.1. The learner will be able to recognize........................
   1.2. The learner will be able to recall.......................
2. Understanding Objectives
   2.1. The learner will be able to see relationship between........ and...........
   2.2. The learner will be able to cite example of.......................
   2.3. The learner will be able to discriminate between............... and.....
   2.4. The learner will be able to classify.......................
   2.5. The learner will be able to interpret.......................
   2.6. The learner will be able to verify.......................
   2.7. The learner will be able to generalize.......................
3. Application Objectives
   3.1. The learner will be able to reason out.......................
   3.2. The learner will be able to formulate hypothesis for.......................

3.3. The learner will be able to establish hypothesis for........................
3.4. The learner will be able to infer about........................
3.5. The learner will be able to predict about........................

4. Creativity Objectives
   4.1. The learner will be able to analyze........................
   4.2. The learner will be able to synthesize........................
   4.3. The learner will be able to evaluate........................

Table 21.10: Instructional Objectives and their Corresponding Mental Processes in RCEM Approach

Knowledge	*Recognize* *Recall*
1. Understanding	1.1. Seeing Relationship 1.2. Cite Example 1.3. Discriminate 1.4. Classify 1.5. Interpret 1.6. Verify 1.7. Generalize
2. Application	2.1. Reason out 2.2. Formulate Hypothesis 2.3. Establish Hypothesis 2.4. Infer 2.5. Predict
3. Creativity	3.1. Analyze 3.2. Synthesize 3.3. Evaluate

How to Write Objectives in RCEM Approach

The writing procedure of instructional objectives in RCEM Approach is as under:

- First of all, have in mind the entry behaviour of the learner.
- Try to think over the element of content, topic or the learning experience to be given to the learner.
- Try to think over the teaching or learning objective or objectives.
- In view of the entry behaviour of the learner, element of content and the particular objective, try to select appropriate mental process or mental abilities for writing the objective in question.
- Try to make use of the seventeen frames or statements of the RCEM approach given here and fill in the blanks in view of the entry behaviour of the learner and learning experiences given to him.

22
Modification of Teacher Behaviour and Analysis of Classroom Interaction

TEACHING OR TEACHER BEHAVIOUR

In simple words, the behaviour maintained and demonstrated by a teacher at the time of teaching is known as his teaching behaviour. Ryans (1969) defined teaching behaviour as *"The term teaching or teacher behaviour may be defined as the behaviour or activities of persons as they go about doing whatever is required of teachers, particularly those activities which are concerned with the guidance or direction of the learning of others."* According to McNergency and Carner (1981), *"teacher behaviour may be regarded as a function of the characteristics of the teacher, his environment and the task in which the teacher engages".*

MODIFICATION OF THE TEACHING OR TEACHER BEHAVIOUR

The term modification of teaching or teacher behaviour stands for the attempts made or processes undergone for bringing desirable improvement or modification in the teaching or teacher behaviour with an objective of making one as a quite effective and competent teacher for performing one's professional duties as effectively as possible. Modification or improvement in one's performance and behaviour is a continuous process.

TECHNIQUES FOR THE MODIFICATION OF TEACHING OR TEACHER BEHAVIOUR

Researches in field of pedagogy and teacher education programme have brought out a number of innovation and techniques especially suitable for bringing planned modification and improvement in teachers' teaching begaviour. These techniques are especially concerned with the process of modifying the ways of interaction of the teacher with the students and improving teacher's behaviour. The following are the main techniques for the modification of teaching or teacher behaviour:

- Interaction Analysis and Transaction Analysis
- Action Research
- Micro-Teaching
- Role Playing (Simulation)
- Teacher Evaluation

Meaning of Interaction

The act of teaching is a kind of reciprocal contact established between the teacher and the pupil. This reciprocal contact can be perceived as a series of events which occur one after another. Classroom interaction refers to these chains of events each one of which occupies a small sequence of time. An event may be defined as the shortest possible act that a trained observer can observe and record. Ned. A. Flanders defines, *"Teaching as an interactive process. Interaction means participation of teacher and students in the process of teaching. In this process, teacher influences the students; students also interact with the teacher. Interaction takes place among the students themselves also. It means, in the process of teaching, everybody interacts with every other person involved in the process."*

Meaning of Interaction Analysis

Interaction analysis is a process of encoding and decoding the pattern of interaction between the communicator and the receiver. In the coding process a code symbol is assigned to each category of behaviour and a trained observer records by jotting down code symbols. In the decoding step, a trained analyst interprets the display of code data and reconstructs the original events on the basis of the encoded data. Interaction analysis is the study of classroom climate and teaching behaviour of the teacher.

According to Ober, *"systematic observation represents a useful means of identifying, classifying, studying and measuring specific variables as they interact with in the instructional learning situation"*. Hence, interaction analysis method is research oriented. It is the scientific and sequential study of all the events in the class-room. The subject matter is not measured in it. Only the interactions between the teacher and the pupils and amongst the peoples are studied.

Classroom interaction analysis can be used for pre-service and in-service education in order to help teachers improve the quality of classroom instruction. This requires some kind of objective feedback to the person who is trying to change his behaviour.

Definitions of Interaction Analysis

The definitions of Interaction Analysis are as under:

1. Classroom interaction analysis may be defined as *"Any system for coding spontaneous verbal communication, arranging the data into a useful display and then analyzing the results in order to study patterns of teaching and learning."*
2. Interaction analysis is *"an approach from group dynamics involving systematic recording of how members of a group react to one another in a situation and analysis of the results with a view to interpretation"*.
3. Interaction analysis is a study of *"interaction between teacher and learner, learner and learner. The variables to be studied will depend on the purpose of research. some researchers join them with pre-specific ideas of what to look for and keep checks on a check list or grid."*
4. *"Interaction analysis is an observational procedure designed to minimize these difficulties, to permit a systematic record of spontaneous acts and to utilize the process of instruction by taking in the account of each small bit of interaction."*

Characteristics of Interaction Analysis

The definitions of interaction analysis given above stress its following characteristic features:

- Interaction analysis relates to group dynamics, which is its super ordinate concept. It therefore involves a study of social interactions that take place in a classroom.
- It studies interactions between the teacher and learner as well as the learner and the learner.
- It involves use of observation systems for collection tabulation presentation of data pertaining to verbal interactions and its analysis and interpretation of results.

Types of Interaction Analysis

Since 1960, the efforts have been made in this direction to develop the system of observation, the work of withal (1949), Flanders and Amidon (1960), Medley and Mitzel (1948) and Galloway (1968) have developed system of observation for studying the classroom teaching activities. The observation systems are of two types:

Sign System

A sign system is composed of a list of behaviour. The observer simply checks or notes in some manner behaviour which occurs during a given period of time. The sign system of the Forida Taxonomy of cognitive behaviour consists of fifty-five items, which are grouped in seven levels as defined by bloom (1956): as (1) Knowledge, (2) Translation, (3) Interpretation, (4) Application, (5) Analysis (6) Synthesis and (7) Evaluation and the behaviour is marked only once as it occurs per six minutes observation period.

Category System

A category system is composed of a discrete set of categories. A behaviour unit is classified into categories. An observer simply encodes the classroom events which occur during a three second of duration, e.g., Flanders's ten categories system of interaction analysis consists of three major units of behaviour: (A) Teacher talk, (B) Pupils talk and (C) None of these or both. Each unit of behaviour is calculated in number of categories. The teacher talk has been classified into seven categories, and pupil-talk into two categories.

TECHNIQUES TO OBSERVE THE CLASSROOM INTERACTION

There are many important techniques to observe the interaction systematically. Some of them are:

- Flinders' Interaction Analysis Categories System (FIACS)
- Reciprocal Category System (RCS)
- Equivalent Talk Categories (ETC)
- Verbal Interaction Category System (VICS)
- Observation Schedule and Record (OSCAR)

FLINDERS' INTERACTION ANALYSIS CATEGORIES SYSTEM (FIACS)

Flanders Interaction Analysis Technique is most suitable and widely used technique of interaction analysis. This system was developed by Ned A. Flanders (1966) in the year 1959 at the University of Minnesota in the form of a teachers training technique. It involves categorization of all the sets of possible verbal behaviours of a teacher in the classroom while interacting with his students.

OBJECTIVES OF FLINDERS' INTERACTION ANALYSIS CATEGORY SYSTEM

The objectives of Flinders' Interaction Category System are:

- To identify teacher's behaviour in the class through interaction analysis.
- To collect the objective data and systematic record of the teacher behaviour by this method.
- To formulate remedial strategies with reference to the teaching methods.

ASSUMPTIONS OF FLINDERS' INTERACTION ANALYSIS CATEGORY SYSTEM

The assumptions of Flinders' Interaction Analysis Category System are:

- In the learning process the class-room environment is the most important.
- Teacher's behaviour influences teaching.
- Democratic behaviour in the class-room is highly appreciated.
- The classroom behaviour can be changed by using feedback.
- The observation of the teacher's class-room behaviour is possible objectively.
- The mutual relationship between the pupil and the teacher carries much importance in the learning process.
- Verbal behaviour can be observed more reliably than the non-verbal behaviour.

MEANING OF FLINDERS' INTERACTION ANALYSIS CATEGORIES SYSTEM (FIACS)

Ned. A. Flanders developed a system of interaction analysis to study what is happening in a classroom when a teacher teaches. It is known as Flanders Interaction Analysis Categories System (FIACS). Flanders and others developed this system at the University of Minnesota, U.S.A. between 1955 and 1960. The interaction category system developed by Flander is easier as compared to the other systems. In order to classify the verbal behaviours of the pupils and the teachers, interaction analysis functions as an observational tool. It has been developed to record the verbal communication. It does not include the non-verbal behaviours. Verbal behaviour comprises teacher talk, student talk and silence or confusion.

DESCRIPTION OF FLINDERS' INTERACTION ANALYSIS CATEGORIES SYSTEM (FIACS)

Flander has divided the class-room behaviour of the pupils and the teachers in ten categories. The ten categories are mentioned as under:

- Teacher Talk—7 categories

- Pupil Talk—2 categories
- Silence or Confusion- 1 category

Thus, the first seven categories include teacher talk. Next two categories include pupil talk. The last tenth category includes the small spans of silence or pause or confusion. The first 7 categories or teacher talk has been bifurcated into a) indirect talk, b) direct talk.

Teacher's Talk - 7 Categories

A) Indirect Talk (4 Categories)

Category-1: Accepts Feelings
Category-2: Praise or Encouragement
Category-3: Accepts or Uses ideas of Pupils
Category-4: Asking Questions

B) Direct Talk (3 Categories)

Category-5: Lecture
Category-6: Giving Directions
Category-7: Criticizing or Justifying Authority

Pupil Talk (2 Categories)

Category-8: Pupil Talk Response
Category-9: Pupil Talk Initiation

Neither Teacher Talk nor Pupil Talk (1 Category)

Category-10: Silence or Pause or Confusion

Meaning of Various Categories

1. Teacher Talk (7 Categories)

(A) Indirect Talk

In this method of analysis, the first four categories represent the teacher's indirect influence.

Category 1: Accepts Feelings

In this category the feelings of the pupils are accepted by the teacner. He feels himself that the pupils should not be punished for exhibiting his feelings.

- In this category, teacher accepts the feelings of the pupils.
- He feels himself that the pupils should not be punished for exhibiting his feelings.
- Feelings may be positive or negative.

Category 2: Praise or Encouragement

The teacher uses the words 'good' better' 'correct' etc. while appreciating the activities of the pupils. He encourages them by saying 'carry on' 'move ahead', 'yes tell more' etc. It also includes joking but not too much.

- Teacher praises or encourages student action or behaviour.
- When a student gives answer to the question asked by the teacher, the teacher gives positive reinforcement by saying words like "good", "very good", "better", "correct", "excellent", "carry on", etc.

Category 3: Accepts or Uses ideas of Pupils

In this category, the pupil's ideas and not his feelings are accepted. If a pupil passes on some suggestion, then the teacher may repeat it in nut shell in his own style or words.

- It is just like 1st category. But in this category, the pupils ideas are accepted only and not his feelings.
- If a pupil passes on some suggestions, then the teacher may repeat in nutshell in his own style or words.
- The teacher can say, "I understand what you mean" etc. Or the teacher clarifies, builds or develops ideas or suggestions given by a student.

Category 4: Asking Questions

This category includes asking questions only. There must be an answer to each question. Sometimes teacher asks the question but he carries on his lecture without receiving any answer. Such questions are not included in this category.

- Asking question about content or procedures, based on the teacher ideas and expecting an answer from the pupil.
- Sometimes, teacher asks the question but he carries on his lecture without receiving any answer. Such questions are not included in this category.

(B) Direct Talk

Next 5th to 7th categories represent the teacher's direct influence.

Category 5: Lecturing/Lecture

It is a sort of verbal interaction used to impart the information's or awareness regarding ideas. When a teacher explains something, consults something or provides information's, this category is used.

- Giving facts or opinions about content or procedure expression of his own ideas, giving his own explanation or citing an authority other than a pupil.

Category 6: Giving Directions

Whatever a teacher asks the pupils to do in the class is called 'giving directions'.

- The teacher gives directions, commands or orders or initiation, with which a pupil/student is expected to comply with:

Ø Open your books.
Ø Stand up on the benches.
Ø Solve 4th sum of exercise 5.3.

Category 7: Criticizing or Justifying Authority

When the teacher asks the pupils not to interrupt with foolish questions, then this behaviour is included in this category. Teachers 'what' and 'why' also come under this category.

When the teacher asks the pupils not to interrupt with foolish questions, then this behaviour is included in this category. Teachers 'what' and 'why' also come under this category.

- When the teacher asks the pupils not to interrupt with foolish questions, then this behaviour is included in this category.
- Teacher's "what" and "why? also come under this category.

2. Pupil Talk (2 Categories)

Category 8: Pupil Talk Response

It includes the pupil's talk in response to teachers talk. The initiates communication or contact but the pupils are not given too much freedom.

- It includes the pupils talk in response to teacher's talk
- Teacher asks question, student gives answer to the question.

Category 9: Pupil Talk Initiation

The pupil initiates the talk and presents his ideas. He starts new subject. He is free to develop his attitude.

- Talk by pupils that they initiate.
- Expressing own ideas; initiating a new topic; freedom to develop opinions and a line of thought like asking thoughtful questions; going beyond the existing structure.

3. Silence or Pause or Confusion (1 category)

Category 10: Silence or Pause or Confusion

Silence or confusion of short spans when no communication is understandable falls under this category.

- Pauses, short periods of silence and period of confusion in which communication cannot be understood by the observer.

PROCEDURE OF OBSERVATION/ENCODING TEACHING PROCEDURE

The procedure of observation/encoding teaching procedure is as follows:

- The observer sits in the classroom in the best position to hear and see the participants.
- At the end of every three seconds he decides which category best represents the communication events just completed. Thus the time involves in coding one tally for every 3 seconds, is 20 tallies in one minute, 100 tallies in 5 minutes and 1200 tallies in one hour.
- In this process only the serial numbers of the categories are recorded.
- The serial number of that category is recorded on the data sheet by the observer.
- When the observation is over, the observer shifts to some other room and prepares the details on the basis of those serial numbers of the categories.
- In this observation process, the writing of serial numbers of the categories is known as Encoding.
- Writing details of behaviour on the basis of these categories is known as Decoding.
- The observers should remember the serial numbers of these categories.

RULES FOR OBSERVATION/RULES FOR RECORDING OR DECODING

Flanders category system has many rules for observation, without following which the observation is not possible. The observer must remember these rules. These rules help in maintaining consistency and making observations uniform. These rules are as follows:

Rule 1: If more than one type of category occurs during a 3 second period, the observer should choose the category that is numerically farther from category 5 (but not category 10). Suppose the observer is in doubt whether the category is 2 or 3; he should write 2 categories.

Rule 2: The observer should not involve his personal viewpoint.

Rule 3: If more than one category is active in a span of 3 seconds, and then all the categories should be recorded. If after 3 seconds, no category changes, then the same serial number should be repeated in the next 3 seconds.

Rule 4: If the time period of silence exceeds 3 seconds, it should be recorded under the category No. 10

Rule 5: When teacher calls a child by name, the observer is supposed to record a 4th category.

Rule 6: When the teacher repeats the student's answer and the answer is a correct, that is recorded as a category No. 2. This tells the student that he has the right answer and therefore functions as praise or encouragement.

Rule 7: When a teacher listens to a pupil and accepts his ideas for a discussion, then this behaviour belongs to category No. 3.

Rule 8: The words "All is ok", "yes", "yah", "hum", "alright" etc. belong to the category No. 2. (Encouragement)

Rule 9: If a teacher jokes without aiming at any pupil, this behaviour belongs to the category No. 2. But if he makes any joke aiming at some particular pupil, then it belongs to the category No. 7.

Rule 10: When all the pupils respond to a very small question collectively, then the serial number of category-8 is recorded.

CONSTRUCTION OF INTERACTION MATRIX

The following guidelines will be helpful for the construction of matrix:

- After encoding or observation procedure of interaction, the coded behaviours are written in 10 x 10 table. This 10 (rows) x 10 (columns) table is known as a matrix.
- The category numbers of the record sheet the tabulated in the matrix table. Each number is entered in the form of sequence pairs, being used twice, first as the first numbers and second as second number.
- The row of the matrix represent the first number and the columns the second number.
- For example an observation recorded is 6, 10, 7, 5, 1, 4, 8, 4.
- Hence, the beginning and end of the coding should have the same number of the categories.
- It is the tradiiion of adding number 10 in the beginning and at the end. Hence the above number will be written in this way 10, 6, 10, 7, 5, 1, 4, 8, 4, 10

1st Pair (10, 6)
2nd Pair (6, 10)
3rd Pair (10, 7)
4th pair (7, 5)
5th Pair (5, 1)
6th Pair (1, 4)
7th Pair (4, 8)
8th Pair (8, 4)
9th Pair (4, 10)

- Sequence of the pair: (10, 6), (6, 10), (10, 7), (7, 5), (5, 1), (1, 4), (4, 8), (8, 4), (4, 10).
- While preparing matrices, one pair is marked at a time.
- The matrices have rows and columns.
- The first number of the pair represents "row" and second number of the pair represents "column".
- For example, in the first pair (10, 6), the number 10 represents row and the number 6 represents column.
- Every pair overlaps the other pair. Total tallies of the matrices is N.
- In the matrices (N-1) i.e. one less number is marked. In the above example, N=10, (N-1) i.e. 9 numbers will be marked.
- Each matrix has 100 cells.

Interaction Matrix Table

	1	*2*	*3*	*4*	*5*	*6*	*7*	*8*	*9*	*10*	*Total*
1				/							1
2											0
3											0
4								/		/	2
5	/										1
6										/	1
7					/						1
8				/							1
9											0
10						/	/				2
Total	1	0	0	2	1	1	1	1	0	2	9(N)

INTERPRETING THE INTERACTION MATRIX

The purpose of interaction analysis is to preserve selected aspects of interaction through observation, encoding, tabulation and then decoding.

The proportion of teacher talk, pupil talk and silence or confusion: The proportion of tallies in columns 1, 2, 3, 4, 5, 6 and 7 columns 8, 9 and column 10 to the total tallies indicates how much the teacher talks, the student talks and the time spent in silence or confusion. After several years of observing, we anticipate an average of 68 percent teacher talk, 20 percent of pupil talk and 11 or 12 percent silence or confusion.

The ratio between indirect influence and direct influence: The sum of column 1,2,3,4, divided by the sum of columns 5, 6, 7 gives this ratio. If the ratio is 1 or more than 1, the teacher is said to be indirect in his behaviour. This ratio, therefore, shows whether a teacher is more direct or indirect in his teaching.

The ratio between positive reinforcement and negative reinforcement: The sum of column 1, 2, 3 is to be divided by the sum of the columns 6, 7 to get this ratio. If the ratio is 1 or more than 1 then the teacher is said to have succeeded in providing positive reinforcement.

Student's participation ratio: The sum of columns 8 and 9 is to be divided by total sum to get this ratio. The answer will reveal how much the students have participated in the teaching-learning process.

Steady State Cells

	1	*2*	*3*	*4*	*5*	*6*	*7*	*8*	*9*	*10*	*Total*
1	1.1										
2		2.2									
3			3.3								
4				4.4							
5					5.5						
6						6.6					
7							7.7				
8								8.8			
9									9.9		
10										10.10	
Total											

The above figure shows the 'steady state' cells along the diagonal from the upper left to the lower right. If these cells are heavily loaded it shows that the teacher remains in a particular category for more than three seconds. The cell with the highest frequency of the entire matrix is typically the 5-5 cell which lies on this diagonal indicating that the teacher frequently stays longer than 3 seconds when he provides information through lecture.

Content cross cell: The cell corresponding to the number pairs (4, 4) and (5, 5) are known as 'content cross' cells. If these cells are overloaded they reflect the teacher's emphasis on the subject matter

Constructive integration cells and vicious cells: Two areas that are most sensitive to the positive and negative aspects of social skill is the teacher-student relationship.

	1	2	3	4	5	6	7	8	9	10	Total
1											
2		A									
3											
4											
5											
6							B				
7											
8											
9											
10											
Total											

Area A might be called "Constructive Integrative Cells" while area B is called the "Vicious Cells". The cells corresponding to number 1,2 and 3 are known as constructive integration cells because they indicate the positive aspect of the social skill of the teacher. Cells of numbers 6 and 7 are known as vicious cells because they reveal the negative aspect of the teacher.

Advantages of Flander's Interaction Analysis Categories System (FIACS)

- It is an effective tool/instrument to measure the social-emotional climate in the classroom.
- It is also used for in-service teachers.
- It provides feedback to the pupil-teachers.
- It is an objective and reliable method for observation of classroom teaching.
- It is used to compare the behaviour of teachers at different age levels, gender, subject etc.
- It is much useful in team teaching and microteaching.

Limitations of Flander's Interaction Analysis Categories System (FIACS)

- It consumes much time in preparing 10 x 10 matrix without which, interpretation is not possible.
- The observers have to be trained in order to code correctly.
- Classroom interaction of pupil-pupil type is not considered here.
- The system of coding and decoding procedure very difficult and expensive.

23
Team Teaching

MEANING OF TEAM TEACHING

Team teaching a style of instruction in which resources as well as interests and expertise of a team of teachers are pooled in order to enhance the effectiveness of instruction/curriculum transaction to the maximum possible by utilizing all facilities available in school.

CHARACTERISTIC OF TEAM TEACHING

The main characteristics of team teaching are as under:

- It utilizes the service of two or more teacher in the process of teaching the same class.
- It is an instructional strategy rather than training strategy.
- In team teaching a group of teachers are responsible for realization of the educational objectives, rather than an individual teacher.
- A team of teachers of the same subjects work together to deal relevant content area to the same group of students.
- It can be termed as co-operative teaching, in which teachers together plan to pool resources, interests and expertise for teaching the same content for the same group of students.
- Every individual teacher of the team gets an appropriate role in the instructional process in accordance with one's special competencies or area of specialization.
- The group of teachers involves have shared responsibilities in planning, organizing, leading, controlling and evaluating.
- In team teaching, the group of teachers has to jointly consider the needs of their pupils.

OBJECTIVES OF TEAM TEACHING

The main objectives of team teaching are as under:

- To make the best use of expertise of a number of teachers.
- To improve the quality of teaching by utilizing the sills of more than one person.
- To develop positive attitude towards co-operation or group in teaching—learning situations.
- To help the student to satisfy the needs and solve the difficulties relating special content areas.
- To develop the sense of shared responsibility in teaching and evaluation.
- To minimize the scope of teaching wrong things to the students by any individual teacher.

TYPES OF TEAM TEACHING

The team teaching can be of different types, given below:

Team Teaching in the Same Class Period: Here the members of the team discuss the various aspects of the same topic to be covered in the same class period and share these aspects in tune with the special knowledge area in which each has expertise.

Team Teaching Based on Ability: In this type, units are shared by different teachers not on the basis of subject matter, but on the basis of special competencies such as lecturing, demonstrating, guiding discussion etc.

Team Teaching Based on Specialization: Teachers with different subject specialization are jointly made responsibilities for instruction, starting from course formation to evaluation. They share the content according to their specialization areas.

Team Teaching on Relay System: Hear one teacher starts the instructional process, when he completes, another follows and so on. Hear the division of work not based on subject competency or skill. Each teacher supplements, enriches and supports what others have done.

PRINCIPLES OF TEAM TEACHING

The main principles of team teaching are as under:

Principle of Size and Composition of the Class: The size of the class should be vary according to the objectives of the team teaching. E.g. To remove the difficulties of students in certain subject, the size of the class should be small.

Principle of Level of Instruction: The entering behaviour of the group of students should be determined so that the presentation of each member of the team in tune with the level of the class.

Principle of Assigning Duties to Teachers of the Work: Duties to the teachers should be appropriate according to their competencies of teaching.

Principle of Learning Environment: Learning environment must be generated by employing appropriate teaching aids and other inputs.

Principle of Time Factor: Time schedule should be prepared by allotting appropriate time to subtopics, lead lecture, group work etc.

Principle of Supervision: The aim of team teaching is to develop mastery over subject matter by utilizing the expertise of teachers. Supervised study is essential for assimilating various items of knowledge of a topic. The nature and duration of supervising students activities depends upon the purpose for which team teaching is employed.

PROCEDURE OF ORGANIZING THE TEAM TEACHING

Team teaching involves three steps

Planning

This step involves the following activities:

- Formulating the objectives of the team teaching session.
- Writing these in behavioural terms.
- Identifying the entering behaviour of the learners.
- Deciding the details of the material to be taught.

- Assigning duties to teachers, such as lead lecture, follow up work and supervision considering their interest and competencies.
- Fixing up the level of instruction.
- selecting appropriate teaching aids and other inputs, if any, for generating learning environment.
- Deciding ways and means to be adopted for evaluating the student performance.

Organizing

The organization of team teaching is decided by considering the needs of the learners. The following are the general activities which are usually performed by a team of teachers:

- Determine the level of instruction. Some questions are asked to explore the background of the learners.
- Selecting the appropriate communication strategy by considering the level of language achievement of the learners.
- Presentation of lead lecture by a competent of the team; other teachers listen the lecture and note down the element of the topic that appear to be not easily understandable to the learners or nor appropriately presented.
- Follow up work. The other teachers have to supplement the lead lecture by explaining the elements of the topic in a simpler way so that the learners can understand easily.
- Providing motivation or reinforcement during both the stages. i.e., during the lead lecture and follow up work.
- Supervision of student activities which are assigned in lead lecture or group work or follow up work. This stage is considered to be important for assimilation.
- Every member of the team should be conscious about time schedule and about the duty assigned to him. He must be well prepared and ready for implementing the plan.

Evaluating

Evaluation is an important aspect of any type of teaching. It will helpful to measure the performance of learners. It also provides reinforcement to the team of teachers as well as to the learners. This stage involves the following activities:

- Asking oral questions. Each question should measure a particular objective envisaged by the team.
- Taking decision about the level of performance and realization of the objectives.
- Diagnosing difficulties of the learners and providing the remediation.
- .Revising the planning and organizing phase of team teaching itself on the basis of evaluation of the student.

ADVANTAGES OF TEAM TEACHING

The main advantages of team teaching are:

Better Planning: Team teaching has to overcome repetition and hence every teacher has to devote more time towards planning and preparation of his unit.

Better Utilization of Resources: It results in the optimum use of available resources, human, material, finance. A number of teachers can work together and make the best use of their specialized knowledge.

Effective Use of Teaching Techniques: Teachers observe each other and thus improve their teaching techniques.

Better Motivation: It provides better motivation for good teachers to become team leaders. Students too are better motivated while they are being taught by a number of teachers. Teachers with greater technical skills influence the performance of their colleagues.

Better Follow-up Work: It ensures better follow-up work as a number of specialists teach the same subject to the same class.

LIMITATIONS OF TEAM TEACHING

The main limitations of team teaching are:

- It is very difficult to ensure co-operation among teachers of a team.
- It is not east to assign powers and responsibilities to a group of teachers. It might happen no one takes care of the responsibilities expected.
- Many teachers do not maintain regard and respect. Every teacher considers himself an expert of the subject and has his own style of teaching.
- Teachers generally do not like to deviate from the routine methods of teaching and they do not prefer any change in the system of education.

24
Classroom Communication

In teaching-learning process, communication plays an effective and essential role. In many ways, teaching is communicating and in this sense good teachers are always good communicators. It is also equally true for the learners. The process of communication involves a two-way interaction between the teacher and the taught. The process of interpersonal communication is both an art and a science. It is an art which involves skills, techniques and has its roots in psychology. It is a science for it involves the use of audio-visual materials.

MEANING OF COMMUNICATION

Etymologically communication has been derived from the Greek word *'communis'* meaning 'to make *'common'*. Thus, when something is communicated, it becomes common knowledge of communicators and receivers. Communication refers to the transmission of thoughts, information and commands by employing the sensory channels. Communication is also considered to be a process of exchange i.e. give and take information by message or otherwise. Communication is a process of sharing or exchanging experiences, information, ideas, opinions, sentiments, thoughts and feelings etc, between the source of communication and the receiver through some mutually agreeable or known media (verbal or non-verbal)

DEFINITIONS OF COMMUNICATION

1. According to Edger Dale, *"Communication is defined as the sharing of ideas and feelings in a mood of mutuality"*.
2. James Carey, *"Communication as a symbolic process whereby reality is produced, maintained, repaired and transformed"*.
3. Keith Davis, *"Communication is the process of passing information and understanding from one person to another"*.
4. D.E. McFarland, *"Communication may be broadly defined as the process of meaningful interaction among human beings, more specifically it is the process by which meanings are perceived and understandings are reached among human beings"*..

CHARACTERISTICS OF COMMUNICATION

The characteristics of communication are as given below:

It Involves at Least Two Persons: It involves at least two persons, a sender and a receiver. The sender is called communicator and the receiver of the message is known as communicate. A person who speaks, writes or issues some instructions is the sender and the person for whom the communication is meant or who receives the message is the receiver.

In It Message is a Must: A message is the subject matter of communication i.e the contents of the letter or speech, order, instructions or the suggestions. A communication must convey some message.

It is Written, Oral or Gestural: Communication is generally understood as spoken or written words. It includes everything that may be used to convey meaning from one person to another ie movement of lips, or the wink of an eye or the wave of hands may convey more meaning.

It is a Two Way Process: It involves both information and understanding. Communication is not complete unless the receiver has understood the message properly and his reaction or response is known to the sender.

Its Primary Purpose is to Motivate a Response: The primary purpose of communication is to motivate a response or influence human behaviour.

It Flows Up and Down and also From Side to Side: Communication flows downward from a superior to subordinates and upward from subordinate to a superior. It also flows between two or more persons operating at the same level of authority.

It is an Integral Part of the Process of Exchange: It refers to the exchange of ideas, feelings, emotions and knowledge and informations between two or more persons.

COMPONENTS OR ELEMENTS OF COMMUNICATION

The components or elements of communication is given in Table 24.1

Table 24.1: Components or Elements of Communication

1. Communication Context	– Overall environment existing i) Physical (the classroom and surroundings) ii) Social (the relationship between teacher and learner) iii) Psychological (formal / informal) iv) Temporal (time and period)
2. Communicator/ Source	A person or an event which provides verbal or nonverbal cues to which some one can respond when the source is a person, he is called a sender (teacher)
3. Receiver	A person who receives and interprets the message (student)
4. Message	A set of verbal or nonverbal symbols, gestures, cues, movements, figures or words sent by the source.
5. Symbol	A symbol is something that denotes an idea / thing / fact etc. They can be verbal or non-verbal (e.q, words are symbols –speech)
6. Channel	It is the means through which message is conveyed. The channels are sense of perception which include sight, hearing, touch, taste and smell.
7. Encoding	It is the process of using symbols to send the message.
8. Decoding	It is the process involves understanding and interpretation of the message sent.
9. Feed back	It is the response the receiver gives to the sender as a result of sender's message.

PRINCIPLES OF COMMUNICATION

Communication as a two way channel requires certain basic principles to be observed for its effective outcomes.

Principles of Readiness and Motivation: The communicator as well as the receiver both should be ready and remain motivated throughout the process of communication. Lack of interest, enthusiasm on the part of either of them or both may affect adversely the process and products of communication.

Principle of Competency: The communicator and receiver both should be quite competent and efficient in terms of communicating and receiving the desired information or message. There is a great need of the development of required communication skills so that the task of communication in terms of transmission and receiving may be performed by them as effectively as possible.

Principle of Sharing and Interaction: Communication is always a two way process. Its success lies in allowing as much as sharing of the ideas and mutual interaction between the source of communication (teacher) and receiver (students) as possible.

Principles of the Suitability of the Communication Contents: What is to be communicated in a communication process should be quite appropriate and suitable on the parts of both the communicator and receiver. The communicated material should be suitable enough for being grasped and responded by the receiver.

Principle of Appropriate Media and Channel: The effectiveness of the process of communication will lie in the appropriateness, quality and strength of the communication media and channel. Therefore it is quite worthwhile to make use of the verbal or nonverbal or both means and media for the efficient and effective flow of communication between the source and receiver.

Principle of Appropriate Feedback: The communication enjoys its effective flow it continues to receive the desired feedback from the receiver and vice versa. In the classroom, if a teacher gets desired feedback from his students in term of the quality of the effectiveness of his teaching efforts, it will definitely boost up his morale and give desired direction to his further efforts in the two-way communication process.

Principle of Facilitators and Barriers of Communication: There are many intervening variables lying in between the source and receiver of communication. The way, positive or negative, favourably or adversely these variables affect the functioning of the source (teacher) and received (students) becomes an important decisive factor for the success or failure of the process of communication. Therefore, it should be always arrived that the learning situations and environment should be so arranged as to eliminate barriers of communication as much as possible for getting effectiveness in the process of communication.

TYPES OF COMMUNICATION

The different types of communication are as follows:

One to One Communication

This type of communication takes place between two individuals. Most of our day-to-day conversation and communication takes place in an informal or formal way e.g. communication between wife and husband, lover and beloved, shopkeeper and customer and between any two relatives, friends, colleagues and even two strategies.

Small Group Communication

This type of communication takes place occurs in formal as well as informal ways among the members of a small group (more than two) e.g. Communication among the members of a family, students of a section/class, passengers of a bus/train.

Large Group or Public Communication

This type of communication involves a large number of people on individual or group basis e.g. communication carried out during morning assembly hall, public functions organized for honouring the individuals, places of worships, addresses by leaders in political gatherings etc.

Organizational or Institutional Communication

This type of communication is carried out within the four walls of the various organizations or institutions like factory/industrial establishments, government offices, army, hospitals. This type of communication is quite formal, systematic, planned and organized.

Mass Communication

This type of communication is quite wide and extensive. It is carried out through different types of mechanical means, appliances and mass media like radio, TV, video, cinema, films, books and literature, newspapers and magazines, E-mail, internet communication and conferencing etc,. Here we don't have any direct face to face natural communication between the sender or receiver yet it is the only way to reach the masses with the meaningful message full of information and education with utmost economy and effectiveness. The masses after receiving the message, information or instruction can send their responses to the source through their writing or may show the impact of the message through their actions and behaviours.

MODES OF COMMUNICATION

There are two modes of communication used in teaching process:

1. Oral Communication (Speaking and Listening Channels) Strategy

The oral communication is largely oral or verbal interaction in classroom teaching. It is based upon audio lingual method. The teacher has to speak something orally the students have to listen the oral communications. It requires content first and expression on the part of teacher and the students listen the expression first than the theme or content.

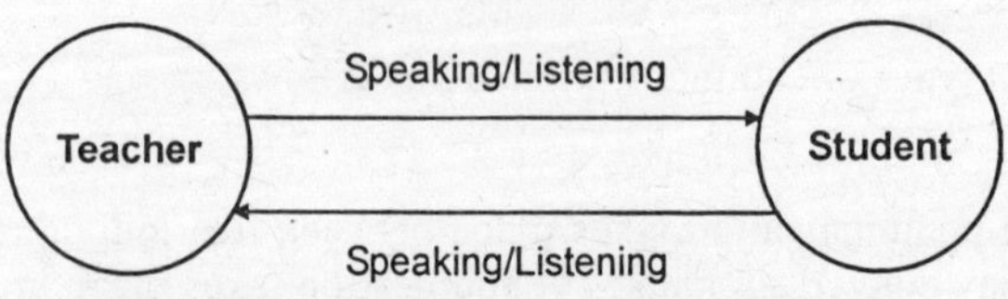

Figure 24.1: Oral Communication Strategy

As shown in the above diagram the oral communication takes place between teacher as student with the help of speaking and listening operations.

2. Written Communication Strategy

While the oral communication strategy does not ensure about the solution of the problem written communication ensures about the correct solution of the problem. It is based upon the cognitive code of method of teaching. Integration between teacher and students takes place through reading and writing activities. In writing, content comes first than expression and sequence is reverse in reading activities. Generally, communications are performed with the help of four activities: speaking and listening, writing and reading.

COMMUNICATION PROCESS/CYCLE

Communication as a two way process involves interaction between the two or more persons (on giving and receiving ends). There are six main components/ elements are involved in any process of communication namely:

The Source of Communication (The Communicator): The process of communication essentially starts with a source of communication. There must be somebody to initiate the process of communication. This source whether in the form of some object/event or person must be in a position to transmit information's, ideas, thoughts, opinions and feelings etc. The source of communication person or object is generally named as 'sender' in the language of communication technology. In the teaching-learning process given inside the classroom, the teacher is to be regarded as the source of communication or sender of the message.

Contents of Communication or Message: What is intended to be communicated or transmitted by the source of communication that is sender from his own stock of knowledge, information, thoughts, opinions and feelings etc., to the other persons/persons (receivers) is known as the contents of communication. These contents may be well organized and structured or unstructured and unstructured.

Media and Channel of Communication: What one wishes to communicate to others is always communicated with the help of some or the other appropriate media or channel. The media is general takes the two distinctive forms—verbal and non-verbal. In any communication process the sender and receiver both are forced to make use of that media/channel of communication which is mutually acceptable as well as effective.

The Receiver of Communication: Receiver is the persons who remains at the receiving end of the communication. He is to receive the encoded intended message of the source of communication, decode it for its proper interpretation and must reach or produce a desired response (feedback) to the source of communication.

Response Material/Feedback: The response material or feedback may be defined as the reaction or response signals in the encoded form transmitted back by the receiver, to the communicated message after its proper decoding, interpretation and understanding in order to maintain the flow of communication between him and the sender. The effectiveness in the flow of communication is dependent much upon the quality and effectiveness of the contents of the response. It is through feedback that one may evaluate the outcomes of his communication.

Facilitators or Barriers of Communication: The quality and effectiveness of the process of communication is affected favourably or adversely through the presence of some or the other intervening variables lying between the source of communication and the receiver. These variables, according to their nature helping or obstructing the path communication, may be termed as facilitators or barriers of communication. Whereas the presence of congenial, physical, and psychological environmental conditions and facilities available for effective communication may facilitate and help in providing desirable effectiveness to the communication system.

FACTORS AFFECTING COMMUNICATION

The different factors that affect the communication are as under:

Factors Related to Sender

- The sender's perception of the receiver
- The sender's concept of the environment
- The sender's self-concept, self-knowledge etc.
- The audiences perception of sender
- The psychological readiness of sender
- Personal factors like age, interest, health, skills etc.

Factors Related to Learner

- Intelligence
- Gender and age
- Needs and motivation
- Attitudes, beliefs and values
- Concentration and interest
- Self-esteem
- Perception of learner about the sender

Factors Related to Atmosphere

- Openness and supportiveness
- Empathic and sympathetic
- Devoid of noise
- Positiveness
- Climate conducive to communication

Factors Related to Messages

(A) Verbal

- Simple, easy to understand words
- Accuracy and precision in use of words
- Simplicity and clarity
- Imagination and Originality

(B) Non verbal

- Style and posture

- Language—speech delivery, intonation
- Gestures and body movements
- Facial expressions and emotions
- Clothing and presentation

BARRIERS OF COMMUNICATION

The main barriers of communication are:

Internal Barriers of Communication

The roots of such barriers lie in the sender and receiver of the message. These can be named as under:

- Poor physical health or illness.
- Poor background in terms of previous learning and general knowledge about the subject of communication.
- Poor mental health and improper psychological make up like affected with prejudices, in attention, feeling or insecurity, anxiety depression and districts etc.,
- Handicapped understands the symbolic expression, verbalism and graphical representation etc.

External Barriers of Communication

The roots of these barriers lie in the environmental conditions prevailing at the time of communication. These conditions can be named as under:

- Noise and other similar distractors (indiscipline, improper physical facilities)
- Polluted environment
- Invisibility
- Environmental and physical discomfort
- Improper functioning of the communication channels involving audio-visual materials and equipment.
- The non-cooperative or unhealthy rivalries and competitions among the participants in the process of communication.
- Lack of proper motivation, incentives, zeal and enthusiasm needed to remain active on the part of the sender and receivers in the process of communication.

ACHIEVING EFFECTIVENESS IN THE CLASSROOM COMMUNICATION

Effective communication is the essential requirement for having an effective interaction or getting maximum advantages from the process of communication. The nature and working of communication components are bring efficiency. A teacher's success is largely depends on his effective communication with his students. Hence, the following points should be kept in mind for achieving effectiveness in the classromm communication:

Source of Communication: Effectiveness of a communication very much depends upon the strengths and qualities of the source of communication. The personality characteristics, his potential in terms of the content of communication and its presentation count very much for the effectiveness of a person as a communicator. The teachers, lawyers, political and religious leaders, writers, actors, artists or any one who wants to communicate his feelings, thoughts and ideas thus always try to imbibe all the essential virtues and qualities of an effective communicator.

Communication Material: The effectiveness and success of the communication process in any classroom situation very much depends upon the quality and nature of the communication material. If the content and message has some attraction, force and value to the receiver, it will surely catch his attention and make him quite attentive and active participant in the communication process.

Communication Media or Channel: Communication media or channel just lies in between the source and the receiver like a bridge or connecting link. What the source of communication says or shows to the receivers, it can be done only with the help of some or the other verbal or non-verbal communication channel. The effectiveness and strength of the communication flow between the communicator and receiver will surely depend upon the nature and quality of the verbal and non-verbal means, media and channels employed in the process of communication.

Receiver of the Communication: Where the initiator or source of communication is the communicator, the receiver lies on the other end for actualizing the process of communication. Actually what is dome through communication is always intended for the benefit of the receiver. That is why it can only be carried out effectively with his active involvement and cooperation. In case he is not interested or not capable of receiving and understanding the meaning of the message or does not respond in a proper way for maintaining the flow of communication, the communication will turn into one sided affair and thus lose its purpose and significance. In this way the actual key of effective classroom communication lies with the receiver.

25
Measurement and Evaluation in Education

MEANING OF MEASUREMENT

The measurement in psychology and education is the origin of twentieth century. The measurement is the process of quantification of a trait or characteristics or assigning numerals. The direct measurement is used in physical and bio-science while measurement is indirect in psychology and education. The traits and attributes are abstract. Measurement can be categorized into two:

- Measurement in Physical Science
- Measurement in Behavioural Science

Measurement in physical science is simple and precise processes of quantification of physical traits of the objects are perceivable and measured directly. The measuring instrument is placed along the traits. For example, height is measured by placing the meter along the height of a person and similarly his weight is also measured. The body temperature is measured by placing thermometer in his mouth. In physical measurement, the units are fixed or definite. The height or length is measured in meter and centimetres. The weight is measured in Kg. and quintals. The zero is the reference point in the physical measurement. It is also known as absolute measurement.

The process of measurement in behavioural science is difficult as well as complex, because it employs the indirect process of measurement. The trait is not measured by the scale, but the trait is measured indirectly by the behaviours. The basis of measurement is the behaviour of a subject. The behaviour sciences measurement is relative, while physical measurement is absolute. The zero mark has no meaning in this area, for e.g., if a student has scored zero, it does not mean that he does not know anything but could not attempt correctly the items given in the test, therefore, zero mark has been assigned to him.

DEFINITIONS OF MEASUREMENT

1. According to J.P. Guilford, *"Assignment of numerals to objects or events according to certain rules is called measurement"*.
2. Bradfield, *"Measurement is a process of assigning symbols to the dimensions of phenomenon in order to characterise the status of the phenomenon as precisely as possible"*.
3. Campbell, *"Assignment of numerals to objects or events according to certain rules is called measurement"*.
4. Tyler, *"Assignment of numerals, according to rules."*
5. Nunnally, *"Measurement is a consistent of rules for assigning number to objects in such a way as to represent the quantities of attributes"*.

EDUCATIONAL MEASUREMENT

The term *"Educational Measurement"* refers to any device for the general study and practice of testing, scaling, and appraising the outcomes of educational process. It includes administration and scoring or tests, scale construction, validation and standardization and application of statistical techniques in the interpretation of obtained measures or test results.

Thus, educational measurement refers to the use of educational assessments and the analysis of data, such as scores obtained from educational assessments, to infer the abilities and proficiencies of students. Educational measurement is the assigning of numerals to traits such as achievement, interest, attitudes, aptitudes, intelligence and performance.

Definition of Educational Measurement

Educational Measurement is the process of assigning numbers to individuals or their characteristics according to specified rules. Measurement requires the use of numbers but does not require the value judgments be made about the numbers obtained from the process. We measure achievement with a test by counting the number of test items a student answers correctly, and we use exactly the same rule to assign a number to the achievement of each, student in the class. Measurements are useful for describing the amount of certain abilities that individuals have. For that reason, they represent useful information for the evaluation process.

Characteristics of Educational Measurement

The six important characteristics of educational measurement are given below:

In Educational Measurement there is No Absolute Zero Point

In educational measurement, there is no absolute zero point. It is relative to some arbitrary standard. For example, a student has secured 'O' in a test of mathematics. It does not mean that he has 'O' knowledge in mathematics. Because he may secured 30 in another test, which is easier than the first one. As the zero point is not fixed, so we cannot say that a student with a score of '60' has doubled the knowledge of a student with a score of '30'.

The Units are not Definite in Educational Measurement

In educational measurement, the units are not definite, so we may not obtain the same value for every person, because, the test vary in their content and difficulty level. Therefore, one individual may per-form differently on different tests and different individuals may perform differently on one test.

It Conveys a Sense of Infinity

It means, we cannot measure the whole of an attribute of an individual. Generally,, the scores obtained from a measurement are observed scores which contains measurement errors. So, that true score is infinite and unknown.

It is a Process of Assigning Symbols

Measurement is a process of assigning symbols to observations in some meaningful and consistent manner. In measurement, generally, we compare with certain standard unit or criteria which have a universal acceptability.

It Cannot be Measured Directly

In case of educational measurement, we cannot measure for attribute directly. It is ob-served through behaviour. For example, the reading ability of an individual can only be measured, when he is asked to read a written material.

It is a Means to an End but not an End Itself

The objective of educational measurement is not just to measure a particular attribute. Rather, it is done to evaluate to what extent different objectives have been achieved.

MEANING OF EVALUATION

Evaluation is the assessment of quality and analyzing and interpreting of all round development of a person. Evaluation is the process by which, we judge the value of something. In the field of education, evaluation is the process of determining the extent to which educational objectives, one attains. It is a systematic process of collecting, analyzing and interpreting evidences of students' progress and achievement both in cognitive and non- cognitive areas of learning for the purpose of taking a variety of decisions. Evaluation, thus, involves gathering and processing of information and decision making.

Evaluation is an important component of the teaching- learning process. Teaching for successful learning cannot occur without high quality evaluation. Evaluation, therefore, needs to be integrated with the process of teaching and learning. The greater the integration, the result is the better the outcomes of learning. Hence, evaluation has to be so designed that it can be used as a powerful means of influencing the quality of what teachers teach and what students learn.

DEFINITIONS OF EVALUATION

Some important definitions of evaluation are as under:

1. According to M.P. Moffat, *"Evaluation is a continuous process and is concerned with more than the general academic achievements of students. It is interested in the development of the individual in terms of desirable behavioural changes in relation to his feelings, thinking and actions"*.
2. According to N. E. Gronlund, *"Evaluation is a systematic process of collecting, analyzing and interpreting information to determine the extent to which pupils are achieving the expected outcome."*
3. From the education point of view, the definition of evaluation can be given as *"Evaluation is any systematic continuous process of determining- the extent to which the specified educational objectives are attained, the effectiveness of the learning experiences provided in the classroom, how well the goals of education can be established."*
4. *"Evaluation is a continuous process where various process of measurement can be utilized. It is a co-operative activity in which the principal, teachers, parents and students participate."*

CHARACTERISTICS OF EVALUATION

The main characteristics of evaluation are as follows:

- Evaluation provides quality control at every stage of the teaching- learning process and therefore, evaluation would be treated as an integral part of the teaching- learning process.
- Evaluation will be humane in nature. It will help students grow as social beings.
- Evaluation will be the responsibility of the teacher who teaches the students and is responsible for developing the requisite healthy attributes in them.
- Evaluation will be consistent with its purpose and will provide a reliable and valid measure of students' performance.
- Evaluation will take into account both the background and the prior experiences of students.
- Procedures for grading and their reporting will be appropriate and easily understood by one and all.

NEED, SCOPE AND IMPORTANCE OF EVALUATION

- The need, scope and importance of evaluation ism as follows:
- Interpretations of the behaviour of the children are done through the right type of evaluation.
- The success/failure of an educational programme is decided through evaluation.
- It determines how far the learning objectives could be achieved.
- It motivates students for better learning.
- It judges effectiveness of instruction.
- It determines the rate of progress of the students.
- It provides the base for certifying the students.
- It helps in classifying the students.
- It predicts the success of students in future.
- It diagnoses strengths & weaknesses of students.

FUNCTIONS OF EVALUATION

Functions of evaluation may be classified into two major categories:

Functions Associated with the Instructional Process

(i) Measurement Function: The measurement function act as the basis for most of the other functions is of primary importance to a teacher. Through evaluation teachers are able to measure the degree of realization of the objectives of classroom teaching, to measure the attributes related to the physical growth, development, health conditions etc, to measure intelligence, aptitudes and other personality traits. These are essential for enhancing the quality of instruction.

(ii) Diagnostic Function: It helps to detect errors committed, deficiencies, gaps that exist in the cognitive structure, limitations of the learning experiences and learning conditions provided, physical and psychological problems etc.

(iii) Guidance and Remediation: This is a natural extension of the diagnostic function. When the difficulties are identified a teacher can help the learners to overcome their difficulties by giving guidance and remediation.

(iv) Motivating Function: Evaluation motivates the learner in two ways. Firstly, it provides immediate feedback about the performance of each learner.

Secondly, the knowledge of the result and the diagnosis of difficulties lead to mastery learning and the thrill of success can act as a motivating force.

(v) Assessment of Final Output: Assessment of the final performance of the learner in terms of quality and quantity of the total attainment with respect to a specific curriculum area is the function of evaluation.

(vi) Classification and Placement: Classification of students on the basis of their level of attainment and abilities, placement of students on the basis of realization of the expected level etc are the functions of evaluation.

(vii) Prognosis, Prediction and Selection: This aims at determining in advance whether a particular student can be expected to succeed in a course of study or job he is intended to take up. This prediction is necessary because each field of study or job demands certain capacities and levels of attainment in all the three domains of behaviour.

(viii) Setting Up of Norms: On many occasions, we will have to compare individuals with reference to standards or norms of a group of which they are members. For example, to select a few girls who have completed SSLC for admission to sports school, the performance will have to be compared with some prescribed standard. By measuring the performance of a large sample, group norms can be established.

Functions Associated with the Educational System as a Whole

(i) Improvement of Inputs and Processes of Education: The inputs include curriculum, text books, instructional material, infrastructure facilities, expertise of teachers etc. Improvement in this field can be done only on the basis of proper analysis and evaluation of inputs and processes.

(ii) Maximization of the Output (Student Development): Evaluation helps in setting goals, re-fixing goals, reinforcing achievements and remediating weaknesses. By improving inputs and processes and by ensuring perfection through diagnosis and remediation, educational evaluation enhances productivity of the system.

MEASUREMENT

Measurement is an important feature of almost every aspect of our life. It is an act or process which ascertains the quantity of something. It is the quantitative description of data. Measurement is the assignment of numerals to entities according to rules. It is the process of obtaining a numerical description of the degree to which an individual possesses a particular characteristic. Educational measurement is the assessing of academic or educational achievement. It includes all aspect of testing and test construction.

Measurement = quantitative description

Evaluation = quantitative description (measurement) + value judgment.

DIFFERENCE BETWEEN MEASUREMENT, EVALUATION, ASSESSMENT AND TEST

The difference between Measurement, Evaluation, Assessment and Test is given below:

1. Measurement refers to process by which attributes or dimensions of some physical object are determined.

2. Evaluation is a process that is designed to provide information that will help us make a judgement about a given situation.
3. Assessment is a process by which information is obtained relative to some known objective or goal.
4. A test is a special form of assessment. All tests are assessments, but not all assessments are tests.

DISTINCTION BETWEEN MEASUREMENT AND EVALUATION

The difference between measurement and evaluation is shown in Table 25.1 given below:

Table 25.1: Difference between Measurement and Evaluation

Measurement	*Evaluation*
Answers to the questions how much	Answers to the questions how good
Quantitative description	Qualitative description
Describes a situation	Judges its value
Objective and impersonal	Subjective and personal
Occasional	Continuous
Independent of evaluation	Dependent on measurement
Process involved is collecting information	Process involved are collecting, analyzing and interpreting information
Concerned with knowing the level of attainment	Concerned with its improvement
Less comprehensive	More comprehensive
Measures scholastic area of an individual	Measures students' achievement in scholastic and co-scholastic areas.

TYPES OF EVALUATION

The two types of evaluation are as under:

1. Formative Evaluation

Formative evaluation is a process by which the achievements of students are judged at every stage of teaching and learning process. It is done during the instructional programme. According to A.J. Nikto *"Formative evaluation is concerned with judgements made during the design and or development of a programme which is directed towards modifying, forming or improving the programme before it is completed."* While teaching, the content to be taught is presented in the form of small teaching units. At the end of each such item students have to be evaluated with respect to the anticipated objectives. Thus difficulties if any should be diagnosed and remediated.

Functions of Formative Evaluation

The important functions of formative evaluation are:

- Provides feedback to an individual in order to improve that individual's performance.
- Identifies areas for improvement and provides specific suggestions for improvement

- Planned corrective action for overcoming learning difficulties.
- To aid in motivating learning.
- To increase retention and transfer of learning.
- To improve the quality of educational institutions.

2. Summative Evaluation

Summative evaluation is done at the end of a course or unit of study. It is the overall assessment or decision with the programme. According to A.J. Nikto *"Summative evaluation describes judgements about the merits of an already completed programme, procedure or product."* It may be done at the end of a term or end of a unit. Summative evaluation is designed to determine the extent to which the instructional objectives have been achieved and is used primarily for assigning the course grade or certifying pupil's mastery or the intended learning outcome. Summative evaluation is useful for teachers to plan their teaching for next year.

Functions of Summative Evaluation

The important functions of summative evaluation are:

- Assigning grades
- Reporting learning programmes to parents, pupils and school personal.
- Improving learning and instruction.
- The results of summative evaluation help students to plan their future.

DIFFERENCE BETWEEN FORMATIVE EVALUATION AND SUMMATIVE EVALUATION

The difference between Formative Evaluation and Summative Evaluation is shown in Table 25.2 given below:

Table 25.2: Difference between Formative Evaluation and Summative Evaluation

Formative Evaluation	*Summative Evaluation*
Process oriented	Product oriented
Internal in nature	Can be internal or external in nature
Aims at immediate feedback, diagnosis and remediation	Aims at overall assessment
Grading, Classification, placement, selection	Setting up of norms etc.
Can be conducted daily	Weekly, termly etc.
Developmental in nature	Judgemental
Timing is during instructional period	End of the course or unit
Methods used are daily assignment, observations etc.	Methods used are tests, projects etc.
Profiles and record of achievements are regularly used	Limits the use of profiles and record of achievements

OBJECTIVE BASED AND COMPETENCY BASED EVALUATION

Objective Based Evaluation

Evaluation is based on predetermined objective is objective based evaluation.

An objective is the statement of a result to be achieved. In objective based evaluation the teacher evaluates the realization of a specific objective. He selects one specific objective he wants to set. Based on these objectives, he selects learning activities and experiences. Then he selects appropriate evaluation procedures to test those objectives. Thus, we find that objectives, learning experiences and evaluation are interrelated as:

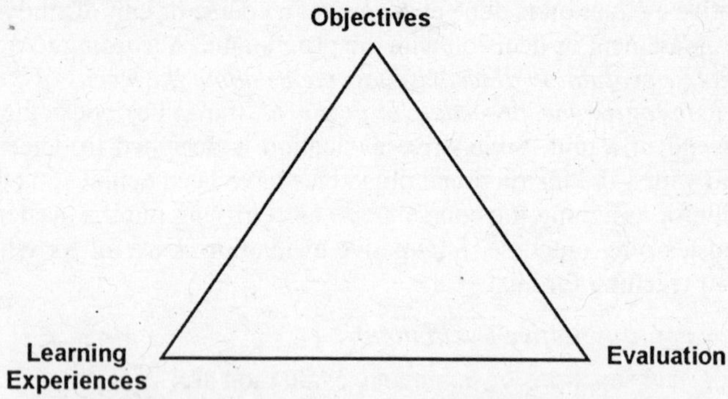

Figure 25.1: Triangular relationship of Objectives, Learning Experiences and Evaluation

Competency Based Evaluation

Competency based evaluation involve testing pupils on the basic skills and setting a satisfactory level of performance as a graduation requirement. Competency is the ability to do something at some level of proficiency and is usually composed of some combination of knowledge, understanding, skill, attitude and values. Competency based evaluation procedure is specially constructed to check the proficiency of an individual in performing a skill in different situations. Competency tests are used as a basis for promotion at the lower grade levels. Competency based assessment is not a set of examinations; it is a basis for certification of competency and it is carried out as a process in order to collect evidence about the performance and knowledge of a person with respect to a competency standard.

Distinction between Objective Based Evaluation and Competency Based Evaluation

The distinction between Objective Based Evaluation and Competency Based Evaluation is given in Table 25.3 given below:

Table 25.3: Distinction between Objective Based Evaluation and Competency Based Evaluation

Objective Based Evaluation	*Competency Based Evaluation*
Emphasis on objectives	Emphasis on what a person can do in the work

SCHOLASTIC AND CO-SCHOLASTIC EVALUATION

Scholastic Evaluation: Scholastic evaluation is the evaluation meant for testing the performance of the learner in scholastic aspects.. Assessment based on the scholastic aspect which includes curricular areas or subject specific area is known as scholastic evaluation. The area of assessment includes the entire school subject i.e. assessment of cognitive growth in subject.

Co-scholastic Evaluation: Co-scholastic evaluation meant to measure the co- scholastic or the objectives other than the academic aspects of the learner. The area of assessment –co-scholastic aspects of pupils growth helping the all round development of the child i.e. growth in affective and psychomotor areas is covered. Co-scholastic areas are required to develop physical growth, development of social personal qualities, interests, attitudes and values etc.

CRITERION-REFERENCED AND NORM-REFERENCED EVALUATION

Criterion-Referenced Evaluation: A test is criterion–referenced when provision is made for translating the test score into a statement about the behaviour to be expected of a person with that score. Evaluation done on the basis of selected criteria indicating specific changes brought about in the learner is said to be criterion-referenced evaluation. Predetermined and well-defined specific objectives act as the criterion. Criterion referenced evaluation are those which are used to ascertain an individual's status with respect to certain criterion i.e. performance standard. It is because the individual is compared with some established criterion, rather than individuals. It aims at qualitative assessment. Whenever evaluation is based on well defined objectives and is done by searching for criteria it is criterion referenced. Most of achievement tests are criterion referenced.

Uses of Criterion-Referenced Evaluation: The main uses of Criterion-Referenced Evaluation are as under:

- To discover the inadequacies in learners learning and assist the weaker section of learners to reach the level of other students.
- To identify the master learners and non-master learners in a class.
- To find out the level at which a particular concept has been learnt.
- To find out the level of attainment of various objectives of instruction.

Norm-Referenced Evaluation: Norm-referenced tests are designed to rank students in the order of achievement, from high to low, so that decisions based on relative achievements(e.g. selection, grouping, grading) can be made with greater confidence. Tests that set goals for students based on the average student's performance are norm-referenced tests.

This test is used primarily for comparing achievement of an examinee to that of a large representative group of examinees at the same grade level. The representative group is known as the norm-group. Norm group can be made up of examinees at the local level, district level, state level, or national level. Since the development of norm-referenced test is expensive and time consuming.

Uses of Norm-Referenced Evaluation: The main uses of Norm-Referenced Evaluation are as under:

- Its basic purpose is to measure student's achievement in curriculum based skills.
- It is prepared for a particular grade level.
- It is administered after instruction.
- It classifies achievement as above average, average or below average.

Distinction between Criterion- Referenced (CRT) and Norm-Referenced Evaluation (NRT)

The distinction between Criterion- Referenced (CRT) and Norm-Referenced (NRT) Evaluation is shown in Table 25.4:

Table 25.4: Distinction between Criterion-Referenced (CRT) and Norm-Referenced Evaluation

Criterion- Referenced (CRT) Evaluation	*Norm-Referenced (NRT) Evaluation*
It stresses what examinees can do and What they Cannot do	It stresses discrimination among individuals.
It contains easy as well as difficult items.	It contains items of average difficulty.
It diagnosis the loopholes in the developmental process.	It stresses the final product of development rather than process.
Remedial instruction is given to the students if the material presented is not mastered.	A norm-referenced test will use questions which were correctly answered by the "best" students and not correctly answered by the "worst" students.
A criterion-referenced test will use questions, which were correctly answered by students who know the specific material.	

Both terms criterion- referenced and norm- referenced were originally coined by Robert Glaser. They differ only to the method of interpreting results. They can and should mutually complement.

CONTINUOUS AND COMPREHENSIVE EVALUATION (CCE)

Evaluation of all the relevant scholastic, co -scholastic and personal qualities of a learner, done all over the period in a school is known as continuous and comprehensive evaluation. i.e. it refers to a particular process of evaluation, which aims at overall development of the child.

The term continuous refers to continuity and regularity of assessment during the whole session. The frequency of class tests, unit tests, and terminal tests make the evaluation regular. The continuity can be made feasible by employing both formal and informal methods of assessment. Education is a continuous process. Therefore, evaluation and development must go hand in hand. Evaluation has to be carried out in every possible situation and throughout the period of formal education of a pupil. Hence, evaluation has to be continuous.

By comprehensive evaluation, we mean that evaluation should cover all the learning experiences of the learner in curricular and non-cognitive areas. It refers to the areas of assessment, which includes both scholastic and co–

scholastic aspects of pupil growth helping in all round development of the child. The scholastic areas are meant for intellectual growth whereas co-scholastic areas are required to develop physical growth, development of social personal qualities, interests, attitudes and values. If we want the teaching – learning process really effective, we should evaluate the learners continuously and comprehensively. The CCE is multi- dimensional as it involves multiple techniques and different persons like teacher, pupil, peer, parent, community etc.

Objectives of Continuous and Comprehensive Evaluation (CCE)

The main objectives of Objectives of Continuous and Comprehensive Evaluation (CCE) are:

- To make evaluation as an integral part of teaching - learning process.
- To use evaluation for improvement of students achievement through diagnosis and remediation.
- To take timely decisions of learners' growth, learning process, learning pace and learning environment.
- To maintain desired standard of attainment.
- To provide scope for self- evaluation.

Components of CCE (Innovative programmes for the promotion of CCE)

On the basis of the recommendations made by different committees and commissions four areas were highlighted for the implementation of new concept CCE. They are:

- Continuous internal assessment
- Introduction of the grading system
- Introduction of the semester system
- Development of question bank

These programmes were used not only for implementing examination reforms but also for revitalizing all aspects of education- curriculum development, curriculum analysis, curriculum transaction-with evaluation.

GRADING

The word grade is derived from the Latin word 'gradus' where it means step. Grading is comparing the performance of one student in relation to his reference group (all the students of same age and class level) on a normative scale. A grading system is a method of communicating measurement of achievement. Fundamentally a grade is a score. It is a process of classifying students on the basis of predefined standard.

Marking is awarding marks for the correct responses of the student. Marks compare a student's performance with a standard or on a scale. Marking system has its own limitations- precise judgement is not possible, subjectivity involved in assigning marks, limitation regarding coverage e of aspects etc.

Distinction between Grading and Marking

The difference between grading and marking is given in table-36.5 given below:

Table 25.5: Difference between Grading and Marking

Grading	*Marking*
Compares the performance of students	Awarding marks for the correct responses of the student
More scientific in the present day system	Marks are great motivators for better performance
Measures scholastic and co-scholastic areas.	Measures only scholastic areas
True representation of a student's ability	Not a true representation of a student's ability
Grades are standard scores	Percentage of marks is not a standard score
Skills of students can be measured	Skills of students cannot be completely measured

Features of Grading

The main features of grading system are as follows:

- In grading classification is made on 5 point, 7 point, and 9 point scale.
- Fundamentally a grade is a score.
- More scientific way of evaluation as it solves the problems of borderline cases by inculcating all the pupils falling with in wider range within a wider range within the same grade.
- Identifies students' performance level with a wide range.
- Grading involves the use of set of specialized symbols.

ACHIEVEMENT TEST

The term achievement is often understood in terms of pupil's score on a certain school test. Achievement means one's learning attainments, accomplishments etc. it is related to pupil's growth in educational situations. Achievement test is an important tool in the school evaluation programme. It is necessary for the teacher to know how far the pupils have attained in a particular subject area. A test designed to assess the achievement in any subject with regard to a set of pre- determined objectives is called an achievement test.

Types of Achievement Tests

Achievement tests are of two types. Teacher made tests and standardized tests. Teacher made tests may be divided into oral and written tests.

Teacher Made Achievement Tests

Oral Tests: It is the oldest form of achievement tests. They are common in lower classes. Viva Voce is an example. An advantage of this test is that a large number of areas can be covered and knowledge of the student can be assessed. But it is difficult to test each pupil on the basis of total curriculum. The examiner does not have any written proof regarding the pupil's attainment.

Written Tests: These can be divided into 3 types Essay type, Short answer type, and objective type.

Functions of Achievement Test

The main functions of an achievement test are:

- Provide basis of promotion to the next grade.
- Help in finding out at the beginning of the year where each student stands in the various academic areas.
- Help in determining the relative position of a student in a particular subject or area of learning.
- Help the teacher to sees for himself how effectively he is doing, what
- Helps the teacher in is getting across to pupils and what is not. identifying pupil's difficulties and arranging for remedial measures.
- Provides the teacher evidence relating to the realization of objectives, effectiveness of learning activities provided and mode of instruction employed.
- Motivate the students before a new assignment is taken up.

Characteristics of a Good Achievement Test

The characteristics of a good achievement test are as follows:

- A good achievement test is tried out and selected on the basis of its difficulty level and discriminating power.
- It should have a description of a measured behaviour.
- It should contain a sufficient number of test items for each measured behaviours.
- It provides equivalent and comparable forms of the test.
- It is accompanied by norms which are developed at various levels and on various age groups.
- Its instructions in regard to its administering and scoring are so clear that they become standardized for different users.

Preparation/Construction of an Achievement Test

If the test is to serve as an efficient and effective tool of evaluation, its preparation should be based on a number of careful considerations. The preparation of a good test is a systematic process having well defined stages. The important steps envisaged in the preparation of a good achievement test are:

Step-1: Planning of the Test

It should be well planned and systematically developed. The paper setter should aim at testing the degree of realization of his objectives and also to determine the maximum time, maximum marks, and the nature of the test. *Planning* implies *preparation of design* for the test or *preparation of blue print.*

Preparation of Design for the Test

Designing is the first and most important step in the test construction. It is at this stage that we plan to build in the test the important qualities: validity, reliability, objectivity and practicality. In order to accomplish this, the test constructor has to take a number of decisions regarding selection of objective, the selection of the content, form of questions, the difficulty level of test items and the weightage to be allotted to them. The set of these decisions will be called the design of the test.

(a) Identification of the Objective and Allotting Weightage to the Objectives: The most important step while planning a test or any evaluation tool is the identification of the instructional objectives and stating them in terms of specific observable behaviour. After the objectives are identified and stated, the test maker has to decide their relative weights in the test. The fundamental principle to be observed here is that the test should reflect the actual emphasis being given to various mental processes during instruction. The simplest basis for assigning the weights could be to weigh them in terms of time devoted for their achievement. Weightages could of course be given in numerical terms, distributing 100 points over the objectives, giving the greatest number to those that are to receive the greatest emphasis.

(b) Selection of the Content and Allotting Weightage to the Content: Content being the means through which objectives are attained, it becomes very necessary to decide the weights to be given to its different parts. The importance of the unit, time devoted to it during instruction etc. will consider while giving relative weightage to units.

(c) Selection of the Form of Questions and Giving Weightage to the Questions: For testing different abilities and sub units different forms of questions-essay type, short answer type and objective type questions may be judiciously used. According to different objectives and different aspect of content the weightage to be given to each form should be decided the marks are allotted to each form in the basis of time needed for answering, difficulty level, and skill involving. However among the objective type questions multiple choice may be given more weightage.

(d) Distribution of Difficulty Level: The distribution of difficulty level in a test will depend upon the purpose of the test as also on the group of students for whom it is designed to get optimum discrimination through a test; most of its questions should be of average difficulty level. A few easy questions, to motivate below average students and a few difficult ones to challenge the gifted.

In short, at preparation stage, we give weightage to the following four important aspects of the achievement test:

(i) ***Weightage to objectives:*** this indicates what objectives are to be tested and what weightage has to be given to each objective.

(ii) ***Weightage to content:*** this indicates the various aspects of the content to be tested and what weightage has to be given to each of these aspects.

(iii) ***Weightage to form of questions:*** this indicates the forms of questions (objective type, short answer type, and essay type) to be included in the test and the weightage to each form of questions.

(vi) ***Weightage to difficulty level:*** the test should cater to the bright, the average, and the dull. Discriminating power i.e. the ability to discriminate high achievers, average achievers, and low achievers is a quality to be maintained by a good test. Hence the test should contain easy, average, and difficult questions.

Preparation of a Blue Print

A blue print gives the details of the design in concrete terms. Blueprint is prepared as a three dimensional chart indicating the distribution of questions objective- wise, content- wise and form- wise. The preparation of the blue print refers to the final stage of the planning of a test. It is a document which gives a complete functional picture of the test. In other words a blue print is a three dimensional chart showing the weightage given to the objectives, content and the form of questions in terms of marks. The units or content spread along the vertical axis while the objectives are listed on horizontal axis. Each column is further subdivided into columns that indicate the forms of question. Thus we get a number of cells each cell having three dimensions, the objective, the content and the form of question. What is required on the part of the test maker is to fit in all the questions in different cells in such a way that the blue print reflects the decisions of the designer.

The uses of Blue Print are

- Helps to improve the content validity of the test.
- Defines as clearly as possible the scope and emphasis of the test.
- Relates objectives to the content.
- It provides greater assurance that the test will measure learning outcomes and course content in a balanced manner.

Planning of the test will be completed by the preparation of design and blue print.

Step-2: Designing the Test Items (Questions)

After preparation of a blue-print, we come to the framing of the test items according to the blue print. It is desirable to prepare more items than the requirement of the blue print (at least 20% excess) so that the test maker may be able to choose the best item to suit the allocation in the blue print.

The blue print gives a very clear picture about the number of questions to be written from each topic, their forms and objectives. On the basis of the blueprint, the paper setter can start writing items according to the requirements.

Step-3: Reviewing and Editing the Test Items

The items can be reviewed with the help of experts keeping in mind the design and blue print and the qualities of good evaluation tool.

Step-4: Arranging the Test Items

When the final selection of items has been completed, arrange the items according to the following guide lines:

- The items should be arranged so that all items of the same type are grouped together.
- The item should be arranged in the order of increasing difficulty.
- It may be desirable to group together items of same pattern.

Step-5: Providing Directions

The direction of an achievement test should be simple and concise general instructions may be given at the beginning of the test. It also include purpose of the test, time allowed to complete the test, how to record the answers and mark allotted for each question and also for each section of the test.

Step-6: Preparation of Scoring Key and Marking Scheme

Scoring key refers to the prepared list of answers to a given set of objective questions. The examiner compares the answers given by the students with those in the scoring key and thus awards marks to students.

In the case of objective type items where the answers are the form of some letter or other symbol, a scoring key is prepared. In the case of short answer and essay type questions, the marking scheme is prepared. In preparing the marking scheme what the examiner has to do is to list out the value points to be credited and then to fix up the mark to be given to each value point.

A Marking scheme is essential in the case of short answer type and essay type questions. It indicates:

- The number of steps or learning points expected in the answer.
- The outline of each point or step expected in the answer.
- The weightage to e ach point or each step.
- The level of accuracy expected of each step.

Step-7: Question/Item wise Analysis

Question wise analysis means making an analysis of each item (question) in terms of objective, specification, form of question, difficulty level, marks and estimated time. This analysis is very helpful to check whether all the aspects envisaged in the design and blueprint are satisfied by the test in its final form. It also gives an insight into the difficulties encountered by students in taking the test

26
Pedagogy and Pedagogical Analysis

In order to be an effective teacher, one must study the science of pedagogy. Learning how to managing activities and instruction in the classroom can empower educators to facilitate courses that optimize the learning potential of every student. Professionals who desire to work with students of all ages usually must complete a course in pedagogy before entering the classroom. Many state teacher examines also evaluate an educator's understanding of pedagogical and instructional theory in the core subject areas.

WHAT IS PEDAGOGY?

The word pedagogy comes from the Greek word '*paidagogeo*', (*Latin paedagogia)* in which '*paidos*' means "child" and '*agogos*' means "lead"; so it literally means "*to lead the child*" or "*to guide the child*". In Ancient Greece, a slave –paidagogos- was assigned to a wealthy master's son, to take him to school, supervise him while in school, and carrying his equipment such as musical instruments, etc. Pedagogy refers to educational schools of thought or philosophies regarding how people learn and how teachers should assist in that learning. Pedagogy is the science and art of education. It is the study of being a teacher. The term generally refers to strategies of instruction or a style of instruction.

According to Webster's dictionary pedagogy means "*the art or profession of teaching*". In terms of teacher training, it means the art or science of being a teacher, which includes the style and strategies of the teacher's instruction. The word '*pedagogue*' means, teacher, schoolmaster, educator, educationalist, etc. Especially, one who is strict, stiff or *old-fashioned*, who stands in the front of the room and lectures for the entire class period.

DEFINITIONS OF PEDAGOGY

Some important definitions of pedagogy are:

1. *"Pedagogy is the science/theory or art/practice of teaching that makes a difference in the intellectual and social development of students."*
2. *"A highly complex blend of theoretical understanding and practical skill"*
3. According to Alexander (2003) - *"Pedagogy is the act of teaching together with its attendant discourse. It is what one needs to know, and the skills one needs to command in order to make and justify the many different kinds of decisions of which teaching is constituted."*

WHAT IS PEDAGOGICAL ANALYSIS?

'*Pedagogical Analysis*' means the logical and systematical breaking up of the curriculum from the point of view of a pedagogue for the purpose of its effective transaction.

DEFINING PEDAGOGICAL ANALYSIS

Pedagogical analysis considers different instructional questions such as how to achieve predetermined educational objectives, which teaching methods should be used and how they should be used, which teaching techniques are necessary foe successful instruction, which teaching aids should be used to help the learners for meaningful learning and how to evaluate the performance of the learners etc.. Jerome Bruner (1977) states his view of instruction as follows:

"A theory of instruction is prescriptive, because it establishes rules concerning the best ways to teach knowledge and skills, normative, because it sets criteria and states the conditions for meeting these rules, and descriptive because it tells what has happened in the instructional process."

This explanation makes clear that instruction or pedagogy is totally practical in its nature.

In the past, pedagogy was silent on many aspects. Whatever was included in pedagogy was severely criticized. All the theories, rules, formulas, methods propagated in the theory were considered to be bookish and impractical. It was considered to be good enough for practice lessons conducted by Colleges of education but not for actual classroom teaching. In recent years, many researches related to teaching were undertaken and conducted in the Western countries. After having considered all the relevant researches, Shulman (1987) has specified a comprehensive map of the process of teaching which comprises the four groups of activities or processes:.

- Teacher's thinking process regarding content knowledge.
- Teacher's activities/skills for teaching specific subject.
- Teacher's subject enrichment.
- Considerations about 'pupil' and 'pupil's thinking processes' in term of subject knowledge.

OPERATIONS INVOLVED IN THE TASK OF PEDAGOGICAL ANALYSIS

Components and operations involved in the task of pedagogical analysis are as follows:

- *Content analysis* of the unit/topic/single concept being taught by the teacher in the subject.
- *Setting of the teaching or instructional objectives* of the content material of the topic in hand by writing them in specific behavioural terms.
- Suggesting methods, techniques, teaching-learning activities, aids and equipments helpful for the teaching learning of the topic in hand quite in tune with the realization of the set instructional objectives.
- *Suggesting appropriate evaluation devices* in the form of oral, written or practical activities and test questions etc for evaluating the outcomes of the teaching learning process carried in relation to the teaching of the topic in hand.

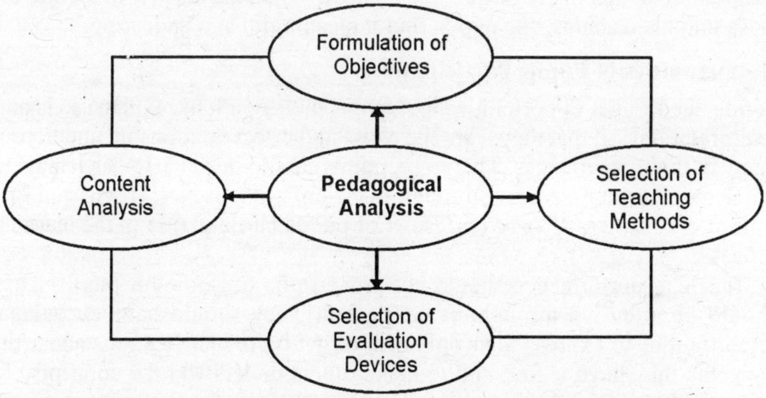

Figure 26.1: Operations Involved in the Task of Pedagogical Analysis

COMPONENTS OF PEDAGOGICAL ANALYSIS

The following are the components of pedagogical analysis:

Goal Awareness

Learning becomes more effective, when the learners know the reasons for studying the lesson, the teacher is about to teach and they know the activities they are to perform. Therefore, this step considers the procedures of making learners aware of the instructional objectives.

It is important to make the pupils aware of the teaching contents before the teacher actually teaches them. Therefore, mere ascertaining of goals, while planning the curriculum is not sufficient. It is more important to think of ways and means to explain them to the pupils. Therefore, it becomes necessary to inform the pupils of the goal of each learning experience. The teachers do verify, if the goal is achieved time-to-time and it also helps pupils understand the significance of learning experiences. Moreover, they realize their utility in achieving the basic goal of teaching content. For this, the teaching skill *'Set Induction'* is significant. An appropriate use of this skill is not only clarifies the goal of the teaching content but also the goal of every teaching-learning activity. Similarly, every learning material should specify the goal/purpose of every activity it recommends. This helps in verifying, if pupils have clearly understood the interrelationships in the activity they perform.

Awareness of Pupil Ideas

Pupils have some ideas about the content knowledge, the teacher is about to teach. The teachers need to know them. Some of the pupil ideas can be supportive to the new learning and others can be obstructive. The knowledge of such ideas helps the teachers in their teaching performance.

The teacher should be aware of content related ideas already existing with pupils. He should know their previous knowledge about the lesson, their ways of thinking about it and the skills they possess. All such considerations are helpful in deciding the teaching strategies. He should have an idea about pupils' general understanding regarding the content. When the teacher integrates all these into his teaching, the pupils find it meaningful and endearing.

Opportunities of Pupils Participation

Pupils need to get opportunities to express their opinions, explanations and interpretations, so that they learn the cause and effect relationship underlying many of their experiences. Therefore, pupils should be made to participate in the actual learning process, through questioning, activities, discussion etc. This step considers *'Where and How'* of pupils participation in the learning process.

Teaching performance should not prove to be tiresome for pupils. They should be attentive throughout the period. They should have occasional opportunities to express their opinions, to get more clarifications about the concepts they have learnt, and to make others understand the concepts. To achieve all this, pupils should be given suitable opportunities. The teachers should provide general suggestions to pupils. For example, when the teacher states, *'Fish cannot live out of water'*, he should ask pupils, *"What makes fish remain alive in water?"* and *"why can it not live out of water?"* He should let them express their opinions. Such a practice promotes their understanding.

The pupils must clearly understand the cause-effect relationship in the experiences they have. In order to enable them to understand the cause-effect relationship, the teacher should ask some questions or prescribe some activities that are based on the experiences.

For example, the teacher wants to explain, why days and nights have differences in their duration. This teaching point is related to the rotation and axis of the earth. To clarify the teaching point, the teacher should show the inclined axis of the earth and the revolution of the earth around the sun by using the globe. It clarifies the effect relationships. The teacher can ask pertinent questions to draw out the cause-effect relationship from pupils.

Developing Abstract Ideas

Pupils need to understand the ideas communicated in teaching. For this, it is necessary to ask pupils to provide evidence, examples relevant to the ideas, and to explain their correlation with other ideas.

The teachers teach many new ideas, concepts, facts etc.. It is not proper to insist that the pupils should believe in them because the teachers have taught them. There is a need to give evidence and supports to whatever the teacher teaches. To let the pupils to understand this fact, the teachers should provide examples and justify the points properly. The content knowledge that seems to be difficult for the pupils to understand should be supported by examples and facts. The support, evidence and examples promote quick understanding.

For example, the teacher can ask a pupil to lift his bag, to break a stick, or to throw a stone when he wants to explain the concept, 'force'. These physical activities will clarify the concept of 'force' quickly.

Sometimes, the pupils come across difficult words and technical terms which adversely affect comprehension of teaching contents. The teachers need to identify such words and terms in advance, and explain them at the proper time.

Activating Pupil's Thinking Process

Pupils interpret the teaching content according to their comprehension ability. Therefore, the teachers need to activate pupils' thinking process to help them to interpret the content knowledge and also check time to time whether their interpretations are correct or not.

Routine teaching is basically a one-way process in which pupils acts as receivers only. It reduces their active participation. Therefore, the teachers need to take necessary steps, so that they become active in their thinking. For this, the teacher should first of all identify the teaching content areas that can activate and challenge pupils' thinking processes. Later, he can think of various ways to make the pupils interpret the information and express their opinions.

The interpretation of knowledge by the pupils is more significant than the knowledge presented by the teacher. The pupils do not necessarily interpret the content, information and ideas in exactly the same way as the teacher does or as the teacher wants them to do. Some pupils might interpret differently. Therefore, it is necessary to let them verify, if their construction of knowledge is accurate and to let them put forward their ideas.

Evaluating Progress

This step expects prescribing of content related evaluation activities in order to verify, if the predetermined goals and objectives of teaching-learning have been achieved or not.

The teacher should have opportunities to verify, if their teaching is proceeding in the right direction. There are three ways for this:

1. The teacher can ask questions that verify content-based specific objective related progress and that help him to check, if the basic objective is achieved or not.
2. The teacher can ask comprehension questions on each point of the content after it has been taught.
3. The teacher can ask questions to verify if the pupils can apply the knowledge taught to them.

Such questions and activities are useful for ascertaining the level of understanding and the knowledge the pupils have acquired.

Creating Supportive Learning Environment

This step recommends the teaching activities for integrating teaching contents, values and core areas of curriculum, for connecting teaching contents with creativity and life practices and for creating joyful atmosphere in the classrooms.

The complementary, supportive, prosperous and healthy environment promotes pupil meaningful learning. Therefore, the teaching performance needs to be pleasant and interesting for the learners. There are numerous methods to do so.

When the teaching content is correlated to other school subjects, it enriches the learning environment. Therefore, such correlations among the subjects should be established.

The pupils should realize the relation between content knowledge and their daily life. Once, they understand it, they find it meaningful. The teachers should clarify such relationships. It makes the learning process more interesting.

For example, the teacher should explain how the mathematical concept, 'Area' is useful for the valuation of a plot or for house construction.

STEPS OF PEDAGOGICAL ANALYSIS

The following are the steps of pedagogical analysis:

Step-1: Divided the contents of the selected unit into suitable sub-units and arrange the selected sub-units in to a number of required periods.

Step-2: Briefly write the essence of the content of the selected sub-unit.

Step-3: Write appropriate previous knowledge required for the sub-unit.

Step-4: Write appropriate instructional objectives to be selected for the sub-unit.

Step-5: Select appropriate teaching strategies for the sub-unit according to the following instructions:

- Write the name of the methods applied.
- Mention the teaching aids required.
- Briefly illustrate the necessary demonstration and/or experimentation required.
- Mention the necessary board work required.
- Write probing questions related to the sub-unit and provide appropriate answers for them.
- Prepare a work sheet for the sub unit.

Step-6: Give suitable examples/illustration/analogies for the sub-unit.

Step-7: Prepare a table of specification for the sub-unit. Write at least six criterion referenced test-items each with specific criteria for the sub-unit.

ADVANTAGES OF PEDAGOGIC ANALYSIS

The advantages of pedagogic analysis are listed as follows:

- Teacher can take steps to motivate students
- It helps the teacher to adopt learner centered instruction
- It makes the instructional programme more systematic and content appropriate
- It helps the teacher to design a plan of action to for immediate feedback, diagnosis and remediation
- It helps the teacher to implement proper evaluation procedure

PEDAGOGY OF THE OPPRESSED

Pedagogy of the Oppressed (Portuguese: *Pedagogia do Oprimido*), written by educator Paulo Freire, proposes a pedagogy with a new relationship between teacher, student and society. It was first published in Portuguese in 1968 and was translated by Myra Ramos into English and published in 1970. The book is considered one of the foundational texts of critical pedagogy.

Dedicated to what is called *"the oppressed"* and based on his own experience helping Brazilian adults to read and write, Freire includes a detailed Marxist class analysis in his exploration of the relationship between what he calls "the colonizer" and "the colonized". In the book Freire calls traditional pedagogy the *"banking model"* because it treats the student as an empty vessel to be filled with knowledge, like a piggy bank. However, he argues for pedagogy to treat the learner as a co-creator of knowledge.

Paulo Freire's Critical Pedagogy

Paulo Freire was a Brazilian educator and philosopher. He was an influential figure in theorizing about '*critical pedagogy*'. His influential work, *Pedagogy of the Oppressed*, lays out the fundamental principles of critical pedagogy. Some of the concepts he develops in his work include:

- Oppressors–oppressed distinction
- Banking model of education
- Culture of silence

Oppressors–oppressed Distinction

Oppressors–oppressed distinction refers to the distinction Freire makes in his *Pedagogy of the Oppressed* between two models of education. Freire contends that education may follow one of two possible models:

- Education may function as a way to integrate generations into the logic of the present system and may work to lead these generations to conform to this logic.
- Education may function as a liberating and transformative tool that leads generations to think critically about reality and contribute to the transformation of their world.

These models represent the positions of the oppressor and the oppressed in an unjust society. He argues that education should aim at providing the oppressed with the tools to improve their condition and, consequently, regain their humanity. This can only occur if:

- the oppressed individual plays a role in their liberation.
- the oppressors understand that they have to rethink their way of life and examine their own role in the oppression.

Freire affirms that:

> "No pedagogy which is truly liberating can remain distant from the oppressed by treating them as unfortunates and by presenting for their emulation models from among the oppressors. The oppressed must be their own example in the struggle for their redemption". (Freire, 1970, p. 54).

He also states that:

> "Education makes sense because women and men learn that through learning they can make and remake themselves, because women and men are able to take responsibility for themselves as beings capable of knowing — of knowing that they know and knowing that they don't" (Freire, 2004, p. 15)

Culture of Silence

According to Freire the dominant system (the oppressors system) tries to instill the model that fits the goals of the oppressors, and encourages a *'culture of silence'*. The aim of education must be to achieve a form of liberation where by the oppressed are prompted to develop the critical awareness necessary to break the pattern of oppression, the culture of silence.

MEANING OF CRITICAL PEDAGOGY

Critical pedagogy is an educational approach proposed by Paulo Friere for developing critical consciousness or critical awareness in the learner. Critical consciousness is the ability to critically perceive the causes of social, political and economic oppression and to take action against the oppressive elements of the society.

> Critical Pedagogy enables student to question and challenge domination, the beliefs and practices that dominate. The aim of Friere's critical pedagogy is to restore to marginalized groups, their stolen 'voice' to enable them recognize identify and give their name the things in the world.

DEFINITIONS OF CRITICAL PEDAGOGY

Some definitions of critical pedagogy are:

1. "Critical pedagogy is a teaching approach which attempts to help students question and challenge domination and the beliefs and practices that dominate them. It tries to help students become critically conscious."
2. *Critical pedagogy* is a philosophy of education described by Henry Giroux and other scholars as an *"educational movement, guided by passion and principle, to help students develop consciousness of freedom, recognize authoritarian tendencies, and connect knowledge to power and the ability to take constructive action"*.
3. "Critical Pedagogy is a form of education in which students are encouraged to question dominant or common notions of meaning and form their own understanding of what they learn. One of the central ideas of this teaching method is that students are able to build their own meaning when learning and teachers should facilitate that process rather than "force" meaning upon the students."
4. "Critical pedagogy is defined as an educational methodology that seeks to increase student awareness of the hidden curriculum's inequalities and multiple from of oppression that exist in the society and encourage them to take step towards creating a more democratic and equitable society."

Characteristics of Critical Pedagogy

The main characteristics of critical pedagogy are as follows:

- Critical pedagogy is based on the presumption that all education is pedagogy.
- It provides the learner with tools to better themselves and define the world.
- Its approach is issue based or problem based.
- It provides the learner with the tools to analyze critically how and on whose benefit the knowledge is constructed.
- Critical pedagogy transforms the learner from objects to subjects.
- It aims to create a more egalitarian and just society.
- It transforms the learner from the role of passive listener to active participants.
- Critical pedagogy argues for an approach to education that is rooted in the experiences of marginalized peoples.
- It is focused on dialogue instead of a one-way transmission of knowledge.
- It envisages a transformed world i.e., a more democratic, more just and more egalitarian world.
- Critical pedagogy needs to create new forms of knowledge through its emphasis on breaking down disciplinary boundaries and creating new spaces where knowledge can be produced.

BANKING SYSTEM OF EDUCATION

The term *'Banking System Education'* is a phrase used ironically by Paulo Freire to describe the prevailing system of education. He called the traditional system of education as 'banking education' because in this system, teachers make deposits of information and knowledge into the empty accounts of students, in a similar manner one operates a bank account. The traditional education, as conceived by Friere is an act of depositing, in which the students are depositories and the teacher is the depositor. In this system of education, the teacher lectures and the students receive, memorize and repeat.

Characteristics of Banking Education

The main characteristics of banking education are given below:

- The teacher teaches and the students are taught.
- The teacher knows everything and the students know nothing.
- The teacher thinks and the students are thought about.
- The teacher talks and the students listen meekly.
- The teacher disciplines and the students are disciplines.
- The teacher chooses and enforces his choice and the students comply.
- The teacher chooses the programme content and the students adapt to it.
- The teacher confuses the authority of knowledge with his own professional authority, which he sets in opposition to the freedom of the students.
- The teacher is the subject of the learning process, while the pupils are mere objects.

PROBLEM POSING EDUCATION (PPE)/DIALOGICAL METHOD

Problem-posing is an alternative method of education, suggested by Paulo

Friere, instead of the existing authoritarian and oppressing banking education. It is based on the principal, that a student learns better when he creates knowledge and when knowledge is created for him. The term problem posing is used because in this type of education, the whole learning is driven by a problem that pop-up from the life situation of the learners. On the other hand, in problem posing education, learning always beings from a problem thrown up in the classroom. The problem is posed, so that the students discover that they need to learn some new knowledge before they can solve the problem. The responsibility of the teacher is to diversify subject matter and to use students' thought and speech as the base for developing critical understanding of personal experience, unequal conditions in society and existing knowledge.

Characteristics of Problem Posing Education

Characteristics of problem-posing education are as follows:

1. Problem-posing education encourages students to become active in thinking about and acting upon their world.
2. It involves co-creation of knowledge in which the teacher and students learn together.
3. Dialogue is the method of problem-posing learning.
4. Problem posing method opens doors to critically analyze the hidden curriculum.
5. The teacher just acts as a mediator and organizer and barely comes up with any ideas.
6. Encourages the students to think critically.
7. It ensures egalitarian teacher-student relations.
8. Problem posing ignites praxis and leads to action.
9. In the problem-posing method teachers and students learn together through dialogue.
10. This method starts from the life situation and reality of learners.

Conscientization

Friere's pedagogy aims to cultivate conscientization or critical consciousness (critical awareness) in the learner. Conscientization is the ability to critically perceive the causes of social, political and economic oppression and to take action against the oppressive elements of society. It is a state of in-depth understanding about the world and resulting freedom from oppression.

Praxis

Praxis means a synthesis of reflection and action (theory and practice) in the learning process. Praxis means the use of a theory in a practical way. Friere considered praxis (informed action) as the goal of problem-posing education. He defined praxis as reflection and action upon the world in order to transform it. It is a complex activity by which individuals create culture and society and become critically conscious human beings. It involves development of critical consciousness combine with social action.

CULTURALLY RELEVANT PEDAGOGY

Teachers who embrace the belief that schools are important in creating a socially just society must teach in culturally relevant ways that take into consideration how all students experience the curriculum. "Students must learn to be critical, understand each other and appreciate other forms of knowledge." Within a context of immigration, globalization and colonization, students' identities are transnational, fluid and emerging. Given this social reality, it is imperative that teachers engage in teaching approaches that are effective in educating today's diverse student population. The research shows that diverse students, particularly students of colour, are not achieving the success in schools that they should, and this has increased calls for teachers to examine the curricula and their teaching practices. Culturally relevant pedagogy has been proven to be an effective set of principles upon which teachers can base their instruction of diverse and students.

Definition of Culturally Relevant Pedagogy

1. According to *Ladson-Billings* (1994)—"Culturally relevant pedagogy is an educational approach that empowers students intellectually, socially, emotionally and politically through the use of cultural and historical references to convey knowledge, impart academic skills and change students' attitudes towards academic instruction".
2. *Ladson-Billings* (1995a) positions culturally relevant pedagogy as a—"pedagogy of opposition...committed to collective, not merely individual empowerment".
3. Culturally relevant pedagogy is a term that describes effective teaching in culturally diverse classrooms. It can be a daunting idea to understand and implement.
4. According to *Gloria Ladson-Billings* (1992)—"It is an approach that serves to empower students to the point where they will be able to examine critically educational content and process and ask what its role is in creating a truly democratic and multicultural society. It uses the students' culture to help them create meaning and understand the world. Thus, not only academic success, but also social and cultural success is emphasized."
5. According to (*Gay*, 2000)—"Culturally relevant pedagogy can be defined as using cultural knowledge, prior experiences, frames of reference, and performance styles of ethnically diverse students to make learning encounters more relevant and effective for them".

Principles of Culturally Relevant Pedagogy (CRP)

Ladson-Billings (1995a; 1995b) identified three principles of culturally relevant teaching:

- First, students must experience academic success and intellectual growth by engaging in activities that require them to pose and solve higher-order problems.
- Second, students must develop cultural competence as a vehicle for learning, and see their identities and cultures as strengths.
- Thirdly, students must develop sociopolitical and critical consciousness that allows them to critique the cultural norms, values and institutions that produce and maintain social inequities.

Goals/Objectives of Culturally Relevant Pedagogy

The main objectives of culturally relevant pedagogy are as follows:

- The primary goal of culturally relevant pedagogy is to empower students to examine critically the society in which they live and to work for social change. In order to do this, students must possess a variety of literacy.
- A culturally relevant pedagogy focuses on the need for teachers to not only value the diverse home cultures of students they teach but explicitly address the home culture and students' understanding of it in the classroom, to teach in a culturally appropriate manner situated within students' funds of knowledge that they bring to school and to be educated with an understanding of the historical legacy of racism in society and its current impact on education.
- The understandings and processes of culturally relevant pedagogy underscore students' connections to their home culture and provide ways for school leaders and teachers to support cultural connections in school and use them to scaffold learning.
- The application of culturally relevant pedagogy in classroom validates and incorporates students' cultural background, ethnic history, and current societal interests into teachers' daily instruction.
- It addresses students' socio-emotional needs and uses ethnically and culturally diverse materials for its pedagogical action in classrooms. In this perspective,

Characteristics of Culturally Relevant Teaching

A number of authors, including Gay and Lipman have identified characteristics of culturally relevant teaching. These characteristics are:

Validating and Affirming: Culturally relevant teaching is validating and affirming because it acknowledges the strengths of students' diverse heritages.

Comprehensive: Culturally relevant teaching is comprehensive because it uses cultural resources to teach knowledge, skills, values, and attitudes.

Multidimensional: Culturally relevant teaching encompasses many areas and applies multicultural theory to the classroom environment, teaching methods, and evaluation.

Liberating: Culturally relevant teachers liberate students.

Empowering: Culturally relevant teaching empowers students, giving them opportunities to excel in the classroom and beyond. Empowerment translates into academic competence, personal confidence, courage, and the will to act.

Transformative: Culturally relevant teaching is transformative because educators and their students must often defy educational traditions and the status quo.

Role of Teacher in Culturally Relevant Pedagogy

- Culturally relevant teaching requires teachers to possess a thorough knowledge of the content and employ multiple representations of knowledge that use students' lived experiences to connect new knowledge to home, community and global settings.

- Teachers need to find pertinent examples in students' experience; they need to compare and contrast new concepts with concepts students already know; they need to bridge the gap between the known (students' personal cultural knowledge) and the unknown (materials and concepts to be mastered).
- Culturally relevant teachers form caring relationships with their students. If you have a true, caring relationship with your students, you will know what their interests are, what information they relate to.
- Culturally relevant teachers recognize that they do not instruct culturally hoitiogenized, generic students in generic school settings.
- They are systemic reformers, members of caring communities, reflective practitioners and researchers, pedagogical content specialists, and anti-racist.
- As systemic reformers, culturally relevant teachers must lead the call for whole school reform. Educating and mentoring peers is part of that.
- Teachers, not just novices, benefit from the expertise and guidance of master teachers who observe their classes and coach them regularly.
- Teachers need release time to observe master teachers in their classes and periods for conferencing and planning.
- Teachers need to reflect on their classroom experiences, which enables them to examine their actions, instructional goals, methods and materials in reference to their students' cultural experiences and preferred learning environments.
- Culturally relevant teachers must also assist students in changing our society. When teachers promote justice they directly confront inequities such as racism, sexism, and classism
- Culturally relevant teachers as action researchers extend the reflection process.

27
Teacher's Diary

MEANING OF TEACHER'S DIARY

Teacher's Diary is a sort of record of his day-to-day activities. It may show him what he has done, what he is doing and what he plans to do in the future. No elaborate lesson plans are to be written in the diary, abstracts and brief outlines are sufficient. In the beginning of a year, the teacher may draw the blueprints of his early work. Schedules of the syllabus to be covered term-wise and month-wise etc. may be prepared in each subject he has to teach.

Teacher diary is a daily record of a teacher's professional experiences, particularly focusing on the events in the classroom. Maintaining a regular diary takes discipline as it does take up some time. But, it is time well spent as it will help to clarify one's thinking. Include in your diary not only the events that occurred during the lesson, but also your own thoughts and feelings about it as well as students' reactions and responses.

A teacher should maintain a teacher diary for the following purposes:

- Blueprint of yearly work
- Schedule of syllabus
- Abstracts and outlines of the lesson
- Weekly programmes
- Academic Records
- Records of Unit Tests
- List of students who need special care
- Records of day-to-day activities

Besides the above, the Teacher's Diary should consist of:

- Weekly programmes as shown in the school time table.
- Other extra mural duties assigned to the teacher.
- Brief record what he has done from time to time.
- Entry of home work assigned to students
- Names of students he teaches class-wise
- Academic records of students
- Peculiarities of class or of individual students
- Remarks about daily or weekly work
- Records of class tests

NEED OF TEACHER'S DIARY

One could say that the teacher diary is, to a certain extent, a continuation of teacher-teaching portfolio The teacher diary provides a real reflection of the school life. It is not a simulation created during student teaching under more ideal conditions. More ideal conditions for example involve also the fact that faculties can choose their own lab schools. The teacher diary is a mirror of reality and of what the teacher in the given moment, in the given situation actually goes through. The beginning teacher can depict problems as well as joys encountered daily which opens up new possibilities for further analyses. The diary serves as a "listening friend" for the given subject.

An internal dialogue takes place during writing which has an important self-reflective value for the teacher. The diary opens the door to a secret, unchartered world, to a fragile reality, which is another reason why it stirs interest in educational research.

The teacher diary is a *"personal document of a subject serving to depict experienced and subjectively perceived situations and events"*. It is the subjective experience of a teacher and all events in school that he/she considers to be important and which he/she believes have an impact on him/her that can bring new knowledge in the life of a beginning teacher. We consider the diary to be the simplest way of targeted reflection of a teacher and his/her reflective instruction. The teacher diary is used in educational research more sporadically. It is because teachers disclose their internal experiences when writing the diary and the processing of statements is often time demanding. The work on one's own teacher diary, though time demanding, is unquestionably important in terms of the teacher's progress, improvement and analyses of one's own processes of self-evaluation. In other words, it is an investment in one's own improvement.

IMPORTANCE OF TEACHER'S DIARY

The teacher's diary is his helpful guide. It will enable him to keep a personal contact with his work, maintaining an active interest in his activities and remind him of his shortcomings, draw-backs, etc. The worth of a diary lies in the regularity with which it is filled and the use to which it is put and also the inspiration which it may give to the teacher to be on his track and to miss his aim and scheduled targets.

The headmaster should occasionally check the diaries and give useful comments orally, if he feels the need. His matured experience will go a long way in making the Teacher's Diary really worthwhile documents. Teacher can use teacher's diary for the following activities:

School Activities

- Curricular
- Co-Curricular

Extra Curricular

- Personal Guidance
- Career Counselling
- Community Service

Conduct of School Activities

- Planning
- Organizing

- Guiding
- Supervising
- Evaluating

ADVANTAGES OF TEACHER'S DIARY

The following are the main advantages of maintain a teacher's diary:

- It enables to describe situations that are harder to handle in person;
- The subject can come back later to his/her statements later (the subject can e.g. add something later);
- It has therapeutic effects;
- It enables reflection of one's own work;
- It minimizes the feeling of the subject that research is involved;
- It creates better conditions for preventing distortion of statements, since they are recorded by the subject him/herself;
- The subject him/herself can decide when the diary is to be written and how much time will be devoted to it;
- The subject can choose the form in which he/she w ill write the diary—electronic, written.

REFLECTIVE TEACHING DIARY

Reflective teaching diary includes the answers of the three reflective questions:

- What?
- So What?
- Now What?

You can run through these in your head and note down the most important points.

What?

- What happened in class (what did you do, what did the students do—just the facts please!)
- Did you achieve your aims?

So What?

- What do you think of what happened (opinions now!)
- Why do you think you achieved/didn't achieve your aims?

Now What?

- How can I improve for the next class?

28
Constructivist Teaching

CONSTRUCTIVIST PEDAGOGICAL THEORY

Constructivism is a way of thinking about knowing, a referent for building models of teaching, learning and curriculum. In this sense it is a learning philosophy and it may also become a teaching philosophy.

PRINCIPLES OF CONSTRUCTIVISM

There are several guiding principles of constructivism.

- First, learning is a quest for understanding and meaning. Learning starts with the problem or question that students are trying to understand or make meaning of.
- Second, learning is centered around main concepts and ideas instead of isolated facts. It is important for students to know and understand both the wholes of a concept, as well as the parts of a concept.
- Third, as teachers, we must understand the mental models of our students, which includes the way they perceive the world, and the assumptions that they make in their understanding of the world. By doing so, we will be able to better guide our students as they construct meaning.
- The last principle in constructivism is that students are constructing meaning as opposed to repeating facts and memorizing answers. The assessment must be tied to the learning process.

BENEFITS OF CONSTRUCTIVISM

The benefits of constructivism are:

- Children learn more, and enjoy learning more when they are actively involved, rather than passive listeners.
- Education works best when it concentrates on thinking and understanding, rather than on rote memorization. Constructivism concentrates on learning how to think and understand.
- Constructivist learning is transferable. In constructivist classrooms, students create organizing principles that they can take with them to other learning settings.
- Constructivism gives students ownership of what they learn, since learning is based on students' questions and explorations, and often the students have a hand in designing the assessments as well. Constructivist assessment engages the students' initiatives and personal investments in their journals, research reports, physical models, and artistic representations. Engaging the creative instincts develops students' abilities to express knowledge through a variety of ways. The students are also more likely to retain and transfer the new knowledge to real life.

- By grounding learning activities in an authentic, real-world context, constructivism stimulates and engages students. Students in constructivist classrooms learn to question things and to apply their natural curiosity to the world.
- Constructivism promotes social and communication skills by creating a classroom environment that emphasizes collaboration and exchange of ideas. Students must learn how to articulate their ideas clearly as well as to collaborate on tasks effectively by sharing in group projects. Students must therefore exchange ideas and so must learn to "negotiate" with others and to evaluate their contributions in a socially acceptable manner. This is essential to success in the real world, since they will always be exposed to a variety of experiences in which they will have to cooperate and navigate among the ideas of others.

MEANING OF CONSTRUCTIVIST TEACHING

Constructivist teaching is based on constructivist learning theory. Constructivist teaching is based on the belief that learning occurs as learners are actively involved in a process of meaning and knowledge construction as opposed to passively receiving information. Learners are the makers of meaning and knowledge. Constructivist teaching fosters critical thinking and creates motivated and independent learners. This theoretical framework holds that learning always builds upon knowledge that a student already knows; this prior knowledge is called a schema. Because all learning is filtered through pre-existing schemata, constructivists suggest that learning is more effective when a student is actively engaged in the learning process rather than attempting to receive knowledge passively. A wide variety of methods claim to be based on constructivist learning theory. Most of these methods rely on some form of guided discovery where the teacher avoids most direct instruction and attempts to lead the student through questions and activities to discover, discuss, appreciate and verbalize the new knowledge.

COMMON TENETS OF CONSTRUCTIVIST PEDAGOGICAL THEORY

Some of the tenets of constructivism in pedagogical terms:

- Learning is a search for meaning. Therefore, learning must start with the issues around which students are actively trying to construct meaning.
- Meaning requires understanding wholes as well as parts. And parts must be understood in the context of wholes. Therefore, the learning process focuses on primary concepts, not isolated facts.
- In order to teach well, we must understand the mental models that students use to perceive the world and the assumptions they make to support those models.
- The purpose of learning is for an individual to construct his or her own meaning, not just memorize the "right" answers and regurgitate someone else's meaning. Since education is inherently interdisciplinary, the only valuable way to measure learning is to make the assessment part of the learning process, ensuring it provides students with information on the quality of their learning.

- Students come to class with an established world-view, formed by years of prior experience and learning.
- Even as it evolves, a student's world-view filters all experiences and affects their interpretation of observations.
- For students to change their world-view requires work.
- Students learn from each other as well as the teacher.
- Students learn better by doing.
- Allowing and creating opportunities for all to have a voice promotes the construction of new ideas.

CHARACTERISTICS OF CONSTRUCTIVIST TEACHING

One of the primary goals of using constructivist teaching is that students learn how to learn by giving them the training to take initiative for their own learning experiences. The main characteristics of a constructivist teaching/classroom are as follows:

- the learners are actively involved
- the environment is democratic
- the activities are interactive and student-centered
- the teacher facilitates a process of learning in which students are encouraged to be responsible and autonomous

CONSTRUCTIVISM IN THE CLASSROOM

In a constructivist classroom, teachers use active techniques to learning. Students learn primarily through experiments, real-world problem solving, reflection and discussion. Unlike traditional classroom instruction where the teacher gives the students the knowledge they need, in a constructivist classroom, the teacher guides the students in their learning. The teacher encourages the students to ask questions and to access their learning. By asking questions, the students work through their learning and not only learn new information, but they learn how to learn. Students are encouraged to evaluate their learning and reflect on their learning progress. Hands on learning is the basis of a constructivist classroom. Students learn by doing. "They become engaged by applying their existing knowledge and real-world experience, learning to hypothesize, testing their theories, and ultimately drawing conclusions from their findings" (Thirteen Ed.). By asking questions and evaluating their learning, students are able to work with their natural curiosity. Students work to understand their world and how it works. Assessment of learning is based on student evaluation of learning.

COMPARISON BETWEEN TRADITIONAL CLASSROOM AND CONSTRUCTIVIST CLASSROOM

In the constructivist classroom, the focus tends to shift from the teacher to the students. The classroom is no longer a place where the teacher ("expert") pours knowledge into passive students, who wait like empty vessels to be filled. In the constructivist model, the students are urged to be actively involved in their own process of learning. The teacher functions more as a facilitator who coaches, mediates, prompts and helps students develop and assess their understanding and thereby their learning. One of the teacher's biggest jobs becomes asking good questions.

In the constructivist classroom, both teacher and students think of knowledge not as inert factoids to be memorized but as a dynamic, ever-changing view of the world we live in and the ability to successfully stretch and explore that view.

The Table 28.1 given below compares the traditional classroom to the constructivist one. You can see significant differences in basic assumptions about knowledge, students and learning.

Table 28.1: Comparison between Traditional Classroom and Constructivist Classroom

Traditional Classroom	*Constructivist Classroom*
Curriculum begins with the parts of the whole. Emphasizes basic skills.	Curriculum emphasizes big concepts, beginning with the whole and expanding to include the parts.
Strict adherence to fixed curriculum is highly valued.	Pursuit of student questions and interests is valued.
Materials are primarily textbooks and workbooks.	Materials include primary sources of material and manipulative materials.
Instructor gives/students receive	Learning is interaction—building on what students already know
Instructor assumes directive, authoritative role	Instructor interacts/negotiates with students
Assessment via testing/correct answers	Assessment via student works, observations, points of view, tests. Process is as important as product
Knowledge is inert	Knowledge is dynamic/change with experiences
Students work individually	Students work in groups Source
Learning is based on repetition.	Learning is interactive, building on what the student already knows.
Teachers disseminate information to students; students are recipients of knowledge.	Teachers have a dialogue with students, helping students construct their own knowledge.
Teacher's role is directive, rooted in authority.	Teacher's role is interactive, rooted in negotiation.
More teacher cantered	More pupil cantered
Content oriented	Process oriented
Based on behaviourist theories of learning	Based on cognitive, constructivist and humanist theories of learning
Leaner is a receiver of knowledge	Learner constructs knowledge
Students primarily work alone.	Students collaborate on tasks.
Adherence to the established curriculum is highly valued.	Student input is highly valued in the teaching-learning process.
Students are treated as empty vessels into which information is poured by the teacher.	Students are treated as thinkers with the ability to construct new knowledge.
Teachers are the experts, disseminating information to students.	Teachers partner with students in the classroom.
Teachers seek the "correct" answer to validate student learning.	Teachers seek students' feedback in order to better understand student learning.
Assessment of student learning is separate from teaching.	Assessment of student learning is integral to the teaching-learning process.

A constructivist perspective views learners as actively engaged in making meaning, and teaching with that approach looks for what students can analyse, investigate, collaborate, share, build and generate based on what they already know, rather than what facts, skills, and processes they can parrot. To do this effectively, a teacher needs to be a learner and a researcher, to strive for greater awareness of the environments and the participants in a given teaching situation in order to continually adjust their actions to engage students in learning, using constructivism as a referent.

It is a fact that a *"traditional classroom"* strictly following pure behaviourist pattern do not exist and similarly a *"constructivist classroom"* with pure constructivist methodology do not exist. Every classroom behaviour is a mix of different methods and different approaches. Anyway, a shift towards the constructivist pattern is appreciated.

BENEFITS OF CONSTRUCTIVIST CLASSROOM

In a constructivist classroom, learning is

Constructed: Students are not blank slates upon which knowledge is etched. They come to learning situations with already formulated knowledge, ideas and understandings. This previous knowledge is the raw material for the new knowledge they will create.

Active: The student is the person who creates new understanding for him/ herself. The teacher coaches, moderates, suggests but allows the students to experiment, ask questions, try things that don't work. Learning activities require the students' full participation (like hands-on experiments). An important part of the learning process is that students reflect on and talk about, their activities. Students also help set their own goals and means of assessment.

Reflective: Students control their own learning process and they lead the way by reflecting on their experiences. This process makes them experts of their own learning. The teacher helps create situations where the students feel safe questioning and reflecting on their own processes, either privately or in group discussions. The teacher should also create activities that lead the student to reflect on his or her prior knowledge and experiences. Talking about what was learned and how it was learned is really important.

Collaborative: The constructivist classroom relies heavily on collaboration among students. There are many reasons why collaboration contributes to learning. The main reason it is used so much in constructivism is that students learn about learning not only from themselves, but also from their peers. When students review and reflect on their learning processes together, they can pick up strategies and methods from one another.

Inquiry Based: The main activity in a constructivist classroom is solving problems. Students use inquiry methods to ask questions, investigate a topic, and use a variety of resources to find solutions and answers. As students explore the topic, they draw conclusions, and, as exploration continues, they revisit those conclusions. Exploration of questions leads to more questions.

Evolving: Students have ideas that they may later see were invalid, incorrect or insufficient to explain new experiences. These ideas are temporary steps in the integration of knowledge. For instance, a child may believe that all trees lose their leaves in the fall, until she visits an evergreen forest. Constructivist teaching takes into account students' current conceptions and builds from there.

What happens when a student gets a new piece of information? The constructivist model says that the student compares the information to the knowledge and understanding he/she already has, and one of three things can occur:

- The new information matches up with his previous knowledge pretty well (it's **consonant** with the previous knowledge), so the student adds it to his understanding. It may take some work, but it's just a matter of finding the right fit, as with a puzzle piece.
- The information doesn't match previous knowledge (it's **dissonant**). The student has to change her previous understanding to find a fit for the information. This can be harder work.
- The information doesn't match previous knowledge, and it is **ignored**. Rejected bits of information may just not be absorbed by the student. Or they may float around, waiting for the day when the student's understanding has developed and permits a fit.

CONSTRUCTIVIST TEACHING PRACTICES

There are twelve teaching practices of constructivist teachers.

- First constructivist teachers encourage and accept student initiative. They guide students as they ask questions, and students are responsible for their own learning.
- Another practice is that teachers use data and primary sources, as well as manipulatives that will help students better comprehend abstract concepts.
- Third, constructivist teachers use cognitive vocabulary such as "classify," "analyze," "predict," and "create." By doing these activities, it requires higher level thinking that will benefit students.
- Fourth, students drive the instruction. Based on their needs, the teacher adapts and seizes the teachable moments that arise on a daily basis.
- In addition, constructivist teachers discover the prior knowledge of their students before sharing their own knowledge.
- A sixth practice is to encourage students to engage in conversation with both the teacher and with each another. Teachers also further knowledge by asking open-ended questions, and getting the students to ask questions of each other.
- Another practice is to encourage students to elaborate after responding. This allows the student more think time, as well as the ability to correct their errors, or better explain their thinking.
- Constructivist teachers engage students in experiences that might cause contradictions to their first or original thoughts or discussion.
- Another practice is for teachers to allow wait time after posing a question. This gives everyone time to think and process his or her thoughts before responding.
- In addition, constructivist teachers allow time for students to make connections and create metaphors, which will help guide their learning.
- The final practice is to nurture a child's natural curiosity through discovery.

COMPONENTS OF CONSTRUCTIVIST PRACTICE

The practical application of constructivist practices in the classroom presents additional challenges and benefits to both the teacher, and the student. The challenge for the teacher is to provide relevant frameworks upon which the student can construct knowledge and understanding, and to act as a facilitator rather than knowledge-bearer during the process Students must become actively engaged in their learning experience, rather than act as passive recipients of information. Some components of constructivist practices include:

Depth vs. Breadth: One of the key issues that a constructivist teacher faces is the need to develop a sense of depth about a concept. This requires longer content modules, greater focus on process rather than product and open-ended questioning techniques that require contemplation and assimilation of information (Brooks & Brooks, 1993).

Learning for Transfer: The constructivist classroom is an environment based on inquiry that leads to deep understanding of the concept under scrutiny. It is also an environment in which students will have enough time to develop mental models of the content, which will assist in moving that knowledge away from the primary content area, so that it can be applied elsewhere (Spiro et al, 1992a, 1992b).

Changing One's Frame of Reference through Experimentation: In traditional classrooms, there is often only one 'right' answer. In the constructivist environment, naive beliefs are often the starting point for further discussion and discovery and are not discounted as being 'wrong'. Though formal scientific experimentation is not often introduced until at least middle school, the process of discovering cause and effect relationships is often employed even in the primary grades. This discovery process allows the child to reevaluate what they know, and to change their understanding based on what they have directly learned from their environment.

Implementation of Cooperative rather than Individual Learning: In many traditional classrooms, cooperative learning would be frowned upon, or might even be viewed as 'cheating'. Constructivism puts cooperation and mutual exploration at the top of the list. This frees students to bounce ideas off of one another, and fosters learning-in-dialogue rather than learning-in-isolation (Lewis, 1993; Brown & Palinscar, 1985).

Holistic Learning Opportunities: The perceived benefits to a constructivist learning environment include holistic learning opportunities, the enhancement of collaborative/cooperative skills and time and appreciation for metacognitive reflection. Holistic learning encompasses absorption and synthesis of individual facts, building relationships between these facts and linking this knowledge with understanding of other knowledge domains. It is a process that involves engaging all of one's perceptual senses, creativity, and intellectual prowess in the learning process (Weisberg, 1988; Kraft & Sakofs, 1989).

Top-Down Vs Bottom-Up Processing: Many lessons are bottom-up oriented (starting with a detailed skill or fact and then building up to the big picture, application or relevance). Constructivist classrooms are top-down. A teacher might present a challenge or problem first, have students think of solutions, and then lastly give the answer or details.

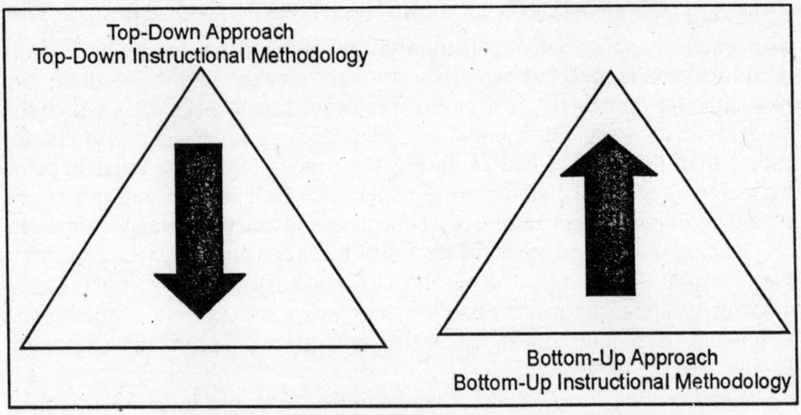

Figure 28.1: Top-Down Vs Bottom-Up Processing

The basic premise of constructivist theories is that people create their own meaning through experience. Constructivism has its roots in the cognitive theories of Piaget and Vygotsky and embraces several aspects of both of those theories. From Piaget we get active learning, schemes, assimilation and accommodation, etc. From Vygotsky we get social constructivism, group work, apprenticeship, etc. Constructivism embraces a *"top-down"* rather than a *"bottom-up"* instructional methodology. This means that, rather than teach all of the details that lead to a main idea; students discover the main idea and then derive the details.

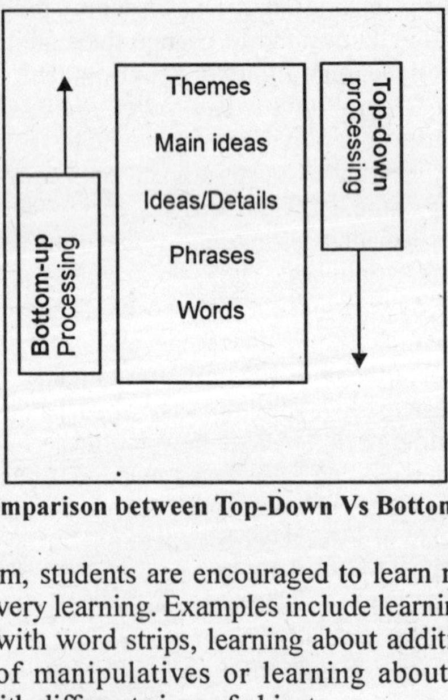

Figure 28.2: Comparison between Top-Down Vs Bottom-Up Processing

In constructivism, students are encouraged to learn main ideas on their own through discovery learning. Examples include learning about compound words by playing with word strips, learning about addition and subtraction through the use of manipulatives or learning about capacity through experimentation with different sizes of objects.

Personal theories or students' own ideas about how things work, play a large role in constructivism as we attempt to provide activities that clarify and correct misconceptions. Additional constructivist strategies include presenting others' viewpoints, promoting dialogue, and emphasizing conceptual understanding rather than rote learning.

Conceptual Change

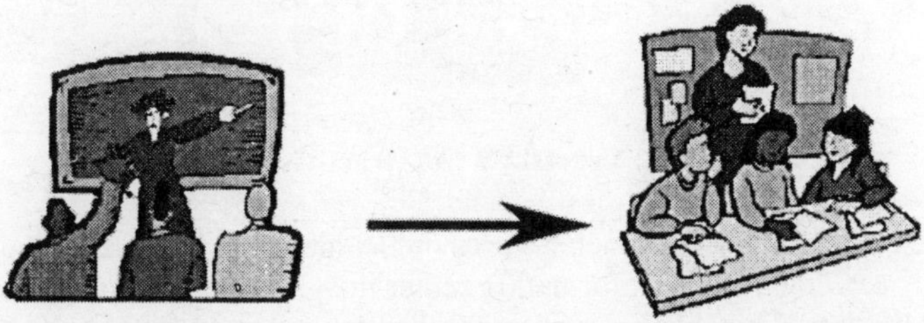

"sage on the stage" "guide on the side"

Figure 28.3: Changing conceptions related to teaching. Instead of the "Sage on the Stage," teachers become the "Guide on the Side" in the Constructivist approach.

Teaching for conceptual change primarily involves:

- Uncovering students' preconceptions about a particular topic or phenomenon and
- using various techniques to help students change their conceptual framework.

The vast majority of research on conceptual change instruction has been confined to science education, while research in other subject areas has been scarce. However, outside of school, students develop strong (mis)conceptions about a wide range of concepts related to non-scientific domains, such as how the government works, principles of economics, the utility of mathematics, the reasons for the Civil Rights movement, the nature of the writing process, and the purpose of the electoral college. Conceptual change instruction can help students overcome misconceptions and learn difficult concepts in all subject areas.

Conceptual change is not only relevant to teaching in the content areas, but it is also applicable to the professional development of teachers and administrators. For example, as constructivist approaches to teaching gain popularity, the role of the teacher changes. Teachers must learn different instructional strategies, but they must also reconceptualize or change their conception about the meaning of teaching. This change implies conceiving of teaching as facilitating, rather than managing learning and changing roles from the "sage on the stage" to a "guide on the side."

VYGOTSKY'S CONSTRUCTIVIST APPROACH

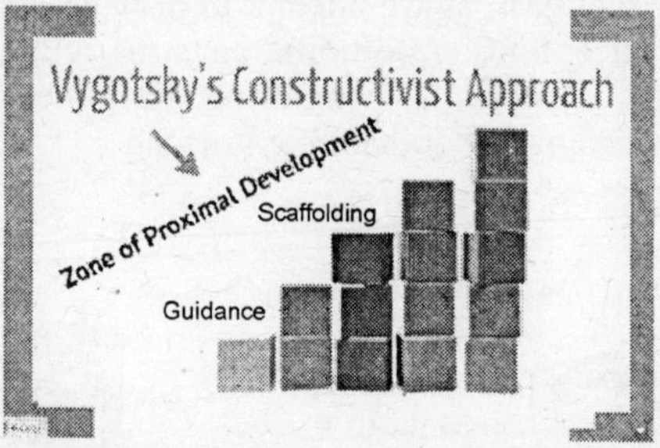

Figure 28.4: Vygotsky's Constructivist Approach

The constructivist approach focuses on the idea that the learner should be actively seeking out new information rather than listening to teachers simply give it to them. This theory emphasizes the idea that students learn best with guidance from the teacher as well as collaboration with classmates. One of Vygotsky's main principles is the zone of proximal development, or ZPD. The ZPD consists of various tasks and skills that are too difficult for an individual to master on their own at a specific time. However, with the assistance of an adult or a skilled peer, the individual may master a specific task. This assistance is often referred to as "scaffolding". There are two limits within the ZPD. The lower limit refers to the level of problem solving an individual may achieve while working on a task without aid. Whereas the upper limit refers to the level of achievement an individual can accept with guidance or assistance from a more-skilled adult or peer. It is important that those providing the "scaffolding" limit the amount of assistance they contribute to the learner. Vygotsky stresses that those providing assistance merely serve as a guide or facilitator, but not a director. This theory warns that if too much assistance is given to a youth they may become too dependent on their help.

The characteristics of a constructivist classroom are as follows:

- the learners are actively involved
- the environment is democratic
- the activities are interactive and student-centered
- the teacher facilitates a process of learning in which students are encouraged to be responsible and autonomous

ROLE OF A CONSTRUCTIVIST TEACHER

The role of a constructivist teacher is as follows:

- Teacher serves as one of many resources for students, not necessarily the primary source of information.
- The teacher engages students in experiences that challenge previous conceptions of their existing knowledge.
- The teacher uses student responses in the planning of next lessons and seeks elaboration of students' initial responses.
- The teacher encourages questions and discussion among students by asking open-ended questions.

- The teacher assists students to understand their own cognitive processes (metacognition) by using cognitive terminology such as classify, analyze, create, organize, hierarchy, etc. when framing tasks.
- The teacher encourages and accepts student autonomy and initiative by being willing to let go of classroom control
- The teacher makes available raw data and primary resources, along with manipulative and interactive physical materials.
- The teacher does not separate knowing from the process of finding out. Nouns and verbs.
- The teacher facilitates clear communication from students in writing and verbal responses, from the point of view that communication comes from ones deep structural understanding of the concepts being communicated. When they can communicate clearly and meaningfully, they have truly integrated the new learning.

ROLE OF THE CONSTRUCTIVIST STUDENT

The expectation within a constructivist learning environment is that the students plays a more active role in, and accepts more responsibility for their own learning.

- The role of the student to actively participate in their own education.
- Students have to accommodate & assimilate new information with their current understanding.
- One important aspect of controlling their own learning process is reflecting on their experiences.
- Students begin their study with pre-conceived notions.
- Students are very reluctant to give up their established schema/idea & may reject new information that challenges prior knowledge.
- Students may not be aware of the reasons they hold such strong ideas/ schemata.
- Learners need to use and test ideas, skills, and information through relevant activities.
- Students need to know how to learn or change their thinking/learning style.
- Because knowledge is so communally-based, learners deserve access to knowledge of different communities.
- For students to learn they need to receive different 'lenses' to see things in new ways.
- Learners need guidance through the ZDP.
- In social constructivism tutors and peers play a vital role in learning.

SUGGESTIONS FOR TEACHING WITH THE CONSTRUCTIVIST LEARNING THEORY

- Encourage and accept student autonomy and initiative.
- Try to use raw data and primary sources, in addition to manipulative, interactive, and physical materials.
- When assigning tasks to the students, use cognitive terminology such as "classify," "analyze," "predict," and "create."
- Build off and use student responses when making "on-the-spot" decisions

about teacher behaviours, instructional strategies, activities, and content to be taught.

- Search out students' understanding and prior experiences about a concept before teaching it to them.
- Encourage communication between the teacher and the students and also between the students.
- Encourage student critical thinking and inquiry by asking them thoughtful, open-ended questions, and encourage them to ask questions to each other.
- Ask follow up questions and seek elaboration after a student's initial response.
- Put students in situations that might challenge their previous conceptions and that will create contradictions that will encourage discussion.
- Make sure to wait long enough after posing a question so that the students have time to think about their answers and be able to respond thoughtfully.
- Provide enough time for students to construct their own meaning when learning something new.

29
Multicultural Education

WHAT IS MULTICULTURALISM?

Multiculturalism is the co-existence of diverse cultures, where culture includes racial, religious, or cultural groups and is manifested in customary behaviours, cultural assumptions and values, patterns of thinking, and communicative styles. Multiculturalism describes the existence, acceptance, or promotion of multiple cultural traditions within a single jurisdiction, usually considered in terms of the culture associated with an ethnic group. This can happen when a jurisdiction is created or expanded by amalgamating areas with two or more different cultures or through immigration from different jurisdictions around the world.

Multicultural ideologies or policies vary widely, ranging from the advocacy of equal respect to the various cultures in a society, to a policy of promoting the maintenance of cultural diversity, to policies in which people of various ethnic and religious groups are addressed by the authorities as defined by the group to which they belong. Multiculturalism that promotes maintaining the distinctiveness of multiple cultures is often contrasted to other settlement policies such as social integration, cultural assimilation and racial segregation. Multiculturalism has been described as a "salad bowl" or "cultural mosaic" rather than a "melting pot"

Definitions of Multiculturalism

The definition of multiculturalism is as follows:

> "Multiculturalism is a philosophy that appreciates ethnic diversity within a society and that encourages people to learn from the contributions of those of diverse ethnic backgrounds."

Meaning of Multicultural Education

Multicultural education is an idea, an educational reform movement, and a process whose major goal is to change the structure of education instructions so that male and female student, exceptional students, and students who are members of diverse social class, ethnic and cultural groups will have an equal chance to achieve academically in school (Banks 1990). Another important idea in multicultural education is that some students because of this characteristic have a better chance to learn in schools as they are currently structured than to students who belong to other groups or who have different cultural characteristics. Multicultural education involves changes in the school or educational environment; it is not limited to curricular changes. This must also be viewed as an ongoing process, and not as something that we "do" and thereby solve the problems that are the target of multicultural educational reform.

Definitions of Multicultural Education

1. According to Sonia Nieto (1992)—*"multicultural education in a sociopolitical context"*
2. *"Multicultural education encompasses theories and practices that strive to promote equitable access and rigorous academic achievement for students from all diverse groups, so that they can work toward social change."*
3. Banks (1993), *"Multicultural Education is an educational reform movement, and process whose major goal is to change the structure of educational institutions."*
4. Baptiste (1986), *"Multicultural education consist of beliefs and explanations that recognizes and values the importance of ethnic and cultural diversity which shapes lifestyles, social experiences, personal identities, and educational opportunities of individuals, groups and nations. Multicultural education also prescribes what should be done to ensure equitable accessibility and treatment for diverse groups in schools and in the society as a whole."*

The Aims of Multicultural Education

Bennett (as cited by Bulankina & Polyankina, 2011) identified six aims of multicultural education, which are:

- To develop multiple historical perspectives
- To strengthen cultural consciousness
- To strengthen intercultural competence
- To combat racism, sexism and all forms of prejudice and discrimination
- To increase awareness of the state of the planet and global dynamics and
- To develop social action skills

CHARACTERISTICS OF MULTICULTURAL EDUCATION

Sonia Nieto (2008) describes on seven characteristics of multicultural education:

- ***Antiracist education*** makes antidiscrimination explicit in the curriculum and teaches students the skills to combat racism and other forms of oppression.
- ***Basic education*** advances the basic right of all students to engage in core academics and arts; it addresses the urgent need for students to develop social and intellectual skills to expand understanding in a diverse society.
- That multicultural education is ***important for all students*** challenges the commonly held misunderstanding that it is only for students of colour, multilingual students, or special interest groups. Rather. all students deserve and need an education that is inclusive and rigorous.
- The ***pervasive*** nature of multicultural education emphasizes an approach

that permeates the entire educational experience, including school climate, physical environment, curriculum, and relationships.

- In education for ***social justice*** teachers and students put their learning into action. Students learn that they have the power to make change as apprentices in a democratic society.
- Multicultural education as a ***process*** highlights the ongoing, organic development of individuals and educational institutions involving relationships among people. It also points to the intangibles of multicultural education that are less recognizable than specific curriculum content, such as expectations of student achievement, learning environments, students' learning preferences, and cultural variables that influence the educational experience.
- ***Critical pedagogy*** draws upon experiences of students through their cultural, linguistic, familial, academic, artistic and other forms of knowledge. It also takes students beyond their own experiences and enables them to understand perspectives with which they disagree, as well as to think critically about multiple viewpoints, leading to praxis, or reflection combined with action.

APPROACHES OF MULTICULTURAL EDUCATION

Christine Sleeter and Carl Grant (1987) explained five approaches of multicultural education as follows:

1. *Teaching the Exceptional and the Culturally Different:* The goal of the first approach, which Sleeter and Grant call *Teaching the Exceptional and the Culturally Different*, is to equip students with the academic skills; *Multicultural education acknowledges and affirms the multiple identities that students bring to their learning* concepts, and values to function in society's institutions and culture. The positive attribute of this approach is that it spurred the movement toward modifying instruction and curriculum, commonly called differentiated instruction.

2. *Human Relations:* The second approach, *Human Relations*, consists of developing positive relationships among diverse groups and individuals to fight stereotyping and promote unity. Reducing prejudice and hostility are admirable goals, but according to its critics this approach tends to simplify culture and identity and avoids analyzing the causes of discrimination and inequality. Without a critical perspective, the Human Relations approach runs the risk of falling into the trap of feel-good tactics that are too soft on academic achievement.

3. *Single-Group Studies: Single-Group Studies* is the third approach in the Sleeter and Grant analysis. The goal is to engage in an in-depth, comprehensive study that moves specific groups from the margins by providing information about the group's history, including experiences with oppression and resistance to that oppression. The hope is to reduce stratification and create greater access to power.

4. *Multicultural Education:* The fourth approach to multicultural education is self-reflexively dubbed *multicultural education*. Sleeter and Grant use this seemingly redundant title to clarify this approach since so many other practices,

such as those described in the first three approaches, are sometimes referred to as multicultural education. They cite Gollnick (1980) to explain that the multicultural education approach promotes a range of goals: the value of cultural diversity, human rights, respect for differences, alternative life choices, social justice, equal opportunity, and equitable distribution of power. There are several criticisms of this approach that are discussed later in this entry.

5. Education that is Multicultural and Social Reconstructionist: The fifth approach, which is the approach Sleeter and Grant advocate, is *Education that is Multicultural and Social Reconstructionist*, which describes a complete redesign of an educational programme.

APPROACHES OF MULTICULTURAL TEACHING

There are four different approaches or practices of multicultural teaching:

1. The Contributions Approach: It is the easiest to implement and makes the least impact on the current curriculum. It does however have significant limitations in meeting the goals of multicultural education because "it does not give students the opportunity to see the critical role of ethnic groups in society.

2. The Additive Approach: Called the ethnic additive approach; it is slightly more involved than the contributions approach, but still requires no major restructuring of the curriculum. While this approach is often a first step towards a more multicultural curriculum, it is still very limited in that it still presents the topic from the dominant perspective. "Individuals or groups of people from marginalized groups in society are included in the curriculum, yet racial and cultural inequalities or oppression are not necessarily addressed".

3. The Transformative Approach: This approach requires pulling in multiple perspectives while discussing a topic. This approach is significantly more challenging to teach than the previous two: "it requires a complete transformation of the curriculum and, in some cases, a conscious effort on the part of the teacher to deconstruct what they have been taught to think, believe, and teach".

4. The Decision Making and Social Action Approach: This approach includes all of the elements of the transformative approach but also challenges students to work to bring about social change. The goal of this approach is not only to make students aware of past and present injustice, but to equip them and empower them to be the agents of change.

STRATEGIES OF MULTICULTURAL INSTRUCTION

Listed below are different strategies that are particularly useful in promoting multicultural/diverse perspective learning in a multicultural classroom:

Questioning: Questioning techniques that personally involve students will allow them to respond in a way that reflects their cultural diversity and that will expose their fellow students to those differences.

Role-Playing: Role-playing is a versatile activity that allows students to express their opinions in a realistic situation. Students can *"trade places"* with a fellow student or a character from a literature selection. Role-playing enables students to express and to examine their attitudes, beliefs and feelings about prejudice and discrimination. Poetry, biography and powerful fiction are excellent sources for both discussion and role-playing.

Cooperative Learning: Many years of research and practice support the use of cooperative groups to focus on students' different strengths and styles. In addition, cooperative learning groups have been found to have strong and consistent positive effects on social relationships between culturally different students (Slavin, 1983). Group members become more accepting of classmates who are different.

Exposure to Different Languages Cultures: It is important for students to recognize that the language that students speak is not the only language. Students should be exposed to speakers of various and languages. In addition to broadening students' perspectives by introducing them to different languages, such speakers can also share with students' ideas and values from other cultures.

Group Discussions: Group discussions stimulate thinking. The notion that thinking originates within individuals—and only after that is it ready to be shared socially—has given way to the belief that some of the best thinking results from a group's collective efforts (Sternberg, 1987). In discussions in which students examine more than one point of view, there is ample opportunity to enrich and refine their understanding by helping them to view their own interpretation in the light of the interpretations of others.

Active Involvement: Instructional techniques that allow for individual differences and that add a spark of excitement to classroom activities should be used in place of fill-in-the-blank activities. Students should be engaged in listening, speaking, reading, writing, and thinking activities that provide opportunities for them to make decisions and solve problems.

MULTICULTURAL CLASSROOM

A multicultural classroom is one in which both the students and the teacher are accepting of all races, cultures and religions.

Implementation of Multicultural Education in the Classroom

Multicultural education is a broad concept with several important dimensions. Teachers can use the dimensions as a way to incorporate culture in their classrooms. These dimensions as explain by (Banks 1995a) are as follows;

Content Integration: Content integration deals with the extent to which teachers use examples and content from a variety of cultures in their teaching. However, the infusion of ethnic and cultural content into subject area should be logical and not contrived.

The Knowledge Construction Process: This relates with the extent to which teachers help students to understand, investigate and determine how the implicit cultural assumptions, frame of references, perspectives and baises within a discipline influences the ways in which knowledge is constructed within it.

Equity Pedagogy: This exists when teachers modify their teaching in ways that will facilitate the academic achievement of students from diverse racial, cultural gender, and social class groups. This includes using a variety of teaching styles and approaches that are consistent with the wide range of learning styles with various cultural and ethnic groups.

Prejudice Reduction: This dimension focuses on the characteristics of student's ethnic attitudes and how they can be modified by teaching methods and materials. Children come to school with many negative attitudes towards and misconception about different ethnic groups (Phinney and Rotheram, 1987). Based on this Banks (1995b) explained that lessons, units, and teaching materials that include content about different ethnic groups can help students to develop more positive intergroup attitudes if certain conditions include positive images of the ethnic groups in the materials and the use of multi-ethnic materials in a consistent and sequential way.

An Empowering School Culture: Grouping and labeling practices, sports participation in achievement and the interaction of the staff and students across ethnic and cultural lines must be examined to create a school culture that empowers students from diverse ethnic and cultural groups.

The school as a social system in implementing a multicultural education cannot be over emphasized; we must think of the school as a social system in which all of its variables are closely interrelated and the formalized curriculum and course of study. Any of these factors may be the focus of initial school reform, but changes must take place in each of them to create and sustain an effective multicultural school environment. Hence, when formulating plans for multicultural education, educators should conceptualize the school as a micro culture that has norms, values, statuses and goals like other social system.

Multicultural education can be implemented on the macro-level with the implementation of programmes and culture at the school-wide or district-wide level and also at the micro-level by specific teachers within their individual classrooms.

CULTURALLY RESPONSIVE TEACHING

Culturally sensitive teaching needs to purposely respond to the needs of the many culturally and ethnically diverse students in their classrooms. Culturally responsive teaching includes implementing specifically student-oriented instructional processes as well as choosing and delivering ethnically and culturally relevant curricula. Culturally sensitive teachers use effective communication which may include translations to other languages in the case of English-Language Learners (ELL) and the use of audio-visual aids when working with ELL and Special Education Serviced Students (SESS). Culturally responsive teaching should include activities that reflect the students' values, cultures, and beliefs.

What is a Culturally Responsive Classroom?

A culturally responsive classroom builds on students strengths and encourages academic success for all students. Within this setting, teachers encompass the whole student. Teachers must have compassion, understanding, giving, and an open mind, provide extended time, and be able to differentiate. Teachers must consider the students' home environment as well as their school environment and make connections. The teachers must also explore how students relate, communicate, learn and solve problem. In addition, teachers must consider each student's personal life, beliefs, values and how they function to truly understand their ideas, thought process and reasoning. To further extend the definition of a culturally responsive classroom Davis (2003) recognizes the importance of building a strong student-teacher relationship and how this relationship can increase academic success as well as socio-emotional support.

Ways to Build a Culturally Responsive Classroom

The following steps will be helpful to build a culturally responsive classroom:

Know Your Students: The first step to building a culturally responsive classroom is to get to know your students on a personal level. Davis (2003) explains that relationships that children have at home extend to their school environment and taking this into account will provide rational for teachers. Davis (2003) further explains the importance of teachers recognizing that they share a similar relationship that students have with their parents. This teacher-child relationship is the key to influencing motivation, success, conflict, and emotions.

Build a Community within the Classroom: The second step is building a community within the classroom. To implement this teachers, must allow for collaboration and encourage activities where students work together in social climates. Teachers can also use team building exercises to build peer relationships and encourage the class to help each other.

Evaluate Your Teacher Style and Reflect on Your Personal Expectations: The third step is to evaluate your teacher style and reflect on your personal expectations of learning. Teachers must evaluate whether they are setting expectations for surface learning or for in depth learning.

The sample reflection questions related to the above are:

- Do I encourage students' questions and curiosity?
- Does my classroom environment encourage students to take risks?
- Am I aware of how culture and gender influence students' interaction and communication styles?
- Am I encouraging the children to listen and respond to the remarks of their peers during large and small groups discussions?
- Am I providing sufficient opportunity and time for the children to work independently, in pairs and in small groups?

Meaning of Culturally Sensitive Teacher

A culturally-sensitive teacher is one that is aware of and addresses the students' cultural and ethnic needs as well as their social, emotional and cognitive needs in order to obtain the students' cooperation. Urban classrooms can present many challenges for teachers due to many factors.

Characteristics of a Multicultural Teacher

With the increasing attention on preparing teachers to work effectively in classrooms having diverse groups of students, a good deal of attention has been given to the characteristics of successful multicultural teachers. The following seven attributes help describe the skills that enable teachers to create environments that respect and draw upon diversity.

Use this model as a self-evaluation tool. Reflect on how you would rate yourself, and what steps you need to take to be a more effective multicultural teacher.

- Understanding one's cultural perspective and how it affects the ongoing teaching/learning relationship and that exploring this cultural issue is an ongoing process.
- Providing and promoting an atmosphere in which cultural differences are respected and explored. This atmosphere is one in which this process is not only academic, but also attitudinal and affective.
- Drawing upon the cultural experiences of students and parents in order to include authentic cultural perspectives in the curriculum.
- Flexibly adjusting and accommodating varied learning styles, building on students' strengths, and avoiding judgments and labels that might otherwise be placed on students.
- Being skeptical when using student evaluation tools and raising questions regarding the validity of all assessment instruments when used with students from culturally different groups than those on whom the norms were calculated.
- Understanding and communicating that all cultures have their own integrity, validity and coherence.
- Expanding students' knowledge of their own cultures and their capacity to appreciate differences in others, and helping them move toward a multicultural and global perspective in their thinking.

30
Teaching as a Profession and Mission

MEANING OF PROFESSION

A profession is a vocation founded upon specialized high educational training, the purpose of which is to supply objective counsel and service to others, for a direct and definite compensation, wholly apart from expectation of other business gain. Goodson (2003) noted that Occupations that have attained professional status share the following characteristics:

- A high level of education and training based on a unique and specialized body of knowledge.
- A strong ideal of public service with an enforced professional code of conduct and high levels of respect from the public at large.
- Registration and regulation by the profession itself
- Trusted to act in the clients' best interests within a framework of accountability
- A supportive working environment
- Similar levels of compensation as other professions.

DEFINITION OF A PROFESSION

While there is no agreed definition of a profession, the Australian Council of Professions (Professions Australia) defines a profession as: *'A disciplined group of individuals who adhere to high ethical standards and uphold themselves to, and are accepted by, the public as possessing special knowledge and skills in a widely recognized, organized body of learning derived from education and training at a high level, and who are prepared to exercise this knowledge and these skills in the interest of others."*

IS TEACHING A PROFESSION?

Not every form of activity is work, even if it brings remuneration to the person engaged in it. It is work only when it produces something of value to others. The business of teachers is to help students to achieve higher standards of knowledge, ability, skills, and moral character. If teachers do their work well, then their work is of great value to others, not simply in a particular time, but also in the future

DUTIES OF A TEACHER

There are many duties a teacher has. The following are the general duties of a teacher:

- Prepare lessons, making them as interesting as possible
- Prepare homework, assignments and assessment

- Research information to ensure the knowledge they impart is current
- Mark homework and pieces of assessment
- Identify the needs of individual students in their classes, and work to help each child develop his or her own potential
- Prepare resources for the classroom
- Confer with students over their work
- Assist children to learn, not judge their inability to learn
- Identify emotional, intellectual, physical, etc issues which may be hindering the student from learning to his/her best potential, and research and recommend courses of action
- Conduct parent-teacher interviews
- Provide a sounding board (for both students and teachers) and allow for open discussion
- Attend professional development sessions to improve his/her own teaching methods and curriculum
- Present a professional but caring persona at all times
- Treat students with respect, and teach them to treat others with respect.

RESPONSIBILITIES OF A TEACHER

The responsibilities of a teacher are as given below:

Responsibilities towards Themselves

- To be a teacher out of choice, and not by default.
- To acquire relevant professional education and training to get the right concepts of teaching.
- Honesty and sincerity towards the profession.
- Accept that being a teacher does not make you a 'know-it-all'; so it's important to become a partner in the learning cycle with the students.
- Accept that no two students will think, act and react alike, and respect that diversity.
- Upgrade knowledge and learn new ways of teaching.
- Avoid indulging in unethical behaviour, and at all times maintain the dignity of a teacher-student relationship.

Responsibilities towards Students

- Inculcate model behaviour and mannerisms by self example.
- Prepare long-term teaching programmes and daily lessons in accordance with the guidelines of the school's education system.
- Provide activities and materials that engage and challenge the students intellectually.
- Understand and implement the use of information technology in lesson preparation and teaching.
- Shift between formal and informal methods of teaching, like debates, discussions, practical activities, experiments, projects and excursions.
- Plan, set and evaluate grade test, exams and assignments.
- Supervise student conduct during class, lunchtime and other breaks.
- Understand the diverse background students come from, their strengths, weaknesses and areas of interest.

- Be honest in student appraisal and avoid favouritism.
- Enforce discipline by firmly setting classroom rules.
- Resolve conflict among students by encouraging positive debate.
- Be ready to adjust teaching styles to meet individual needs of students.

Responsibilities towards Parents

- Keep parents well-informed about their ward's progress.
- Take time out to discuss an issue, or a problematic behaviour.
- Encourage parents to promote various diverse interests of their children.
- Inform parents about after-school activities like excursions, meetings, as well as detention.
- Keep the parent feedback journal updated.
- Encourage parent participation in parent-teacher meets.
- Finally, work with parents for the betterment of their child's future.

Responsibilities towards Management

- Actively involved in staff meetings, educational conferences, and school programmes.
- Voluntarily participate in organizing sporting events, and other excursions like camping trips, picnics, educational tours, etc.
- Maintain a healthy relationship with all teaching and non-teaching staff members.
- Help out in formulating school policies.
- Carry out administrative duties relevant to your position in the school.

ROLE OF THE CONSTRUCTIVIST TEACHER

Constructivist teachers do not take the role of the "sage on the stage." Instead, teachers act as a "guide on the side" providing students with opportunities to test the adequacy of their current understandings

- The educator should consider the knowledge and experiences students bring to class
- Learners construct their knowledge through a process of active enquiry
- 'Discovery' is facilitated by providing the necessary resources
- Knowledge is actively constructed & learning is presented as a process of active discovery
- Provide assistance with assimilation of new and old knowledge
- Learning programme should be sufficiently flexible to permit development along lines of student enquiry
- Due to its interpretivist nature, each student will interpret information in different ways
- Create situations where the students feel safe questioning and reflecting on their own processes
- Present authentic tasks to contextualize learning through real-world, case-based learning environments
- Support collaboration in constructing knowledge, not competition
- Encourage development through Inter-subjectivity
- Providing Scaffolding at the right time and the right level

- Provide opportunities for more expert and less expert participants to learn from each other

TEACHER ROLES

In modern age we are using different smart and active teaching learning methodologies. Several researchers have been searching innovative ideas in education. In so many countries there is a crunch in educational research. We see that the teacher's role is going to be modified. We have to understand the different roles of the teacher.

An interactive teacher is by definition one that is fully aware of the group dynamics of a classroom. As Dörnyei and Murphey (2003) explained, the success of classroom learning is very much dependent on:

- How students relate to each other and their teacher
- What the classroom environment is
- How effectively students cooperate and communicate with each other
- The roles not only the teacher plays but the learners engage in

Brown, H. Douglas (2007) mentions that *"teachers can play many roles in the course of teaching and this might facilitate learning. Their ability to carry these out effectively will depend to a large extent on the rapport they establish with their students, and of course, on their own level of knowledge and skills."*

Teacher as Planner: Teachers are planners. This is the essential role of successful teaching. Before all else, the teacher must develops a "plan." Like any good plan, it must lay out a destination and the path to that destination. A well conceived plan is fundamental to a successful learning experience. Without a good plan, the inexperienced teacher crashes. Planning is preparing a course of action to achieve specific objectives.

Teacher as Facilitator: The role of teacher is changing in smart and active learning methodologies. Now teacher is as a facilitator in learning. Teaching is the well known word for teachers. Teachers know the meaning of this word and know how to perform teaching. Sometimes they do not know the difference between teaching and facilitating in learning and it make a distance between the students and teachers. We have to understand the difference between "teaching" and 'facilitating in learning". Teaching is an activity which is helping the student in learning. In several classes teachers go to the class, teach the students, supply the homework and do some daily routine activities and "finish". How much achieve the students, it is another question and it is not a matter for teacher.

The term *'facilitator'* is used by many authors to describe a particular kind of teacher, one who is democratic (where the teacher shares some of the leadership with the students) rather than autocratic (where the teacher is in control of everything that goes on in the classroom) and one who fosters learner autonomy (where students not only learn on their own, but also take responsibility for that learning) through the use of group and pair work and by acting as more of a resource than a transmitter of knowledge.

Teacher as Coach: Coaching is typically practiced with individuals, and tends to be bit more directive than facilitation. Coaching focuses on helping individuals get into immediate action, while addressing barriers and support they may need to get moving quickly. Coach usually asks more of the group than pure Facilitation–often challenging the group to produce more or be more.

Teacher as Trainer: Training requires that the trainer have specific knowledge in the subject of the training. The job of the trainer is to impart knowledge or skills to her students using a variety of methods at her disposal. Effective trainers will often employ facilitation and coaching skills.

Teacher as a Learner: Teaching and learning are processes that are inseparably linked together. Teachers are professional learners. Good teachers are able to incite students with a desire to learn. Effective teachers are able to stimulate students to learn specific types of things. You cannot learn somebody something. Teaching is guiding another person to opportunities for them to learn something. Designed properly, these experiences will result in learning with the desired outcome. There are a number of factors involved in designing the learning experience. Most often teachers need to rely on their own instincts to develop these learning experiences.

Teachers are the expert learners. They must transfer their abilities of learning to their students. The single most important consideration to keep in mind is that students do learn in different ways. There has been a wealth of studies performed about this idea. Teachers have always known that students do learn in different styles

Teacher as Communicator: Teachers are communicators. In fact, communication is what teachers do. Successful teachers go hand in hand with good communicators. Effective teachers communicate in more than one way. Communication is a skill that separates a mediocre teacher from the professional teacher/educator. Effective teachers are skilled at more in communication. Teachers use communication for everything that occurs in the classroom. The role of the teacher as communicator is vital to the success of that teacher.

Teacher as Model: The importance of teacher as model cannot be overstated. Social Learning Theory, a broad field of human research, is based almost completely on the effect of the things we see others do and the ways that children learn to behave like people. Who we are as teachers and people will most assuredly send a louder message than anything else we hope to teach. And after all, what could be more important to teach, than how to be a wonderful, self fulfilled, caring human being?

Teacher as a Guide: The teacher carries out guidance in different ways. He will vary his method according to the capacity of the individual pupil, needs and according to the subject matter. The teacher guides more definitely and deliberately by means of discussion, by giving advice on concrete problems, and personal one to one conversation with his pupils.

Teacher as Manager: https://fm44.files.wordpress.com/2007/12/bosslogogif.gifManagers handle people, events, materials and time. Teachers are managers. This is the teacher's first and most challenging role. Classroom management is probably the most common cause for a teacher becoming frustrated and turning to a new field of endeavour. Classroom management is perhaps the least significant role of the teacher but it is the role that allows teachers to teach.

Teacher as Mentor: Mentoring involves instructing, guiding, coaching someone seeking to master a particular field that you have already mastered. Though mentoring is very "content" focused, it will also often employ teaching, training, and coaching as well.

Teacher as Controller: The teacher is in complete charge of the class, what students do, what they say and how they say it. The teacher assumes this role when new concept is being introduced and accurate reproduction and drilling techniques are needed. In this classroom, the teacher is mostly the centre of focus, the teacher may have the gift of instruction and can inspire through their own knowledge and expertise.

Teacher as Prompter: The teacher encourages students to participate and makes suggestions about how students may proceed in an activity. The teacher should be helping students only when necessary. When learners are literally *'lost for words'*, the prompter can encourage by discreetly nudging students. Students can sometimes lose the thread or become unsure how to proceed; the prompter in this regard can prompt but always in a supportive way.

Teacher as a Friend: Good teaching should enable children to develop emotional stability. To do this, the child needs affection. It is not the job of the school alone to provide an atmosphere of affection. It is the principal task of the home. But, whatever the role the home plays, the school must do its best in taking the children into confidence that, in the school, they enjoy their due place and identity. Teaching will lose its value, unless it brings to the child the sense that he matters to the teacher, and the teacher is his supporter against many odd things with which he has to struggle.

Teacher as Relater: As a relater, the teacher cares about, supports and encourages each child; therefore he:

- makes himself readily available to each child in the group and focuses his utmost attention to the physical, psychological and scholastic needs of each and every child.
- talks to each child as a good human being and draw him out in frank, meaningful conversation.
- listens and shows an absorbing interest in what each child is saying.
- responds with honest consideration to the ideas, inventions and discoveries of each child.
- expresses confidence firmly in each child's specific ability to progress. makes positive statements of recognition regarding each child's co-curricular and extra-curricular achievements.
- controls his negative and bitter feelings in a responsible way and allows children know what his feelings are.
- displays honesty and fairness in his interaction and transaction with children.
- approaches his work with willingness, confidence and optimism.
- sees situations through the eyes of the child and looks for the goals of each child's actions.

Teacher as a Mediator: As a Mediator, the teacher lays the platform for the teaching-learning process. Mediation means interposing. The teacher interposes something within the environment with which child interacts. The problem for the teacher is to make appropriate stimuli available for the child's interaction and to help the child select and organize these stimuli in ways that develop his thought processes.

The teacher helps children see realistic purposes for school activities in relationship to their own needs and goals.

Teacher as Educational Diagnostician: There may be enough scope for informal diagnosis in classrooms or at other instructional areas. The teacher diagnoses day in and day out as he helps the child with his thinking process and guides him in achieving the objective of his choice. At times, he looks thoroughly into areas of concern and adopts the scientific tools in order to make a formal diagnosis. He predicts a problem through observing the child's movements over an adequate period of time. In baffling situations, the teacher may decide to maintain anecdotal details of the child's behaviour, socio-metric devices and periodical examinations.

Teacher as Educational Leader: The teacher as Educational Leader is a role of paradox and presumes a sense of humility, of clarity, of flexibility. The research on leadership has brought recognition that being able to assume different roles, to fit the leadership style to the time, place, task, ability of followers, is the most crucial skill. We cannot validate the model of one personality type being best at bossing, but rather the greatest potential for leadership is show in the ability to delegate, to step away and to have implicit faith in human nature combined with recognition of the best hat for the situation show the greatest potential. This is referred to as situational leadership.

Teacher as Resource: The teacher is a kind of walking resource center ready to offer help if needed or provide learners with whatever knowledge they lack when performing activities. The teacher must make her/himself available so that learners can consult her/him when (and only when) it is absolutely necessary. As a resource, the teacher can guide learners to use available resources such as the library, internet, for themselves, it certainly isn't necessary to spoon-feed learners, as this might have the down side of making learners reliant on the teacher.

Teacher as Assessor: Teachers draw a distinction between assessment and evaluation. Assessment refers to the tools and resulting measurements. Evaluation is using those assessments to find the value in certain events. Teachers use assessment to determine where the child is in the learning process and what teaching processes have worked. Tests, quizzes, papers, discussion, observation are a few examples of assessments. The assessments are used by teachers to evaluate the pupils with grades and/or parent conferences.

Teacher as Organizer: Perhaps it is the most difficult and important role the teacher has to play. The success of many activities depends on good organization and on the students knowing exactly what they are to do next. Giving instructions is vital in this role as well as setting up activities. The organizer can also serve as a demonstrator, this role also allows a teacher to get involved and engaged with learners. The teacher also serves to open and neatly close activities and also give content feedback.

Teacher as Participant: This role improves the atmosphere in the class when the teacher takes part in an activity. However, the teacher takes a risk of dominating the activity when performing it. Here the teacher can enliven a class; if a teacher is able to stand back and not become the center of attention, it can be a great way to interact with learners without being too overpowering.

Teacher as Tutor: The teacher acts as a coach when students are involved in project work or self-study. The teacher provides advice and guidance and helps students clarify ideas and limit tasks. This role can be a great way to pay individual attention to a student. It can also allow a teacher to tailor make a course to fit specific student needs. However, it can also lead to a student becoming too dependent or even too comfortable with one teacher and one method or style of teaching.

Teachers as Motivator: There is another role also for a teacher that is teacher as a motivator. Motivation in teaching is an essential process of effective teaching. Motivation is a very strong factor for the teachers to educate the people. If the motivation is powerful and strong, the rest of process will be easy and comfortable. Students affect from the different factors. They attracts by different things. If they find anything attractive and useful, they pay a proper attention but if they feel anything useless they get tired and bored. So, a proper motivation moves them to grasp the lesson carefully and seriously. In a school or college we see that the students like the specific teachers because those teachers always use the interesting presentation and sometimes he maintains the pleasant personality. So, we can understand the role of motivation in educating in our schools. A teacher has to play different roles in his journey.

Teacher as an Evaluator: Teaching, like learning, is cyclic. It is a continuous process. There are three aspects to the teaching cycle: *planning, implementing and evaluating.* Teachers approach these tasks as a one step at a time process. But, in actuality, these three aspects of teaching are so interrelated that the teacher weighs all three aspects at one time. Effective teaching requires that the teacher be involved in all three phases of the cycle. This role of a teacher- to evaluate- is vital to a teacher's success. It is this role that allows the teacher to discover the worth of their work.

31
Learning Style vs. Teaching Style

Each person has different learning preferences and styles that benefit them. Some may find they even have a dominant learning style. Others, that they prefer different learning styles in different circumstances. There is no right or wrong answer to which learning style is best for you – or mix of learning styles. However, by discovering and better understanding your own learning styles, you can employ techniques that will improve the rate and quality of your learning.

MEANING OF LEARNING STYLE

Each of us is unique. We see things differently. We have our own opinions, our own personalities, even our own fingerprints. Just like our unique fingerprint, we all have a unique *learning style.* A learning style is a series of theories that explain the differences in our individual patterns of understanding information. We all learn differently, and we prefer information to be presented to us in a particular way - a way that makes it easiest for us to understand.

A learning style is a student's consistent way of responding to and using stimuli in the context of learning. Learning styles is a term that refers to different ways in which we learn, process, and retain information. All young children learn through meaningful hands-on experiences—through touching, doing, and moving. And children also learn through seeing and hearing. A student's style of learning, if accommodated, can result in improved attitudes toward learning and an increase in thinking skills, academic achievement, and creativity.

The term *"learning styles"* speaks to the understanding that every student learns differently. Technically, an individual's learning style refers to the preferential way in which the student absorbs processes, comprehends and retains information. For example, when learning how to build a clock, some students understand the process by following verbal instructions, while others have to physically manipulate the clock themselves. This notion of individualized learning styles has gained widespread recognition in education theory and classroom management strategy. Individual learning styles depend on cognitive, emotional and environmental factors, as well as one's prior experience. In other words: everyone's different. It is important for educators to understand the differences in their students' learning styles, so that they can implement best practice strategies into their daily activities, curriculum and assessments.

Thus, learning styles are not really concerned with *what* learners learn, but rather *how* they prefer to learn.

There are seven key learning styles. These include:

- *Visual (spacial)* – learning through imagery and spacial understanding
- *Aural (auditory)* – learning through listening, sound, and music
- *Verbal (linguistic)* – learning through speech and writing
- *Physical (kinesthetic)* – learning through hands-on, tactile interaction
- *Logical (mathematical)* – learning through logic, reasoning and systems
- *Social (interpersonal)* – preference for learning in groups or working with other people
- *Solitary (intrapersonal)* – preference for learning alone via self-study

DEFINITIONS OF LEARNING STYLE

Some definitions of learning style are given below:

- According to Wikipedia, *"Learning styles are different ways that a person can learn. It's commonly believed that most people favour some particular method of interacting with, taking in and processing stimuli or information."*
- Stewart and Felicetti (1992) define learning styles as those *"educational conditions under which a student is most likely to learn."*
- Keefe (1979) defines learning styles as the *"composite of characteristic cognitive, affective, and physiological factors that serve as relatively stable indicators of how a learner perceives, interacts with, and responds to the learning environment."*
- "The manner in which a learner perceives, interacts with, and responds to the learning environment. Components of learning style are the cognitive, affective and physiological elements, all of which may be strongly influenced by a person's cultural background."
- "A preferential mode, through which a subject likes to master learning, solve problems, thinks or simply react in a pedagogical situation."
- "A consistent pattern of behavior and performance by which an individual approaches educational experiences; learning style is derived from cultural socialization and individual personality as well as from the broader influence of human development."

On the basis of the above definitions, learning styles can be defined as a student's preferred method of acquiring and assimilating information. Most researchers find that successful learners are those with the ability to adjust their learning style to the subject matter and instructor teaching style. Hayes and Allen contend that *"exposing learners to learning activities that are mismatched with their preferred learning style will help them develop the learning competencies necessary to cope with situations involving a range of different learning requirements" (cited in Brown, 2003).*

TYPES OF LEARNING STYLES

How many ways are there to learn about a subject? According to the latest findings by several leading psychologists, there are seven specific types of learning styles. This means that in order to maximize learning advantages, one must define the type of learner that he/she have, and cater the lesson to that particular learning style. For example, if the child is primarily a linguistic learner, teacher/parents could incorporate several novels into his curriculum. We could encourage short stories to explain scientific developments, or allow the student to rewrite a difficult math problem into a story problem. If he/she is primarily logical, we will want to emphasize charts, tables, and diagrams. Venn diagrams work well with a logical learner.

1. Visual Learning Style (Visual – Look and Learn)

Visual learners prefer to use pictures, diagrams and images and have good spatial understanding. Such learners tend to visualize information and will easily remember something that they have seen, such as writings on a whiteboard or drawings.

Characteristics of Visual Learning Style

Children with a visual learning style:

- Like to use pictures and diagrams
- Easily visualize information and processes
- Have good map reading skills
- Remember what they see, including images and words written on a whiteboard
- Prefer reading and writing to listening
- Sometimes tune out when trying to focus and need quiet study
- Good at spelling
- Usually sit near the front of the class so they can see the teacher and the board
- Notice small details
- Ask for things to be described so they can form a mental image

Strengths of Visual Learners

Children with a visual learning style may tend to have a good sense of direction, due to excellent map reading skills. As visual learners like to see words written down, they tend to be good at spelling and have excellent essay writing skills. Visualization often requires concentration, therefore, children with a visual learning style may remain focused for long periods of time and they may keep their workspace tidy and organized in order to avoid visual distractions. Another strength of visual learners is that they are very good at remembering people's faces.

Struggle of Visual Learners

It is important to remember that no learning style is better than another. There are areas in which all children will struggle. Children with a visual learning style may daydream, which means they aren't always paying attention. This can especially be the case with listening exercises, which don't provide any visual stimuli. Whilst visual learners are very good at remembering faces, they may easily forget people's names. Additionally, many visual learners can be very quiet and shy in class and therefore may not join in with class discussions.

Teaching Strategies to Help Visual Learners

There are lots of strategies that can be put in place to help visual learners to excel. Children with a visual learning style use visual information to help them learn and remember facts. Therefore when studying, they could:

- Make mind maps to organize information
- Write notes in different colours
- Replace words with drawings
- Use a wall planner
- Watch videos
- Use flashcards
- Highlight and underline notes in bright colours
- Draw diagrams
- Write timelines
- Use visual materials such as pictures, charts, maps, graphs, etc.
- Have a clear view of your teachers when they are speaking so you can see their body language and facial expression
- Use color to highlight important points in text
- Take notes or ask your teacher to provide handouts
- Illustrate your ideas as a picture or brainstorming bubble before writing them down
- Write a story and illustrate it
- Use multi-media (e.g. computers, videos, and filmstrips)
- Study in a quiet place away from verbal disturbances
- Read illustrated books
- Visualize information as a picture to aid memorization

2. Aural/ Auditory Learning Style (Hear and Learn)

Some children may have an auditory learning style. Auditory learning is not strictly related to being musical. Rather, it means that children learn best from listening to information. Aural learners enjoy listening to sounds and have a good sense of rhythm. Often, aural learners will speak or read out loud to help them remember information. Aural learners' ability to hear different sounds easily might make them good at music or foreign languages.

Characteristics of the Auditory Learning Style

Children with an auditory learning style:

- Have a good sense of pitch and rhythm
- Like background noise
- Can easily identify different sounds
- Easily follow spoken instructions
- Like listening to someone explain things
- Enjoy discussion
- Enjoy reading aloud
- Tend to be very vocal in class
- May read more slowly
- Can remember past conversations in great detail

- Participate in class discussions/debates
- Make speeches and presentations
- Use a tape recorder during lectures instead of taking notes
- Read text out aloud
- Create musical jingles to aid memorization
- Create mnemonics to aid memorization
- Discuss your ideas verbally
- Dictate to someone while they write down your thoughts
- Use verbal analogies, and storytelling to demonstrate your point

Strengths of Auditory Learners

There are unique strengths to each of the seven learning styles. Children with an auditory learning style tend to very good at learning grammar and foreign languages since they like to hear how things sound. Additionally, such children may enjoy oral reports and explaining things aloud to a group or another individual. Auditory learners often say things to themselves, which makes them very good at memorizing poems, scripts and people's names.

Struggle of Auditory Learners

Auditory learners love sound. However, there can be some areas that they may struggle in. For example, they may struggle to read silently or understand information when they do not read it out loud. Children with an auditory learning style may appear disruptive in class, as they don't like to keep quiet for long periods of time. As auditory learners prefer hearing information to seeing it, they may struggle to visual information and diagrams and they may struggle to write under timed or silent conditions.

Teaching Strategies to Help Auditory Learners

Some teaching strategies for auditory learners are:

- Use rhyming or rhythmic mnemonics
- Read aloud, record and play back notes
- Listen to podcasts
- Have a study group or study buddy
- Have your child explain the information to you, or to another child
- Repeat facts with their eyes closed, to avoid visual distractions
- Give them opportunities to ask questions or discuss what they've been taught
- Don't work with loud music as this is particularly distracting for aural learners

3. Verbal Learning Style (Learn with Words)

Children with a verbal learning style tend to use spoken or written words to help them to learn information. Verbal learners are those who use either spoken or written words to help them learn information. Such learners also tend to think about the meaning of words and prefer things to be written in an explanatory paragraph, rather than in a chart or diagram, which a visual learner might prefer.

Characteristics of Verbal Learning Style

Children with a verbal learning style are similar to visual learners because they like to have words written down. However, they are also similar to auditory learners because they like to hear words spoken. The key traits of verbal learners are:

- Enjoy reading
- Enjoy writing
- Enjoy drama
- Think about the meaning of words
- Express self through words
- Write in a diary
- Prefer to work in a quiet environment
- Prefer words to diagrams
- Often ask "why"
- Link word puns, rhymes and tongue twisters

Strengths of Verbal Learners

Children with a verbal learning style enjoy information when it is presented with a lot of words. As they enjoy listening to speech, they may develop good memories and be able to learn foreign languages easily. Children with a verbal learning style may also be very good at explaining information and tend to develop into very fast readers and good writers.

Struggle of Verbal Learners

Although verbal learners have some similarities to visual learners, a key difference is that verbal learners may have poor spatial-navigation skills. This is because they do not like diagrams and drawings. Moreover, as verbal learners are sensitive to words, they may be easily distracted by music with lots of lyrics or other people talking when they are working.

Teaching Strategies to Help Verbal Learners

As verbal learners are very good with words, many of the traditional learning methods may suite them well. Those with a verbal learning style may benefit from:

- Writing notes or information in their own words
- Talking through and explaining ideas with another person
- Memorizing phrases
- Reading notes aloud in different voices
- Using acronyms
- Using flashcards
- Re-reading notes and books several times
- Using the dictionary, internet or reference books for research
- Incorporating facts they need to remember in a made up story

4. Tactile/Physical/Kinaesthetic Learning Style (Do and Learn)

Children with a kinaesthetic learning style like to use their hands, body and sense of touch when they are learning. Physical learners like to use their hands, body and sense of touch when they are learning. Physical learners may be able to remember the details of an object or model they have held in their hands or been able to touch.

Characteristics of Kinaesthetic Learning Style

Traits of children with a kinaesthetic learning style include:

- Enjoying hands on activities
- Likes science projects
- Uses hand gestures when explaining things
- Likes sport
- Likes to feel things and make models
- May fidget or doodle when listening in class
- Enjoys dance and drama
- Remembers things that they do
- Chooses to read adventure books
- Take frequent study breaks
- Move around to learn new things (e.g. read while on an exercise bike, mold a piece of clay to learn a new concept)
- Work at a standing position
- Chew gum while studying
- Use bright colors to highlight reading material
- Dress up your work space with posters
- If you wish, listen to music while you study
- Skim through reading material to get a rough idea what it is about before settling down to read it in detail.

Strengths of a Kinaesthetic Learning Style

Children with a kinaesthetic learning style like to make their body do different things as this helps them to remember information. This makes them very good at sport and dance. As kinaesthetic learners tend to feel things in their hands a lot, they may also be very good at construction.

Struggle of Kinaesthetic Learners

Generally, if a child has a kinaesthetic learning style, they do not like to keep their body still. This makes prolonged tasks such as essays difficult for them. Additionally, children with a kinaesthetic learning style may not like visual or aural tasks. This may cause them to struggle with spelling and handwriting.

Teaching Strategies to Help Kinaesthetic Learners

Here are some suggestions:

- Use physical objects when explaining information
- Act out information or role play
- Make models to represent what has been learnt
- Relate information to your child's own feelings or experiences
- Have study breaks. In this time, they could do something physical like a quick run around outside
- Go on trips

- Have they do something whilst studying like squeeze a ball

5. Logical Learning Style (Learn with Systems)

Children with a logical learning style thrive when they see how information is lined to each other. Having a logical learning style is different to having high logical intelligence. If a child has a logical learning style it means that they approach a task in a systematic or logical way. Having logical intelligence means being able to understand sequences and numbers. Although these are similar, they should not be confused. A person with logical intelligence could be a visual learner rather than a logical learner, for example. Logical learners tend to follow a rational approach and easily understand systems and sequences. Such learners thrive when they see how things link to each other and work together.

Characteristics of Logical Learning Style

There are some common traits that children with a logical learning style may have. These include:

- Likes patterns
- Likes Maths and numbers
- Is very organized
- Plays strategy games
- Deep thinker – wonder's how things work
- Enjoys science
- Asks for rational explanations
- Will choose to do a puzzle
- Will do things the same way each time

Strengths of Logical Learning Style

As children with a logical learning style like things to be rational and make sense, they may develop good analysis and reasoning skills. Due to their learning style, logical learners may become very good at Maths and science.

Struggle of Logical Learners

Children with a logical learning style do not like activities that do not seem to follow strict rules all the time. This may cause them to struggle to participate in creative tasks, including writing. Additionally, logical learners may not like to learn foreign languages due to grammar rule exceptions.

Teaching Strategies to Help Logical Learners

Those with a logical learning style tend to do best when they feel that the work they are doing has a reason and a logical purpose. It can be helpful to:

- Give child an organized work space
- Break down larger tasks into smaller ones and explain how they are relevant to each other
- Give a reason for why they are learning something
- Have your child conduct their own research and experiments
- Open up discussions and opportunities to ask questions

6. Social / Interpersonal Learning Style (Learn with Others)

Social learners may lack focus when they work alone but do well when they work in a group or with a partner. As group work helps children to develop good communication and listening skills, social learners can also be very engaged when simply listening to a person give a presentation.

Characteristics of Social Learners

The characteristics of interpersonal or social learners are:

- Communicate and listen well
- Like group work
- Like team sports
- Show empathy
- Have lots of friends
- Like group work
- Use lots of body language
- May have a strong personality
- Don't like being alone

Strengths for Social or Interpersonal Learners

Social or interpersonal learners like to engage with other people. There are lots of advantages for this. For example, your child may develop good leadership and problem solving skills. They may also develop become very good at reading body language.

Teaching Strategies to Help a Social Learner

There are different learning strategies for interpersonal learners. Social learners are benefited from:

- Study group or study buddy
- Role play
- Explaining information to another person
- Brainstorming
- Discussion
- Clubs or group activities

7. Solitary /Intrapersonal Learning Styles (Learn When Alone)

Solitary learners may struggle to work in a group but thrive when they work by themselves. Such learners may enjoy teaching themselves new skills or finding things out for themselves, rather than asking another person.

Characteristics of Solitary/Intrapersonal Learning Style

The main characteristics of solitary learning style are:

- Intrapersonal or solitary learners tend to:
- Self-reflect
- Like working independently
- Make plans
- Write in a diary

- Can be introverted
- Is self motivated
- Like to be in control
- Prefers their own company
- Be a perfectionist
- Be quiet in class

Strengths for Solitary or Intrapersonal Learners

Intrapersonal learners enjoy their own company. This may lead your child to be very observant, focus for long periods of time and produce excellent work when they work independently. Children, who are interpersonal and intrapersonal learners, may enjoy the advantages of both of these learning styles.

Teaching Strategies to Help Solitary Learners

The Intrapersonal / solitary learning methods are:

- Have personal goals to reach
- Work at their own pace and in their own space
- Record what they have achieved in a diary
- Relate facts to their own feelings and experiences
- Learn for themselves – do their own research
- Crete self-assessments
- Write summaries about what they've learnt

Struggle of Interpersonal and Intrapersonal Learners

Interpersonal and intrapersonal learners tend to struggle in conflicting areas. Interpersonal learners may not work well independently and can be argumentative. Intrapersonal learners may not work well in a group and may not ask for help. Children, who are both interpersonal and intrapersonal learners, may struggle in these areas, depending on which method they have chosen to approach the task and the situation they are in. For example, a child may be an interpersonal learner at school. This means, in a classroom situation, they love working in a group but do not work well independently. However, at home they may be an intrapersonal learner. This means that they work excellently by themselves and may not ask for help from a parent.

TEACHING STYLE

Just as students have individual learning styles; teachers have teaching styles that works best for them. It is important to be aware of teachers' preferences when creating and delivering instruction. The most effective teachers vary their styles depending on the nature of the subject matter, the phase of the course and other factors. By so doing, they encourage and inspire students to do their best at all times throughout the Class or course. There is no one best teaching style. Effective teachers use a variety of styles and they know how and when to choose the most appropriate one for the specific situation.

DEFINITIONS OF TEACHING STYLE

1. Teaching Style refers to the way various teaching approaches are combined.
2. Daniel K. Schneider thinks that "*teaching style* refers to the teaching strategies and methods employed plus use of certain kinds of rhetorics."
3. According to Galton et al, (1980) - The term itself has no agreed definition but the more widely accepted definition refer to it as "a set of teaching tactics".
4. *Teaching Style* refers to the way various teaching approaches are combined.

TYPOLOGIES OF TEACHING STYLE

Anthony Grasha (1996) identified five potential approaches of teaching style for classroom teachers:

- Expert
- Formal Authority,
- Personal Model
- Facilitator
- Delegator

Behar-Horenstein (2006) and many other studies distinguish between:

- teacher-centered
- student-centered

Moston and Ashworth (1986) define 10 types of teaching styles:

1. Style A Command - teacher makes all decisions.
2. Style B Practice - Students carry out teacher-prescribed tasks.
3. Style C Reciprocal - Students work in pairs: one performs, the other provides feedback.
4. Style D Self-check - Students assess their own performance against criteria
5. Style E Inclusion - Teacher planned. Student monitors own work.
6. Style F Guided Discovery - Students solve teacher set movement problems with assistance.
7. Style G Divergent - Students solve problems without assistance from the teacher.
8. Style H Individual - Teacher determines content. Student plans the programme.
9. Style I Learner Initiated - Student plans own programme. Teacher is advisor.
10. Style J Self Teaching - Student takes full responsibility for the learning process.

TYPES OF TEACHING STYLES

Teaching styles can be categorized as:

Formal Authority Teaching Style

Teachers who have a formal authority teaching style tend to focus on content. This style is generally teacher-centered, where the teacher feels responsible for providing and controlling the flow of the content and the student is expected to receive the content.

One type of statement made by a teacher with this teaching style is *"I am the flashlight for my students; I illuminate the content and materials so that my students can see the importance of the material and appreciate the discipline."*

Teachers with this teaching style are not as concerned with building relationships with their students nor is it as important that their students form relationships with other students. This type of teacher doesn't usually require much student participation in class.

Demonstrator or Personal Model Teaching Style

Teachers who have a demonstrator or personal model teaching style tend to run teacher-centered classes with an emphasis on demonstration and modeling. This type of teacher acts as a role model by demonstrating skills and processes and then as a coach/guide in helping students develops and apply these skills and knowledge.

A teacher with this type of teaching style might comment: *"I show my students how to properly do a task or work through a problem and then I'll help them master the task or problem solution. It's important that my students can independently solve similar problems by using and adapting demonstrated methods."*

Teachers with this teaching style are interested in encouraging student participation and adapting their presentation to include various learning styles. Students are expected to take some responsibility for learning what they need to know and for asking for help when they don't understand something.

Facilitator Teaching Style

Teachers who have a facilitator model teaching style tend to focus on activities. This teaching style emphasizes student-centered learning and there is much more responsibility placed on the students to take the initiative for meeting the demands of various learning tasks.

This type of teaching style works best for students who are comfortable with independent learning and who can actively participate and collaborate with other students. Teachers typically design group activities which necessitate active learning, student-to-student collaboration and problem solving. This type of teacher will often try to design learning situations and activities that require student processing and application of course content in creative and original ways.

Delegator Teaching Style

Teachers who have a delegator teaching style tend to place much control and responsibility for learning on individuals or groups of students. This type of teacher will often give students a choice designing and implementing their own complex learning projects and will act in a consultative role.

Students are often asked to work independently or in groups and must be able to maintain motivation and focus for complex projects. Students working in this type of setting learn more than just course specific topics as they also must be able to effectively work in group situations and manage various interpersonal roles.

MATCHING TEACHERS' TEACHING STYLE WITH LEARNERS' LEARNING STYLE

Teaching and learning styles are the behaviors or actions that teachers and learners exhibit in the learning exchange. Teaching behaviors reflect the beliefs and values that teachers hold about the learner's role in the exchange (Heimlich and Norland 2002). Learners' behaviors provide insight into the ways learners perceive, interact with, and respond to the environment in which learning occurs. Now, some questions arises here about the congruence of teaching and learning styles: Do the teaching styles of teachers match students' learning styles? Can individuals learn effectively when instructional delivery does not match their preferred learning style? Can teaching and learning styles be adapted or modified?

In all academic classrooms, no matter what the subject matter, there will be students with multiple learning styles and students with a variety of major, minor and negative learning styles. An effective means of accommodating these learning styles is for teachers to change their own styles and strategies and provide a variety of activities to meet the needs of different learning styles. Then all students will have at least some activities that appeal to them based on their learning styles, and they are more likely to be successful in these activities.

Much research supports the view that when students' learning preferences match their teacher's teaching styles, student motivation and achievement usually improves. Research has shown the uniqueness of different teaching and learning styles and identified the characteristics associated with each style. Although there are benefits to the matching of teaching style and learning style, it appears that this alone does not guarantee greater learner achievement. Age, educational level, and motivation influence each student's learning so that what was once preferred may no longer be the student's current preferred learning style. Teachers need to examine their belief structure regarding education and engage in an *"ongoing process of diagnosis, with self and with learners, including observation, questioning, obtaining evaluative feedback, and critical reflection"*. According to Heimlich and Norland (2002) - *"Each teacher is unique and can use his or her style to be as effective an educator as possible"*.

PRACTICAL STRATEGIES TO MATCH TEACHING STYLE WITH LEARNING STYLE

Teaching styles are made up of methods and approaches with which teachers feel most comfortable; if they try to change to completely different approaches, they would be forced to work entirely with unfamiliar, awkward, and uncomfortable methods. Fortunately, teachers who wish to address a wide variety of learning styles need not make drastic changes in their instructional approach. Regular use of some the instructional techniques given below should suffice to cover some specified learning style categories:

Diagnosing Students' Learning Styles

Effective matching between teaching style and learning style can only be achieved when teachers are, first of all, aware of their learners' needs, capacities, potentials and learning style preferences in meeting these needs.

Altering the Teaching Style to Create Teacher-Student Style Matching

In all academic classrooms, no matter what the subject matter, there will be students with multiple learning styles and students with a variety of major, minor and negative learning styles. An effective means of accommodating these learning styles is for teachers to change their own styles and strategies and provide a variety of activities to meet the needs of different learning styles. Then all students will have at least some activities that appeal to them based on their learning styles, and they are more likely to be successful in these activities. Fr example, multimedia methodology approach is effective in tapping a variety of learning modalities. By consciously accommodating a range of learning styles in the classroom in this way, it is possible to encourage most students to become successful language learners.

Providing Activities with Different Groupings

In a class made up of students with various learning styles and strategies, it is always helpful for the teacher to divide the students into groups by learning styles and give them activities based on their learning styles. This should appeal to them because they will enjoy them and be successful.

Finally, no matter how students are to be grouped, teachers should make a conscious effort to incl ide various learning styles in daily lesson plan. One simple way to do this is to code the lesson plans so that a quick look at the completed plan shows if different learning styles have been included.

HOW A TEACHER CAN MODIFY HIS TEACHING STYLE ACCORDING TO LEARNERS' LEARNING STYLE

Pratt (2002) presents five perspectives on teaching and urges teachers to use these perspectives to identify, articulate and justify their teaching approaches rather than simply adopting one practice or another.

Transmission: Teachers focus on content and determine what students should learn and how they should learn it. Feedback is directed to students' errors.

Developmental: Teachers value students' prior knowledge and direct student learning to the development of increasingly complex ways of reasoning and problem solving.

Apprenticeship: Teachers provide students with authentic tasks in real work settings.

Nurturing: Teachers focus on the interpersonal elements of student learning-listening, getting to know students, and responding to students' emotional and intellectual needs.

Social Reform: Teachers tend to relate ideas explicitly to the lives of the students.

32
Information and Communication Technology (ICT)

CONCEPT OF ICT

Information and communication technologies (ICTs), which include radio and television, as well as newer digital technologies such as computers and the Internet have been proven as potentially powerful tools for educational change and reform. When used appropriately, different ICTs can help expand access to education, strengthen the relevance of education to the increasingly digital workplace and raise educational quality by helping make teaching and learning into an active process connected to real life.

MEANING OF ICT

ICTs stand for information and communication technologies and are defined, for the purposes, as a *"diverse set of technological tools and resources used to communicate, and to create, disseminate, store, and manage information."* These technologies include computers, the Internet, broad casting technologies (radio and television), and telephony.

Information and Communication Technologies refers to technologies that provide access to information through telecommunications such as the Telephony, Internet, wireless networks, cell phones, etc. It is an integration of telecommunications such as telephone lines, wireless signals, computers, necessary software, storage devices, audio-visual systems, etc. which enable us to access, retrieve, store, transmit, and manipulate information. Information and Communication Technology in education is the processing of information its communication facilities and features that variously support teaching, learning and a range of activities in education.

DEFINITIONS OF ICT

1. "ICT is defined, as a diverse set of technological tools and resources used to communicate, and to create, disseminate, store, and manage information."
2. "ICT implies the technology which consists of electronic devices and associated human interactive materials that enable the user to employ them for a wide range of teaching - learning processes in addition to personal use." These technologies include computers, the Internet, broadcasting technologies, and telephony.
3. "Information and communications technology (ICT) in education is the processing of information and its communications facilities and features that variously support teaching, learning and a range of activities in education."

CHARACTERISTICS OF ICT

Some important characteristics of ICT are:

- Support teaching and learning process
- Enhancing teacher training
- Cater to individual differences
- Minimize psychological barriers
- Effective audiovisual effects
- Motivating to learn
- Uses of contemporary devices
- Brings about changes and reforms in education
- Educate both formal and informal settings
- Real time access to information.
- Connecting Geographically dispersed regions
- Facilitating acquisition of basic skills
- Wider range of communication media.
- Expanding learning opportunity
- Facilitator of higher-order thinking skills

SCOPE OF ICT IN EDUCATION

The scope of ICT in education can be best understood with the help of the following points:

Anytime, Anywhere Learning

One defining feature of ICTs is their ability to transcend time and space. ICTs make possible asynchronous learning, or learning characterized by a time lag between the delivery of instruction and its reception by learners. Online course materials, for example, may be accessed 24 hours a day, 7 days a week. ICT-based educational delivery (e.g., educational programming broadcast over radio or television) also dispenses with the need for all learners and the instructor to be in one physical location. Additionally, certain types of ICTs, such as teleconferencing technologies, enable instruction to be received simultaneously by multiple, geographically dispersed learners (i.e., synchronous learning).

Authentic and up to date Information

The information and data which are available on the NET is purely correct and up to date.

Access to Variety of Learning Resources

In the era of technology, ICT aids plenty of resources to enhance the teaching skills and learning ability. It facilitate easy and quick access to rich teaching and learning resources including ICT systems and services, computing resources, online learning materials, e-learning, and other education centered applications.

E-Learning

ICT encourage the use of e-Learning and adoption of its tools and technologies to facilitate widening access to learning and improving educational achievements.

Distance Learning

Distance learning is a method of learning at a distance rather than in a classroom. It is a home-based learning and part-time learning.

Online Library

Internets support thousands of different kinds of operational and experimental services one of which is online library. We can get plenty of data on this online library.

Lifelong Learning

ICT develop a framework for web enabled lifelong learning through continuous education and training.

Multimedia Approach to Education

Audio-visual education helps for planning, preparation and use of devices and materials that involve sight, sound, or both, for educational purposes. It enhances and enriches learning with variety of individual needs.

Administrative Tool

Different types of systems and software are useful educational management and school administration.

Better Accesses to Children with Disabilities

Information technology has brought drastic changes in the life of disabled children. ICT provides various software and technique to educate these poor peoples.

Prepare Individuals for the Workplace

One of the most commonly cited reasons for using ICTs in the classroom has been to better prepare the current generation of students for a workplace where ICTs, particularly computers, the Internet and related technologies, are becoming more and more ubiquitous. Technological literacy, or the ability to use ICTs effectively and efficiently, is thus seen as representing a competitive edge in an increasingly globalizing job market.

ADVANTAGES OF ICT IN EDUCATION

Here are some of the benefits which ICT brings to education according to recent research findings.

General benefits of ICT

- Greater efficiency throughout the school.
- Communication channels are increased through email, discussion groups and chat rooms
- Regular use of ICT across different curriculum subjects can have a beneficial motivational influence on students' learning.

ICT Benefits for Teachers

- ICT facilitates sharing of resources, expertise and advice
- Greater flexibility in when and where tasks are carried out

- Gains in ICT literacy skills, confidence and enthusiasm.
- Easier planning and preparation of lessons and designing materials
- Access to up-to-date pupil and school data, any time and anywhere.
- Enhancement of professional image projected to colleagues.
- Students are generally more 'on task' and express more positive feelings when they use computers than when they are given other tasks to do.
- Computer use during lessons motivated students to continue using learning outside school hours.

ICT Benefits for Students

- Higher quality lessons through greater collaboration between teachers in planning and preparing resources .
- More focused teaching, tailored to students' strengths and weaknesses, through better analysis of attainment data
- Improved pastoral care and behaviour management through better tracking of students
- Gains in understanding and analytical skills, including improvements in reading Comprehension.
- Development of writing skills (including spelling, grammar, punctuation, editing and re-drafting), also fluency, originality and elaboration.
- Encouragement of independent and active learning, and self-responsibility for learning.
- Flexibility of 'anytime, anywhere' access (Jacobsen and Kremer, 2000)
- Development of higher level learning styles.
- Students who used educational technology in school felt more successful in school, were more motivated to learn and have increased self-confidence and self-esteem
- Students found learning in a technology-enhanced setting more stimulating and student-centred than in a traditional classroom
- Broadband technology supports the reliable and uninterrupted downloading of web-hosted educational multimedia resources
- Opportunities to address their work to an external audience
- Opportunities to collaborate on assignments with people outside or inside school

ICT Benefits for Parents

- Easier communication with teachers
- Higher quality student reports – more legible, more detailed, better presented
- Greater access to more accurate attendance and attainment information
- Increased involvement in education for parents and, in some cases, improved self-esteem
- Increased knowledge of children's learning and capabilities, owing to increase in learning activity being situated in the home
- Parents are more likely to be engaged in the school community

EXAMPLES OF ICT-BASED ACTIVITIES

What kind of classroom activities is suited to the use of ICT? The following is a brief discussion to some of the most common uses of ICT in teaching and learning:

Finding Out

Students can use ICT to find out information and to gain new knowledge in several ways. They may find information on the Internet or by using an ICT-based encyclopedia such as Microsoft Encarta. They may find information by extracting it from a document prepared by the teacher and made available to them via ICT, such as document created using Microsoft Word or a Microsoft PowerPoint slideshow. They may find out information by communicating with people elsewhere using email, such as students in a different school or even in a different country.

Processing Knowledge

Students can use ICT as part of a creative process where they have to consider more carefully the information which they have about a given subject. They may need to carry out calculations (eg. by using Microsoft Excel), or to check grammar and spelling in a piece of writing (perhaps using Microsoft Word), or they may need to re-sequence a series of events (for example by re-ordering a series of Microsoft PowerPoint slides).

Sharing Knowledge

Students can use ICT to present their work in a highly professional format. They can create documents and slideshows to demonstrate what they have learned, and then share this with other students, with their teacher, and even via email with people all around the world.

COMPUTERS AND THE INTERNET USE FOR TEACHING AND LEARNING

There are three general approaches to the instructional use of computers and the Internet, namely:

Learn about Computers and the Internet

Learning about computers and the Internet, in which technological literacy is the end goal. Learning about computers and the Internet focuses on developing technological literacy. It typically includes:

- Fundamentals: basic terms, concepts and operations
- Use of the keyboard and mouse
- Use of productivity tools such as word processing, spreadsheets, data base and graphics programs
- Use of research and collaboration tools such as search engines and email
- Basic skills in using programming and authoring applications such as Logo or HyperStudio
- Developing an awareness of the social impact of technological change.

Learning with Computers and the Internet

Learning with computers and the Internet, in which the technology facilitates learning across the curriculum. Learning with the technology means focusing on how the technology can be the means to learning ends across the curriculum. It includes:

- Presentation, demonstration, and the manipulation of data using productivity tools
- Use of curriculum-specific applications types such as educational games, drill and practice, simulations, tutorials, virtual laboratories, visualizations and graphical representations of abstract concepts, musical composition, and expert systems
- Use of information and resources on CD-ROM or online such as encyclopedia, interactive maps and atlases, electronic journals and other references.
- Technological literacy is required for learning with technologies to be possible, implying a two-step process in which students learn about the technologies before they can actually use them to learn.

Learning through computers and the Internet mean

Learning through computers and the Internet, integrating technological skills development with curriculum applications. Learning through computers and the Internet combines learning about them with learning with them. It involves learning the technological skills "just-in-time" or when the learner needs to learn them as he or she engages in a curriculum-related activity.

LIMITATIONS OF ICT

Some limitations of ICT are:

- Setting up the devices can be very troublesome and also expensive.
- Lack of confidence and experience among teachers to use ICT devices.
- Over-reliance on ICT limits students' critical thinking and analytical skills.
- Computers can be misused. Students may be easily distracted from their learning and may visit unwanted sites.
- Computers limit students' imaginations and creativity.
- Computer-based learning has negative physical side-effects.
- Students tend to neglect learning resources other than the computer and internet.
- Students often have only a superficial understanding of the information they download.
- Students may have less opportunity to use oral skills and hand writing and tend to copying data from the internet.
- Use of ICT may be difficult for weaker students, because they may have problems with working independently and may need more support from the teacher.

33
E-Learning and M-Learning

ELECTRONIC LEARNING OR E-LEARNING

E-learning is an approach to administering education and training through the use of modern technology. This is a type of teaching and learning that one can be obtained by the means of online technology. Instead of going to school and attend a regular class, e-learning is done in the comfort of users own home wherein users can also gain intellectually.

MEANING OF E-LEARNING

E-learning is the computer and network-enabled transfer of skills and knowledge. It is specifically used to encompass the use of digital computers and the Internet to support learning and teaching process. It includes all forms of electronically supported learning and teaching, including educational technology. Abbreviations like CBT (Computer-Based Training), IBT (Internet-Based Training) or WBT (Web-Based Training) have been used as synonyms to e-learning.

E-learning applications and processes include Web-based learning, computer-based learning, virtual education opportunities and digital collaboration. Content is delivered via the Internet, intranet, audio or video tape, satellite TV, CD-ROM, etc. It can be self-paced or instructor-led and includes media in the form of text, image, animation, streaming video and audio.

DEFINITIONS OF E-LEARNING

1. According to Oxford English Dictionary, *"E-learning is defined as the learning conducted via electronic media, typically on the Internet."*
2. According to Ministry of Communication and Technology of New Zealand (2008), *"E-learning is defined as learning facilitated by the use of digital tools and content that involves some form of interactivity, which may include online interaction between the learner and their teacher or peers."*
3. According to Jereb & Šmitek (2006), *"E-learning refers to educational processes that utilize information and communications technology to mediate synchronous as well as asynchronous learning and teaching activities."*

FEATURES OF E-LEARNING

The main features of electronic learning are as listed below:

- Learning is self-paced and gives students a chance to speed up or slow down as necessary
- Learning is self-directed, allowing students to choose content and tools appropriate to their differing interests, needs, and skill levels

- Accommodates multiple learning styles using a variety of delivery methods geared to different learners; more effective for certain learners
- Designed around the learner
- Geographical barriers are eliminated, opening up broader education options
- 24/7 accessibility makes scheduling easy and allows a greater number of people to attend classes
- On-demand access means learning can happen precisely when needed
- Travel time and associated costs (parking, fuel, vehicle maintenance) are reduced or eliminated
- Overall student costs are frequently less (tuition, residence, food, child care)
- Potentially lower costs for companies needing training, and for the providers
- Fosters greater student interaction and collaboration
- Fosters greater student/instructor contact
- Enhances computer and Internet skills
- Draws upon hundreds of years of established pedagogical principles
- Has the attention of every major university in the world, most with their own online degrees, certificates, and individual courses

BENEFITS OF E-LEARNING

There are many significant advantages for the student who learns online. Here are just a few to consider:

Convenience and Portability

- Courses are accessible on learner schedule
- Online learning does not require physical attendance
- Learning is self-paced (not too slow, not too fast)
- Learners are unbound by time - courses are available 24/7
- Users are unbound by place - study at home, work, or on the road
- Read materials online or download them for reading later

Cost and Selection

- Choose from a wide range of courses to meet your needs
- Degree, Vocational and Certificate programs
- Continuing Education
- Individual courses
- Wide range of prices to fit learner budget
- Go back to school to get a degree, learn a new skill, learn a new craft, or just have fun.
- From art to zoology you can do it all online in a price range to fit learner budget.

Flexibility

- Online learning accommodates learner preferences and needs - it's student-centered
- Choose instructor-led or self-study courses
- Skip over material learner already know and focus on topics you'd like to learn
- Use the tools best suited to learner learning styles

Higher Retention

Online learning will draw user to topics user like and enjoy. Studies show that because of this and the variety of delivery methods used to reach different types of learners, retention is frequently better than in a traditional classroom.

Greater Collaboration

Technology tools make collaboration among students much easier. Since many projects involve collaborative learning, the online environment is far easier (and often more comfortable) to work in since learners don't have to be face-to-face.

Global Opportunities

The global learning community is at learner fingertips with online learning. The technologies used give online instructional designers the ability to build in tools that take learner to resources you may never see in a traditional classroom.

DISADVANTAGES OF E-LEARNING

- Learners with low motivation or bad study habits may fall behind
- Without the routine structures of a traditional class, students may get lost or confused about course activities and deadlines
- Students may feel isolated from the teacher and classmates
- Teacher/Instructor may not always be available when students are studying or need help
- Slow Internet connections or older computers may make accessing course materials frustrating
- Managing computer files and online learning software can sometimes seem complex for students with beginner-level computer skills
- Hands-on or lab work is difficult to simulate in a virtual classroom

MOBILE LEARNING OR M-LEARNING

In our "information society" education is taking advantage of computer technology which can enhance and improve the teaching and learning process. The traditional classroom, teacher, textbooks, blackboard can no longer satisfy the needs of generations of students used to handling technological tools from a very young age. Mobile phone – the recent and innovative technological device which represents a revolution in education gives the opportunity to learn "in motion", making the learning process more appealing, interesting and motivating. No generation is more at ease with online, collaborative technologies than today's young people – "digital natives", who have grown up in an immersive computing environment. Where a notebook and pen may have formed the toolkit of prior generations, today's students come to class armed with smart phones, laptops and iPods.

MEANING OF MOBILE LEARNING

M-learning or mobile learning is defined as *"learning across multiple contexts, through social and content interactions, using personal electronic devices"*. A form of distance education, m-learners use mobile device educational technology at their time convenience. M-learning technologies include handheld computers, MP3 players, notebooks, mobile phones and tablets. M-learning focuses on the mobility of the learner, interacting with portable technologies. Using mobile tools for creating learning aids and materials becomes an important part of informal learning.

M-learning is convenient in that it is accessible from virtually anywhere. Sharing is almost instantaneous among everyone using the same content, which leads to the reception of instant feedback and tips. M-learning also brings strong portability by replacing books and notes with small devices, filled with tailored learning contents.

Mobile learning is the delivery of learning, education or learning support on mobile phones, PDAs or tablets. E-Learning has provided the ability for traditional learning to break out of the classroom setting and for students to learn at home. Mobile learning has enhanced upon e-learning by taking it a step further and allowing students to learn virtually anywhere a mobile signal is available.

Research outcomes reported in Attewell's (2005) summary of the 2001 Mlearn project, suggest that the use of mobile learning may have positive contributions to make in the following areas:

- Mobile learning helps learners to improve their literacy and numeracy skills and to recognize their existing abilities.
- Mobile learning can be used to encourage both independent and collaborative learning experiences.
- Mobile learning helps learners to identify areas where they need assistance and support.
- Mobile learning helps to combat resistance to the use of ICT and can help bridge the gap between mobile phone literacy and ICT literacy.
- Mobile learning helps to remove some of the formality from the learning experience and engages reluctant learners.
- Mobile learning helps learners to remain focused for longer periods.
- Mobile learning helps to raise self-esteem.
- Mobile learning helps to raise self-confidence (Attewell, 2005, p. 13).

DEFINITIONS OF MOBILE LEARNING

1. Pinkwart, et al. (2003) defines e - learning as *'learning supported by digital "electronic" tools and media', and by analogy, mobile learning as 'e-learning that uses mobile devices and wireless transmission'.*
2. According to Quinn (2000), *"learning that takes place with the help of mobile devices, or the intersection of mobile computing (the application of small, portable, and wireless computing and communication devices) and e-learning (learning facilitated and supported through the use of information and communications technology)."*
3. Traxler (2005) defined it as *"any educational provision where the sole or dominant technologies are handheld or palmtop devices."*

CHALLENGES OF MOBILE LEARNING

Some challenges of mobile learning are as follows:

Technical Challenges

- Connectivity and battery life

- Screen size and key size
- Meeting required bandwidth for nonstop/fast streaming
- Number of file/asset formats supported by a specific device
- Content security or copyright issue from authoring group
- Multiple standards, multiple screen sizes, multiple operating systems
- Reworking existing E-Learning materials for mobile platforms
- Limited memory
- Risk of sudden obsolescence
- Security
- Work/life balance
- Cost of investment

Social and Educational Challenges

- Accessibility and cost barriers for end users: digital divide.
- How to assess learning outside the classroom
- How to support learning across many contexts
- Content's security or pirating issues
- Frequent changes in device models/technologies/functionality etc.
- Developing an appropriate theory of learning for the mobile age
- Conceptual differences between e-learning and m-learning
- Design of technology to support a lifetime of learning
- Tracking of results and proper use of this information
- No restriction on learning timetable
- Personal and private information and content
- No demographic boundary
- Disruption of students' personal and academic lives
- Access to and use of the technology in developing countries
- Risk of distraction

VALUE OF MOBILE LEARNING

Teachers who have used m-learning programs and techniques have made the following value statements in favor of m-learning:

- It is important to bring new technology into the classroom.
- Devices used are more lightweight than books and PCs.
- Mobile learning can be used to diversify the types of learning activities students partake in (or a blended learning approach).
- Mobile learning supports the learning process rather than being integral to it.
- Mobile learning can be a useful add-on tool for students with special needs. However, for SMS and MMS this might be dependent on the students' specific disabilities or difficulties involved.
- Mobile learning can be used as a 'hook' to re-engage disaffected youth.

BENEFITS OF MOBILE LEARNING

The benefits of mobile learning are:

Easy Access

Mobile learning provides easy access to the learning at any place and any time, which is more convenient to the learners. Learners have an advantage of spending their free time during travelling, in between meetings or during weekends to focus on subject they want to learn.

Collaborative Learning

M-Learning encourages collaborative learning allowing the learners at different locations to get in touch with their peers or others teams to discuss and learn.

Learner Engagement

Mobile learning is another platform to be engaged in training. Training at the work place consists of mostly verbal and desktop communication, but adapting mobile learning can bring several opportunities to engage the learner on a digital and social level outside of the work.

Self-Pace Learning

No two learners are the same. Each one has his or her own way of understanding the content or strategies to learn. With mobile learning, learners are now able to learn in their own style at their own pace.

Address All Learning Styles

Mobile learning can fit in to different learning styles as it allows them to do the following:

- Reading
- Learning through Videos
- Listening to podcast (Audio)
- Research on the Internet

LIMITATIONS OF MOBILE LEARNING

Connectivity

There may be some connectivity problems while uploading and downloading of data and because of poor mobile network signals.

Screen Size

As the screen size is too small, it can strain the eyes of the learners if they use it for long period of time. Also only less information or just the gist of content can be provided due to size constraints.

Device

Learners must possess the mobile device that is supporting the courseware and this device may be expensive. As technology keeps changing at a rapid rate, these devices should be upgraded frequently. In addition to the cost of these devices, there are monthly data charges from mobile network providers; so downloading large content not only takes time but also costs a lot.

Distraction

While accessing the course through mobiles, if the learner gets a call or SMS or social media updates, then they are bound to get distracted.

References

Aggarwa J.C. (1995). *Essential of Educational Psychology*, Vikas Publication, New Dehli.

Allen, D.W. and Ryan, K.A. (1969). *Micro-teaching Reading Mass.*: Addison Wesley.

Allen, D.W. (1969). *Micro-teaching: A Description*. Stanford University Press.

Ambrose, S.A., Bridges, M.W., DiPietro, M., Lovett, M.C., and Norman, M.K. (2010). *How Learning Works: 7 Research-based Principles for Smart Teaching*. San Francisco, CA: Jossey- Bass.

Andresen, L., Boud, D. and Cohen, R. (2000). Experience-based Learning (PDF), in G. Foley (ed.), *Understanding Adult Education and Training*, 2nd edn, Sydney, Allen & Unwin, 225-239.

Association for Experiential Education. (2007-2014). http://www.aee.org/.

Bass, R. (2012). Disrupting Ourselves: The Problem of Learning in Higher Education. *EDUCAUSE Review*, 47(2).

Baumgartner, L.M. and Johnson-Bailey, J. (2008). Fostering Awareness of Diversity and Multiculturism in Adult and Higher Education. *New Directions for Continuing Education*. 120. 45-53.

Bednar, A.K., Cunningham, D., Duffy, T.M., & Perry, J.D. (1991). Theory into Practice: How Do We Link? In G.J. Anglin (Ed.), *Instructional technology: Past, present, and future*. Englewood, CO: Libraries Unlimited.

Biggs, J. and Tang, C. (2007) *Teaching for Quality Learning at University*, 3rd edition, New York, Society for Research into Higher Education and Open University Press.

Bloom, B.S., Engelhart, M.D., Furst, E.J., Hill, W.H., and Krathwohl, D.R. (Eds.). (1956). *Taxonomy of Educational Objectives – The Classification of Educational Goals – Handbook 1: Cognitive Domain*. London, WI: Longmans, Green & Co. Ltd.

Boud, D., Cohen, R., and Walker, D. (Eds.). (1993). *Using Experience for Learning*. Bristol, PA: Open University Press.

Bower, G.H., and Hilgard, E.R. (1981). *Theories of Learning* (5th ed.). Englewood Cliffs, NJ: Prentice-Hall.

Brown, J.S., Collins, A., and Duguid, P. (1989). Situated cognition and tne culture of learning. *Educational Researcher*, 18(1), 32–42.

Bruce, R. Joyce and Marsha, Weil (2008). *Models of Teaching* (8th Edition), Publisher: Allyn & Bacon.

Bruce, R. Joyce, Marsha Weil and Emily, Calhoun (2005). *Models of Teaching* (7th Edition) My Lab School Edition.

Bruner, J.S. (1971). The process of education revisited. *Phi Delta Kappan, 53*, 18-21.

Castagno, A., and Brayboy, B. (2008). Culturally Responsive Schooling for Indigenous Youth: A Review of the Literature. *Review of Educational Research*, 78(4), 941-993. doi:10.3102/0034654308323036.

Churchill, R. (2011). *Teaching: Making a Difference*. Milton, Australia: John Wiley and Sons Australia.

Clancey, W.J. (1986). *Review of Winograd and Flores' Understanding Computers and Cognition: A favorable interpretation*. (STAN-CS-87-1173) Palo Alto, CA: Department of Computer Science, Stanford University.

Cunningham, D.J. (1991). Assessing Constructions and Constructing Assessments: A Dialogue. *Educational Technology, 31*(5), 13–17.

Diller, J., and Moule, J. (2005). *Cultural Competence: A Primer for Educators*, Thomson Wadsorth: Belmont, California.

Duffy, T.M., and Jonassen, D. (1991). Constructivism: New implications for instructional technology? *Educational Technology, 31*(5), 3–12.

Erickson, H. L. (2007). *Concept-based Curriculum and Instruction for the Thinking Classroom*, Thousand Oaks, CA, Corwin Press.

Eyler, Janet and Giles, Dwight (1996) A Practitioners Guide to Reflection in Service Learning

Freire, P. (1970). *Pedagogy of the Oppressed*. New York, Continuum.

Freire, P. (2004). *Pedagogy of Indignation*. Boulder: Colorado, Paradigm.

Gagné, R.M. & Driscoll, M.P. (1988). *Essentials of Learning for Instruction (2nd Edition)*. New Jersey: Prentice-Hall Inc.

Gagné, R.M. (1985). *The Conditions of Learning and Theory of Instruction (4th Edition)*. New York: CBS College Publishing.

Galton, M. (2013). *Learning and Teaching in the Primary Classroom* (2nd ed.). London, England: SAGE Publications Ltd.

Gardner, H. (2011). *The Unschooled Mind: How Children Think and How Schools Should Teach*. New York, NY: Basic Books.

Gay, G (2010). Culturally Responsive Teaching, 2nd Ed. New York, New York: Teachers College Press.

Gillespie, H., Boulton, H., Hramiak, A., and Williamson, R. (2007). *Learning and Teaching with Virtual Learning Environments*. SAGE Publications.

Gray, C., and MacBlain, S. (2012). *Learning Theories in Childhood*. UK: SAGE Publications.

Gray, C., and MacBlain, S. (2012). *Learning Theories in Childhood*. UK: SAGE Publications.

Grewal, J.S. and Singh R.P. (1979). A Comparative Study of the Effects of Standard MT With Varied Set of Skills Upon General Teaching Competence and Attitudes of Pre-service Secondary School Teachers. In R.C. DAS, *et al.* Differential Effectiveness of MT Components, New Delhi, NCERT.

Gropper, G.L. (1987). A lesson based on a behavioral approach to instructional design. In C.M. Reigeluth (Ed.), *Instructional theories in action* (pp. 45–112). Hillsdale, NJ: Lawrence Erlbaum Associates.

Haythornthwaite, C., and Andrews, R. (2011). *E-learning Theory and Practice*. UK: SAGE Publications.

Haythornthwaite, C., and Andrews, R. (2011). *E-learning Theory and Practice*. UK: SAGE Publications.

Hopkins, K.R. (2010). *Teaching How to Learn in a What-to-Learn Culture*. San Francisco, CA: Jossey-Bass.

Hopkins, K.R. (2010). *Teaching How to Learn in a What-to-Learn Culture*. San Francisco, CA: Jossey-Bass.

Hulse, S.H., Egeth, H., and Deese, J. (1980). *The psychology of learning* (5th ed.). New York: McGraw-Hill.

Illeris, K. (2008). *Contemporary Theories of Learning: Learning theorists... in their own words*. Abingdon, England: Routledge.

Indiana University. (2006). Experiential Learning Notations on Indiana University Official Transcripts. http://registrar.iupui.edu/experiential-learning.html.

Johnson, J.K. (1992). Advancing by degrees: Trends in master's and doctoral programs in educational communications and technology. *Tech Trends, 37*(2), 13–16.

Jonassen, D.H. (1991a). Evaluating constructivistic learning. *Educational Technology, 31*(9), 28–33.

Jonassen, D.H. (1991b). Objectivism vs constructivism: Do we need a new philosophical paradigm. *Educational Technology Research and Development, 39*(3), 5–14.

Keller, J.M. (1979). Motivation and instructional design: A theoretical perspective. *Journal of Instructional Development, 2*(4), 26–34.

Klein, S.B. (2011). *Learning: Principles and Applications* (6th ed.). California, CA: SAGE Publications.

Kolb, D.A. (1984). *Experiential Learning: Experience as the Source of Learning and Development.* Englewood Cliffs, NJ: Prentice-Hall.

Krause, K.L., Bochner, S., and Duchesne, S. (2006). *Educational Psychology for Learning and Teaching* (4th ed.). Sydney, Australia: Cengage Education.

Ladson-Billings, Gloria (1995). Toward a Theory of Culturally Relevant Pedagogy. *American Research Journal*. 32(3) 465-491.

Latham, G. (2006). *Learning to Teach: New Times, New Practices*. Melbourne; New York, Oxford University Press.

Lave, J., and Wenger, E. (1991). Situated Learning: Legitimate Peripheral Participation. New York: Cambridge University.

Lynch, J.M. (1945). The applicability of psychological research to education. *Journal of Educational Psychology, 43*, 289–296.

Mangal S. K . (2006). *Advanced Educational Psychology*, Prentice Hall of India, New Delhi.

Margetts, K. (2002). The Developing Child in Today's World: Issues and Care in Education. *Educare News*, Issue 127(July), 10-13

Marshal, Weil and Bruce, Joyce (1978). *Information Processing Models of Teaching: Expanding Your Teaching Repertoire*.

Martin, D.J., and Loomis, K.S. (2012). *Building Teachers: A Constructivist Approach to Introducing Education* (2nd ed.). Australia: Wadsworth Publishing Company, Cengage Education.

Merrill, M.D., Kowalis, T., and Wilson, B.G (1981). Instructional design in transition. In F.H. Farley, and N.J. Gordon (Eds.), *Psychology and education: The state of the union* (pp. 298–348). Berkeley: McCutchan.

Moore, D.T. (2010). Forms and Issues in Experiential Learning. In D. M. Qualters (Ed.) *New Directions for Teaching and Learning* (pp. 3-13). New York City, NY: Wiley.

Passi, B.K. (1976). *Becoming Better Teachers. Baroda: Centre for Advanced Study in Education*, M.S. University of Baroda.

Perkins, D.N. (1991). Technology meets constructivism: Do they make a marriage? *Educational Technology*, 31(5), 18–23.

Reigeluth, C.M. (1983). Instructional Design: What is it and why is it? In C.M. Reigeluth (Ed.), *Instructional theories in action* (pp. 3–36). Hillsdale, NJ: Lawrence Erlbaum Associates.

Reigeluth, C.M. (1989). Educational technology at the crossroads: New mindsets and new directions. *Educational Technology Research and Development,* 37(1), 67–80.

Resnick, L.B. (1987). Learning in school and out. *Educational Researcher, 16*(9), 13–20.

Richey, R.D. (1986). *The theoretical and conceptual bases of instructional design.* New York: Nichols.

Robson, S. (2006). *Developing Thinking and Understanding in Young Children: An Introduction for Students*. Abingdon, England: Routledge.

Santrock W.J. (2001). *Adolescence* (8th ed), McGraw-Hill Companies.

Scherff, L., and Spector, K. (2011). *Culturally Relevant Pedagogy*, Rowman & Littlefield Education: Lanham, Maryland.

Schon, D. (1983). *The Reflective Practitioner: How Professionals Think in Action.* New York City, NY: Basic books.

Schon, D.A. (1987). *Educating the Reflective Practitioner.* San Francisco: Jossey-Bass.

Schunk, D.H. (1991). *Learning theories: An educational perspective.* New York: Macmillan.

Shah, G.B. (1984). *Micro-teaching: Without Television*, Nutan Shikshan.

Sharma, N.L. (1984). *Micro-teaching: Integration of Teaching Skills in Sahitya Paricharya*, Vinod Pustak Mandir, Agra.

Shuell, T.J. (1986). Cognitive Conceptions of Learning. *Review of Educational Research, 56*, 411–436.

Shuell, T.J. (1990). Phases of Meaningful Learning. *Review of Educational Research,* 60, 531–547.

Singh, L.C. *et al.* (1987). *Micro-teaching: Theory and Practice*, Agra: Psychological Corporation.

Smith, P.L., and Ragan, T.J. (1993). *Instructional Design.* New York: Macmillan.

Snelbecker, G.E. (1983). *Learning Theory, Instructional Theory and Psychoeducational Design.* New York: McGraw-Hill.

Snelbecker, G.E. (1989). Contrasting and Complementary Approaches to Instructional Design. In C.M. Reigeluth (Ed.), *Instructional Theories in Action* (pp. 321–337). Hillsdale, NJ: Lawrence Erlbaum Associates.

Spiro, R.J., Feltovich, P.J., Jacobson, M.J., and Coulson, R.L. (1991). Cognitive Flexibility, Constructivism and Hypertext: Random access instruction for advanced knowledge acquisition in ill-structured domains. *Educational Technology, 31*(5), 24–33.

Stepich, D.A., and Newby, T.J. (1988). Analogical Instruction within the *Information Processing Paradigm: Effective Means to Facilitate Learning. Instructional Science, 17*, 129–144.

Taylor, G. R., and MacKenney, L. (2008). *Improving Human Learning in the Classroom: Theories and Teaching Practices*. Lanham, MA: Rowman & Littlefield Education.

Thomas, R. M. (2005). *Comparing Theories of Child Development.* Cengage Learning.

Thompson, A.D., Simonson, M.R., Hargrave, C.P. (1992). *Educational technology: A review of the research.* Washington DC: Association for Educational Communications and Technology.

Tyler, R.W. (1978). How schools utilize educational research and development. In R. Glaser (Ed.), *Research and development and school change.* Hillsdale, NJ: Lawrence Erlbaum.

Vaidya, N. (1970). Micro-teaching: An Experiment in Teacher Training. The Polytechnic Teacher, Technical Teacher, Technical Training Institute, Chandigarh.

Vygotsky, L (1986). *Thought and Language*. Cambridge, M. A. the MIT press.

Vygotsky, L.S. (1978). *Mind in Society*. Cambridge, MA: Harvard University Press.

Warries, E. (1990). Theory and the Systematic Design of Instruction. In S. Dijkstra, B. van Hout Wolters, & P.C. van der Sijde, (Eds.), *Research on instruction: Design and eff ects* (pp. 1–19). Englewood Cliffs, NJ: Educational Technology.

Wertsch, J.V. (1985). Cultural, Communication, and Cognition: Vygotskian Perspectives. Cambridge University Press.

West, C.K, Farmer, J.A., & Wolff, P.M. (1991). *Instructional Design: Implications from Cognitive Science*. Englewood Cliffs, NJ: Prentice Hall.

Winn, W. (1990). Some Implications of Cognitive Theory for Instructional Design. *Instructional Science, 19*, 53–69.

Winn, W. (1991). The Assumptions of Constructivism and Instructional Design. *Educational Technology, 31*(9), 38–40.

Winne, P.H. (1985). Cognitive Processing in the Classroom. In T. Husen and T.N. Postlethwaite (Eds.), *The International Encyclopedia of Education* (Vol. 2, pp. 795–808). Oxford: Pergamon.

Wurdinger, D.D., and Carlson, J.A. (2010). *Teaching for Experiential Learning: Five Approaches that Work.* Lanham, MD: Rowman & Littlefield Education.